METHADONE TREATMENT FOR
OPIOID DEPENDENCE

METHADONE TREATMENT FOR OPIOID DEPENDENCE

EDITED BY

Eric C. Strain, M.D.

Associate Professor
Department of Psychiatry and Behavioral Sciences
Johns Hopkins University School of Medicine
Baltimore, Maryland

AND

Maxine L. Stitzer, Ph.D.

Professor
Department of Psychiatry and Behavioral Sciences
Johns Hopkins University School of Medicine
Baltimore, Maryland

THE JOHNS HOPKINS UNIVERSITY PRESS
Baltimore & London

© 1999 The Johns Hopkins University Press
All rights reserved. Published 1999
Printed in the United States of America on acid-free paper
9 8 7 6 5 4 3 2 1

The Johns Hopkins University Press
2715 North Charles Street
Baltimore, Maryland 21218–4363
www.press.jhu.edu

Library of Congress Cataloging-in-Publication Data will be found at the end of this book.
A catalog record for this book is available from the British Library.

ISBN 0-8018-6136-5
ISBN 0-8018-6137-3 (pbk.)

Contents

CONTRIBUTORS

George E. Bigelow, Ph.D., *Professor and Director, Behavioral Pharmacology Research Unit, Department of Psychiatry and Behavioral Sciences, Johns Hopkins University School of Medicine, Baltimore, Maryland.*

Robert K. Brooner, Ph.D., *Associate Professor, Department of Psychiatry and Behavioral Sciences, Johns Hopkins University School of Medicine, Baltimore, Maryland.*

Mary Ann Chutuape, Ph.D., *Assistant Professor, Department of Psychiatry and Behavioral Sciences, Johns Hopkins University School of Medicine, Baltimore, Maryland.*

Michael I. Fingerhood, M.D., *Assistant Professor, Department of Medicine, Johns Hopkins University School of Medicine, Baltimore, Maryland.*

Louise A. Glezen, M.S., *Senior Research Program Coordinator and Clinic Manager, Department of Psychiatry and Behavioral Sciences, Johns Hopkins University School of Medicine, Baltimore, Maryland.*

Rolley E. Johnson, Pharm.D., *Associate Professor, Department of Psychiatry and Behavioral Sciences, Johns Hopkins University School of Medicine, Baltimore, Maryland.*

Hendrée E. Jones, Ph.D., *Instructor, Department of Psychiatry and Behavioral Sciences, Johns Hopkins University School of Medicine, Baltimore, Maryland.*

Michael Kidorf, Ph.D., *Assistant Professor, Department of Psychiatry and Behavioral Sciences, Johns Hopkins University School of Medicine, Baltimore, Maryland.*

Van L. King, M.D., *Assistant Professor, Department of Psychiatry and Behavioral Sciences, Johns Hopkins University School of Medicine, Baltimore, Maryland.*

Connie A. Lowery, R.N., C.A.R.N., *Advanced Clinical Nurse, Department of Psychiatry and Behavioral Sciences, Johns Hopkins University School of Medicine, Baltimore, Maryland.*

Mary E. McCaul, Ph.D., *Associate Professor, Department of Psychiatry and Behavioral Sciences, Johns Hopkins University School of Medicine, Baltimore, Maryland.*

Elias Robles, Ph.D., *Postdoctoral Fellow, Department of Psychiatry and Behavioral Sciences, Johns Hopkins University School of Medicine, Baltimore, Maryland.*

Kenneth Silverman, Ph.D., *Associate Professor, Department of Psychiatry and Behavioral Sciences, Johns Hopkins University School of Medicine, Baltimore, Maryland.*

Kenneth B. Stoller, M.D., *Instructor, Department of Psychiatry and Behavioral Sciences, Johns Hopkins University School of Medicine, Baltimore, Maryland.*

Dace S. Svikis, Ph.D., *Associate Professor, Department of Psychiatry and Behavioral Sciences, Johns Hopkins University School of Medicine, Baltimore, Maryland.*

Martha L. Velez, M.D., *Parenting Coordinator, Center for Addiction and Pregnancy, Johns Hopkins Bayview Medical Center, Baltimore, Maryland.*

Sharon L. Walsh, Ph.D., *Associate Professor, Department of Psychiatry and Behavioral Sciences, Johns Hopkins University School of Medicine, Baltimore, Maryland.*

PREFACE

It is estimated that in the United States, there are at least 600,000 persons dependent on illicit opioids, and more than 100,000 persons have received methadone treatment. In addition, there are probably at least another 100,000 methadone patients in other countries. Methadone, which has been clinically used as a treatment for opioid dependence for more than 30 years, is the most commonly used pharmacologic treatment for opioid dependence. However, despite its long history of use and the substantial number of methadone patients, methadone treatment remains controversial. Opinions about methadone treatment are varied and not always based on the numerous scientific studies supporting the efficacy of this treatment approach. The purpose of this book is to provide an objective and comprehensive overview of methadone treatment that utilizes the extensive body of research available on this modality to support clinical recommendations. Thus, we hope that colleagues in the treatment community will find this book a useful resource in their clinical practice and that researchers may find new clinically based questions that need to be answered through empirical study.

It is important to note that methadone itself provides pharmacologic support that specifically leads to the reduction or elimination of heroin use. However, the use of methadone does not address other, concurrent drug use and psychosocial problems that opiate-dependent patients bring to treatment. Thus, comprehensive treatment is more than simply the delivery of methadone medication. Effective methadone treatment is a combination of pharmacologic and nonpharmacologic methods, and the latter can include individual and group therapies, urine testing, education and vocation training, medical and psychiatric treatment of comorbid conditions, and other services appropriate to the needs of the individual patient. When delivered properly, *methadone treatment is a highly effective intervention,* decreasing illicit drug use and increasing prosocial behaviors in patients. Yet, despite the long and extensive use of methadone for the treatment of opioid dependence, there have been few attempts to provide a single textbook that provides integrated information about the various aspects of an effective comprehensive methadone treatment program.

This book addresses both the pharmacologic and nonpharmacologic aspects of methadone treatment and provides a historical overview to methadone treatment, as well as a review of the regulations associated with treatment delivery, and information about the operation of a methadone clinic. It also provides clinically valuable information about the pharmacology of methadone, including issues of proper maintenance dosing, and about how a patient should be started on and withdrawn from methadone. Several chapters address the nonpharmacologic aspects of treatment, including the management of medical and psychiatric disorders, delivery of individual and group counseling, behavioral treatments, and special issues for women. Finally, information about the use of other, newer pharmacotherapies for opioid dependence, such as LAAM, buprenorphine, and naltrexone, is provided. The book provides a mixture of clinical experience and a review of scientific studies and is a focused, comprehensive review of the use of methadone treatment for opioid dependence. This information should be valuable to directors, physicians, counselors, and other staff who work in methadone programs. It is also important for persons in the public policy arena to understand methadone treatment and appreciate the extensive body of evidence that supports its efficacy. Thus, we hope that this book is read by those who are in a position to influence public policy, funding, and expansion of treatment.

We would like to take this opportunity to thank the authors who took the time to write the chapters of this book. They are colleagues and friends, and readily agreed to this project with a level of enthusiasm that we appreciated. In addition, we would like to acknowledge our grateful thanks to the methadone patients who have participated in various treatment/research studies at the Johns Hopkins Behavioral Pharmacology Research Unit over the last 20 years. These projects have been funded through a series of grants from the National Institute on Drug Abuse, and its support is greatly appreciated. Similarly, the Department of Psychiatry at Johns Hopkins University School of Medicine has been an invaluable support. Finally, we would like to thank our families (Grace, Andrew, Kate, and Duncan) for their patience and good cheer during the many evenings and weekends we have been working on this and other projects.

LIST OF ABBREVIATIONS

APD	antisocial personality disorder
ASI	Addiction Severity Index
AUDIT	Alcohol Use Disorders Identification Test
BCP	Behaviorally Contingent Pharmacotherapy
BDI	Beck Depression Inventory
CALDATA	California Drug and Alcohol Treatment Assessment
CNS	central nervous system
CSAT	Center for Substance Abuse Treatment
DEA	Drug Enforcement Agency
DIS	Diagnostic Interview Schedule
ECG	electrocardiogram
FDA	Food and Drug Administration
GAD	generalized anxiety disorder
HIV	human immunodeficiency virus
LAAM	L-alpha-acetylmethadol
MAST	Michigan Alcoholism Screening Test
NIDA	National Institute on Drug Abuse
SAMHSA	Substance Abuse and Mental Health Services Administration
SAODAP	Special Action Office for Drug Abuse Prevention
SCID	Structured Clinical Interview for DSM-IV
STD	sexually transmitted disease
$t_{1/2}$	half life

METHADONE TREATMENT FOR OPIOID DEPENDENCE

Introduction and Historical Overview

Eric C. Strain, M.D., and Kenneth B. Stoller, M.D.

The most extensively used medication for the treatment of opioid dependence is methadone. Methadone was not developed for the treatment of opioid dependence; rather, it was developed in Germany during the 1940s for use as an analgesic, and it continues to be used as an effective analgesic today. Not until the 1960s did studies and reports of using methadone for the treatment of opioid dependence first begin to appear in the scientific literature.

For many years methadone was the most *effective* medication for the treatment of opioid dependence because it was the *only* medication available. Whereas this chapter and book focus primarily on methadone, one must recognize that other medications are available and approved for the treatment of opioid dependence (such as naltrexone and L-alpha-acetylmethadol [LAAM]) and that more medications will probably become widely available in the near future (such as buprenorphine). This chapter focuses on the development of methadone for the treatment of opioid dependence and provides the more recent history of the development of these other medications.

Opiate Abuse before Methadone Treatment

Development and Recognition of an Opioid Problem

Opioids have been abused for hundreds of years; contemporary problems associated with opioid use are not unique to the present era. Nor has abuse of opioids been isolated to a single culture or region of the world.

However, from the late nineteenth to the twentieth centuries, the United States has often occupied a unique position in terms of the total consumption and prevalence of opioid abuse, and a review of the history of opioid use in the United States provides a useful, illustrative example of the context in which methadone was developed for the treatment of opioid dependence.

During the second half of the nineteenth century, the use of opioids markedly increased in the United States (Musto 1987; Jonnes 1996)—primarily for medical use—and this increase reflected a common social and medical perception that opioids were safe and effective. In addition to being prescribed by physicians, a substantial amount of opioids was consumed, often unknowingly, in the form of patent medications, whose manufacturers were not required to list the ingredients. At this time, most opiate addiction in the United States occurred among middle- and upper-class Caucasian women, although some opiate-containing patent medications were marketed specifically for use by children.

By the turn of the century, it is believed that there were at least 250,000 opiate addicts in the United States, perhaps a conservative estimate. (The population of the United States at that time was about 75,000,000, so about 1 in 300 persons was an opiate addict. By comparison, in the early 1990s the population was about 225,000,000, and the number of opiate addicts has been estimated to be about 600,000—about 1 in 375 persons.) However, society's perception of the safety of opioids was in flux, prompted in part by the publication of exposés, at the turn of the century, that reported on the analytic results of the contents of commonly used patent medications. As the public became aware of these results, interest grew in regulating this industry and culminated in the passage of the Pure Food and Drug Act of 1906.

The Pure Food and Drug Act of 1906 required manufacturers to list the contents of medications that would be shipped across state lines. The act resulted both in withdrawal from the market of a large number of medications and in a suddenly heightened awareness by consumers of the actual content of medications previously thought to be safe. Within a few years of the act's passage, sales of these patent medications dropped by about a third, and the number of people dependent on opiates also began to drop.

As the use of opiates began to decline, there was also a shift in the perception of who was using opiates. Whereas opiate use had previously been primarily among white middle- and upper middle-class women, now illicit opiate use became associated with minorities (especially Chinese immigrants), who often lived in the inner cities. Furthermore, while opiate use in the nineteenth century had mainly been restricted to morphine and opium, heroin now became a popular form of opioid to abuse. Heroin was introduced to the public in 1898 (initially marketed as a cough suppressant by the Friedrich Bayer Company), and in the early 1900s, this new form of opioid quickly became a popular drug of abuse for young males living in the inner cities.

Thus, by the turn of the century two major changes were occurring in opiate use: First, the demographics of those addicted were changing from middle-class white females to inner-city minorities and poor, young males; and, second, concurrent with this demographic shift, the overall number of people using opiates was declining.

The Harrison Narcotics Act

Despite this overall decline in drug use, there was a rising political interest to limit the international opium trade. This interest culminated in the Harrison Narcotics Act of 1914—federal legislation sponsored by Representative Francis Burton Harrison—which controlled domestic trade in opiates. The Harrison Act is best understood as a response to international events, even though it addressed domestic rather than international issues.

During the early 1900s, the United States actively participated in a series of international conferences that sought to regulate international trade in narcotics. The United States wanted other countries to exert greater local control over the production and distribution of opiates. However, the United States was placed in an awkward position, because it could hardly argue that other nations should improve opiate-related laws when its own laws were weak and ineffective. The Harrison Act provided a federal mechanism for the control of opiates (previously handled at the state level), and once the act had been passed the United States was able to confront other nations that did not have similar antiopiate laws. While passage of the act served a useful purpose for international conferences, enforcement of the act by the Treasury Department also resulted in a further tightening of opiate use in the United States.

As the Harrison and Pure Food and Drug acts produced further control over opiate distribution and use in the United States, programs for the treatment of opiate abusers through the provision of maintenance opioids began to be established in various cities. These programs, which operated in areas such as New York, Connecticut, Ohio, Texas, and Louisiana, continued into the 1920s and can be viewed as the forerunners of methadone treatment. Although the provision of maintenance or detoxification opioids to addicts was initially acceptable under the provisions of the Harrison Act, subsequent rulings allowed the Treasury Department to shut down programs offering such support, and by the mid- to late-1920s maintenance treatment for opioid dependence had effectively ended in the United States.

Prohibitive Enforcement

In 1930 the Federal Bureau of Narcotics (FBN) was established and given the task of enforcing the Harrison Act and representing the nation in foreign conferences concerning narcotics control. Harry Anslinger led the FBN from the time of its creation until his retirement in 1962. Anslinger believed in strict enforcement of laws and the active discouragement of medicalization of opioid treatments (such as substitution therapies). However, despite his approach to the management of opioid dependence, a review of Anslinger's tenure suggests that, under his leadership, the FBN failed to provide effective control of illicit opiate use. The FBN operated within the Treasury Department until 1968, when it was turned over to the Justice Department. This turnover was prompted, in part, by the belief that a single agency with domestic and international responsibilities would be more effective in performing enforcement duties, preventing smuggling, and, at the same time, acting as a model to other nations.

Both the use of illicit opiates and the intolerance regarding such use intensified after World War II (much as it had following World War I). There was a notable increase in heroin addiction in New York City—which probably had the greatest concentration of opiate addicts in the United States during this period—a trend that was apparent in other cities throughout the United States during the 1950s as well. As the number of heroin addicts rose, so did drug-related crime against property. Governmental action during this time culminated in the 1956 Narcotic Control Act, which mandated minimum sentencing for first conviction drug charges, as well as the threat of the death penalty for some cases.

In 1955 the American Bar Association (ABA) and the American Medical Association (AMA) joined in studying the narcotics problem, and the Joint Committee of the ABA and the AMA on Narcotic Drugs was appointed. In 1958 the committee's Interim Report recommended that an outpatient facility prescribing narcotics be established on a controlled, experimental basis. The report also criticized the intimidation of physicians by federal agents and suggested that, through maintenance therapy, crime might be prevented. The FBN aggressively criticized the Joint Committee, whose recommendations were seen as a threat that would lead to softened penalties, increased prescribing of opioids, and/or the establishment of maintenance clinics.

Transition toward Medicalization

Increasing concern about drug use mounted in the 1960s, spawned by the increased use of heroin (as well as amphetamines and marijuana), and the emergence of new drugs such as LSD. Increased drug use during this period led to elevated morbidity and mortality associated with drug use. In New York City, by the mid-1960s heroin-related mortality was the leading cause of death of persons between the ages of 15 and 35. Hepatitis transmitted through intravenous drug injection was increasing, as were drug-related crimes. These problems developed during a time when President John F. Kennedy was advocating increased resources for research and treatment of the mentally ill and the retarded. The understanding of drug addiction by those in the mental health field differed tremendously from the prevailing view at the FBN, where drug abuse was seen as a problem to be handled through more vigorous law enforcement and punishment of those breaking the laws. Physicians and mental health care workers viewed addiction as a medical problem, placing the responsibility for finding solutions within the arena of health care providers and medical researchers.

Although these attitudes in the health care field had become increasingly prevalent prior to the 1960s, it was only with the clear failure of prohibitive enforcement that the existing policy of punishment was questioned. In 1962 the Supreme Court declared that addiction in itself was a disease, not a crime. Subsequently, courts became more lenient, mandatory sentencing was opposed, and funding for drug abuse research increased. In 1962 the president called for a White House conference on drug abuse, followed by the President's Advisory Commission on Narcotic and Drug Abuse (the Prettyman Commission). The commission recommended the relaxation of mandatory minimum sentences and intensified research for all aspects of narcotic abuse, including the effectiveness of outpatient dispensing of narcotics for addiction. It also recommended the dismantling of the FBN, making Health, Education, and Welfare (HEW) responsible for distribution and research, and the Justice Department responsible for the investigation of illicit trafficking. The medical profession would now determine what constituted legitimate medical treatment. This changing perception of opiate abuse as a medical disorder and not simply a problem of law enforcement prompted the study of methadone treatment in the late 1960s.

The Development of Methadone

Methadone was developed by German chemists at I. G. Farbenindus-trie, during World War II, as a substitute for morphine. In August 1947 the pharmaceutical company Eli Lilly and Company was granted a New Drug Application (NDA) by the Food and Drug Administration (FDA) for the use of methadone as an analgesic and antitussive (anticough) medication. Its trade name for methadone was Dolophine (derived from *dolor* for pain or sorrow). However, because of the drug's link to Germany, some in the addict community have believed that this name—Dolophine—was a de-rivative of Adolf Hitler's name.

Studies of the pharmacologic effects of methadone began appearing in the scientific literature in the late 1940s. These early studies characterized the abuse liability of methadone and indicated that it was an opioid simi-lar to morphine in many aspects. However, methadone was also noted to differ in important ways from morphine, such as in its duration of action and the withdrawal syndrome produced upon sudden discontinuation of chronic dosing. (See Chapter 3 for a full discussion of the pharmacologic effects of methadone.) These early studies did not identify the therapeutic potential of methadone for the treatment of opioid dependence. But, even if this potential had been appreciated, the regulatory environment most likely would have precluded its use for this indication.

Early Methadone Treatment for Opioid Dependence

While many reports on the early use of methadone for the treatment of opioid dependence begin with the work conducted in the 1960s by Vin-cent Dole and Marie Nyswander (Figure 1.1) at Rockefeller University in New York, it is interesting to note that other sites were also experimenting with its use and had been doing so even before Dole and Nyswander had begun their studies. For example, a program providing extended methadone treatment was started in 1963 in Vancouver, British Columbia, and this site first began experimenting with methadone as a short-term treatment for opiate addicts as early as 1959 (Williams 1971). However, Dole and Nyswander have generally been considered as the innovators of methadone treatment for opioid dependence. To understand this, it is use-ful to place their work in the context of time, location, and scientific suc-cess.

First, after World War II there was rising opiate use in the United States, especially in New York City. This increase occurred despite the efforts of

Figure 1.1. Drs. Vincent Dole and Marie Nyswander.

the Treasury Department's FBN. The head of the FBN, Harry Anslinger, was a tough-talking bureaucrat who actively worked to prevent the medicalization of addiction and who tended to portray drug abuse in the United States based on his beliefs rather than on data and scientific studies. Although Anslinger maintained that drug use was under control (through his efforts and the efforts of the FBN), by the late 1950s and early 1960s it was clear that this was not the case. Because efforts to control illicit opiate use through the persecution of users was not successful, there was renewed interest in studying possible treatments for opioid dependence. It was not simply a fringe element of society that advocated this study of treatment: as previously described, the AMA, the ABA, and the White House itself were reevaluating how opiate abuse was being managed.

Second, Dole and Nyswander were in a place that was receptive to their work. New York was a city with a rising population of opiate addicts. Furthermore, they were in the right academic location—Rockefeller University. Despite efforts by the FBN to intimidate them, they were able to continue their studies and treatments with the backing of the university (and its lawyers).

Finally, the ultimate importance of Dole and Nyswander's work rests on the work conducted and the results shown. Starting in late 1963, Dole and Nyswander began treating opiate addicts at an inpatient unit at Rockefeller. While their earlier efforts had examined the potential efficacy of morphine maintenance, Dole and Nyswander observed that patients who transferred to methadone from morphine appeared to function more effectively on methadone. This observation led to their initial studies of treating patients with methadone and to a series of published scientific reports on their success (Dole and Nyswander 1965; Dole, Nyswander, and Kreek, 1966a, 1966b). These results, in the mid- to late-1960s, quickly gained the attention and interest of the medical community, both in the United States and in other countries, and led to the institution and rapid expansion of methadone treatment worldwide. For example, in 1969, in New York City almost 2,000 patients were in methadone treatment, whereas by 1970 the number of patients had reached 20,000. In addition, programs were begun in Sweden in 1966, Holland in 1968, Australia in 1970, Hong Kong in 1972, Italy and Switzerland in 1975, and France in 1983. (In some cases, clinicians initially trained with Dole and Nyswander in New York, then returned to their home countries to begin methadone programs.)

Contemporary Methadone Treatment

When methadone treatment became popular during the late 1960s and early 1970s, the medical community hoped and believed that it would provide a solution to the problems of opiate addiction. The early successes in methadone treatment, which occurred in small populations of selected patients treated under specific circumstances (e.g., living in a hospital, initially for long periods of time), were not replicated as treatment expanded rapidly. Success rates in some clinics were poor, and treatment practices across clinics were highly variable. During the 1980s the previous enthusiasm for methadone treatment waned, and expansion of treatment programs virtually halted in the United States. However, not all countries had the same experience, and during this time some countries (such as Australia) continued to develop and expand methadone treatment programs (Table 1.1).

Table 1.1 **Countries Using Methadone Treatment**

Australia	Greece	Portugal
Austria	Ireland	Scotland
Belgium	Italy	Slovenia
Bulgaria	The Netherlands	Sweden
Canada	New Zealand	Switzerland
Denmark	Norway	Thailand
England	Lithuania	Spain
France	Poland	United States
Germany		

By the mid-1990s an estimated 250,000 patients were in methadone treatment worldwide, with the United States continuing to have the largest population of methadone patients. The National Drug and Alcoholism Treatment Unit Survey (NDATUS), conducted annually in the United States, estimated that on a single day in 1994 there were 111,501 patients who received methadone treatment in the United States (SAMHSA 1996). Although new methadone treatment programs rarely open in the United States, continued interest in methadone treatment has led to the opening of new programs in other countries. Worldwide, the spread of human immunodeficiency virus (HIV) infection through injecting-drug use has sparked a new interest in methadone treatment, because studies conducted in the late 1980s and in the 1990s have demonstrated that methadone treatment can significantly decrease this HIV-risk behavior.

WHAT IS METHADONE TREATMENT?

The defining feature of methadone treatment is the use of the medication methadone. However, as methadone treatment is rarely limited to methadone pharmacotherapy, the label "methadone treatment" may be less than optimal because it provides undue emphasis on the pharmacologic aspects of treatment.

Thus, although methadone treatment includes a pharmacotherapy (methadone), one must recognize that methadone treatment represents both pharmacologic and nonpharmacologic therapies; it is a combination of the two, and optimal outcomes are obtained when both are provided. Since the inception of methadone treatment, as designed by Dole and Nyswander at Rockefeller University, nonpharmacologic aspects of treatment have been included in virtually all methadone programs. The importance of these treatment components deserves special emphasis, because for most patients cessation of illicit drug use is not achieved simply by ingesting a daily dose of methadone. As stated by Vincent Dole,

> Some people became overly converted. They felt, without reading our reports carefully, that all they had to do was give methadone and then there was no more problem with the addict. . . . I urged that physicians should see that the problem was one of rehabilitating people with a very complicated mixture of social problems on top of a specific medical problem, and that they ought to tailor their programs to the kinds of problems they were dealing with. The strength of the early programs as designed by Marie Nyswander was in their sensitivity to individual human problems. The stupidity of thinking that just giving methadone will solve a complicated social problem seems to me beyond comprehension. (quoted in Courtwright, Joseph, and Des Jarlais, 1989:338)

These nonpharmacologic aspects of methadone treatment are considered in other chapters of this book (e.g., Chapters 8–11). They can include individual counseling, group therapy, couples counseling, urinalysis testing, contingency contracting, vocational rehabilitation, education programs, parenting classes, HIV testing and counseling, primary medical care services, and psychiatric assessments and treatment of comorbid disorders. The methadone clinic may be best viewed as a site for the comprehensive treatment of patients.

Although methadone treatment represents a combination of pharmacotherapy and nonpharmacotherapy, there has been interest in the development of programs that provide methadone medication without concurrent nonpharmacologic services (often referred to as "medical methadone"). As a methadone clinic builds up a stable group of patients who are doing well, it is not uncommon for such patients to be given special privileges such as take-home doses of medication for several days each week. It may be possible for such patients to transfer into a specialized unit that provides only methadone, after documentation over a sustained period indicates that the patients demonstrate good social functioning and absence of illicit drug use (and no evidence of problematic licit drug use). However, for patients entering methadone treatment, the need to address multiple problem areas related to their drug use requires treatment services beyond simply their daily dose of methadone.

History of the Development of Other Medications for the Treatment of Opioid Dependence

In addition to methadone, several other medications either are available for the treatment of opioid dependence or are in active development and probably will be available in the near future. More details about these medications can be found in Chapter 13, but the history of their development is briefly summarized here.

After methadone treatment was launched, the next available medication for the treatment of opioid dependence was naltrexone. During the period that methadone treatment was undergoing rapid expansion, interest in the substance abuse research and treatment communities turned to the possibility of developing an opioid antagonist for the treatment of opioid dependence. A concern was that some methadone doses meant to be taken outside the supervision of the clinic were being diverted and sold to addicts not in treatment. Therefore, an alternate medication that would have a low-abuse potential was needed, and interest focused on an opioid *antagonist* (vs. methadone, an opioid *agonist*). A patient maintained on an opioid antagonist medication would not experience drug effects if an abused opiate were taken (e.g., would block the effects of heroin), and the antagonist itself should have no abuse potential (i.e., it would not produce a subjective feeling of being high). If there was no abuse potential, then the antagonist could be prescribed and taken at home with no concern about diversion onto the street.

In 1971 President Richard M. Nixon created the Special Action Office for Drug Abuse Prevention (SAODAP), a government office that predated the National Institute on Drug Abuse (NIDA). One of the SAODAP's early interests (specifically included in the legislation that created SAODAP), in collaboration with the Division of Narcotic Addiction and Drug Abuse (DNADA) (located within the National Institute for Mental Health [NIMH]), was the development of an opioid antagonist. Although several possible compounds were considered, the most promising was EN-1639A (initially synthesized at Endo Laboratories), an orally active, relatively long duration opioid antagonist subsequently named naltrexone (Julius and Renault 1976).

In the late 1970s and early 1980s, naltrexone underwent a series of studies, sponsored by the U.S. government, to examine both its safety and efficacy. It was eventually approved in 1984 for use in the treatment of opioid dependence in the United States by the FDA. Naltrexone never gained widespread use comparable to methadone; however, studies in the early 1990s suggested that it decreased alcohol use and craving in patients with alcohol dependence, and in 1995 it gained approval for this indication.

After the approval of naltrexone in 1984, nine years passed before another medication—LAAM—was approved by the FDA for the treatment of opioid dependence. Initial work with LAAM actually occurred before the development of naltrexone, dating back to the late 1940s and early 1950s, and in the 1960s Merck and Company studied LAAM's possible use as an analgesic, but this indication was eventually abandoned (because of delayed onset of effects and long duration of action).

However, near the end of the 1960s Jaffe and co-workers began studying the clinical use of LAAM on a thrice-weekly basis for the treatment of opioid dependence (Jaffe et al. 1970, 1972). The results from this early work were promising and led the DNADA to sponsor, in the 1970s, further studies of LAAM for the treatment of opioid dependence. Several important clinical trials with LAAM were conducted under the sponsorship of NIDA (which grew out of the DNADA) in the mid- and late-1970s (and are described in detail in Chapter 13).

But, in the 1980s LAAM languished, with little clinical research or further movement toward its development or approval. In 1990 the Medications Development Division (MDD) at NIDA was created, and one of its early objectives was the approval of LAAM for the treatment of opioid dependence. In consultation with the FDA, the MDD sponsored a final clinical trial with LAAM (called the Labeling Assessment Study), and in 1993 received FDA approval for LAAM.

While the MDD successfully completed the approval of LAAM, it also began sponsoring work with buprenorphine for the treatment of opioid dependence. Buprenorphine, an opioid with mixed agonist-antagonist properties, gained the attention and interest of the research and treatment communities because its unique pharmacologic profile suggested advantages over opioid agonist medications such as methadone and LAAM (see Chapter 13). Early human studies with buprenorphine were conducted in the late 1970s, with subsequent small clinical trials in the 1980s. However, it was not until the late 1980s and early 1990s that reports from large clinical trials on the efficacy and safety of buprenorphine in the treatment of opioid dependence began to appear. Whereas previous medications for the treatment of opioid dependence (methadone, naltrexone, and LAAM) had primarily been approved for use initially in the United States, buprenorphine was first approved for use in France. It is expected that the MDD will seek FDA approval for the use of buprenorphine in the treatment of opioid dependence in the United States sometime in 1999.

Two other medications used in the treatment of opioid dependence need to be briefly mentioned in this overview: clonidine and lofexidine, both alpha$_2$-adrenergic agonists (see Chapter 13). Clonidine is available as an antihypertensive in several countries, but is generally not approved for use in the treatment of opioid dependence. However, several studies in the 1980s showed that it could be effective in attenuating opioid withdrawal, making it a popular nonopioid detoxification agent. Lofexidine is approved for opioid withdrawal in the United Kingdom (as BritLofex). Interestingly, while the development of naltrexone, LAAM, and buprenorphine have involved substantial governmental support, it appears that lofexidine has developed primarily through the sponsorship of the private sector.

SUMMARY

Methadone treatment represents the first pharmacotherapy targeting opioid dependence to have gained wide acceptance and availability. Although attempts were made at the turn of the century to treat opioid-dependent persons at clinics that used substitution therapies such as morphine, these clinics were relatively short-lived and closed in response to political pressures. Early studies of the efficacy of methadone treatment produced markedly good outcomes, leading to the rapid expansion of methadone treatment in the United States and in other countries. And although this expansion ended in the United States in the late 1970s and early 1980s, steady expansion of methadone treatment continues throughout the world. Renewed interest in methadone treatment in the late 1980s was prompted in part by the rise of HIV infection among injection drug users, and by a resurgence of interest in methadone treatment as a highly effective means for decreasing high-risk behaviors. In addition to methadone, other medications such as naltrexone, LAAM, buprenorphine, clonidine, and lofexidine are available for the treatment of opioid dependence in some countries, and their use continues to expand as clinicians gain familiarity with their application. However, despite these newer medications, methadone continues to be the most widely used pharmacotherapy for the treatment of opioid dependence.

References and Suggested Further Reading

Courtwright D., Joseph H., Des Jarlais D. 1989. *Addicts Who Survived: An Oral History of Narcotics Use in America, 1923–1965*. University of Tennessee Press, Knoxville.

Dole V.P., Nyswander M. 1965. A medical treatment for diacetylmorphine (heroin) addiction: a clinical trial with methadone hydrochloride. *JAMA* 193:80–84.

Dole V.P., Nyswander M.E., Kreek M.J. 1966a. Narcotic blockade—a medical technique for stopping heroin use by addicts. *Trans. Assoc. Am. Physicians* 79:122–36.

———. 1966b. Narcotic blockade. *Arch. Intern. Med.* 118:304–9.

Farrell M. 1996. A Review of the Legislation, Regulation and Delivery of Methadone in 12 Member States of the European Union—Final Report. Office for Official Publications of the European Communities, Luxembourg.

Fulco C.E., Liverman C.T., Earley L.E., eds. 1995. *The Development of Medications for the Treatment of Opiate and Cocaine Addictions: Issues for the Government and Private Sector.* Institute of Medicine, National Academy Press, Washington, DC.

Jaffe J.H., Schuster C.R., Smith B.B., Blachley P.H. 1970. Comparison of acetylmethadol and methadone in the treatment of long-term heroin users: a pilot study. *JAMA* 211:1834–36.

Jaffe J.H., Senay E.C., Schuster C.R., Renault P.R., Smith B.B., DiMenza S. 1972. Methadyl acetate vs methadone: a double-blind study in heroin users. *JAMA* 222:437–42.

Jonnes J. 1996. *Hep-cats, Narcs, and Pipe Dreams: A History of America's Romance with Illegal Drugs.* Scribners, New York.

Julius D., Renault P., eds. 1976. Narcotic Antagonists: Naltrexone Progress Report. NIDA Research Monograph 9. U.S. Department of Health, Education, and Welfare, Public Health Service, Rockville, MD.

Musto D.F. 1987. *The American Disease: Origins of Narcotic Control.* Oxford University Press, New York.

Substance Abuse and Mental Health Services Administration (SAMHSA), Office of Applied Studies. 1996. National Drug and Alcoholism Treatment Unit Survey (NDATUS): Data for 1994 and 1980–1994. U.S. Department of Health and Human Services, Public Health Service, Rockville, MD.

Williams H.R. 1971. Low and high methadone maintenance in the out-patient treatment of the hard core heroin addict. In: Einstein S., ed. *Methadone Maintenance.* Marcel Dekker, New York.

2

Regulatory, Cost, and Policy Issues

Kenneth B. Stoller, M.D., and George E. Bigelow, Ph.D.

With the dramatic increase in the prevalence of HIV, hepatitis B and C viruses, and tuberculosis among injecting-opiate users during the past two decades, the delivery of effective treatments for opiate addiction should be of critical importance. After almost four decades of experience and scientific inquiry, the efficacy and safety of methadone in the treatment of opiate dependence are indisputable. Even so, public misperception and the stigma associated with opiate addiction and treatment continue to prevail. Excessive concern over the possible diversion of methadone from treatment clinics has been a significant driving factor behind an enduring policy of regulation. Rather than focusing on how best to deliver treatment to those who could benefit from it, public policy has centered on controls to limit delivery. As a result, methadone treatment is readily available to only a small portion of individuals with opiate dependence.

The regulation of methadone treatment has varied over time, across countries, and among localities. Methadone maintenance is the most highly regulated of all medical treatments. The governmental bodies and agencies involved in its regulation are often numerous, as are the relevant laws and regulations. For example, in the United States methadone treatment is regulated at local, state, and federal levels. Even within the federal level, multiple agencies, such as the FDA and the Drug Enforcement Agency (DEA), are involved in the operation and surveillance of methadone treatment.

This chapter, organized into three sections, addresses regulatory as well as cost and policy issues as they pertain to methadone. The first part examines regulatory issues as they pertain to methadone's use in the United States, where the regulation of methadone treatment is uniquely complex. The largest population of methadone patients is in the United States, where the treatment originated. However, it is important to recognize that methadone treatment is also available in many other parts of the world, including eastern and western Europe, Asia, Australia, and Canada (see Table 1.1). Regulatory issues in other countries where methadone is available for the treatment of opioid dependence is also briefly reviewed.

The second part of this chapter examines the cost-related issues of methadone treatment. While regulatory and policy issues regarding methadone treatment have played a prominent role in the use and expansion of methadone treatment, cost issues also have played an important role in the use of methadone for the treatment of opioid dependence. Numerous studies have demonstrated that methadone treatment is cost-effective when a broad array of cost-saving measures are included (e.g., decreases in crime, increases in employment). However, in countries such as the United States, it is not clear how methadone treatment will operate and be adequately reimbursed in an evolving environment of managed health care. These issues become increasingly important when governmental-supported services for uninsured people are decreased or withdrawn, because a large population of patients entering drug abuse treatment rely on treatment subsidized by the government.

Creative and more cost-effective mechanisms for the delivery of methadone treatment continue to be proposed and investigated. The third part of this chapter examines novel approaches to treatment, including medical methadone (the delivery of methadone without concurrent nonpharmacologic treatments), mobile methadone treatment, and the designation of methadone clinics as primary health care sites. These and other approaches may be utilized in the future as part of a medically and economically effective delivery system.

REGULATORY ISSUES IN THE UNITED STATES

In the United States, the regulation of methadone (and more recently LAAM) is extensive and unique (IOM 1995). No other medications approved by the FDA in the United States are regulated in a similar fashion. There have been periodic discussions and appeals to relax methadone's regulations—including recent efforts to have methadone programs certified or licensed through some other governmental agencies—so that physicians could prescribe it under the same circumstances that they prescribe other medications. However, substantial changes in methadone regulations will require considerable bureaucratic change (although it is hoped that regulations for buprenorphine treatment may be less stringent; see Chapter 13 for a discussion about buprenorphine).

Federal Levels of Control

In 1972 methadone was approved by the FDA for use in the maintenance treatment of opiate addiction in the United States. The basic framework for methadone regulation was issued by the FDA in December 1972, and became effective in March 1973 (37 FR 26790; IOM [1995]). During this time, Congress approved a series of bills that became known as the Narcotic Addict Treatment Act (NATA) of 1974. The NATA was driven by concerns about the diversion of methadone to illicit channels, and it established the statutory role of the Secretary of the Department of Health and Human Services (DHHS) over methadone treatment. Guidelines established by the secretary defined a unique, third level of federal control, beyond the usual regulations (FDA and DEA) for controlled substances, and the NATA resulted in the still existing closed system of methadone distribution.

The NATA also defined the differences between detoxification and maintenance treatments. Detoxification was defined as the use of methadone in decreasing doses to reach a drug-free state in not more than 21 days. Maintenance treatment was to be restricted to methadone treatment programs and was defined as the use of methadone "at relatively stable doses" for more than 21 days, along with social and medical services. (Notably, subsequent revisions have changed the definitions of detoxification and maintenance treatment; see Chapter 11 for a discussion of current regulations regarding methadone detoxification and maintenance treatment in the United States.)

These regulations between 1972 and 1974 created a closed system of delivery, defining "methadone treatment programs," which provided comprehensive services for methadone detoxification or maintenance, as well as initial patient evaluation. Also defined were "methadone treatment medication units," which were facilities within treatment programs that were restricted to dispensing methadone and collecting urine samples to test for narcotics. This system limited the dispensing of methadone to treatment programs with specific prior FDA and state approval and to hospital pharmacies.

This early and unique form of regulation for methadone treatment in the United States has persisted, with some modifications to the present-day regulations. Currently, methadone (and now LAAM) manufacturers and treatment providers must comply with four levels of regulatory control.

First, as with all prescription drugs, the manufacturing, labeling, and dispensing must meet the requirements of the FDA under the Federal Food, Drug, and Cosmetic Act. The primary intent of this first level of control is to protect the consumer. Second, as with all schedule II controlled sub-

Table 2.1 **Program Aspects Required or Described by U.S. Federal Regulations (DHHS, FDA, 21 CFR Part 291) for Methadone**

Program Approval and Structure
　Submission of applications (to FDA and state authorities)
　Compliance with special DEA security requirements
　Organizational structure (e.g., primary facility, medication unit, program sponsor, medical director)
　Notification of FDA and state authorities of changes in organizational structure
Use of "Narcotic Drugs"
　Designation of approved medications
　Security of drug stocks (standards as required by the DEA)
　Dosing (initial dose, justification for high doses, who may dispense, form and route of medication, packaging of take-home doses)
　Dispensing to patients enrolled in other programs
　Hospital detoxification treatment
Clinical Standards and Required Services
　Admission standards (addiction history, physiologic dependence, voluntary participation, informed consent; exceptions if coming from penal or chronic care institutions, pregnant patients, previously treated patients; limitations if under 18 years of age)
　Admission evaluation (psychologic and sociologic background)
　Medical services (e.g., confirm patient suitability, medical evaluations, laboratory studies, countersign orders and treatment plans, justify take-home medications, physician review of treatment plan)
　Contents of medical evaluation (including history, physical examination, laboratory examinations)
　"Initial treatment plan" and "periodic treatment plan evaluation" (describes treatment and rehabilitative service needs)
　Referral to vocational rehabilitation, education, and employment services
　Minimal frequency of attendance (quantity of take-home medication)
　Drug testing
Administrative
　Clinical and administrative record keeping
　Staffing pattern considerations
　Conduct of research
Special Populations
　Services for pregnant patients
　Special standards for short-term detoxification treatment
　Special standards for long-term detoxification treatment

Note: See Chapter 11 for a more detailed description of specific areas under regulation.

stances, DEA regulations govern the manufacturing, distribution, and dispensing of methadone. The objective of the DEA in this role is to prevent the diversion of drugs with abuse potential.

A third tier of regulation is unique for methadone. The office of the Secretary of DHHS has been assigned the task of establishing standards regarding the methods and circumstances for the use of methadone. These regulations are now implemented by FDA regulations, jointly with the Substance Abuse and Mental Health Services Administration (SAMHSA). This extensive system of regulations was first issued in 1972 and continues to persist, with periodic revisions (e.g., using language that is more clinically relevant and allowing provisions for LAAM treatment). Table 2.1 lists programmatic areas currently under federal regulatory control (DHHS, FDA, 21 CFR Part 291; see Parrino [1993]).

State and Local Levels of Control

The final level of control over methadone treatment is at the local level, and involves individual states, counties, and municipalities. These local levels of government often codify their own controls, further restricting the use of methadone for the treatment of opiate addiction. At times extremely restrictive local regulations have resulted in essentially a banning of methadone treatment altogether in some parts of the country.

The additional regulation of methadone treatment on the state level is actually mandated by federal regulations. These regulations state that no prescribing, administering, or dispensing of a narcotic drug for the treatment of narcotic addiction may occur without prior approval by the Food and Drug Administration and the State authority (21 CFR 291.505; Parrino [1993]). This requirement represents a level of control imposed by current federal regulation that exceeds the usual requirements for the prescribing and dispensing of medication.

The local control of methadone treatment may itself consist of multiple layers involving state, county, and local interests in treatment programs. These entities comprise governmental agencies and local organizations and are involved in many aspects of professional practice and program operation. These aspects can include regulation, financing, licensing of practitioners, quality assurance, data collection, use of controlled substances, control of diversion, and control of illicit drugs. Beyond adhering to federal regulatory requirements, states may, and do, impose more restrictive measures. Areas of clinical operation affected by these measures include urinalysis collection and testing, take-home doses of methadone, issues of patient rights, record keeping, staffing, and admission criteria. In addition, issues involving patient registry, treatment duration, and treatment plan reviews are often addressed.

Each state, and localities within each state, have highly variable requirements; however, it is impractical to review such measures in depth. But, it is worthwhile to consider in brief one example of control at this level. In 1993 the FDA approved LAAM for the treatment of opioid dependence, and federal regulations were issued for LAAM treatment. However, because of additional local regulation, programs were still unable to dispense LAAM. First, existing state regulations had to be modified to include LAAM. Although LAAM was reclassified as a schedule II drug by the federal government, state law often mandated similar reclassification procedures. Only then might LAAM be added to state formularies as a medication approved for the treatment of opioid dependence. Second, many county and local entities overseeing program operation mandated review proceedings for the approval of LAAM treatment, further delaying its availability. Thus, despite FDA approval of LAAM in 1993, only about 3,000 patients were being treated with it in the United States four years later. This slow process of making LAAM available highlights the complex process required to institute changes in the pharmacologic treatment of opioid dependence in the United States.

REGULATORY ISSUES IN OTHER PARTS OF THE WORLD

It is difficult to summarize the regulatory and policy issues of methadone treatment in the numerous other countries where methadone treatment is provided. At least 20 countries have methadone treatment programs and, as in the United States, the regulation of this treatment undergoes periodic revision in many of these countries. A brief summary of the history of methadone treatment and regulation for several countries can be found in the third edition of the Swiss Methadone Report (Uchtenhagen 1996).[1]

Most countries that developed methadone treatment programs in the 1970s based their model of treatment on the early work done by Dole and Nyswander. For example, the first European methadone treatment program was started in Sweden in 1966 and was essentially a replication of the model used by Dole and Nyswander in New York. However, there has been considerable variability in methadone treatment practices across countries and over time, and it is no longer unusual for some countries (such as Australia) to allow individual physicians to prescribe methadone (rather than to establish centralized treatment programs such as those in the United States).

While generalizations across countries concerning the regulation of methadone treatment should be recognized *as* generalizations, a few points do seem to appear consistently. First, most countries use oral methadone (rather than injections), and more often the liquid rather than tablet formulation. Second, many countries either require or recommend that methadone treatment be delivered in the context of other, nonpharmacologic treatment services. And finally, it is not uncommon to find countries regulating specific aspects of methadone practice, such as dosing and urinalysis testing. Thus, the heavy regulation of methadone treatment in the United States is not unique. Interestingly, many countries have made substantial efforts to find the best means for regulating methadone treatment.

Cost-Benefit Analysis of Drug Abuse Treatment

Calculating the cost of drug abuse and the benefit of treatment can be exceedingly complicated. Many areas are impacted by drug abuse beyond simply the individual user. Certainly drug use adversely affects the individual user; but it also affects the family, the local community, the broader community, and society at large. Effective treatment can produce both savings in cost and a broad array of other benefits at each of these levels.

Financial loss from drug use stems from the direct cost of drugs, as well as lost earnings, decreased workforce productivity, primary and secondary medical costs, increased law enforcement and prison costs, and societal, drug-related theft and violence (Table 2.2). Untreated opiate addiction in the United States costs an estimated $20 billion per year. However, dollar figures often fail to capture the magnitude of personal suffering, familial pain, and societal woes produced by drug use. Hence, the justification of drug abuse treatment is not simply an economic one; patients, families, and society benefit as well.

Financing of drug abuse treatment can come from a variety of sources, including patients, insurance companies, community entities such as foundations and churches, hospitals, and most significantly, local, state, and federal governments. The cost of treatment is affected by many factors, including the incidence and severity of the disorder; the modality, efficiency, and efficacy of the particular treatment delivery system; the availability of treatment programs; and the willingness of society and policy makers to fund programs. These elements are in turn influenced by factors such as drug availability, the efficacy of prevention, scientific research findings, outcome measures, societal priorities and attitudes toward addiction, and the political atmosphere.

Table 2.2 Costs of Drug Abuse

Criminal Justice System	Victim Losses	Theft Losses	Health Care Service Utilization	Lost Legitimate Earnings	Income Transfers
Cost of police protection, prosecution, adjudication, public defense, and corrections (incarceration and parole/probation)	Victim expenditures on medical care, repairs of damaged property, and lost time from work resulting from predatory crimes	Value of property or money stolen during a crime, excluding any property damage or other victim losses	Economic value of avoidable inpatient, outpatient, and emergency medical and mental health care	Value of legitimate productivity lost because individuals pursue income through crime or live off the resources of friends, families, or others	Resources moved from nonsubstance-abusing taxpayers to others via gifts, public assistance, or public and private disability insurance

Source: Adapted from Gerstein et al. (1994), fig. 1.

The California Drug and Alcohol Treatment Assessment (CALDATA)

Before discussing the specific costs of methadone treatment, this section provides a brief review of a comprehensive cost-benefit analysis for general substance abuse treatment conducted in the early 1990s in California. The study, titled "Evaluating Recovery Services: The California Drug and Alcohol Treatment Assessment" (more commonly referred to as CALDATA), was published in 1994 (Gerstein et al. 1994). The study's objective was to evaluate the effectiveness, benefits, and costs of alcohol and drug abuse treatment. A voluntary survey was conducted of approximately 3,000 participants in 97 residential, residential "social model," general outpatient, and outpatient methadone treatment programs in 16 counties in California. Participants were in treatment or were discharged from treatment between October 1991 and September 1992 and were randomly selected to represent the nearly 150,000 statewide patients in treatment. More than 1,850 of the survey participants were successfully contacted and interviewed for follow-up after nine months.

The cost of treating the 150,000 statewide patients was $209 million, and the one-year benefits to taxpaying citizens, mostly owing to reductions in crime, were worth approximately $1.5 billion. This 1:7 average cost-benefit ratio ranged from 1:4 to greater than 1:12, depending on the type of treatment. However, it was evident that the populations served by the various modalities were quite different. Therefore, comparisons across the modalities of the relative costs and benefits should be made with caution.

Table 2.3 gives data regarding the cost and benefits of "continuing" and "discharged" methadone patients. The "methadone discharge" group was composed of short-term methadone detoxification patients in addition to long-term maintenance patients who began maintenance but left treat-

Table 2.3 Total Benefits and Costs to Taxpayers, by Treatment Modality

	Methadone Discharge	Methadone Continuing
Savings per day during treatment	$20.59	$30.47
Savings per day after treatment	$11.32	n/a[a]
Length of stay (average days)	60	365
Cost per day of treatment	$6.79	$6.37
Total cost per treatment episode	$405	$2,325
Total benefits	$5,093	$11,122
Cost-to-benefit ratio	1:12.58	1:4.78

Source: Adapted from Gerstein et al. (1994), table 35.
[a]Posttreatment values not applicable for continuing participants.

ment. All "methadone continuing" patients had been in treatment for at least four months at the time of the follow-up interview. Of all treatment modalities studied, the most favorable cost-to-benefit ratio (1:12.58) was for discharged methadone patients. However, this ratio largely reflects the low total cost incurred per treatment episode ($405), despite a lower (relative to the other treatment modalities) total benefit ($5,093). Total benefits reported for the methadone continuing group were $11,122, yielding a cost-to-benefit ratio of 1:4.78. Furthermore, benefits persisted after treatment through the second year of follow-up for participants monitored longer than one year. Thus, longer-term benefits are likely to be substantially higher than outcomes found after one year.

The results from the CALDATA, in which a comparison was made of patients before and after their treatment episode, demonstrated a two-thirds decrease in criminal activity, with longer treatment duration associated with greater improvement. Alcohol and drug use fell by approximately two-fifths. Hospitalizations were reduced by about one-third, with significant improvements in other health indicators. Additionally, longer lengths of stay in treatment had a positive effect on employment.

These results from the CALDATA provide an exceedingly important message: substance abuse treatment results in remarkable savings, even when patients are followed for relatively short periods of time. As noted in the final report, $1 spent on treatment resulted in $7 in savings to the community. Although that benefit figure represents a variety of treatment modalities, analyses of only the methadone patients in CALDATA show a benefit of $4–$13 per $1 spent.

Other studies have shown similar substantial savings associated with methadone treatment. For example, a study of methadone treatment conducted in the late 1980s showed that a 16-week course of methadone maintenance therapy resulted in striking decreases in drug use, criminal activity, and economic costs to the community (Strain et al. 1993). For instance, there was a 96 percent reduction in money spent on drugs, a 96 percent reduction in days with illegal activity, and a 95 percent reduction in the amount of money obtained through illegal activities. Illegal income fell, on average, from $1,504 to $73 per month—a social benefit of $1,431 per month during treatment.

Regarding the health-related cost benefits of methadone treatment, the potential reduction in HIV transmission is of paramount importance. In November 1997, The National Institutes of Health (NIH) convened a consensus development conference during which data were presented on this issue. One study tracked HIV seroconversion rates over time among subjects both in and out of methadone maintenance therapy in Philadelphia,

Pennsylvania, during the late 1980s and early 1990s (Merrill 1997). After four years, those who had received no treatment were 4.2 times more likely (13.5 vs. 3.2%) to have seroconverted to HIV positive than those who had received two or more years of methadone treatment. Currently, the annual incidence of seroconversion to HIV for injection drug users is 3–4 percent per year, based on Centers for Disease Control surveillance data. These data suggest that putting all opiate-dependent persons into methadone maintenance treatment would result in a decrease of 55,000 to 70,000 individuals who would become HIV positive over a four-year period, resulting in a cumulative savings in health care costs of $1.325–$1.75 billion.

Cost of Methadone Treatment

Methadone pharmacotherapy alone is relatively inexpensive. In the United States, in the mid-1990s, a 60-mg daily dose of methadone (not including costs of medication preparation or administration, counseling, etc.) cost a little more than $200 per year. The annual cost for LAAM is slightly higher, but this difference in cost is minimal when all other costs are factored in, as described next.

Annual costs for comprehensive methadone treatment can easily exceed 15 to 20 times the cost of the medication. The Office of Applied Studies of SAMHSA conducts an annual survey of substance abuse treatment programs, including methadone facilities, called the National Drug and Alcoholism Treatment Unit Survey (NDATUS; DHHS 1993a). Among the information collected are data on the financing of methadone treatment. Using 1991 NDATUS data adjusted for inflation, Harwood (as described in IOM [1995]) estimated that in fiscal year 1993 payments for methadone treatment from all sources totaled $480 million. Assuming that there were 117,000 patients in outpatient methadone maintenance treatment during that time, the average cost per patient was $4,100 per year. Similarly, Bradley, French, and Rachal (1994), in a study involving three methadone treatment programs (one hospital based and two freestanding clinics), determined the average annual cost per patient to be between $3,750 and $4,400 for standard treatment (i.e., methadone pharmacotherapy plus counseling and urinalysis testing).

This difference between the cost of medication alone and costs for full methadone treatment is owing to the other components of methadone treatment (Table 2.4). The largest cost associated with methadone treatment is staffing of the program. (A discussion of personnel requirements for methadone treatment can be found in Chapter 11.) Other costs that can represent substantial outlays include rent and utilities, security, and urinalysis testing. In the study by Bradley, French, and Rachal (1994), expenditures for labor, professional consultants, and contracted services such as laboratory analyses amounted to 69–81 percent of the total annual cost of treatment.

Those individuals most in need of methadone treatment often do not have the resources to pay for it. Although government sources such as state and local grants often helped to underwrite the costs of methadone treatment in the past, these sources of funding are declining. Innovative mechanisms for lowering the cost of methadone treatment are needed, so that methadone treatment remains an attractive and viable option for funding sources such as managed care organizations. At the same time, communicating the benefits of methadone treatment to funding sources is also vital (Table 2.4), and it is important to stress that the robust efficacy of methadone treatment is achieved by adequately funding the full array of services provided at successful programs.

***Table 2.4* Cost Factors and Benefits of Methadone Treatment**

Cost Factors
- Staff wages and benefits[a]
- Rent and utilities
- Licensing and credentialing
- Medical supplies
- Staff training
- Medication (methadone)
- Urinalysis testing
- Security
- Documentation and record keeping

Benefits
- Reduced illicit drug consumption
- Improved general health
- Improved access to health care
- Reduced spread of infectious diseases
- Improved psychologic well-being
- Reduced violence
- Reduced theft and property damage
- Acquired/maintained employment
- Decreased reliance on public assistance
- Improved domestic relations
- Improved childrearing
- Improved social functioning

[a]See Chapter 11 for a discussion of staff requirements for a methadone clinic.

Revenue Sources for Methadone Treatment

The primary sources of funding for methadone treatment programs in the United States are federal block grants, Medicare, Medicaid, state agencies, self-pay (out-of-pocket), and private insurance. The percentage of total revenue dollars that each source contributes to methadone treatment varies among individual states and programs and is largely a function of program type (e.g., hospital based, public, for-profit, etc.), patient population, and resource availability.

Three sources of public funding of substance abuse treatment in the United States—federal block grants, Medicaid, and state funding—are all administered by state agencies. The State Alcohol and Drug Abuse Profile (SADAP), administered by the National Association of State Alcohol and Drug Abuse Directors, Inc., surveys the financing of programs that receive state funding, with the exception of most private-for-profit, some not-for-profit, and Department of Veterans Affairs programs. The SADAP has shown that the majority (68–78% between 1987 and 1992) of financing for all alcohol and drug abuse programs (not just methadone) has come from public sources. During this time, federal block grants increased at a more rapid rate than state agency funding, so that by 1992 the two sources of funding were approximately equal.

Medicaid's role in the funding of treatment is significant. The Drug Services Research Survey of Brandeis University, published in 1992, estimated that Medicaid was the expected source of payment for 27 percent of methadone patients upon admission for treatment (Batten et al. 1992). About 30 percent of the revenues in Medicaid-certified methadone programs were from Medicaid (as described in IOM [1995]).

Increasingly, Medicaid funding will be through assignment to managed care organizations; managed care has typically taken a negative view of long-term treatment for substance abuse. Psychiatric and substance abuse treatments preferred by managed care have been oriented toward short-term crisis intervention. Methadone maintenance, by its nature, is therefore not a favored modality of treatment despite its proven efficacy. When Medicaid dollars are under public control, the societal benefits of treatment such as decreases in crime enter the cost-benefit equation. However, decision makers in managed care do not view such societal benefits as being relevant to their corporate cost-benefit decisions.

In time, managed care may come to appreciate more fully the value of long-term substance abuse treatment, including methadone treatment, if substance abuse treatment dollars become a part of all health care dollars (rather than "carved out"). Then, managed care may recognize that failure to invest in effective, long-term treatment of addiction can result in increased total expenditures owing to medical complications from continued drug use. For example, by avoiding the morbidity associated with a single case of HIV/AIDS, a savings of approximately $157,811 in health care dollars could be realized (French et al. 1996).

Treatment programs must do their part in teaching managed care about the clinical and economic benefits of treatment, for example, by demonstrating decreases in risk behaviors (such as HIV-related) associated with treatment, and also by showing the advantages of funding sustained treatment rather than paying for multiple, brief admissions. Providers also must be increasingly willing to work effectively with utilization review and management, and to justify intensity and duration of treatment (McCarty 1997).

Self-pay, private insurance, and, for a select group of patients, the Department of Veterans Affairs comprise most of the remaining payment sources. Using NDATUS data, investigators have estimated that self-pay and private insurance contribute 17 percent and 2.5 percent, respectively, of total expenditures for methadone treatment (IOM 1995). When one examines different types of treatment programs, it is evident that for-profit programs derive a significantly higher proportion of revenue from patient out-of-pocket payments than do not-for-profit programs (Batten et al. 1992; IOM 1990). Regarding the Veterans Affairs system, one study found that 26 percent of all inpatients were diagnosed with a substance abuse disorder (Peterson et al. 1993), indicating a large population in need of treatment. In 1993 approximately 36 Veterans Affairs medical centers were providing methadone maintenance to 5,886 patients, or 5 percent of all U.S. methadone patients (IOM 1995). The estimated cost of this treatment was about $22 million (Department of Veterans Affairs 1993), or $3,700 per patient.

Summary of Cost and Financing of Methadone Treatment

Methadone treatment is the combination of a pharmacotherapy and nonpharmacologic treatment services. Both of these aspects of methadone treatment are expensive. Special regulatory issues associated with methadone treatment increase the cost of delivery of this effective treatment.

Efforts in three areas may help to make this effective treatment more widely available to those who could benefit from it. First, mechanisms for lowering the costs of traditional systems of methadone delivery without reducing efficacy should be explored; however, because of current regulatory excesses, feasibility of this approach is severely limited. Second, the benefits of methadone treatment must be effectively communicated to funding sources, policy makers, and the general public. And third, new and innovative means for the delivery of methadone treatment should be systematically studied and developed. Some possible future directions for methadone treatment are described in the next section.

POSSIBLE FUTURE DIRECTIONS AND IMPLICATIONS REGARDING POLICY

Modifications of Current Methadone Treatment Systems

Some changes within the current framework of treatment may result in improved efficiency of operation in existing programs, thus resulting in improvements independent of external factors. Staff optimization through organizational efficiency, computerized tracking and documentation, and state-of-the-art automated pouring systems for methadone delivery are potential means for increasing efficiency. However, sufficient restructuring to achieve substantial improvement in efficiency would be possible only in an atmosphere of reduced regulatory encumbrance.

In the meantime, novel treatment modalities can be integrated within existing clinics utilizing tools such as formalized behavioral contingencies (Kidorf et al. 1994; Silverman et al. 1996; Brooner et al. 1997; Brooner et al. 1998; also see Chapter 10). After all, the fundamental objective of a methadone maintenance clinic is to provide a context that encourages behavioral change. These behavioral contingency models have promise in enhancing the effectiveness of treatment, thereby increasing the proportion of patients who are stable in their recovery and require less intensive services. Clinic resources are thus freed, allowing enhanced treatment for unstable patients, increased census, or a reduction in resource expenditures.

Finally, the use of LAAM can affect program operating costs. The NIDA has estimated that LAAM costs about $2.85 more per patient per week ($148 annually) than methadone. Monthly pregnancy tests, mandatory for LAAM patients, cost about $90 per patient annually. However, less frequent dispensing of medication and clinic attendance of LAAM patients may translate into increased program efficiency and reduced per capita costs (Prendergast et al. 1995).

Alternative Delivery Systems

Innovations of the type that fall outside the realm of the typical comprehensive methadone program, though controversial, are worth considering. There has been some experience with all of the modalities discussed here.

Interim Methadone Maintenance (IMM)

A proposal for IMM in the United States was initially issued in 1989 by the NIDA and the DEA, and eventually regulations for IMM were published in the revised 1993 regulations (58 FR 495; IOM [1995]). IMM involved the dispensing of methadone on a temporary basis to individuals awaiting treatment placement in a comprehensive program. With IMM other services required by existing regulations in the United States were not required. IMM was provided by comprehensive treatment programs that were required to provide medical evaluation and service as well as counseling on HIV risk. Random drug screening was not required, and take-home doses were prohibited. Transfer to comprehensive treatment occurred after a "relatively brief period."

The only program providing IMM services, Beth Israel in New York City, was forced to close in 1993. Opposition to the Beth Israel program was largely based on evidence that interim treatment was not as effective as comprehensive treatment, and on the fear that these less costly programs would set precedents, resulting in decreased funding for existing programs. Treatment in such limited service (or "low-threshold") methadone programs, though not as effective, has been associated with reduced heroin use and transition into comprehensive treatment (Yancovitz et al. 1991). IMM may be used as a way to engage individuals who are awaiting or have not yet committed to comprehensive services. Such reduced-service units may also be utilized for selected stable maintenance patients during periods in which they are judged not to require rehabilitative services.

Mobile Treatment

Another novel method for engaging opioid-dependent individuals in treatment is through mobile treatment—a medical, van-based clinic on wheels. Mobile methadone treatment has been used in Baltimore, Maryland, and Springfield, Massachusetts (Brady 1996). By bringing services into the addicted individual's neighborhood, treatment becomes more available to those not able or willing to travel to clinics. Coordination with needle-exchange programs may create a system whereby individuals are gradually initiated into the role of patient, stabilized in terms of their dependence and social situation, and eventually enrolled in more traditional comprehensive clinics. Mobile treatment also avoids the problem of the "not in my backyard" attitude prevalent in communities surrounding non-mobile clinics.

The Methadone Clinic as a Comprehensive Primary Care Clinic

Substance abuse patients often have comorbid medical problems. However, despite the high medical needs of this population, patients often slip through the cracks in the health care delivery system. Referring patients from the methadone clinic to other sites for medical or psychiatric care often results in poor compliance rates in attending such off-site appointments. Methadone treatment programs that operate as sites for primary medical care address this problem, by utilizing a "one-stop shopping" model for health care delivery (Umbricht-Schneiter et al. 1994). Daily attendance for methadone treatment can enhance compliance with medical appointments and treatments. By using the methadone clinic as a site for primary medical care services, enhanced preventive and problem-oriented medical care can result in less frequent hospitalizations and emergency department visits, which, in turn, can lead to better quality of life for patients, as well as decreased medical costs.

Medical Maintenance

Medical maintenance refers to the provision of maintenance methadone within the context of general medical practice. Novick et al. (1991) reported on a study of such a model. One hundred methadone maintenance patients meeting study criteria were transferred to practices where they received methadone treatment from their physicians rather than at a traditional methadone treatment program. The participants met with their physicians about once a month and submitted urine samples and drank methadone in the presence of staff at the time of each visit. Then each participant received a prescription for a 28-day supply of methadone, which was filled at a hospital pharmacy. In initial analyses of the first 40 patients, treatment retention was high (82% at 12 months), and only 12.5 percent were returned to traditional methadone programs for unfavorable response.

Office-based physicians prescribing with pharmacy pickup of methadone may be especially valuable for two populations: (1) socially rehabilitated patients, to further reduce contact with current abusers, and (2) residents in rural areas, where it is not feasible to require them to travel long distances for clinic-based treatment.

Under current U.S. regulations, medical maintenance is theoretically possible through two routes. A treatment provider may apply for a research IND ("investigational new drug") exemption, which would permit a non-conventional delivery system. However, the FDA requires that a clear *research* purpose and methodology be demonstrated. Alternatively, an individual physician, or even a pharmacy, may apply to the FDA and the DEA to become a narcotic treatment program, and required services such as intake history, counseling, and urinalysis may be contracted out. At the time of application, or any time thereafter, a program is permitted to request exemption from specific program standards. The Federal Register cites an example in which such an exemption might be granted: "A private practitioner who wishes to treat a limited number of patients in a nonmetropolitan area with few physicians and no rehabilitative services geographically accessible and requests exemption from some of the staffing and service standards" (21 CFR 291.505; Parrino [1993]). However, the process of an individual physician or pharmacy becoming a narcotic treatment program requires considerable imagination and innovation on the part of the provider and has been perceived as too burdensome to have been used to a meaningful extent. While medical methadone remains an interesting idea that may be particularly suitable for certain patient populations, in practicality, it is unavailable in the United States under current regulatory circumstances.

Buprenorphine

Buprenorphine has shown promise as a new pharmacotherapy for opioid addiction, and as a partial agonist it appears to offer certain advantages when compared to methadone (see Chapter 13 for a review of buprenorphine's use in the treatment of opioid dependence). Buprenorphine's opioid agonist activity provides sufficient reinforcement to make it acceptable to patients, but its ceiling on the magnitude of these effects results in greater safety. It has a reduced abuse liability relative to full opioid agonists. Combination buprenorphine/naloxone products that are being developed may further reduce abuse liability. Buprenorphine has a slow onset and a long duration of receptor binding, which results in a relatively mild abstinence syndrome and which makes less than daily dosing a possibility. Studies of alternate-day dosing have shown that this regimen is safe, effective, and acceptable to patients (Amass et al. 1994; Johnson et al. 1995), and preliminary results of other studies may support even less frequent dosing. Such a schedule permits less frequent clinic attendance, which may result in cost savings to clinics and enhanced convenience for patients, without the potential for diversion inherent in take-home doses. The relatively lower abuse potential, along with the enhanced safety profile and less than daily dosing, may make the dispensing of buprenorphine outside traditional methadone clinics more feasible; buprenorphine can potentially serve as a model for alternative dispensing of other opioid substitution pharmacotherapies.

Encouraging Improved Resource Allocation

Probably the most important intervention the substance abuse treatment community could make toward improving the system of care delivery is to make drug abuse treatment more attractive and acceptable to the general public, as well as to decision makers and funding agencies. This can be accomplished through teaching, advocacy, and outreach to the community, as well as through continued, rigorous economic evaluations of cost-effectiveness and net benefits of treatment (French 1995). Disseminating the message that substance abuse treatment including methadone treatment is effective continues to be needed—both to decision makers in government and, especially, to the general public. Publicizing the value of treatment is of critical importance; this information will affect those who allocate managed care dollars as well as policy makers who assign public resources and control treatment regulations. The Institute of Medicine recommends that DHHS "conduct a review of its priorities in substance abuse treatment, including methadone treatment, in a way that integrates changes in regulations and the development of practice guidelines with decisions about treatment funding" (IOM 1995). These priorities would ideally be determined by a rational drug policy based on sound research and the demonstration of medical, economic, and social value.

International Experience

Several countries have utilized alternatives to the United States' "comprehensive methadone clinic" model (Farrell 1996). For example, in Denmark general practitioners initiate 50 percent of methadone prescriptions without consulting a treatment center, in the United Kingdom community pharmacists dispense approximately 95 percent of methadone prescriptions (with subsequent consumption outside the pharmacy), and in the Netherlands mobile methadone treatment dates from as early as 1978. In contrast to these relatively open systems, in Italy methadone is available only through specialist services, and in Germany virtually all methadone is consumed on-site at clinics.

Summary

Methadone maintenance is the most highly regulated of medical treatments. In the United States, there is a growing consensus in the medical community that the current regulatory system should be revised. In 1997 a consensus panel on the treatment of heroin addiction, sponsored by the NIH, pointed out that federal regulations prevent treatment from being tailored to the needs of the individual patient by requiring an inflexible system of delivery, unproductive paperwork, and excessive administrative costs (NIH 1997). The panel recommended that the regulations be eliminated and that some alternate means, such as accreditation, be instituted to ensure safe and effective practice. (The process of transferring the oversight of methadone treatment from the FDA to the Center of Substance Abuse Treatment [CSAT] is currently under way; the new structure is, in fact, expected to be in the form of guidelines and accreditation.) In addition, the panel suggested a revision that would permit more physicians and pharmacies to prescribe and dispense methadone, at least to more stable patients. Furthermore, they recommended that federal, state, and local agencies coordinate their efforts, examine programs with poor performance, reduce the scrutiny of programs consistently performing well, and address the problem of slow state approval of medications.

Many studies have demonstrated that methadone treatment is cost-effective when a broad array of cost-saving measures are included (e.g., decreases in crime, increases in employment). However, it is not yet clear how methadone treatment will operate and be adequately reimbursed in the current environment of managed health care. This issue becomes increasingly important as state and federally supported insurance programs assume a greater managed care orientation.

Creative and more cost-effective mechanisms for the delivery of methadone treatment continue to be proposed and investigated. These alternative treatment approaches have sought to decrease costs, improve outcomes, and increase availability of treatment, and have included operations such as medical methadone, mobile methadone treatment, and the designation of methadone clinics as primary-care sites. In addition, the future use of other pharmacotherapies such as LAAM and buprenorphine may affect treatment delivery significantly.

Methadone treatment can appear to be an expensive intervention to agencies that fund substance abuse treatment—especially since many benefits are social, and not directly economical to the funding agency. To maintain and improve the availability of methadone treatment, the medical profession must demonstrate and publicize justification for costs and explain the savings incurred through treatment. Effectively communicating the value of methadone treatment—to the general public as well as funding agencies—is critical if methadone treatment is to remain an available option for a significant number of patients with opioid dependence.

Note

1. Copies of the third edition of the Swiss Methadone Report are available, in English, from the Addiction Research Foundation, 33 Russell Street, Toronto, Ontario M5S 2S1, Canada (telephone 1-800-661-1111). German and French copies are available through the Swiss Federal Office of Public Health, CH 3003 Bern, Switzerland.

References and Suggested Further Reading

Amass L., Bickel W.K., Higgins S.T., Badger G.J. 1994. Alternate-day dosing during buprenorphine treatment of opioid dependence. *Life Sci.* 54:1215–28.

Anglin M.D., Speckart G.R., Booth M.W., Ryan T.M. 1989. Consequences and costs of shutting off methadone. *Addict. Behav.* 14:307–26.

Batten H., Prottas J., Horgan C.M., Simon L.J., Larson M.J., Elliott E.A., Marsden M.E. 1992. Drug Services Research Survey, Final Report: Phase II Revised. Contract number 271-90-8319/1. Submitted to the National Institute on Drug Abuse, Feb. 12.

Bigelow G.E. 1995. Forward. In: Cowan A., Lewis J.W., eds. *Buprenorphine: Combating Drug Abuse with a Unique Opioid.* Wiley-Liss, New York, pp. xi–xiii.

Bradley C.J., French M.T., Rachal J.V. 1994. Financing and cost of standard and enhanced methadone treatment. *J. Subst. Abuse Treat.* 11:433–42.

Brady J.V. 1996. Enhancing Drug Abuse Treatment by Mobile Health Services; Final Report to the National Institute on Drug Abuse. Substance Abuse Center, Institutes for Behavior Resources, Baltimore, MD.

Brooner R.K., Kidorf M.S., King V.L., Bigelow G.E. 1997. Using behaviorally contingent pharmacotherapy in opioid abusers enhances treatment outcome. In: Harris L.S., ed. Problems of Drug Dependence 1996. Proceedings of the 58th Annual Scientific Meeting of College on Problems of Drug Dependence. National Institute on Drug Abuse Research Monograph, U.S. Government Printing Office, Washington, DC.

Brooner R.K., Kidorf M.S., King V.L., Stoller K.B. 1998. Preliminary evidence of improved treatment response in antisocial drug abusers. *Drug Alcohol Depend.* 49:249–60.

Department of Health and Human Services (DHHS). 1993a. National Drug and Alcoholism Treatment Unit Survey (NDATUS): 1991 Main Findings Report. DHHS Publication No. (SMA) 93–2007, Washington, DC.
———. 1993b. State Resources and Services Related to Alcohol and Drug Abuse Problems, Fiscal Years 1987, 1988, 1989, 1990, 1991. DHHS Publication No. (SMA) 93–1989, Washington, DC.

Department of Veterans Affairs. 1993. Annual Cost Distribution Report for FY 1993. U.S. Government Printing Office, Washington, DC.

Farrell M. 1996. A Review of the Legislation, Regulation and Delivery of Methadone in 12 Member States of the European Union—Final Report. Office for Official Publications of the European Communities, Luxembourg.

French M.T. 1995. Economic evaluation of drug abuse treatment programs: methodology and findings. *Am. J. Drug Alcohol Abuse* 21:111–35.

French M.T., Mauskopf J.A., Teague J.L., Roland E.J. 1996. Estimating the dollar value of health outcomes from drug-abuse interventions. *Med. Care* 34:890–910.

Gerstein D.R., Johnson R.A., Harwood H.J., Fountain D., Suter N., Mallow K. 1994. Evaluating Recovery Services: The California Drug and Alcohol Treatment Assessment (CALDATA) General Report. California Department of Alcohol and Drug Programs, Sacramento.

Institute of Medicine (IOM). 1990. *Treating Drug Problems*. Gerstein D., Harwood H., eds. National Academy Press, Washington, DC.
———. 1995. *Federal Regulation of Methadone Treatment*. National Academy Press, Washington, DC.

Johnson R.E., Eissenberg T., Stitzer M.L., Strain E.C., Liebson I.A., Bigelow G.E. 1995. Buprenorphine treatment of opioid dependence: clinical trial of daily versus alternate-day dosing. *Drug Alcohol Depend.* 40:27–35.

Joseph H., Appel P. 1993. Historical perspectives and public health issues. In: *Center for Substance Abuse Treatment, Treatment Improvement Protocol Series, Vol. 1: State Methadone Treatment Guidelines*. Substance Abuse and Mental Health Services Administration, Rockville, MD, pp. 11–24.

Kidorf M., Stitzer M.L., Brooner R.K., Goldberg J. 1994. Contingent methadone take-home doses reinforce adjunct therapy attendance of methadone maintenance patients. *Drug Alcohol Depend.* 36:221–26.

McCarty D. 1997. Narcotic Agonist Treatment as a Benefit Under Managed Care. Paper presented at the NIH Consensus Development Conference on Effective Medical Treatment of Heroin Addiction, Nov. Bethesda, MD.

Merrill J. 1997. Impact of Methadone Maintenance on HIV Seroconversion and Related Costs. Paper presented at the NIH Consensus Development Conference on Effective Medical Treatment of Heroin Addiction, Nov. Bethesda, MD.

National Institutes of Health (NIH). 1997. Consensus Statement Online 15(6): Nov. 17–19, in press.

Novick D.M., Joseph H. 1991. Medical maintenance: the treatment of chronic opiate dependence in general medical practice. *J. Subst. Abuse Treat.* 8:233–39.

Novick D.M., Joseph H., Salsitz E.A., Kalin M.F., Keefe J.B., Miller E.L., Richman B.L. 1991. Outcomes of treatment of socially rehabilitated methadone maintenance patients in physicians' offices (medical maintenance): follow-up at three and a half to nine and a fourth years. *J. Gen. Intern. Med.* 9:127–30.

Parrino M.W. 1993. *State Methadone Treatment Guidelines; Treatment Improvement Protocol (TIP) Series 1.* Substance Abuse and Mental Health Services Administration, Center for Substance Abuse Treatment, Rockville, MD.

Peterson K., Swindle R., Paradise M., Moos R. 1993. *Substance Abuse Treatment Programming in the Department of Veterans Affairs: Staffing, Patients, Services, and Policies.* Program Evaluation Resource Center, Department of Veterans Affairs Medical Center, Palo Alto, CA.

Prendergast M.L., Grella C., Perry S.M., Anglin M.D. 1995. Levo-Alpha-Acetylmethadol (LAAM): clinical, research, and policy issues of a new pharmacotherapy for opioid addiction. *J. Psychoactive Drugs* 27:239–47.

Silverman K., Higgins S.T., Brooner R.K., Montoya I.D., Cone E.J., Schuster C.R., Preston K.L. 1996. Sustained cocaine abstinence in methadone maintenance patients through voucher-based reinforcement therapy. *Arch. Gen. Psychiatry* 53:409–15.

Strain E.C., Stitzer M.L., Liebson I.A., Bigelow G.E. 1993. Methadone dose and treatment outcome. *Drug Alcohol Depend.* 33:105–17.

Uchtenhagen A., ed. 1996. *Swiss Methadone Report: Narcotic Substitution in the Treatment of Heroin Addicts in Switzerland,* 3rd ed. Swiss Federal Office of Public Health, Zurich.

Umbricht-Schneiter A., Ginn D.H., Pabst K.M., Bigelow G.E. 1994. Providing medical care to methadone clinic patients: referral vs on-site care. *Am. J. Public Health* 84:207–10.

Yancovitz S.R., Des Jarlais D.C., Peyser N.P., Drew E., Friedmann P., Trigg H.L., Robinson J.W. 1991. A randomized trial of an interim methadone maintenance clinic. *Am. J. Public Health* 81:1185–91.

3

The Pharmacology of Methadone

Sharon L. Walsh, Ph.D., and Eric C. Strain, M.D.

The pharmacologic effects of methadone were characterized in humans and other species more than fifty years ago. It is now known that methadone exerts its actions as an analgesic and euphoriant through binding with mu opioid receptors similarly to other mu opioid agonists such as morphine. This chapter begins by defining and providing a brief overview of opioid receptors and the basic principles of drug action, to set the stage for reviewing the pharmacologic actions of methadone in humans.

Overview of Opioid Receptors and Opioid Pharmacology

To understand the pharmacologic actions of opioid drugs, in general, and methadone, in particular, one must first be familiar with some basic facts of drug action at receptors and with the characteristics of opioid receptors. Receptors are specially configured proteins that can produce a specific physiologic effect when activated. Opioid receptors are found on the exterior surface of cells in the brain and in the periphery. There are actually a number of subtypes of opioid receptors that differ in their structure, including the mu, kappa, and delta receptors. For each opioid receptor subtype, there are distinct endogenous or naturally occurring neurotransmitter substances or chemicals that interact with the receptor, and these subtypes exhibit differential sensitivity to a variety of opioid drugs. The second fact critical for understanding opioid drugs and their effects on the body is that an opioid drug can either produce physiologic effects or block the physiologic effects mediated by a receptor, depending on whether the drug is classified as an agonist or antagonist, respectively. Each of these points is briefly reviewed here. (The reader can learn more about opioid pharmacology and opioid receptors by reviewing the excellent textbooks available on pharmacology and psychopharmacology listed at the end of this chapter.)

Agonists and Antagonists

Drugs that occupy a receptor and activate that receptor are called *agonists*. In general, as the dose of an agonist drug increases, the effect being measured increases until a maximal effect is achieved. Drugs that occupy and activate a receptor are said to have *intrinsic activity* at that receptor, but the degree of intrinsic activity can vary across drugs. Some agonist drugs are partial agonists; they occupy a receptor and activate it, but even at high doses they do not produce an effect as great as a full agonist drug, hence the term *partial agonist,* indicating a *partial* effect. These partial agonist drugs are said to have less intrinsic activity than a full agonist drug. The features of partial agonists are considered in Chapter 13 in the section on buprenorphine, an opioid that has partial agonist features.

A second type of drug that can occupy a receptor is an *antagonist*. These drugs occupy a receptor but produce no activation of that receptor; in other words, they have no intrinsic activity. However, such medications can block the effects of other agonist drugs subsequently ingested. In an opioid-naive individual, an antagonist will produce no effects since it has no intrinsic activity. However, in a person who is physically dependent on an opioid agonist such as heroin, administration of a sufficient dose of an antagonist will reverse the effects of the agonist and can produce withdrawal symptoms (described further in Chapter 13).

Although not the focus of this discussion, a final feature of drugs is worth mentioning here. Different drugs can have different *affinities* for a receptor. Affinity is a measure of how well a drug and a receptor fit when they are bound together. Thus, even though a drug might have a low intrinsic activity (i.e., it is a partial agonist), it could have a high affinity for the receptor, making it difficult to uncouple, or separate, the drug from the receptor to reverse its effects. Buprenorphine is believed to be just that type of drug—a partial agonist at the mu receptor, with high affinity for that receptor (see Chapter 13 for more details about buprenorphine).

Multiple Opioid Receptors

The classification of a particular receptor as an opioid receptor is based on the observation that naloxone, a pure opioid antagonist, will reverse the effects of a compound acting at that receptor. Three distinct types of opioid receptors have been identified, and these are labeled as mu, kappa, and delta receptors. Researchers once thought that there was another opioid receptor, called the sigma receptor, but it is now accepted that the sigma receptor is not an opioid receptor. It appears that there are further subtypes for each of the three major opioid receptors, such as mu_1 and mu_2 receptors and $kappa_1$ and $kappa_3$ receptors. However, a review of these subtypes of receptors is not necessary for understanding methadone's pharmacologic effects.

The prototypic or classic mu opioid agonist is morphine (mu for *mor*phine), although there are many other compounds that function as an agonist at the mu receptor (including methadone, heroin, opium, and codeine). While many of these drugs primarily activate mu receptors, at sufficiently high doses they may also interact with other opioid receptors. Activation of mu receptors results in a wide variety of effects in humans, as shown in Table 3.1. The two effects of primary interest that are produced by the activation of mu receptors are analgesia and euphoria. Mu opioid antagonists can block or reverse the effects of morphine and other mu agonists. Naloxone (Narcan®), nalmefene (Revex®), and naltrexone (ReVia™) are marketed and widely known for their antagonist properties; naloxone and nalmefene are commonly used to reverse narcotic overdose, whereas naltrexone, a much longer-acting agent, is marketed for use as an opioid-blocking treatment for heroin abuse and more recently for the treatment of alcoholism.

The prototypic or classic kappa opioid agonist is ketocyclazocine (kappa for *k*etocyclazocine). This drug was given to humans in past studies but

Table 3.1   Effects Produced by Mu and Kappa Opioid Agonists in Humans

Mu Agonist Effects	Kappa Agonist Effects
Analgesia	Analgesia (mediated primarily via the spinal cord)
Drowsiness	Psychotomimesis (?)
Constipation	Respiratory depression[a]
Nausea and vomiting	Dysphoria
Itching	Miosis[a] (pupillary constriction)
Miosis (pupillary constriction)	
Mental clouding or confusion	
Euphoria	
Respiratory depression	

Note: Effects are dose related and can vary depending on the circumstances of the individual (i.e., dependent on opioids, experiencing pain).
[a]These effects are less than those seen with mu agonist opioids.

was never used clinically, and it is no longer available for investigations. Pure kappa agonists in humans reportedly produced dysphoria and perceptual distortions, and these effects led to a loss of interest in developing kappa agonists for use in humans as analgesic agents. Thus, whereas there are several pure mu agonist opioids available for licensed use in humans, such as morphine, there are currently no pure kappa agonists that can be prescribed for humans. However, there is renewed interest in the possible use of kappa opioids in humans as possible treatments for head injury, analgesia, and cocaine dependence, and therefore, kappa agonists are being studied once again. Activation of kappa receptors also results in a variety of effects (Table 3.1). Notably, the analgesia produced by their activation is not the same as that produced by the activation of mu receptors. For example, animals made tolerant to the analgesic effects of a mu opioid will still have analgesic effects from a kappa opioid. Although there are no marketed pure kappa agonists, some prescribed analgesic agents, such as butorphanol (Stadol®), produce their actions through the activation of both kappa and mu receptors.

Delta opioid receptors are less well characterized than mu and kappa receptors, especially in humans. Early in the discovery of delta receptors, investigators used isolated mouse vas deferens (a duct from the testicle) and found high concentrations of delta receptors in this tissue. Hence, the term delta originated from the use of the *deferens* in these studies. Delta receptor activation, like mu and kappa receptor activation, can produce analgesia in animals. To date, no pure or selective delta opioid agonists have been studied in humans. However, experimental delta agonists have been studied in animals and appear to be reinforcing (animals self-administer the drug), suggesting that pure delta receptor agonists may have abuse potential in humans. Thus, since one of the goals of medications development with opioids is to find nonabusable analgesics, pharmaceutical companies may not find it worthwhile to pursue delta agonists either for analgesic or for drug abuse treatments.

Methadone's Opioid Receptor Properties

Based on the preceding review of opioid pharmacology, the characterization of methadone as a pure mu opioid agonist can now be understood. Methadone acts upon and activates mu opioid receptors, producing the characteristic profile of effects of mu opioid agonists (Table 3.1). Furthermore, it is a full agonist, not a partial agonist, and at sufficiently high doses methadone will therefore produce maximal physiologic effects. Clinically, this means that in someone who is not tolerant to the effects of opioids, severe respiratory depression, and even death, can occur in the case of methadone overdose. The remainder of this chapter reviews the effects of methadone in both animals and humans in more detail.

PHARMACOLOGY OF METHADONE: OVERVIEW

The Structure of Methadone

Like many other medications, methadone actually exists in two different forms or isomers, known as the *d*-form for dextrorotary and the *l*-form for levorotary. When methadone is shown as a two-dimensional structure (Figure 3.1), the *d*- and *l*-forms appear identical; however, when viewed as a three-dimensional structure, their conformations or configurations differ. These two isomers also differ in their pharmacologic activity. *l*-Methadone is about 50 times more potent as an analgesic than *d*-methadone (Scott, Robbins, and Chen 1948). Studies have reported that *d*-methadone can produce effects at higher doses; for example, *d*-methadone given at doses as high as 1,000 mg/day can partially suppress opioid withdrawal symptoms (Fraser and Isbell 1962). The methadone formulation that is used clinically contains both the *d*- and *l*-forms ("*d,l*-methadone" or racemic methadone), but *l*-methadone appears to account for most of the pharmacologic effects when given in typical clinical doses. Subsequent descriptions of methadone in this chapter refer to the racemic combination or *d,l*-methadone unless otherwise specified.

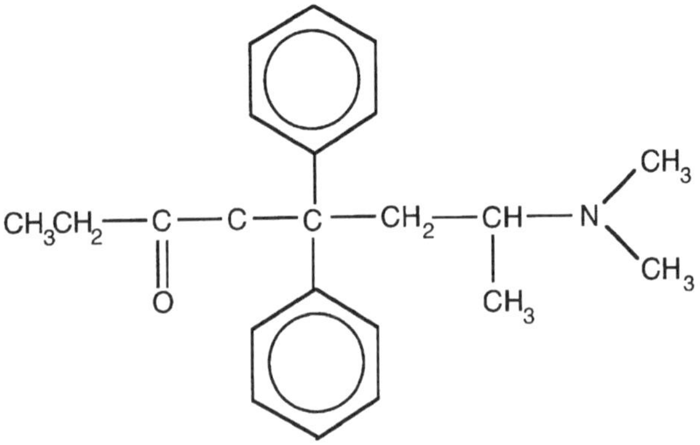

Figure 3.1. The structure of methadone.

Absorption, Metabolism, and Excretion

Methadone can be ingested orally or administered parenterally (by injection). In addition, it can be absorbed from the buccal mucosa, or mouth, although this is not the typical route for administering methadone, and it can be given rectally. The oral route of ingestion results in good bioavailability; although estimates vary, it is typically accepted that an oral dose of methadone results in about 50 percent of the analgesic effect produced by an injection of equal dose (i.e., about 50% of the drug is bioavailable or available for the body to use). However, at least one study suggests that perhaps as much as 80–95 percent of an oral methadone dose is bioavailable; note, however, that differences among subjects in the bioavailability of methadone varied widely in that study. The bioavailability of oral methadone does not markedly change as a person is stabilized on methadone or given the drug chronically.

In humans who are not opioid dependent and who receive a single oral dose of methadone, the medication typically is detected in plasma 30 minutes after ingestion, and the peak, or highest, concentrations of drug occur about two hours after ingestion (Inturrisi and Verebely 1972). Methadone blood levels then decline slowly over the next 72 hours, and continued excretion of methadone and its metabolites can be found in the urine 96 hours after a single dose.

The half-life ($t_{1/2}$) of methadone, or the time required for one-half of the dose to disappear from plasma, is reported to be between 15 and 31 hours in humans, with most studies reporting an average $t_{1/2}$ of 24 hours or longer. There can be marked variability among individuals in the $t_{1/2}$ of methadone, and several possible factors may contribute to these interindividual differences, including gender, urine pH, the duration of chronic exposure, and whether a patient is initiating treatment or has been maintained on methadone for some time. For some patients stabilized on methadone for at least one month, the rate of methadone metabolism may increase, thereby actually decreasing the duration of its effects (Nilsson et al. 1982). This does not occur in all patients, but may occur for a significant minority—perhaps about one-third—and suggests that these patients may benefit from dosing at intervals more frequent than 24 hours, or that an alternate pharmacotherapy should be considered.

Methadone is extensively bound to plasma proteins (about 70–90%), and it also binds to proteins in tissues throughout the body. Methadone can be found in the blood and brain and also in other tissues such as the kidneys, spleen, liver, and lungs; these concentrations of methadone are typically higher than those found in blood. This binding results in the accumulation of methadone over time in the body, so that the drug gradually builds up in a patient who is receiving regular daily dosing with methadone. It also results in a relatively gradual decline in circulating methadone over time when a person stops taking methadone. Despite this gradual decline, abrupt discontinuation of methadone does lead to a withdrawal syndrome, which can be extremely distressing to the patient.

Methadone is metabolized in the liver, where it undergoes N-demethylation followed by cyclization that leads to its major metabolic product known as M1 (2-ethylidene-1,5-dimethyl-3,3-diphenylpyrrolidine). In addition, other metabolites of methadone have been found including M2 (2-ethyl-5-methyl-3,3-diphenyl-1-pyrroline), produced by N-demethylation followed by cyclization and then another N-demethylation. There are several other minor metabolites of methadone, but methadone and M1 appear to be the primary compounds that are eliminated. Estimates suggest that approximately 10 percent of methadone is eliminated as the unchanged drug. Methadone's metabolites have been found in urine, feces, plasma, and bile and do not appear to be pharmacologically active.

The primary routes for the elimination of methadone and its metabolites are through the urine and feces. In addition, methadone has been found in the sweat, semen, and saliva of patients maintained on methadone. For relatively low doses of methadone, the fecal route can be a significant means of elimination for methadone and its metabolites. However, for higher doses renal elimination predominates. Significant differences in the plasma $t_{1/2}$ of methadone can be induced by marked changes in urinary pH. If urine is acidic, then the ratio of M1 to methadone decreases in urine (an increase in the clearance of the parent compound methadone); conversely, if urine is basic, there is an increase in the ratio of M1 to methadone (a decrease in the clearance of methadone). These observations have led some investigators to suggest that in patients who complain that their dose is not effective (or "holding" them) for a full 24 hours, reducing the pH of their urine may improve therapeutic efficacy; however, no known studies have systematically tested this theory.

Patients with liver disease may exhibit a number of changes in their metabolism of methadone. Metabolic rate may actually decrease, leading to a subsequent increase in the $t_{1/2}$ of methadone. However, patients with liver disease may have a reduced capacity to store methadone in the liver, so that the overall pool of methadone is decreased; this reduction in storage capacity can compensate for the change in methadone $t_{1/2}$.

Several other factors can influence methadone metabolism. There is some evidence that methadone may induce or speed up its own metabolism, since the excretion of the M_1 metabolite increases as a patient is stabilized on methadone. However, it is not clear if this observation has been controlled for possible variations in the pH of the subjects' urine samples, which may account for the sometimes variable results found in such studies. In addition, methadone metabolism is greater when it is taken by the oral route versus intramuscular injection. Finally, there is some evidence suggesting that women may metabolize methadone faster than men (although this observation may again be confounded by factors such as urinary pH, and not all results from the studies are consistent with this finding).

PHARMACOLOGY OF METHADONE: CLINICAL FEATURES

Analgesic Effects

Methadone is an effective analgesic when administered by either the oral, rectal, or parenteral routes. The recommended dose for pain relief in a nonopioid-dependent patient is 2.5–10 mg of methadone orally every 3 to 4 hours. Onset of analgesic effects occurs within 30 to 60 minutes after oral administration, and about 20 minutes after parenteral administration. The peak analgesic effect produced by the parenteral route is greater than that produced by the oral route, but both oral and parenteral routes produce their peak pain relief about 1 hour after administration. Although the duration of analgesia is somewhat greater for the oral versus parenteral route, both oral and parenteral methadone produce analgesic effects that last about 3–5 hours.

When given acutely by the intramuscular route, the analgesic potency of methadone is about equal to or slightly greater than the potency of morphine. Interestingly, the duration of a single dose of methadone's analgesic effects is also about the same as morphine's, despite methadone's longer $t_{1/2}$. However, in patients with chronic pain treated with methadone, the dosing interval can be lengthened (e.g., to 8–12-hour intervals) and still provide excellent pain relief. If methadone is to be used in the treatment of chronic pain, the initial dosing should be based on whether a patient is already dependent on other opioids (e.g., previous treatment with morphine), the source and degree of the patient's pain, and whether oral administration is possible. Although initial doses should be relatively low and close monitoring of respiratory status should be conducted, regular increases of dose should be made until adequate pain relief is achieved. As with other actions of methadone, over repeated administrations tolerance may develop to the analgesic efficacy of the methadone, necessitating dose increases in patients requiring chronic treatment.

When methadone is used for the treatment of pain, it must be prescribed using another DEA license (i.e., not a methadone clinic license). In addition, it is a good idea for the physician to write on the prescription a statement about the indication (e.g., for pain treatment), thereby ensuring that the physician will not be suspected of illegally maintaining an opioid-dependent patient on methadone for substitution treatment.

If methadone is to be used in the treatment of patients with chronic pain who are already taking another opioid, conversion to a methadone dose equivalent needs to be estimated. Although some studies have suggested that oral methadone and oral morphine are equipotent, and that parenteral methadone and parenteral morphine are also equipotent, these results generally reflect those from acute- rather than chronic-dosing studies. In general, reports from clinical experience suggest that the dose of methadone should be significantly less than the dose of morphine previously used. Similarly, reports on the conversion of patients treated with chronic hydromorphone (Dilaudid®) to treatment with methadone suggest that methadone is also more potent than hydromorphone. This finding may be related to evidence suggesting that oral methadone is better absorbed from the gastrointestinal tract than oral hydromorphone.

Methadone offers several advantages over other medications used in the treatment of chronic pain, including its good oral bioavailability (decreasing the need for injections), its low cost, and its widely demonstrated efficacy. Because of its apparently greater analgesic potency versus other opioids when used in the treatment of chronic pain, the dosing of methadone should be individualized for each patient. While methadone is an attractive analgesic, its association with the treatment of opioid abuse may inhibit some patients from appropriately using it for pain relief. If a patient expresses such a concern, this should be addressed with a candid discussion about the excellent efficacy of methadone as a well-studied analgesic.

Respiratory Depression

Like other mu opioid agonists, methadone can produce respiratory depression when a dose is taken in excess of a person's level of dependence. In a person who is not physically dependent on opioids, the recommended analgesic dose is 2.5–10 mg orally. This dose should not produce significant respiratory depression in patients without preexisting respiratory compromise. If respiratory depression results from methadone dosing, reversal with an opioid antagonist such as intravenous naloxone should be instituted.

Opioid Blockade or Cross-Tolerance

One of the features of methadone that makes it a useful medication in the treatment of opioid dependence is that methadone maintenance produces blockade or cross-tolerance to the effects produced by other ingested mu opioid agonists (such as heroin or morphine). One of the first studies on methadone's clinical use in the treatment of opioid dependence included a report on these blockade effects of methadone (Dole, Nyswander, and Kreek 1966). In that study, the investigators reported that methadone decreased the euphoria produced by intravenous injection of other opioids, such as morphine, and increased the magnitude of blockade at higher doses of methadone.

Similar results have been shown in a variety of studies that have either directly or indirectly assessed the blockade abilities of methadone. In an elegant study conducted more than 20 years ago (Jones and Prada 1975), a group of inpatient subjects with histories of opioid dependence who were not currently opioid dependent were allowed to "earn" intravenous doses of 4 mg of hydromorphone each day by riding an exercise bicycle. The amount of hydromorphone self-administered was determined before the group started taking methadone (i.e., at baseline), and then repeatedly over time as the methadone treatment dose was increased. The initial dose of methadone was 5 mg per day, and increased over six weeks to a final stable dose of 100 mg per day. Before methadone treatment began, essentially all the subjects were riding the exercise bicycle and earning all of the hydromorphone available. As methadone treatment was initiated and the dose gradually increased, the amount of riding and hydromorphone self-administration, the self-reported "liking" of the hydromorphone, and the change in pupillary diameter produced by an injection of hydromorphone all decreased. After about four weeks of maintenance on 100 mg of daily methadone, there were days when none of the subjects in the study group rode the bicycle (although there were still occasional days when one subject rode the bicycle to earn an injection). Thus, this study demonstrated how maintenance on an adequate dose of methadone could block the effects of an injection of an opioid, resulting in marked and sustained decreases in opioid drug taking.

Other studies have shown that subjects maintained on 30 mg of daily methadone report drug effects from 10 mg of intramuscular hydromorphone, but that subjects maintained on 60 mg of daily methadone report essentially no drug effects from this same dose of hydromorphone. These results demonstrate that methadone can block the effects of opioids and that higher doses of methadone produce greater blockade than lower doses. Methadone's ability to produce blockade of other opioids is considered to be the critical feature that leads to its ability to suppress or reduce the use of illicit opioid abuse during maintenance therapy. Similar to the observation that the degree of opioid blockade is positively related to methadone dose in the laboratory, the reduction of illicit opioid use in clinical populations has been shown to be positively related to methadone maintenance dose (Strain et al. 1993). However, some residual opioid use observed during treatment suggests that opioid blockade by methadone maintenance may be incomplete.

Withdrawal Suppression

In addition to blockade or cross-tolerance effects, another feature of methadone's pharmacology that makes it highly useful in the treatment of opioid dependence is its effectiveness in suppressing the signs and symptoms of opioid withdrawal for 24 hours or longer. This characteristic of methadone was demonstrated in a study conducted in the 1940s (Isbell et al. 1948), in which inpatient subjects were maintained on daily morphine and then abruptly had their morphine discontinued. Thirty-two hours later, when they were in moderate to severe withdrawal, the subjects received an injection of methadone. The injection of methadone resulted in marked and immediate decreases in withdrawal that persisted for at least 10 hours (the length of time observations were recorded), and suppressed withdrawal for a longer period than that achieved with an injection of morphine. The ability of methadone to suppress withdrawal makes patients comfortable, especially at the start of treatment when first initiating abstinence from heroin use.

Physiologic Effects

Acute doses of methadone produce pupillary constriction (miosis), which is a telltale sign of opioid use. In humans without physiologic dependence on opioids, pupillary constriction can persist for 24 hours after a single dose. In methadone-maintained patients, pupils are somewhat constricted on a chronic basis although pupil size will fluctuate during the daily dosing cycle, decreasing after dose ingestion and increasing between doses. Methadone, like other mu opioid agonists, can produce respiratory depression by inhibiting the responsivity of cells that control respiratory rate in the brain stem. In patients who are chronically treated with methadone, respiratory depression is not commonly seen at therapeutic doses. However, in nontolerant individuals methadone administration can lead to respiratory failure and death at higher doses. Reports on the relationship between chronic methadone dosing and blood pressure are equivocal, with evidence of slight increases as well as slight decreases in both systolic and diastolic blood pressure. However, the magnitude of these blood pressure changes (whether increased or decreased) does not appear to be clinically important. No changes in the electrocardiogram (ECG) are seen in patients receiving chronic methadone administration, but slight decreases in hemoglobin and hematocrit can be seen, probably secondary to hemodilution. And finally, there is no evidence to suggest that methadone is hepatotoxic or harmful to the liver.

Methadone, like morphine and heroin, can cause nausea and vomiting following acute administration; however, patients who receive chronic treatment and who are susceptible to the nausea-producing properties of methadone usually develop tolerance to these effects. Methadone can also cause significant itchiness of the skin owing to histamine release; other histamine-related effects can include flushing, sweating, and increased skin temperature. Another common problematic, but not dangerous, side effect associated with methadone administration is constipation. Constipation occurs because methadone inhibits peristaltic movement in the gut, slowing the transit of food through the intestines, while simultaneously increasing the muscular tone of the anal sphincter. Constipation can become severe for some individuals during chronic treatment and is best treated by a change in diet, although pharmacologic aids and fiber supplements are sometimes needed.

Psychological Effects

In subjects who have a history of opioid dependence but are not currently opioid dependent, acute doses of 10–60 mg of oral methadone produce increased ratings of "liking" of the medication and euphoria. The euphoriant effects of methadone have been shown to be qualitatively similar to those of morphine (Jasinski and Preston 1986). These effects peak during the first 5 hours after the dose is ingested and dissipate within 24 hours. These doses also produce sedation in nondependent individuals, which is characterized, in part, by "nodding" or head bobbing. Patients receiving chronic methadone treatment do not typically experience sedation or lethargy at low methadone doses; however, at high doses (e.g., 100 mg orally per day) patients can report increased ratings of lethargy, weakness, and decreased motivation (Martin et al. 1973). These effects are usually mild, and clinical experience suggests that patients are able to function well when maintained on doses of methadone up to 100 mg. Interestingly, despite the development of tolerance to many of methadone's actions during chronic treatment, it has been shown that patients will choose to self-administer supplemental methadone doses when given the opportunity, suggesting that the reinforcing or euphoric properties of methadone are still detectable even in chronically maintained and tolerant patients (Stitzer et al. 1983).

Antianxiety, Antidepressant, and Antipsychotic Effects

Some evidence suggests that methadone and opioids in general can have antianxiety, antidepressant, and antipsychotic effects. Such effects, if present, are probably mild and may reflect the general, acute sedating effects of opioids such as methadone, rather than a specific therapeutic response. These effects have primarily been reported in early clinic reports, and controlled studies of methadone for use in the treatment of anxiety, depression, or psychosis have not been conducted.

Effects on Psychomotor and Cognitive Function

Patients maintained on methadone do not show evidence of impairments in psychomotor reaction time, attention, or other measures of intellectual functioning. This is important because methadone-maintained patients can continue to function normally in work and social environments with no restriction of activities. However, acute doses of methadone given to nondependent individuals have been shown to impair psychomotor performance, and the extent of the impairment increases as a function of dose.

SUMMARY

Methadone is a full agonist whose effects are mediated through activation of the mu opioid receptor system. Like other mu opioid agonists, methadone is an effective analgesic and can also produce an array of side effects when given to nondependent individuals, including pupillary constriction, respiratory depression, sedation, nausea, and vomiting. Several pharmacologic features of methadone make it particularly useful for the treatment of opioid dependence. These features include its good bioavailability through the oral route, permitting easy dosage administration (typically through a liquid vehicle); its long $t_{1/2}$, allowing dosing on a once per day basis; its effective suppression of the opioid withdrawal syndrome, improving compliance with treatment; and its cross-tolerance to the effects of illicit opioid use, decreasing their use when patients are maintained on methadone.

References and Suggested Further Reading

Bigelow G.E., Preston K.L. 1995. Opioids. In: Bloom F.E., Kupfer D.J., eds. *Psychopharmacology: The Fourth Generation of Progress.* Raven Press, New York, pp. 1731–44.

Cooper J.R., Bloom F.E., Roth R.H. 1991. *The Biochemical Basis of Neuropharmacology,* 6th ed. Oxford University Press, New York.

Dole V., Nyswander M.E., Kreek M.J. 1966. Narcotic blockade. *Arch. Intern. Med.* 118:304–9.

Fraser H.F., Isbell H. 1962. Human pharmacology and addictiveness of certain dextroisomers of synthetic analgesics: I. d-3-hydroxy-N-phenethylmorphinan. II. d-3-methoxy-N-phenethylmorphinan. III. d-methadone. *Bull. Narcotics* 14:25–35.

Inturrisi C.E., Verebely K. 1972. Disposition of methadone in man after a single oral dose. *Clin. Pharmacol. Ther.* 13:923–30.

Isbell H., Wikler A., Eisenman A.J., Daingerfield M., Frank K. 1948. Liability of addiction to 6-dimethylamino-4-4-diphenyl-3-heptanone (methadone, "amidone" or "10820") in man. *Arch. Intern. Med.* 82:362–92.

Jaffe J.H. 1992. Opiates: clinical aspects. In: Lowinson J.H., Ruiz P., Millman R.B., Langrod J.G., eds. *Substance Abuse—A Comprehensive Textbook,* 2nd ed. Williams & Wilkins, Baltimore, pp. 186–94.

Jasinski D.R., Preston K.L. 1986. Comparison of intravenously administered methadone, morphine and heroin. *Drug Alcohol. Depend.* 17:301–10.

Jones B.E., Prada J.A. 1975. Drug-seeking behavior during methadone maintenance. *Psychopharmacology (Berl.)* 41:7–10.

Martin W.R., Jasinski D.R., Haertzen C.A., Kay D.C., Jones B.E., Mansky P.A., Carpenter R.W. 1973. Methadone—a reevaluation. *Arch. Gen. Psychiatry* 28:286–95.

Nilsson M.-I., Anggard E., Holmstrand J., Funne L.-M. 1982. Pharmacokinetics of methadone during maintenance treatment: adaptive changes during the induction phase. *Eur. J. Clin. Pharmacol.* 22:343–49.

Preston A. 1996. *The Methadone Briefing.* ISDD, London.

Reisine T., Pasternak G. 1996. Opioid analgesics and antagonists. In: Hardman J.G., Limbird L.E., Molinoff P.B., Ruddon R.W., Gilman A.G., eds. *Goodman and Gilman's The Pharmacological Basis of Therapeutics,* 9th ed. McGraw-Hill, New York, pp. 521–56.

Scott C.C., Robbins E.B., Chen K.K. 1948. Pharmacologic comparison of the optical isomers of methadon. *J. Pharmacol. Exp. Ther.* 93:282–86.

Stitzer M.L., McCaul M.E., Bigelow G.E., Liebson I.A. 1983. Oral methadone self-administration: effects of dose and alternative reinforcers. *Clin. Pharmacol. Ther.* 34:29–35.

Strain E.C., Stitzer M.L., Liebson I.A., Bigelow G.E. 1993. Dose-response effects of methadone in the treatment of opioid dependence. *Ann. Intern. Med.* 119:23–27.

4

Beginning and Ending Methadone Dosing

Induction and Withdrawal

Eric C. Strain, M.D.

In general, there are three phases of methadone dosing for a patient: dose induction (the phase during which the patient starts on methadone), dose stabilization, or maintenance (the phase during which the patient receives a stable dose of methadone), and dose withdrawal, or detoxification (the phase during which methadone is gradually decreased and then discontinued). This chapter reviews methadone dosing during induction and withdrawal. A separate chapter (Chapter 5) is devoted to issues associated with methadone stabilization, including a review of evidence that methadone is effective and that this efficacy is dose related.

METHADONE DOSE INDUCTION

Before starting a patient on methadone, it is necessary to determine whether or not the patient qualifies for methadone treatment. This topic is addressed in Chapter 11, and will not be repeated here. Subsequent recommendations in this chapter assume that the patient has been adequately evaluated and fulfills the necessary criteria for treatment with methadone.

Surprisingly, there has been virtually no research on the best way to start a patient on methadone. In the pathbreaking work by Dole and Nyswander, methadone was initially given in doses of 10–20 mg twice per day and gradually increased over a period of four weeks to a total daily dose of 50–150 mg (and then eventually changed to a single daily dose). The initial use of methadone on a twice daily basis may provide better relief from withdrawal during the first days of treatment, because it may take 5–10 days for methadone to accumulate in tissues (IOM 1995). However, one report states that split dosing at the start of treatment is no more effective than single daily dosing (Goldstein 1971).

Other early investigators adopted procedures using a single daily dose, and with a quicker induction. For example, Goldstein (1970) administered 30 mg of methadone on the first day of treatment and then increased the dose by 10 mg per day until a daily dose of 100 mg was achieved. This schedule was generally well tolerated, although patients were noted to be excessively drowsy. Ultimately Goldstein modified the schedule so that 10-mg dose increases occurred every other day rather than every day, which decreased reports of drowsiness.

It appears that there have been no double-blind controlled studies examining the optimal dose-induction procedure for methadone. In general, clinical experience suggests that patients tolerate doses of 20–30 mg of methadone on the first day of treatment without adverse effects. If possible, the patient should be monitored for several hours, and a second dose (5–10 mg) can be administered if there is evidence of opioid withdrawal (Payte and Khuri 1993). In the United States, federal regulations stipulate that the first dose of methadone cannot be greater than 30 mg and that the total dose the first day should not be greater than 40 mg (unless the treating physician documents the reason for giving a higher dose the first day).

The goal of methadone dosing in the induction phase is to provide relief from opioid withdrawal, but, unfortunately, initial doses of methadone may fail to "hold" the patient for 24 hours because insufficient levels have accumulated in tissue stores. Although split dosing can address this problem, it is usually not possible to administer doses twice per day during outpatient treatment. As previously noted, there have been no controlled studies examining the optimal initial dosing of methadone, so it is not known if patients might benefit more by rapidly increasing their dose during the first few days of treatment.

Thus, a methadone dose-induction procedure might begin with a first-day dose of 20–40 mg, with subsequent daily dosing increased by 5–10 mg increments. The rate of increase can vary, and a determination of this rate should include daily clinical assessments of the patient. Slow rates of increase, such as 10-mg dose increases once per week, are usually well tolerated and safe. However, a disadvantage of such slow increases is that patients may continue illicit opiate use because of withdrawal and may drop out of treatment. Goldstein's (1970) procedure of rapid dose increases (10-mg increases daily) probably represents the extreme in rapid dose induction on an outpatient basis and may produce drowsiness as an unwanted side effect. Thus, an intermediate schedule (e.g., 10 mg every other day) is recommended.

A final clinical point regarding methadone induction should be made. On the first day of methadone treatment, it is good clinical practice to monitor patients after their first dose of methadone. Patients with a clear history of current opioid dependence should tolerate the first methadone dose without problems. However, occasionally some patients will react with excessive sedation following this first dose, and therefore it is important to monitor the patient for at least one to two hours afterward. Conversely, patients who have objective evidence of continued or worsening opioid withdrawal two hours after their first dose of methadone could receive a second, smaller dose of methadone (5 or 10 mg) later that day.

Methadone Dose Withdrawal

Patients who benefit from stable maintenance on methadone and who qualify for maintenance treatment may never undergo methadone withdrawal. Indefinite maintenance treatment can be clinically indicated and appropriate for such patients, especially if previous attempts at methadone withdrawal have resulted in a relapse to drug use. However, methadone withdrawal also may be indicated in selected cases.

Several studies have examined the optimal procedure for methadone withdrawal (also known as detoxification, although technically patients are not undergoing a process of toxin removal). Issues associated with methadone withdrawal include the length of time and rate of methadone withdrawal, the optimal size of decrease in methadone dose, whether the dose should be decreased in equal intervals or at some other rate (such as a percentage of the previous dose), and whether or not patients should be informed about the details of their withdrawal schedule. Each of these points is addressed in the following sections.

Length of Time and Rate of Methadone Withdrawal

In the United States, federal regulations of methadone programs stipulate the maximum treatment time allowed for a patient who qualifies for methadone detoxification but not for maintenance treatment (see Chapter

11). Whereas earlier regulations limited methadone detoxification to a 90-day period, subsequent revisions have increased this time to 180 days (or six months). This increase reflects the recognition that better outcomes are associated with longer withdrawal schedules.

Several studies have examined different time periods over which methadone is withdrawn, and, in general, results from these studies show that better outcomes are associated with longer lengths of time over which methadone is withdrawn. For example, patients receiving a 10-day withdrawal had higher peak withdrawal scores and higher dropout rates after withdrawal was completed when compared with patients receiving a 21-day withdrawal (Gossop et al. 1989). Similarly, for outpatients randomly assigned to either a three- or six-week methadone withdrawal, better results during treatment for the patients in the six-week withdrawal group were found (e.g., for treatment retention and percentage of opioid-positive urine samples), although these benefits were not sustained during post-treatment follow-up (Sorensen, Hargreaves, and Weinberg 1982).

Finally, Senay et al. (1977) conducted an elegant study examining the relative efficacy of a 10-week withdrawal from methadone (i.e., dose reductions of 10% per week) versus a more gradual 30-week withdrawal (i.e., 3% per week). In that study patients could request interruptions in their double-blind withdrawal, either as a temporary increase in methadone dose for one week or as a stabilization in the schedule for one week. Results from the study show that patients in the 10-mg per week reduction group requested significantly more detoxification schedule interruptions and had a higher rate of opioid-positive urine samples than did patients in the gradual dose-reduction group. Thus, the study concludes that a gradual, 3 percent methadone dose reduction per week is more efficacious than a more rapid 10 percent weekly reduction.

Size of Decrease in Methadone Dose

Most studies examining methadone withdrawal have examined dose decreases that occur at some fixed rate, such as the 10 percent weekly decrease used in the Senay et al. (1977) study. That is, dose decreases are 10 percent of a patient's starting methadone dose. Thus, if a patient were on a 50-mg dose of methadone, decreases would be 5 mg per week using such a schedule. Early in the withdrawal, a 5-mg dose decrease would represent a small percentage of the previous week's dose (i.e., in the first week 5 mg would be 10% of 50 mg, in the second week 5 mg would be 11% of 45 mg, and in the third week 5 mg would be 13% of 40 mg). However, by the end of the 10-week period, 5 mg would represent a significant proportion of the previous week's dose (i.e., in the ninth week 5 mg would be 50% of the previous week's dose of 10 mg). Would an alternate schedule, in which dose decreases become smaller as the withdrawal progresses, provide better treatment outcomes?

Strang and Gossop (1990) examined this question in a 10-day inpatient methadone withdrawal study. In this study one group of patients received daily dose reductions representing 10 percent of their starting dose, and another group received daily dose reductions representing 20 percent of their previous day's dose. For the latter dosing, large decreases occur during the first few days of the withdrawal, whereas much smaller absolute dose reductions occur at the end of the withdrawal. Interestingly, results showed that self-reports of opioid withdrawal symptoms for the two groups were quite similar, both in terms of the time course and in the peak withdrawal produced (which occurred three days after the end of the withdrawal).

Similar investigations comparing alternate forms of detoxification schedules have not been conducted on an outpatient basis, nor over longer time periods. Since most methadone detoxification is done with outpatients over longer periods, studies under these circumstances are needed to establish whether there are clinically significant differences across alternate types of withdrawal schedules. Until such work has been done, it is recommended that methadone dose decreases occur at a fixed percentage of the starting dose. Table 4.1 provides examples of 21-, 91-, and 182-day methadone withdrawal schedules for a patient who is initially dependent on illicit opioids.

Informing the Patient About the Methadone Withdrawal Schedule and Self-Regulation

Several studies have examined outcome in methadone withdrawal when withdrawals are done under blind (i.e., patients are unaware of the dosing schedule) versus open conditions (i.e., patients are aware of their daily dose; Senay et al. 1977; Stitzer, Bigelow, and Liebson 1981; Green and Gossop 1988). In general, these studies show that outcomes are better when patients are aware of the details of their dosing withdrawal schedule. Interestingly, in studies comparing who decides the rate of withdrawal (staff versus the patient), researchers have generally found no advantage in allowing patients to determine their methadone withdrawal schedule (e.g., see Stitzer, Bigelow, and Liebson 1981; Senay et al. 1984).

Table 4.1 **Examples of Methadone Withdrawal Schedules**

Day in Treatment	Week in Treatment	21-Day Schedule		91-Day Schedule		182-Day Schedule	
		Lower Dose (mg)	Higher Dose (mg)	Lower Dose (mg)	Higher Dose (mg)	Lower Dose (mg)	Higher Dose (mg)
1	1	30	40	40	40	40	40
2	1	30	38	40	40	40	40
3	1	30	36	50	50	50	50
4	1	25	34	50	60	60	60
5	1	25	32	60	70	60	70
6	1	25	30	60	70	60	70
7	1	20	28	60	80	60	80
8	2	20	26	60	80	60	80
9	2	20	24	60	80	60	80
10	2	20	22	60	80	60	90
11	2	15	20	60	80	60	90
12	2	15	18	60	80	60	90
13	2	15	16	60	80	60	90
14	2	10	14	60	80	60	100
15	3	10	12	60	80	60	100
16	3	10	10	60	80	60	100
17	3	10	8	60	80	60	100
18	3	5	6	60	80	60	100
19	3	5	4	60	80	60	100
20	3	5	2	60	80	60	100
21	3	0	0	60	80	60	100
22–28	4			54	72	60	100
29–35	5			48	64	60	100
36–42	6			42	56	60	100
43–49	7			36	48	57	95
50–56	8			30	40	54	90
57–63	9			24	32	51	85
64–70	10			18	24	48	80
71–77	11			12	16	45	75
78–84	12			6	8	42	70
85–91	13			0	0	39	65
92–98	14					36	60
99–105	15					33	55
106–112	16					30	50
113–119	17					27	45
120–126	18					24	40
127–133	19					21	35
134–140	20					18	30
141–147	21					15	25
148–154	22					12	20
155–161	23					9	15
162–168	24					6	10
169–175	25					3	5
176–182	26					0	0

Efficacy of Methadone Withdrawal and Predictors of Treatment Success

If successful outcome from methadone withdrawal is defined as abstinence from opioids, then the overall efficacy of methadone withdrawal is quite poor. Although at least one early report suggested that methadone withdrawal could be quite successful (Cushman and Dole 1973), several other studies have reported high rates of relapse to opioid use during and following the completion of methadone withdrawal (e.g., Wilson, Elms, and Thomson 1975; Sorensen, Hargreaves, and Weinberg 1982; Stitzer et al. 1983).

Although many patients relapse to opioid use after withdrawal from methadone, rates of use are generally lower than those before methadone treatment (Strain et al. 1994). Success following methadone withdrawal is not related to prewithdrawal rates of illicit opioid use (Stitzer et al. 1983), nor the prewithdrawal dose of methadone (Gossop, Bradley, and Phillips 1987). Posttreatment success is equally likely if withdrawal occurs on an inpatient versus an outpatient basis (Wilson, Elms, and Thomson 1975), although, not surprisingly, achievement of complete initial abstinence is more likely if the withdrawal is done on an inpatient basis (Gossop, Johns, and Green 1986).

SUMMARY AND CONCLUSIONS

Starting a patient on methadone is relatively simple. Once it has been determined that the patient qualifies for methadone treatment, a first-day dose of 20–40 mg can be given. If a low dose is used (i.e., 20 mg), then there is the option of giving a second, smaller dose on the same day. Subsequent dose increases of 5–10 mg every other day should be given, until the patient is either stabilized on a dose of 50–60 mg per day or there is evidence of excessive dosing. There is relatively little variability in the procedures used for methadone dose induction.

By contrast, there is considerable variability in the procedures used for methadone withdrawal. However, several lessons can be drawn from the studies of methadone withdrawal reviewed in this chapter. First, for many patients methadone withdrawal does not result in sustained, complete abstinence from illicit opioid use. However, it can result in a decrease in opioid use following completion of withdrawal. Second, there is little benefit derived from conducting the withdrawal on an inpatient versus an outpatient service; although initial rates of abstinence are higher for inpatients (since they are under constant supervision), long-term rates of abstinence do not appear to be any better. Third, better outcomes are associated with more gradual, longer withdrawals. Thus, a 90-day withdrawal is better than a 21-day withdrawal, and a 180-day withdrawal is probably even better. Finally, in general it is better if methadone withdrawals are not done blindly; that is, it is better to inform patients about the dosing changes in their withdrawal.

References

Cushman P., Dole V.P. 1973. Detoxification of rehabilitated methadone-maintained patients. *JAMA* 226:747–52.

Goldstein A. 1970. Dosage, duration, side effects: blind controlled dosage comparisons with methadone in 200 patients. In: Proceedings of the Third National Conference on Methadone Treatment, National Association for the Prevention of Addiction to Narcotics, Rockville, MD, pp. 31–37.

———. 1971. Blind dosage comparisons and other studies in a large methadone program. *J. Psychedelic Drugs* 4:177–81.

Gossop M., Bradley B., Phillips G.T. 1987. An investigation of withdrawal symptoms shown by opiate addicts during and subsequent to a 21-day in-patient methadone detoxification procedure. *Addict. Behav.* 12:1–6.

Gossop M., Griffiths P., Bradley B., Strang J. 1989. Opiate withdrawal symptoms in response to 10-day and 21-day methadone withdrawal programmes. *Br. J. Psychiatry* 154:360–63.

Gossop M., Johns A., Green L. 1986. Opiate withdrawal: inpatient versus outpatient programmes and preferred versus random assignment to treatment. *Br. Med. J.* 293:103–4.

Green L., Gossop M. 1988. Effects of information on the opiate withdrawal syndrome. *Br. J. Addictions* 83:305–9.

Institute of Medicine (IOM). 1995. *Federal Regulation of Methadone Treatment*. National Academy Press, Washington, DC.

Payte J.T., Khuri E.T. 1993. Principles of methadone dose determination. In: Parrino M.W., ed. *State Methadone Treatment Guidelines, Treatment Improvement Protocol (TIP) Series 1*. Substance Abuse and Mental Health Services Administration, Center for Substance Abuse Treatment, United States Department of Health and Human Services, Rockville, MD, pp. 47–58.

Senay E.C., Dorus W., Goldberg F., Thornton W. 1977. Withdrawal from methadone maintenance: rate of withdrawal and expectations. *Arch. Gen. Psychiatry* 34:361–67.

Senay E.C., Dorus W., Showalter C. 1984. Methadone detoxification: self versus physician regulation. *Am. J. Drug Alcohol Abuse* 10:361–74.

Sorensen J.L., Hargreaves W.A., Weinberg A. 1982. Withdrawal from heroin in three or six weeks: comparison of methadyl acetate and methadone. *Arch. Gen. Psychiatry* 39:167–71.

Stitzer M.L., Bigelow G.E., Liebson I.A. 1981. Comparison of three outpatient methadone detoxification procedures. In: Harris, L.S., ed. Problems of Drug Dependence, 1981. Proceedings of the 43rd Annual Scientific Meeting, Committee on Problems of Drug Dependence. NIDA Research Monograph 41, Department of Health and Human Services, National Institute on Drug Abuse, Rockville, MD, pp. 239–45.

Stitzer M.L., McCaul M.E., Bigelow G.E., Liebson I.A. 1983. Treatment outcome in methadone detoxification: relationship to initial levels of illicit opiate use. *Drug Alcohol Depend.* 12:259–67.

Strain E.C., Stitzer M.L., Liebson I.A., Bigelow G.E. 1994. Outcome after methadone treatment: influence of prior treatment factors and current treatment status. *Drug Alcohol Depend.* 35:223–30.

Strang J., Gossop M. 1990. Comparison of linear versus inverse exponential methadone reduction curves in the detoxification of opiate addicts. *Addict. Behav.* 15:541–47.

Wilson B.K., Elms R.R., Thomson C.P. 1975. Outpatient vs. hospital methadone detoxification: an experimental comparison. *Int. J. Addictions* 10:13–21.

5

Methadone Dose during Maintenance Treatment

Eric C. Strain, M.D.

Despite more than 30 years of clinical use of methadone for the treatment of opioid dependence, appropriate dosing remains controversial. For virtually all other classes of pharmacotherapies used in medicine, such as antibiotics, antihypertensives, and antidepressants, clear guidelines exist for appropriate drug dosing. Even medications used to treat other substance abuse disorders, such as nicotine replacement products for smoking cessation, have well-established recommendations for dosing. However, the average dose of methadone can vary widely, with some clinics practicing low-dose philosophies and others using high doses. For example, a survey by the U.S. General Accounting Office (GAO) of dosing practices in 24 methadone programs in eight states found that the average daily maintenance doses ranged from 21 to 68 mg (GAO 1990). Similar evidence of dosing practices in other countries is not readily available, so it is not clear if the wide variations in methadone dosing are unique to the United States.

There have been many studies and reports on methadone dosing, but it is beyond the scope of this chapter and book to present a comprehensive examination of these studies. Studies of methadone dosing generally fall into one of two categories: surveys of the methadone dose used in treatment settings, and controlled clinical trials. Surveys report results from the use of methadone in clinical settings, in which patients and staff are aware of the doses used, doses are individualized based on each patient's clinical response, and the effectiveness of the dose can be influenced by nonpharmacologic treatments provided. Controlled clinical trials, on the other hand, provide a more focused assessment of medication effect. However, the results are not completely transferable back to the clinical setting, since the methods used in these trials differ in some respects from the usual clinical practice. For example, patients and staff do not know the doses, and both medication and nonpharmacologic treatments are standardized across doses, not individualized by treatment response. However, these and other features of clinical trials (e.g., strict random assignment to study conditions), are essential for a scientifically valid assessment. Controlled clinical trials seek to determine a medication's "true" effect, uninfluenced by expectations and biases (e.g., special encouragement or discouragement from staff) and the type or intensity of nonpharmacologic treatments. In actual practice, the effectiveness of a medication can be better or worse than what is shown in clinical trials because of these factors. While the methods of controlled clinical trials are different from usual clinical practice, it is encouraging that studies of methadone dosing show similar outcomes whether the data are collected from surveys of community treatment clinics or from controlled clinical trials in treatment research clinics. However, many of the clinical trials with methadone have methodological limitations that compromise the scientific conclusions, for example, being nonblind or single-blind rather than double-blind, not randomly assigning patients to dose conditions, or not providing a standard form of nonpharmacologic treatment. For an excellent, but somewhat dated review of methadone dosing studies, see Hargreaves (1983) in the reference list at the end of this chapter.

The primary question behind the issue of methadone dosing is whether or not higher doses are more effective than lower doses: if 50 mg per day is good, is 100 mg per day even better? However, underlying this question is the assumption that methadone is effective in treating opioid dependence. This assumption can be tested by finding out whether patients on active methadone have better outcomes than those on placebo. Although this chapter's main focus is on treatment outcome across active methadone doses, this more fundamental question will also be addressed.

This chapter has four sections. First, a historical overview of methadone dosing helps place subsequent issues into a larger context. The second examines the efficacy of methadone treatment based on surveys. The third section reviews controlled clinical trials of methadone dosing—first as compared to placebos, then trials that have tested different doses of methadone. Finally, the last section addresses a series of topics related to methadone dosing such as the value of predictors of treatment outcome, the use of methadone blood levels in treatment, and the side effects that can be associated with methadone. The chapter concludes with recommendations regarding the optimal dosing of methadone.

Historical Overview of Methadone Dosing

One of the first evaluations of methadone's effects in humans was published in 1948 by a team of investigators from the U.S. Public Health Service Hospital in Lexington, Kentucky (Isbell et al. 1948). This evaluation described a set of studies, including the assessment of direct addiction to methadone in 15 former morphine addicts. Methadone was given by injection four times each day, and daily doses reached levels as high as 600–800 mg per day in 2 subjects. However, at this high dose signs of toxicity, which were not specifically described, appeared and therefore the amount was decreased to 200–400 mg per day. Thus, results from this early study show that humans can tolerate remarkably high doses of methadone when the dose is gradually increased under careful supervision.

Although the first clinical use of methadone for the treatment of opioid dependence is generally associated with reports in the early 1960s by Vincent Dole and Marie Nyswander (as described subsequently), methadone treatment was, in fact, initiated in Canada in the late 1950s and early 1960s (Williams 1971). In 1959 the Narcotic Addiction Foundation of British Columbia began dispensing methadone for brief, 12-day detoxifications and in early 1963 expanded this program to include a more prolonged period of outpatient methadone treatment. The average methadone dose used in this expanded program was 40 mg per day.

However, this early use of methadone for the outpatient treatment of opioid dependence gained little attention in the medical treatment and research communities. Not until studies by Dole and Nyswander were published in the American Medical Association's journal *JAMA* did methadone treatment gain widespread attention and interest. These studies were conducted at the Rockefeller Institute, in New York, in the 1960s. Small groups of patients were admitted to an inpatient research ward where they lived for relatively long periods of time (i.e., six weeks; Dole and Nyswander 1965; Dole, Nyswander, and Warner 1968). Doses of methadone were initially given twice each day, starting at 10–20 mg per dose, and gradually increased over a period of several weeks to stabilization doses of 50–150 mg per day (although doses as high as 180 mg were reported). Clearly, these techniques (long inpatient hospitalizations, divided doses, gradual escalation of doses over time, intensive supervision of treatment by physicians and staff) are not typical of today's methadone treatment. Outcomes were good, both with respect to illicit drug use and with other, nondrug-related measures such as employment.

After these promising results, a number of scientific papers reported on the outcomes from the use of different doses of methadone in more-controlled clinical trials conducted in the 1970s. In addition, reports by clinicians about their experiences with low- versus high-dose methadone were published. These articles reported on the evaluation of a variety of widely dispersed daily methadone doses. Conclusions from these studies as well as numerous other methadone dosing studies and surveys are described next.

METHADONE'S EFFICACY: EVIDENCE FROM SURVEYS

There have been several investigations of methadone efficacy utilizing surveys of methadone clinics, as well as clinicians' reports of their experience with methadone dosing. This section reviews the results from several of these reports.

Drug Abuse Reporting Program (DARP)

The DARP assessed patients entering a variety of treatment modalities in the United States, including methadone maintenance treatment, between 1969 and 1973. Patients were subsequently followed for various periods of time (e.g., Simpson and Sells [1990] published a summary of 12-year follow-up reports for patients with opioid dependence). In general, results from the DARP show that three different treatment interventions—methadone maintenance, therapeutic communities, and outpatient drug-free counseling—are all effective for opioid dependence. Patients in each of these modalities did better than patients who only attended an intake assessment but failed to follow through with treatment, or patients who received a detoxification without follow-up treatment. Furthermore, results from the DARP showed favorable outcomes when patients remained in treatment for at least three months; those who remained in the three effective modalities for less than three months had outcomes similar to those who went through intake alone, or detoxification alone. Finally, outcomes from the DARP showed that the longer patients remained in treatment, the better the outcomes. Note that the DARP did not evaluate different methadone doses; therefore, conclusions about different outcomes for different methadone doses cannot be drawn from these reports. However, the DARP does provide results from an early, large survey showing that methadone treatment is effective.

Treatment Outcome Prospective Study (TOPS)

The TOPS was a survey of drug abuse treatment outcome for the period 1979–81, and it shared many features of the DARP (Hubbard et al. 1989). Like DARP, patients entering treatment programs were assessed (i.e., there was no random assignment of patients to particular treatments), a variety of treatment modalities were evaluated (including methadone maintenance), and follow-up assessments were conducted at regular intervals. The TOPS assessed patients enrolled in 37 treatment programs in 10 cities in the United States.

The TOPS did collect data about methadone dosing. After 3 months in methadone treatment, 40 percent of patients were receiving methadone doses below 30 mg per day, and doses were highly variable across treatment programs. Despite these relatively low doses, results from the TOPS indicate marked improvements associated with methadone treatment, especially for those patients who remained in treatment longer. Interestingly, whereas the DARP results suggested 3 months as the minimum time needed to effect positive changes from methadone treatment, the TOPS found that at least 6–12 months of treatment were needed. Among methadone patients who stayed in treatment for at least 3 months, 64 percent were regular (weekly or daily) heroin users in the year prior to treatment entry; 3–5 years after methadone treatment, about 18 percent of these patients were regular heroin users.

Drug Abuse Treatment Outcome Study (DATOS)

The DATOS represents the most recent effort in the United States to monitor outcome for substance abuse treatment. This survey grows out of the previous efforts of the DARP and the TOPS. Subject enrollment began in November 1991, and follow-up interviews were scheduled to be completed by March 1995. A total of 10,010 patients were enrolled in the DATOS.

Effectiveness of Methadone Maintenance Treatment Study

Unlike the previous three reports, the Effectiveness of Methadone Maintenance Treatment Study (sometimes referred to as the Ball and Ross study), conducted in the mid-1980s, examined specifically and only methadone treatment. In this study, six methadone programs in three East Coast cities of the United States (Baltimore, New York, and Philadelphia) were intensively investigated (Ball and Ross 1991). The programmatic aspects of each clinic as well as the patients in each program were evaluated. Patients were assessed in their methadone program, then followed for one year, with a second assessment at the end of that year, regardless of whether they were still in treatment at the program.

The results provide a wealth of information about patients in methadone treatment and about the programs. There were wide variations in dosing practices in the six programs, with mean doses as low as 26 mg in one program, and as high as 66 mg in another. Aggregating the results for all programs, the majority of patients were prescribed a daily methadone dose between 30 and 69 mg, and the average dose for all patients evaluated was 47 mg per day. Notably, methadone dose level was inversely related to self-reported heroin use in the 30 days prior to the follow-up interview; that is, patients receiving higher doses of methadone reported fewer days of heroin use. However, methadone dose was not associated with other outcome measures assessed in this study (e.g., cocaine use, days of criminal activity).

Institute for Social Research Survey

The Institute for Social Research Survey, conducted in the fall of 1988, was a survey of 172 methadone treatment programs in the United States (D'Aunno and Vaughn 1992). Interestingly, the average daily dose of methadone was between 43 and 48 mg, virtually identical to the results of the Ball and Ross study, and to the U.S. GAO report mentioned at the beginning of this chapter, which found an average dose of 48 mg. Again, wide variations in dosing practices were found, and like other studies described in this chapter, longer retention in treatment was positively associated with higher doses of methadone.

Other Survey Studies

A multitude of other reports have examined the relationship between methadone treatment and outcome based on results from naturalistic studies. These studies have generally shown that higher doses result in better treatment retention (e.g., Craig 1980; Caplehorn and Bell 1991) and a decrease in illicit opioid use (e.g., Caplehorn et al. 1993; Bell, Chan, and Kuk 1995; Hartel et al. 1995). But not all studies have uniformly found such positive results (e.g., Siassi, Angle, and Alston 1977; Maddux et al. 1991). Negative studies have often involved smaller numbers of patients, and therefore these exceptions may be attributed to such study limitations.

Conclusions from Survey Studies

These survey studies provide valuable information about the use of methadone treatment in community-based treatment clinics. Their strength lies in the large numbers of patients assessed in these studies and the inclusion of other treatment modalities that can function as comparison conditions. Overall, results from survey studies produce two conclusions: first, methadone treatment is effective (as measured by treatment retention and illicit opioid use), and second, higher methadone doses are more effective than lower doses. However, the limitations of survey studies can best be addressed through controlled clinical trials. The next section reviews results from these complementary studies of methadone's efficacy.

Methadone's Efficacy: Evidence from Controlled Clinical Trials

The first half of this section is a review of controlled clinical trials in which active methadone was compared to placebo methadone. However, only a limited number of such placebo-controlled studies have been conducted. The second half of this section reviews controlled clinical trials testing the relative efficacy of different doses of methadone, a research topic that has been studied much more extensively.

Methadone Compared to Placebo

There are only two known placebo-controlled studies examining the efficacy of methadone treatment. Although this is surprising, it is understandable, given the history of the development of methadone for opioid dependence. Most early methadone clinical trials implicitly accepted that methadone worked, in part because there were no other available effective medications for opioid dependence at the time of methadone's development. In addition, placebo-controlled studies of the treatment of opioid dependence could be difficult to implement if the design required patients to start on placebo, since the inevitable opioid withdrawal would result in high rates of dropout from the study. However, one must bear in mind that the robust outcomes found in the early studies of methadone treatment may have partly reflected the enthusiasm and intensive attention given to patients by the investigators and acknowledged by the authors of these reports. Thus, how patients respond when given placebo medication would be of extreme interest, since the relative efficacy of only nonpharmacologic factors, such as counseling, could then be quantified.

The first placebo-controlled study was conducted in Hong Kong between 1972 and 1975. In this study, 100 opioid abusers enrolled in a double-blind clinical trial (Newman and Whitehill 1979). "Double-blind" means that neither the patients nor the staff having contact with the patients knew to which group the patients had been assigned. All subjects were initially hospitalized for two weeks and stabilized on 60 mg of daily methadone. Upon discharge from the hospital, patients assigned to the placebo group received dose reductions of 1 mg per day for 60 days, and then were maintained on placebo. Patients maintained on methadone could have double-blind dose adjustments, with a maximum daily dose of 130 mg. The mean dose at the end of the first year of the study was 97 mg for this group (range 30–130 mg).

At the end of 32 weeks, only 10 percent of the placebo group remained in the study, versus 76 percent of the methadone group. Most of the patients in the placebo group were removed from the study because of persistent illicit opioid use based on urine testing, although a substantial proportion of patients in the placebo group also dropped out of the study and treatment. In addition to evidence of better treatment retention and decreased illicit opioid use for patients receiving methadone, rates of criminal activity were markedly higher for patients in the placebo group.

Thus, results from this study provide strong evidence that methadone is superior to placebo in the outpatient treatment of opioid dependence. One liability to this study is that the nonpharmacologic treatment was poorly described. However, the treatment staff had no prior experience with methadone treatment. Thus, placebo response rates could be higher if patients were to receive a baseline level of nonpharmacologic treatment from staff familiar with counseling opioid-dependent patients. Also, since patients in the placebo group knew they could get active methadone if they dropped out, these results provide further evidence that active methadone treatment is not just acceptable but desirable to opioid-dependent individuals.

The second placebo-controlled study of methadone treatment was conducted in Baltimore, Maryland, in the late 1980s. In this study, 247 opioid-dependent subjects enrolled in a treatment/research clinic (Strain et al. 1993a, 1993b). There was no inpatient portion to this study, and patients were street addicts randomly assigned to one of three dose groups: 0, 20, or 50 mg per day of methadone. All subjects were initially maintained on methadone, with dose adjustments made during the first 6 weeks so that final stabilization doses were achieved during week 6 of treatment. Patients assigned to the 0-mg dose group were maintained on double-blind placebo medication, and the stable dosing period lasted 14 weeks. All subjects were assigned to an experienced counselor for individual therapy, were given the opportunity to participate in group therapy, and had access to on-site primary care medical services.

Results from this study clearly showed that patients receiving 50 mg of methadone per day did better than patients who received 0 mg per day (Figure 5.1). Interestingly, about 20 percent of the patients receiving placebo methadone remained in treatment through the 14 weeks of the study, suggesting that significant elements of methadone treatment are the non-pharmacologic aspects of treatment. Finally, this study found that methadone treatment also produced improvements in a broad array of other areas (Strain et al. 1993b). These improvements were seen for patients on doses of both 50 and 0 mg of methadone, but the greatest improvements occurred for patients assigned to the 50-mg dose group. Thus, for example, the number of crimes committed decreased dramatically, as did illegal income and days of illegal activity. In addition, self-reports showed marked reductions in depressive symptoms as well as reductions in complaints of withdrawal symptoms (although these complaints did rise again over time for patients in the 0-mg dose group). Overall, the two controlled clinical trials described provide compelling evidence that methadone is superior to placebo in the outpatient treatment of opioid dependence.

Methadone Dose Effects

Results from survey studies show that higher doses appear to produce better outcomes than lower doses. This section reviews the relationship between specific methadone doses and treatment outcome. While methadone would be expected to produce favorable outcomes on measures of illicit opiate use, other outcome measures associated with a lifestyle of illicit drug use have also been examined in several of these studies and are reviewed. This is not an exhaustive review of the methadone dosing literature; rather, selected topics and illustrative studies are presented. Results from single-blind studies of methadone dosing are reviewed first, followed by outcomes from double-blind studies.

Outcomes from Single-Blind Methadone Dosing Studies

There are several reports based on single-blind dose studies of methadone treatment. Single-blind studies are not as methodologically rigorous as double-blind studies, since staff having contact with study patients sometimes know the dose assignment. Thus, it is possible that staff biases

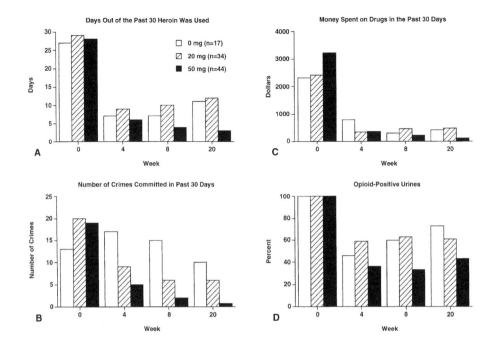

A Days Out of the Past 30 Heroin Was Used

Days / Week

□ 0 mg (n=17)
▨ 20 mg (n=34)
■ 50 mg (n=44)

C Money Spent on Drugs in the Past 30 Days

Dollars / Week

B Number of Crimes Committed in Past 30 Days

Number of Crimes / Week

D Opioid-Positive Urines

Percent / Week

Figure 5.1.   Results from a double-blind outpatient clinical trial comparing 0, 20, and 50 mg of daily methadone in the treatment of opioid dependence. (*A–C*) Data from the Addiction Severity Index; (*D*) results from urine testing conducted three times per week. *Source:* Data from Strain et al. (1993a, 1993b).

can influence outcome in single-blind studies, and it is also possible that staff may inadvertently (or intentionally!) inform patients about their dose assignment, which can create biases within patient groups as well.

Two of these studies examined doses of 30, 50, and 100 mg (Goldstein 1970; Garbutt and Goldstein 1972), whereas the third study tested doses of 40, 80, and 160 mg per day (Goldstein and Judson 1973). Results from these early clinical trials suggest that differences among widely different doses are only slight. Thus, there was no difference among doses of 30, 50, and 100 mg with respect to treatment retention, although patients in the higher-dose groups had somewhat lower rates of opioid-free urines. Another surprising observation was that 80- and 160-mg doses produced very similar outcomes.

Conclusions from Single-Blind Studies of Methadone Dosing

These single-blind studies are of historical interest, especially since they frequently concluded that there were few significant clinical differences between high and low doses of methadone—an observation that probably contributed to the eventual decision to use lower doses of methadone in some treatment programs. However, one must recognize that these studies have methodological limitations and that dose differences are best addressed in more rigorous, double-blind clinical trials.

Outcomes from Double-Blind Studies of Methadone Dosing

Several well-designed and conducted double-blind clinical trials of methadone dosing have been conducted, and six of these studies are briefly summarized here (Table 5.1). Several other early studies testing methadone dose in double-blind clinical trials have also been conducted (e.g., Jaffe 1971; Berry and Kuhn 1975), and are included in Table 5.1. Note, however, that some of these studies have other methodological limitations despite their use of double-blind dosing; the limitations of earlier studies are well summarized in the review by Hargreaves (1983).

In the early 1970s an important double-blind study of methadone dose effects was conducted as part of the assessment of the efficacy of LAAM for the treatment of opioid dependence (Ling et al. 1976). This was a multisite Veterans Affairs cooperative study comparing LAAM to two doses of methadone: 50 and 100 mg per day. Four hundred thirty patients enrolled in the 40-week study (288 were on methadone). With respect to treatment retention, the 100-mg group fared slightly better than the 50-mg group at the end of the 40 weeks. Similarly, results from urine testing for opioids showed that the 100-mg group did better than the 50-mg group. Notably, differences between the two methadone dose conditions were not great, but the results from this study do provide evidence that differential outcome between 50 and 100 mg of methadone occurs.

Four studies designed to test the efficacy of buprenorphine (a medication being developed for the treatment of opioid dependence; see Chapter 13) included two methadone dose groups, so conclusions regarding the efficacy of different doses of methadone can be found in these studies. The first study, conducted in the late 1980s, examined outcomes for patients assigned to doses of either 20 or 60 mg per day of methadone and found significantly better treatment retention and lower rates of opioid-positive urines for patients in the 60-mg group versus the 20-mg group (Johnson, Jaffe, and Fudala 1992). In the second study, patients were assigned doses of either 35 or 65 mg per day of methadone and similar outcomes for some measures were found, such as the rate of opioid-negative urines, although it appears that the lower methadone dose group actually had better results than the higher-dose group for other measures (Kosten et al. 1993). In the

Table 5.1 Summary of Double-Blind Methadone Dosing Studies

Study	Number of Patients[a]	Methadone Doses Studied	Treatment Retention	Illicit Opioid Use
Jaffe (1971)	63	Varied; averages were 36 and 100 mg	No difference between groups	No difference between groups
Berry and Kuhn (1975)	52	50 and 100 mg	No difference between groups	No difference between groups
Ling et al. (1976)	288	50 and 100 mg	100-mg group had slightly better retention	100-mg group had less illicit opioid use
Johnson, Jaffe, and Fudala (1992)	109	20 and 60 mg	60-mg group had better retention	60-mg group had less illicit opioid use
Kosten et al. (1993)	69	35 and 65 mg	No difference between groups	No difference between groups
Strain et al. (1993a, 1993b)	166	20 and 50 mg	50-mg group had better retention	50-mg group had less illicit opioid use
Banys et al. (1994)	38	40 and 80 mg	No difference between groups	Trend for 80-mg group to have less illicit opioid use
Ling et al. (1996)	150	30 and 80 mg	80-mg group had better retention	80-mg group had less illicit opioid use
Schottenfeld et al. (1997)	58	20 and 65 mg	65-mg group had better retention (but unknown if significant)	65-mg group had less illicit opioid use
Strain et al. (1997)	192	Range of 40–50 and 80–100 mg	No difference between groups	80–100 mg group had less illicit opioid use

[a]Total number of patients who received methadone in the study.

third study, the outcomes of patients assigned to either 30 or 80 mg of daily methadone were compared and significantly better treatment retention and rates of illicit opioid use were found for patients in the 80-mg group compared with the 30-mg group (Ling et al. 1996). Finally, in the fourth study, the outcomes of patients randomly assigned to doses of either 20 or 65 mg of daily methadone were compared and significantly lower rates of illicit opioid use for patients in the 65-mg dose group were found compared with the 20-mg condition (Schottenfeld et al. 1997).

Strain et al. (1993a, 1993b) conducted a double-blind study of methadone dosing (discussed in a previous section) that included a comparison between 20 and 50 mg of daily methadone in addition to a 0-mg dose condition. Results from the study showed differences in treatment retention between the 20- and 50-mg dose groups, with the higher dose having better treatment retention than the lower dose. (At the end of the 20-week study 52% of the patients in the 50-mg dose group were still in treatment, compared with 42% of the patients in the 20-mg dose group.) Subjects in this study provided urines for testing three times per week—an intensive schedule that is highly sensitive to detecting any illicit drug use, but relatively insensitive to detecting changes in drug use. There was a significantly lower rate of opioid-positive urine samples for the 50-mg dose group (56%) compared with the 20-mg dose group (68%; Figure 5.1). Interestingly, results for patients in the 20-mg group were not equivalent to those for patients in the placebo group. The 20-mg group had better treatment retention than the 0-mg group and lower rates of opioid use. Thus, even a low dose of methadone can exert some mild beneficial effects.

Several of the previously described studies used fixed dosing schedules. However, a follow-up study to the report by Strain et al. (1993a) examined the efficacy of moderate-dose methadone (40–50 mg per day) versus high-dose methadone (80–100 mg per day) using a flexible dosing procedure (Strain et al. 1997). Patients randomly assigned to the moderate-dose group were initially stabilized on 40 mg of daily methadone, but could receive double-blind dose increases (to a maximum of 50 mg per day) if they continued to have opioid-positive urine samples. Patients assigned to the high-dose group were initially stabilized on 80 mg of daily methadone, but could receive double-blind dose increases (to a maximum of 100 mg per day) if they continued to have opioid-positive urine samples. Results from this study showed that there was no difference in treatment retention for the moderate- versus high-dose conditions—a surprising finding given the dose effects seen for treatment retention in the earlier study using 0, 20, and 50 mg daily doses of methadone. However, there was a significantly lower rate of opioid-positive urine samples for the high-dose group.

Conclusions from and Recommendations Based on Double-Blind Studies of Methadone Dosing

The controversy regarding optimal methadone dosing becomes more understandable after reviewing results from clinical trials that have attempted to address whether higher doses of methadone are more effective than lower doses. The limited number of such studies, along with the strong recommendations from early single-blind studies that little difference exists between moderate- and high-dose methadone, provided little reason to challenge the wide variations in dosing found across treatment clinics.

The double-blind studies suggest that there can be benefits in using high-dose methadone (arbitrarily defined as doses of about 100 mg per day) compared with moderate-dose methadone (about 50 mg per day); the primary benefit is in further decreases in illicit opioid use (relative to moderate-dose methadone). But, although the difference may be in a decrease in illicit opioid use, high-dose methadone does not seem to improve treatment retention. However, moderate doses are definitely better than low doses (about 20 mg per day), both on measures of treatment retention and on rates of illicit opioid use, as determined by urine testing.

A few other points are worth discussing. First, there are no good data on the use of methadone doses greater than 100 mg per day, although there are intriguing early reports suggesting that the administration of doses of 160 mg or even 200 mg per day is feasible. It may be possible to achieve better outcomes with higher doses of methadone, but adequate research studies have not yet been conducted. Second, extrapolating from well-designed and well-conducted clinical trials to actual clinical use should be done with extreme caution. Outcomes certainly can be improved when features of a clinical trial such as double-blind dosing are not present, more intensive nonpharmacologic treatments are used, and dosing is adjusted based on the purity and quantity of heroin being used by a particular patient. Thus, results from these double-blind studies represent treatment outcomes that are obtained under artificial circumstances, and it should be possible to achieve even better treatment results in a community methadone clinic that provides more individualized treatment for each patient.

The results from these studies, along with other reviewed work (i.e., the various survey studies that have been conducted), suggest that substantial clinical gains, as defined by treatment retention and decreases in opioid-positive urine samples, can be achieved by raising doses from 20 mg per day to at least 50 mg per day. Further decreases in illicit opioid use can occur if the dose is increased up to a maximum of 100 mg per day. Thus, a target dose of at least 50 mg per day is clinically indicated, and doses as high as 100 mg per day should be considered, especially for patients who continue using opiates during treatment; anecdotal reports suggest that doses greater than 100 mg per day may be indicated for some patients.

ISSUES RELATED TO METHADONE DOSING

Predicting Outcome in Methadone Treatment

Finding pretreatment characteristics of patients, or early in-treatment factors such as methadone dose, that could be useful in identifying success in treatment would be extremely valuable. However, no single characteristic or set of characteristics can fully predict who will do well (or poorly) in treatment. This fact suggests that allocating treatment slots based solely upon predictor characteristics would not be practical at this time because this method would exclude patients who could do well and include patients who could do poorly. Thus, one must recognize the limitations of using pretreatment variables in predicting outcome in methadone treatment. Still, some characteristics of patients *are* associated with better outcomes, and some early treatment results do appear to have clinical utility in predicting subsequent in-treatment behavior. (For an excellent, although somewhat dated, review of this topic see McLellan [1983] in the references at the end of this chapter.)

The characteristic most consistently associated with treatment outcome is age: older patients tend to have better outcomes than younger patients. In addition, race (being nonwhite) and marital status (being married) are often associated with better treatment outcomes. Other characteristics sometimes associated with poor treatment retention can include a history of criminal activity, psychological problems, and poor employment history (McLellan 1983; Farley et al. 1992).

In addition to these pretreatment factors, in-treatment predictors can influence treatment outcome. Thus, as reviewed in the foregoing, higher methadone dose is associated with better treatment outcome. In addition, some evidence suggests that greater amounts of counseling services are associated with better outcomes (McLellan et al. 1993; Strain et al. 1998). Finally, one study has shown that the amount of illicit opioid use, as determined by intensive urine testing during the first two weeks of treatment, was highly predictive of subsequent rates of opioid-positive urine samples (Strain et al. 1998). A similar relationship was also found for cocaine use; that is, the amount of illicit cocaine use, as determined by intensive urine testing during the first two weeks of treatment, was highly predictive of subsequent rates of cocaine use as determined by urine testing. These relationships suggest that intensive urine monitoring for illicit drug use during the first weeks of methadone treatment may be useful in determining which patients should have subsequent intensive counseling and urine monitoring, and which need not be as closely monitored. For example, patients who have no cocaine use during the first two weeks of treatment are more likely to have no subsequent cocaine use later in treatment.

Conclusions Regarding Predictors of Treatment Outcome

Several patient characteristics are often associated with treatment success, such as age, marital status, and race, but none of these are definitively associated with success in methadone treatment. Similarly, some in-treatment factors, such as dose of methadone, amount of counseling contact, and early in-treatment drug use, can be associated with subsequent treatment success. However, none of these in-treatment factors are definitively associated with success.

Methadone Blood Levels

Details regarding methadone's pharmacodynamic and pharmacokinetic effects can be found in Chapter 3. This section provides a review of the role of methadone blood levels in the management of patients.

It is not at all uncommon in medicine to obtain blood levels of medications in order to determine the optimal dosing of the medication. Indeed, for many medications, such as certain anticonvulsants and antidepressants, well-defined ranges for optimal therapeutic effects have been determined and dosing is titrated to achieve a blood level in that range. Given the wide variations in methadone dosing practices, it was a logical step to determine whether these differences in doses simply reflected individual differences in absorption or metabolism and whether clinical response was associated with particular blood levels of methadone.

Several studies have examined methadone blood levels in patients receiving chronic doses of methadone and found that there are marked individual differences in blood levels for patients receiving the same dose of methadone (e.g., Kreek 1973a; Horns, Rado, and Goldstein 1975; Holmstrand, Änggard, and Gunne 1978). For patients maintained on a stable dose of methadone, some evidence suggests that better outcomes are associated with 24-hour postdose plasma concentrations greater than 150–200 ng/ml (Holmstrand, Änggard, and Gunne 1978; Tennant et al. 1983; Loimer and Schmid 1992), and levels below 50 ng/ml appear to be related to poor treatment outcome (Bell et al. 1988). Note, however, that methadone blood levels peak around the eighth day of dosing and then decline over the subsequent days, so determinations should not be made before the first 3 to 4 weeks of treatment (Holmstrand, Änggard, and Gunne 1978).

In addition to varying during the initial time of stabilization on methadone, blood levels can also change if a patient is treated with certain other medications (see Table 7.1). Thus, for example, enzyme-inducing medications such as phenobarbital or phenytoin can lower blood levels (Tong et al. 1981; Bell et al. 1988), as can rifampin (Kreek et al. 1976). Other medication interactions with methadone are less well characterized, although there is some evidence that they may alter methadone's effects (e.g., Plummer et al. 1988).

Methadone blood levels may be particularly useful under certain circumstances. For example, sometimes patients report that their dose of methadone fails to provide adequate, 24-hour suppression of withdrawal. The clinician should check first for concurrent treatment with enzyme-inducing medications such as phenobarbital or dilantin (Bell et al. 1988), which can lower blood levels. However, rapid declines in blood levels have been found in some patients not treated with such medications (Tennant 1987). For patients who complain that their dose does not provide 24-hour suppression of withdrawal, several methadone blood level tests done over a 24-hour period may show a rapid decline in blood levels and provide a biological confirmation of the self-reports (Walton, Thornton, and Wahl 1978; Nilsson et al. 1983). Such patients may benefit from a split dosing of methadone, so that they are dosed twice per day.

However, under most circumstances methadone blood levels are not routinely used in clinical practice. Their use is probably best reserved for specialized conditions, such as when patients who are receiving an appropriate dose of methadone continue to complain of inadequate dosing and appear to be in opioid withdrawal when they return to the clinic, or when patients need treatment for other conditions with a medication that can alter methadone blood levels (see Table 7.1).

Methadone Side Effects (Table 5.2)

The use of methadone in the treatment of opioid dependence is extremely safe and has few side effects. Formerly opioid-dependent subjects enrolled in the first human laboratory study of methadone were maintained on methadone for several weeks or months and intensively monitored for side effects (Isbell et al. 1948). The most common effect initially noted was sedation, which occurred during the first days of methadone administra-

Table 5.2 Side Effects Associated
with Methadone Treatment

Changes in systolic blood pressure[a]
Constipation
Decrease in ejaculate volume
Decrease in heart rate[b]
Decrease in hemoglobin and hematocrit[b]
Decrease in pupil diameter[b]
Decrease in respiratory rate[b]
Decrease in seminal vesicular and prostatic secretions
Increase in sweating
Lower serum testosterone in males
Sedation[c]
Sleep disturbances (primarily insomnia)
Slowing on EEG

[a]Direction varies depending on length of time taking methadone.
[b]Mild and not clinically significant.
[c] Tolerance develops to this effect.

tion; tolerance to this effect quickly developed. Constipation was also
noted, but tolerance did not develop. In addition, subjects showed mild decreases in heart rate (about 10 beats per minute) and respiratory rate (about
4 breaths per minute), and systolic blood pressure was initially slightly decreased during the first few months of methadone administration, but then
slightly increased during subsequent months (although this increase does
not appear to be clinically significant). Thus, results from this first study
show that methadone produced no significant adverse side effects.

The first report by Dole and Nyswander (1965) noted only constipation and self-reported increased sweating as side effects to methadone
treatment, which is especially significant given the intensive monitoring of
these patients (e.g., bone marrow biopsies in four patients, various blood
and urine tests). Other early studies of methadone also reported constipation and excessive sweating, as well as sexual difficulties (e.g., Goldstein
1970; Kreek 1973b).

More systematic studies of the side effects of methadone have tended
to replicate these early results. Thus, physiologic measures such as blood
pressure, heart rate, respiratory rate, and pupil diameter tend to have mild
decreases with chronic methadone dosing, whereas body temperature
shows a mild increase (Martin et al. 1973; Gritz et al. 1975). All these effects appear to be small and not clinically significant. No abnormalities on
ECGs appear with chronic methadone treatment, although there is slowing on the electroencephalogram (EEG) (Isbell et al. 1948; Martin et al.

1973; Gritz et al. 1975). There can be mild decreases in hemoglobin and hematocrit associated with chronic methadone treatment (i.e., a decrease of about 2.5–3.0 in hematocrit), but, again, these changes do not appear to be clinically significant (Martin et al. 1973).

Serum testosterone levels are lower than normal in men maintained on methadone (Cicero et al. 1975). Testosterone levels are also lower in subjects who use heroin regularly (Mendelson et al. 1975), although levels may be lower yet in men on methadone than in men using heroin regularly (Cicero et al. 1975). Ejaculate volume and seminal vesicular and prostatic secretions can be markedly reduced in men maintained on methadone (Cicero et al. 1975), and these physiologic effects may contribute to patient complaints of decreased sexual functioning while maintained on methadone. However, evidence indicates that rates of sexual activity in men return to baseline rates (i.e., premethadone and pre–opioid dependence rates) as time on methadone progresses (Martin et al. 1973). Comparable data on the rates of sexual activity in women are not available.

Patients with opioid dependence often have liver disease before entering methadone treatment; therefore, the assessment of changes in liver function status owing to methadone use can be confounded by this preexisting dysfunction. In addition, high rates of concurrent alcohol abuse while in methadone treatment can lead to new-onset liver disease that can be wrongly attributed to methadone use. When these factors are considered in studies of liver function in patients maintained on methadone, no evidence is found that methadone has hepatotoxic effects (Kreek et al. 1972; Kreek 1973b; Novick et al. 1993).

Finally, it is important to note one set of side effects not present with chronic methadone dosing: impairments in cognitive functioning. Patients on methadone generally do not have significantly different scores on tests of intellectual functioning when compared with abstinent patients, nor do they have differences in psychomotor tasks such as reaction time (Gordon, Warner, and Henderson 1967; Gordon 1970; Gritz et al. 1975).

Conclusions Regarding Side Effects of Methadone

Methadone has been extensively used for the treatment of opioid dependence in numerous clinics throughout the world. This extensive clinical experience provides considerable information about methadone's side effects. Based on this experience, there appear to be three clinically significant side effects to methadone: constipation, increased sweating, and sexual dysfunction. Several other effects have been noted, but tolerance typically develops to these effects, and some represent clinically insignificant changes. This mild side-effects profile is one of the attractive features of methadone: it is a safe and well-tolerated medication.

Summary and Conclusions

Results both from surveys of methadone use in the treatment of opioid dependence and from controlled clinical trials demonstrate that methadone is an effective medication that produces favorable outcomes both directly related to drug use (i.e., decreases in illicit opioid use) and indirectly related to drug use (e.g., decreases in criminal activity). The minimally effective dose of methadone appears to be about 20 mg per day, as this dose will produce better retention than placebo methadone. However, outcomes can be substantially improved by using doses greater than 20 mg per day, and initial stabilization doses in methadone maintenance should probably be *at least 50 mg per day.* For patients who do not respond in this dose range, further increases *up to 100 mg per day should be considered,* because there is considerable individual difference in the response to different doses of methadone. In addition, assessment using methadone blood levels may be indicated, especially if a patient appears to be experiencing withdrawal prior to the next dose of methadone. Doses in excess of 100 mg per day could be useful in the treatment of opioid dependence, although well-designed and conducted studies of doses greater than 100 mg per day need to be done. In programs that adhere to a "low-dose" philosophy, the clinicians should understand and discuss these outcome data, examine their own retention and drug use results, and consider whether they are providing the best possible services to their patients.

References

Ball J.C., Ross A. 1991. *The Effectiveness of Methadone Maintenance Treatment.* Springer-Verlag, New York.

Banys P., Tusel D.J., Sees K.L., Reilly P.M., Delucchi K.L. 1994. Low (40 mg) versus high (80 mg) dose methadone in a 180-day heroin detoxification program. *J. Subst. Abuse Treat.* 3:225–32.

Bell J., Chan J., Kuk A. 1995. Investigating the influence of treatment philosophy on outcome of methadone maintenance. *Addiction* 90:823–30.

Bell J., Seres V., Bowron P., Lewis J., Batey R. 1988. The use of serum methadone levels in patients receiving methadone maintenance. *Clin. Pharmacol. Ther.* 43:623–29.

Berry G.J., Kuhn K.L. 1975. Dose-related response to methadone: reduction of maintenance dose. In: Proceedings of the Fifth National Conference on Methadone Treatment, National Association for the Prevention of Addiction to Narcotics, Washington, DC, pp. 972–79.

Caplehorn J.R.M., Bell J. 1991. Methadone dosage and retention of patients in maintenance treatment. *Med. J. Aust.* 154:195–99.

Caplehorn J.R.M., Bell J., Kleinbaum D.G., Gebski V.J. 1993. Methadone dose and heroin use during maintenance treatment. *Addiction* 88: 119–24.

Cicero T.J., Bell R.D., Wiest W.G., Allison J.H., Polakoski K., Robins E. 1975. Function of the male sex organs in heroin and methadone users. *N. Engl. J. Med.* 292:882–87.

Craig R.J. 1980. Effectiveness of low-dose methadone maintenance for the treatment of inner city heroin addicts. *Int. J. Addictions* 15:701–10.

D'Aunno T., Vaughn T.E. 1992. Variations in methadone treatment practices: results from a national study. *JAMA* 267:253–58.

Dole V.P., Nyswander M. 1965. A medical treatment for diacetylmorphine (heroin) addiction: a clinical trial with methadone hydrochloride. *JAMA* 193:80–84.

Dole V.P., Nyswander M.E., Warner A. 1968. Successful treatment of 750 criminal addicts. *JAMA* 206:2708–11.

Farley T.A., Cartter M.L., Wassell J.T., Hadler J.L. 1992. Predictors of outcome in methadone programs: effect of HIV counseling and testing. *AIDS* 6:115–21.

Garbutt G.D., Goldstein A. 1972. Blind comparison of three methadone maintenance dosages in 180 patients. In: Proceedings of the Fourth National Conference on Methadone Treatment, National Association for the Prevention of Addiction to Narcotics, New York, pp. 411–14.

General Accounting Office (GAO). 1990. Methadone Maintenance: Some Treatment Programs Are Not Effective; Greater Federal Oversight Needed. United States General Accounting Office, Washington, DC.

Goldstein A. 1970. Dosage, duration, side effects: blind controlled dosage comparisons with methadone in 200 patients. In: Proceedings of the Third National Conference on Methadone Treatment, National Association for the Prevention of Addiction to Narcotics, Rockville, MD, pp. 31–37.

Goldstein A., Judson B.A. 1973. Efficacy and side effects of three widely different methadone doses. In: Proceedings of the Fifth National Conference on Methadone Treatment, National Association for the Prevention of Addiction to Narcotics, Washington, DC, pp. 21–44.

Gordon N.B. 1970. Reaction-times of methadone treated ex heroin addicts. *Psychopharmacology (Berl.)* 16:337–44.

Gordon N.B., Warner A., Henderson A. 1967. Psychomotor and intellectual performance under methadone maintenance. In: Committee on Problems of Drug Dependence, Minutes of the Twenty-Ninth Meeting. National Academy of Sciences, Washington, DC.

Gritz E.R., Shiffman S.M., Jarvik M.E., Haber J., Dymond A.M., Coger R., Charuvastra V., Schlesinger J. 1975. Physiological and psychological effects of methadone in man. *Arch. Gen. Psychiatry* 32:237–42.

Hargreaves W.A. 1983. Methadone dosage and duration for maintenance treatment. In: Cooper J.R., Altman F., Brown B.S., Czechowicz D., eds. *Research on the Treatment of Narcotic Addiction: State of the Art.* United States Department of Health and Human Services, Public Health Service, Rockville, MD.

Hartel D.M., Schoenbaum E.E., Selwyn P.A., Kline J., Davenny K., Klein R.S., Friedland G.H. 1995. Heroin use during methadone maintenance treatment: the importance of methadone dose and cocaine use. *Am. J. Public Health* 85:83–88.

Holmstrand J., Änggard E., Gunne L. 1978. Methadone maintenance: plasma levels and therapeutic outcome. *Clin. Pharmacol. Ther.* 23:175–80.

Horns W.H., Rado M., Goldstein A. 1975. Plasma levels and symptom complaints in patients maintained on daily dosage of methadone hydrochloride. *Clin. Pharmacol. Ther.* 17:636–49.

Hubbard R.L., Marsden M.E., Rachal J.V., Harwood H.J., Cavanaugh E.R., Ginzburg H.M. 1989. *Drug Abuse Treatment: A National Study of Effectiveness.* University of North Carolina Press, Chapel Hill.

Isbell H., Wilker A., Eisenman A.J., Daingerfield M., Frank K. 1948. Liability of addiction to 6-dimethylamino-4,4-diphenyl-3-heptanone (methadon, "amidone" or "10820") in man. *Arch. Intern. Med.* 82:362–92.

Jaffe J.H. 1971. Further experience with methadone in the treatment of narcotic users. In: Einstein S., ed. *Methadone Maintenance.* Marcel Dekker, New York.

Johnson R.E., Jaffe J.H., Fudala P.J. 1992. A controlled trial of buprenorphine treatment for opioid dependence. *JAMA* 267:2750–55.

Kosten T.R., Schottenfeld R., Ziedonis D., Falcioni J. 1993. Buprenorphine versus methadone maintenance for opioid dependence. *J. Nerv. Ment. Dis.* 181:358–64.

Kreek M.J. 1973a. Plasma and urine levels of methadone: comparison following four medication forms used in chronic maintenance treatment. *N.Y. State J. Med.* 73:2773–77.

———. 1973b. Medical safety and side effects of methadone in tolerant individuals. *JAMA* 223:665–68.

Kreek M.J., Dodes L., Kane S., Knobler J., Martin R. 1972. Long-term methadone maintenance therapy: effects on liver function. *Ann. Int. Med.* 77:598–602.

Kreek M.J., Garfield J.W., Gutjahr C.L., Giusti L.M. 1976. Rifampin-induced methadone withdrawal. *N. Engl. J. Med.* 294:1104–6.

Ling W., Charuvastra C., Kaim S.C., Klett J. 1976. Methadyl acetate and methadone as maintenance treatments for heroin addicts. *Arch. Gen. Psychiatry* 33:709–20.

Ling W., Wesson D.R., Charuvastra C., Klett J. 1996. A controlled trial comparing buprenorphine and methadone maintenance in opioid dependence. *Arch. Gen. Psychiatry* 53:401–7.

Loimer N., Schmid R. 1992. The use of plasma levels to optimize methadone maintenance treatment. *Drug Alcohol Depend.* 30:241–46.

Maddux J.F., Esquivel M., Vogtsberger K.N., Desmond D.P. 1991. Methadone dose and urine morphine. *J. Subst. Abuse Treat.* 8:195–201.

Martin W.R., Jasinski D.R., Haertzen C.A., Kay D.C., Jones B.E., Mansky P.A., Carpenter R.W. 1973. Methadone: a reevaluation. *Arch. Gen. Psychiatry* 28:286–95.

McLellan A.T. 1983. Patient characteristics associated with outcome. In: Cooper J.R., Altman F., Brown B.S., Czechowicz D., eds. *Research on the Treatment of Narcotic Addiction: State of the Art.* United States Department of Health and Human Services, Public Health Service, Rockville, MD.

McLellan A.T., Arndt I.O., Metzger D.S., Woody G.E., O'Brien C.P. 1993. The effects of psychosocial services in substance abuse treatment. *JAMA* 269:1953–59.

Mendelson J.H., Meyer R.E., Ellingboe J., Mirin S.M., McDougle M. 1975. Effects of heroin and methadone on plasma cortisol and testosterone. *J. Pharmacol. Exp. Ther.* 195:296–302.

Newman R.G., Whitehill W.B. 1979. Double-blind comparison of methadone and placebo maintenance treatments of narcotic addicts in Hong Kong. *Lancet* 2(8141):485–88.

Nilsson M.-I., Grönbladh L., Widerlöv E., Änggard E. 1983. Pharmacokinetics of methadone in methadone maintenance treatment: characterization of therapeutic failures. *Eur. J. Pharmacol.* 25:497–501.

Novick D.M., Richman B.L., Friedman J.M., Friedman J.E., Fried C., Wilson J.P., Townley A., Kreek M.J. 1993. The medical status of methadone maintenance patients in treatment for 11–18 years. *Drug Alcohol Depend.* 33:235–45.

Plummer J.L., Gourlay G.K., Cherry D.A., Cousins M.J. 1988. Estimation of methadone clearance: application in the management of cancer pain. *Pain* 33:313–22.

Schottenfeld R.S., Pakes J.R., Oliveto A., Ziedonis D., Kosten T.R. 1997. Buprenorphine vs methadone maintenance treatment for concurrent opioid dependence and cocaine abuse. *Arch. Gen. Psychiatry* 54:713–20.

Siassi I., Angle B.P., Alston D.C. 1977. Maintenance dosage as a critical factor in methadone maintenance treatment. *Br. J. Addiction* 72:261–68.

Simpson D.D., Sells S.B. 1990. *Opioid Addiction and Treatment: A 12-Year Follow-up.* Robert E. Krieger, Malabar, FL.

Strain E.C., Stitzer M.L., Liebson I.A., Bigelow G.E. 1993a. Dose-response effects of methadone in the treatment of opioid dependence. *Ann. Intern. Med.* 119:23–27.

———. 1993b. Methadone dose and treatment outcome. *Drug Alcohol Depend.* 33:105–17.

———. 1997. Moderate versus high dose methadone in the treatment of opioid dependence. In: Harris L.S., ed. Problems of Drug Dependence 1996. Proceedings of the 58th Annual Scientific Meeting. College on Problems of Drug Dependence. NIDA Research Monograph 174, Department of Health and Human Services, National Institute on Drug Abuse, Rockville, MD, p. 300.

———. 1998. Useful predictors of outcome in methadone-treated patients: results from a controlled clinical trial with three doses of methadone. *J. Maint. Addict.* 1:15–28.

Tennant F.S. 1987. Inadequate plasma concentrations in some high-dose methadone maintenance patients. *Am. J. Psychiatry* 144:1349–50.

Tennant F.S., Rawson R.A., Cohen A., Tarver A., Clabough D. 1983. Methadone plasma levels and persistent drug abuse in high dose maintenance patients. *Subst. Alcohol Actions/Misuse* 4:369–74.

Tong T.G., Pond S.M., Kreek M.J., Jaffery N.F., Benowitz N.L. 1981. Phenytoin-induced methadone withdrawal. *Ann. Intern. Med.* 94:349–51.

Walton R.G., Thornton T.L., Wahl G.F. 1978. Serum methadone as an aid in managing methadone maintenance patients. *Int. J. Addictions* 13:689–94.

Williams H.R. 1971. Low and high methadone maintenance in the out-patient treatment of the hard core heroin addict. In: Einstein S., ed. *Methadone Maintenance.* Marcel Dekker, New York.

6

Other Substance Use Disorders in Methadone Treatment

Prevalence, Consequences, Detection, and Management

Maxine L. Stitzer, Ph.D., and Mary Ann Chutuape, Ph.D.

Among methadone maintenance patients, the use of other drugs is common. The chemical substances abused by methadone patients during treatment include those that are legally available—tobacco and alcohol—as well as drugs that can be obtained only on the illegal market—heroin and cocaine. The use of oral prescription medications is also seen in methadone patients, prominently including, but not limited to, benzodiazepine tranquilizers. Finally, new compounds surface periodically within the panoply of drugs favored by methadone patients, clonidine being a recent example, so clinicians must always be alert to new trends in drug use in their clinic. This chapter reviews the prevalence, consequences, and detection methods for drugs commonly used by patients during methadone treatment. It focuses on heroin, cocaine, benzodiazepines, alcohol, marijuana and tobacco and makes recommendations for the clinical management of patients using various drug combinations.

Prevalence and Patterns of Polydrug Use

Table 6.1 shows representative data from a large sample survey of patients enrolled in methadone maintenance at a community treatment program in Baltimore, Maryland (Brooner et al. 1997). Although there may

Table 6.1 Substance Abuse Disorders among Methadone Maintenance Patients

Abuse or Dependence	Lifetime Rates (%)	Current Rates (%)
Opioid	100.0	100.0
Cocaine	77.1	43.6
Alcohol	63.3	26.5
Cannabis	65.7	18.6
Sedative	57.6	18.4
Stimulant	30.7	0.3
Hallucinogen	27.3	0.7
Other[a]	20.4	3.2

Source: Adapted from Brooner et al. (1997).
Note: Based on Structured Clinical Interview for DSM-III-R (SCID) interviews with 716 methadone patients in a Baltimore community clinic.
[a]Primarily inhalants, clonidine, and promethazine.

be regional and population differences in drug use among methadone patients, this study makes the important point that the majority of opioid-dependent patients have a history of using multiple drugs. Each methadone patient may have as many as four to five substance abuse or dependence disorders, and for patients who have any comorbid psychiatric disorder (including antisocial personality disorder) this number is even greater. The Baltimore study also illustrates the relative prevalence of use across different types of drugs. In this study, cocaine was by far the more prevalent secondary drug of abuse among methadone patients, with a lifetime prevalence of 77 percent and current prevalence of 43 percent. Alcohol dependence is seen in about one-quarter of methadone maintenance patients and poses another challenge for rehabilitation. Two other drugs with significant prevalence in the opioid-dependent population are cannabis (marijuana) and sedatives (usually benzodiazepine tranquilizers). About 20 percent of the treatment population were dependent on each of these two drugs in the Baltimore sample, although higher rates of marijuana use have been reported in other samples (Nirenberg et al. 1996). The prevalence of tobacco dependence was not assessed in the Baltimore study, but another study conducted with this same population found that 92 percent of patients were cigarette smokers (Clemmey et al. 1997). This finding is consistent with the high rates of cigarette smoking reported for other groups of drug abusers.

As previously discussed, methadone blocks or attenuates the effects of heroin. Nevertheless, up to 60 percent of methadone patients continue to use heroin during treatment. The amount and frequency of heroin use during methadone treatment is clearly lower than the amount and frequency of use prior to treatment. Also, rates of heroin use are influenced by treatment factors including maintenance dose of methadone (see Chapter 5), time in treatment (rates tend to decrease over time), and the clinic's tolerance of this behavior. It is not entirely clear why some methadone patients continue to use heroin, or to what extent they can feel the effects of the drug when they do use it. One association consistently observed, however, is that between heroin and cocaine use. For example, it has been shown that methadone patients who used cocaine in the last three months of treatment were six times more likely to have used heroin compared with those patients who had not used cocaine (Hartel et al. 1995). It is possible that heroin continues to boost or otherwise modulate cocaine's effects even though patients are maintained on methadone.

Changes over Time in Treatment

It has been suggested that alcohol or other drug use may increase after entry into methadone maintenance treatment, but the validity of this belief is debatable. Several factors could explain such an increase. For example, patients who stop or greatly reduce heroin use after entering methadone treatment may now have more time and money to expend on drugs such as cocaine and alcohol. Drugs such as benzodiazepines may become more readily available because of new associations formed at the methadone clinic. Finally, drug use could start or escalate because of the interaction between that drug and methadone. For example, methadone may increase the high obtained from using cocaine (Preston et al. 1996) and benzodiazepines can enhance the effects produced by methadone (Preston et al. 1984).

However, studies examining this issue have generally failed to document any increases in secondary drug use over time during methadone treatment; in fact, trends toward decreasing rates of drug use are more often reported. Decreases over time have been especially documented for opiate-positive urines, indicating that heroin use declines over time in treatment. For example, in a study conducted by Hartel et al. (1995), heroin use was reported by 40–50 percent of patients who had been in treatment for less than two years, but by only 12–20 percent of those in treatment for more than two years. However, because such studies are generally cross-sectional rather than longitudinal, it is not entirely clear whether individual patients actually decrease their use over time or whether it is simply that those who stop using drugs early in treatment are more likely to remain in treatment (so that higher rates of abstinence later in treatment simply reflect the result of drug users dropping out of treatment). The main point is that most methadone patients come to treatment with an extensive history of multiple drug use and that, on the whole, drug use appears to decrease rather than increase during time in treatment.

CONSEQUENCES OF POLYDRUG USE DURING METHADONE TREATMENT

There are medical, psychological, and behavioral risks inherent in using all drugs of abuse, and these risks continue when methadone patients use licit and illicit drugs of abuse during treatment. This section provides a brief overview of some of the risks and adverse consequences that methadone patients face when they continue to use chemical substances during treatment.

Heroin

Although heroin has no direct toxic effects, there may be several important adverse consequences of continued heroin use during treatment. One consequence, if use is by the intravenous route, is the potential for exposure to HIV infection, hepatitis B and C infections, abscesses, and other infections when drug preparations or intravenous equipment is contaminated. A second potential risk, which is currently based on speculation rather than research, is that patients who continue to use heroin will tend to become even more physically dependent through exposure to the added short-acting opiate. This dependency in turn could result in increasing levels of withdrawal discomfort and the need to continue the use of short-acting opiates for withdrawal symptom relief. In this scenario, increasing the methadone dose could be a beneficial treatment strategy, because suppression of the excess withdrawal symptoms should result. Continued association with drug users and a drug-using lifestyle could be listed as a final adverse consequence of heroin, as well as cocaine, use during treatment.

Cocaine

Cocaine has substantial medical risks (reviewed in Benowitz 1993). The most serious risks are related to intense central nervous system (CNS) stimulation and vasoconstriction, which can result in severe hypertension. This in turn can produce serious consequences such as aortic rupture or restricted blood flow to organs that can lead to heart attacks and damage to the kidneys and intestines. Pregnant abusers who use cocaine can experience spontaneous abortions and placental abruption. Most deaths that result from cocaine use are sudden and occur before medical help can be found. However, despite these potentially serious complications, cocaine use may actually be associated more with traumatic deaths and injuries (including homicide, suicide, and accidents) than with medical complications. Cocaine intoxication can also produce mental confusion and other symptoms including anxiety, panic attacks, agitated delirium, and paranoid psychosis. Symptoms produced by cocaine, including chest pains and mental confusion, are a common cause of visits to inner-city emergency rooms.

Benzodiazepines

Problems associated with benzodiazepine use can include sedation, memory impairments, overdose, and physical dependence. Although tolerance develops to the sedative effects of these drugs, the use of benzodiazepines may be a factor in road accidents, particularly when they are used in combination with other sedative drugs such as alcohol. Memory impairment is one of the most striking adverse effects of benzodiazepines (see Curran 1991), and it is not clear how much tolerance develops to this effect. Clinically, memory impairment could be disruptive or dangerous to the extent that a person may forget important events or information, or engage in risky behaviors while under the influence of drugs. While an overdose with benzodiazepines alone is generally not lethal, an overdose of a benzodiazepine combined with another sedating drug (including methadone) can be fatal. Thus, benzodiazepines are routinely found in toxicology screens of suicide victims, or attempters, and suicide risk should be closely assessed and monitored in methadone patients who are taking benzodiazepines.

Perhaps the most prominent and relevant risk associated with benzodiazepine use in a drug-abusing population is that of physical dependence and withdrawal symptoms following discontinuation. When regular use of benzodiazepines is discontinued, patients can experience rebound anxiety and agitation, insomnia, tension, sweating, tremulousness, ringing in the ears, increased sensitivity to noises and to light, and sensory and perceptual distortions (Busto et al. 1986). In cases of severe dependence, withdrawal delirium and seizures (like those seen in severe alcohol withdrawal) may be observed. The extent and timing of symptoms will depend in part on the amount and duration of previous use as well as on the type of benzodiazepine being used. Because of the potentially dangerous symptoms that can appear, benzodiazepine detoxification should be conducted only under medical supervision (Alling 1992).

Alcohol

Heavy alcohol use among opiate addicts has been associated with health problems, increased mortality, and disruptive behaviors at the clinic. Other common alcohol-related problems include blackouts, aggressive or violent behaviors, arrests, accidents, loss of employment, disruption of family life, and deterioration of mental and physical health. In one study in which a sample of methadone-maintained problem drinkers were enrolled in an alcoholism treatment project, half of the subjects had been hospitalized with an alcohol-related illness in the three months prior to participation (Ling et al. 1983). Liver disease is the best known and most common complication associated with excessive drinking. However, alcohol use is well known to produce toxic effects on other organs and can result in both acute and chronic cognitive impairment, as well as heart, kidney, and blood disorders. Alcohol use is a leading cause of death in methadone patients, estimated in different studies to account for 18–60 percent of all mortalities (see Bickel, Marion, and Lowinson 1987). In a 12-year follow-up study of individuals previously enrolled in drug abuse treatment, heavy drinkers died at a rate seven times higher than an age-adjusted general population (Sells and Simpson 1987). Alcohol use is also a strong contributing factor to premature treatment discharges and has been estimated to account for about 25 percent of discharges from methadone programs, primarily because of its association with absenteeism and disruptive behavior at the clinic (Bickel and Amass 1992).

Marijuana

Adverse effects of marijuana use include motor incoordination and memory impairment. These effects may interfere with a patient's ability to perform tasks and could contribute to accidents. Marijuana can also have adverse psychologic consequences, including anxiety and panic attacks, perceptual distortions, and in extreme cases, toxic psychosis. The primary physiologic effects of marijuana are increased heart rate, increased appetite, and bloodshot eyes. Although increased heart rate could be a problem for persons with cardiovascular disease, dangerous cardiovascular reactions to marijuana are rare. A well-confirmed danger of marijuana, however, is its effects on the lungs. Marijuana smoke contains the same carcinogens as tobacco smoke, usually in somewhat higher concentrations. Marijuana is inhaled deeply and held in the lungs longer than tobacco smoke, so there can be an increased risk of lung diseases including bronchitis, emphysema, and lung cancer. These effects add to the potential damage caused by nearly universal cigarette smoking in the methadone population. Interestingly, little evidence has emerged linking marijuana use during methadone treatment with the use of other illicit drugs or with poor treatment response. By contrast, other secondary drugs of abuse, most notably cocaine and benzodiazepines, are clearly associated with higher rates of heroin use, greater risk-taking behaviors, and poor treatment response. Thus, in at least two studies, patients who tested positive for marijuana were no more likely than those who tested negative to be using other drugs of abuse such as cocaine and heroin during methadone treatment (Saxon et al. 1993; Nirenberg et al. 1996). Nor were treatment outcomes for marijuana users either better or worse than those for patients who did not use marijuana. However, these conclusions are based on a very small amount of research, and the role of marijuana smoking in methadone maintenance patients needs to be evaluated further.

Tobacco

Tobacco use is associated with elevated risk of morbidity and mortality in the general population, with over 400,000 persons dying annually from smoking-related causes, including heart attack, stroke, lung cancer, and other chronic lung diseases. Comparable morbidity and mortality information is not specifically available for methadone patients, but it would be expected that these patients have a similar elevated risk of mortality related to their cigarette smoking as has been demonstrated for the general population. Thus, even if drug abusers discontinued all of their illicit drug use and decreased their alcohol consumption, they would still be at risk for premature death and disease from their cigarette smoking.

Detection of Secondary Drugs

It is clearly important to assess accurately the rates and patterns of secondary drug use among methadone patients in order to establish individual treatment plans and targets for intervention. Both self-report and objective assessment methods are available to evaluate a methadone patient's secondary drug use.

Self-Report Assessments

Most clinics have their own questionnaires so that new patients can provide information about their drug use histories as well as rates, patterns, and routes of current use. The ASI (McLellan et al. 1980, 1992) is an interview-based instrument that has been widely adopted in the drug abuse treatment community for assessment of overall patient functioning. It contains detailed questions on drug and alcohol use, with a 30-day time frame assessment. Thus, the instrument gathers systematic information about the number of days within the past 30 that a patient has used each of a variety of abused drugs, including heroin, methadone, alcohol, barbiturates, other sedatives and tranquilizers, cocaine, amphetamines, marijuana, hallucinogens, and inhalants. New patients are also asked how much money they spent in the past 30 days on drugs and on alcohol. Because the ASI is so widely used, clinics should consider adopting it or at least incorporating the 30-day assessment time frame into their own questionnaires in order to gather data that can be compared with other treatment sites. Training in the administration of the instrument is available from the test developers (Treatment Research Institute, 1 Commerce Square, 2005 Market St., Suite 1120, Philadelphia, PA 19103; telephone: 1-800-238-2433).

More in-depth and sophisticated information can be obtained by the administration of the Structured Clinical Interview for DSM-IV (First et al. 1995). This clinical interview provides information for making lifetime and current diagnoses of both mood (e.g., depression, anxiety) and personality (e.g., antisocial) disorders that are common among drug abusers as well as substance use diagnoses (abuse or dependence) for a range of drugs commonly used by methadone patients. Although often used in research to characterize drug abusers, this interview is lengthy and requires extensive training and the ability to make clinical judgments based on information derived from the interview and, therefore, is infrequently used as a tool in clinical practice.

Because of the high rates of documented alcohol dependence among methadone patients, careful clinical assessment should be included early in treatment to identify those patients with current and past alcohol problems. The Michigan Alcoholism Screening Test (MAST) and the Alcohol Use Disorders Identification Test (AUDIT), two brief assessment instruments, are the most commonly used and convenient instruments to administer; both have been shown to be useful for detecting current, excessive drinking in methadone maintenance populations (Bickel and Amass 1992; Maisto, Connors, and Allen 1995; Skipsey, Burleson, and Kranzler 1997). The MAST is a 25-item instrument that assesses physical, behavioral, and psychosocial problems commonly associated with the drinking of alcohol (Table 6.2). The AUDIT is a shorter, 10-item instrument that includes an assessment of the amount of drinking as well as drinking-related problems (Table 6.3). Both have norms and cutoffs that can be used to iden-

Table 6.2 **Michigan Alcoholism Screening Test (MAST)**

Answer each question below with a YES or NO

1. Do you feel you are a normal drinker? (No-2)
2. Have you ever awakened the morning after some drinking the night before and found that you could not remember a part of the evening before? (Yes-2)
3. Does your wife (or do your parents) ever worry or complain about your drinking? (Yes-1)
4. Can you stop drinking without a struggle after one or two drinks? (No-2)
5. Do you ever feel bad about your drinking? (Yes-1)
6. Do friends and relatives think you are a normal drinker? (No-2)
7. Do you ever try to limit your drinking to certain times of the day or to certain places? (0)
8. Are you always able to stop drinking when you want to? (No-2)
9. Have you ever attended a meeting of Alcoholics Anonymous (AA)? (Yes-5)
10. Have you ever gotten into fights when drinking? (Yes-1)
11. Has drinking ever created problems with you and your wife? (Yes-2)
12. Has you wife (or other family member) ever gone to anyone for help about your drinking? (Yes-2)
13. Have you ever lost friends or girlfriends/boyfriends because of drinking? (Yes-2)
14. Have you ever gotten into trouble at work because of drinking? (Yes-2)
15. Have you ever lost a job because of drinking? (Yes-2)
16. Have you ever neglected your obligations, your family, or your work for two or more days in a row because you were drinking? (Yes-2)
17. Do you ever drink before noon? (Yes-1)
18. Have you ever been told you have liver trouble? Cirrhosis? (Yes-2)
19. Have you ever had delirium tremens (DTs), severe shaking, heard voices, or seen things that weren't there after heavy drinking? (Yes-2)
20. Have you ever gone to anyone for help about your drinking? (Yes-5)
21. Have you ever been in a hospital because of drinking? (Yes-5)
22. Have you ever been a patient in a psychiatric hospital or on a psychiatric ward of a general hospital where drinking was part of the problem? (Yes-2)
23. Have you ever been seen at a psychiatric or mental health clinic, or gone to a doctor, social worker, or clergyman for help with an emotional problem in which drinking had played a part? (Yes-2)
24. Have you ever been arrested, even for a few hours, because of drunk behavior? (Yes-2)
25. Have you ever been arrested for drunk driving after drinking? (Yes-2)

Source: "The Michigan Alcoholism Screening Test (MAST): The Quest for a New Diagnostic Instrument," *Am. J. Psychiatry* 127:1653–58, 1971. Copyright 1971, the American Psychiatric Association. Reprinted by permission.

Note: Responses shown in parentheses after each question indicate the direction for a significant answer, and the score for that answer. Question 7 is not scored and is dropped from some forms of the MAST. Total scores of 5 or greater are considered indicative of possible alcoholism.

Table 6.3 **Alcohol Use Disorders Identification Test (AUDIT)**

1. How often do you have a drink containing alcohol? (0) Never. (1) Monthly or less. (2) 2 to 4 times a month. (3) 2 to 3 times a week. (4) 4 or more times a week.
2. How many drinks containing alcohol do you have on a typical day when you are drinking? (0) 1 or 2. (1) 3 or 4. (2) 5 or 6. (3) 7 to 9. (4) 10 or more.
3. How often do you have six or more drinks on one occasion? (0) Never. (1) Less than monthly. (2) Monthly. (3) Weekly. (4) Daily or almost daily.
4. How often during the last year have you found that you were not able to stop drinking once you had started? (0) Never. (1) Less than monthly. (2) Monthly. (3) Weekly. (4) Daily or almost daily.
5. How often during the last year have you failed to do what was normally expected from you because of drinking? (0) Never. (1) Less than monthly. (2) Monthly. (3) Weekly. (4) Daily or almost daily.
6. How often during the last year have you needed a first drink in the morning to get yourself going after a heavy drinking session? (0) Never. (1) Less than monthly. (2) Monthly. (3) Weekly. (4) Daily or almost daily.
7. How often during the last year have you had a feeling or guilt or remorse after drinking? (0) Never. (1) Less than monthly. (2) Monthly. (3) Weekly. (4) Daily or almost daily.
8. How often during the last year have you been unable to remember what happened the night before because you had been drinking? (0) Never. (1) Less than monthly. (2) Monthly. (3) Weekly. (4) Daily or almost daily.
9. Have you or someone else been injured as a result of your drinking? (0) No. (2) Yes, but not in the last year. (4) Yes, during the last year.
10. Has a relative or friend, or a doctor or other health worker been concerned about your drinking or suggested you cut down? (0) No. (2) Yes, but not in the last year. (4) Yes, during the last year.

Source: Saunders J.B. et al., " Development of the Alcohol Use Disorders Identification Test (AUDIT): WHO Collaborative Project on Early Detection of Persons with Harmful Alcohol Consumption," *Addiction* 1993; 88:791–804. (Reproduced with permission from Carfax Publishing Limited, P.O. Box 25, Abingdon, Oxfordshire OX14 3UE, United Kingdom.)
Note: Numbers in parentheses are scoring weights. AUDIT Core total score is the sum of the scoring weights. A score of 8 or more indicates a strong likelihood of hazardous or harmful alcohol consumption. The AUDIT manual contains scoring procedures and interpretation (Babor T.F., De La Fuente J.R., Saunders J., Grant M. *AUDIT—The Alcohol Use Disorders Identification Test: Guidelines for Use in Primary Health Care.* WHO Pub. No. 89.4, Geneva: World Health Organization, 1989).

tify problem drinkers. The AUDIT has received more recent evaluation and has been specifically recommended for the identification of hazardous or harmful drinking in drug-dependent populations (Skipsey, Burleson, and Kranzler 1997). These screening instruments are not designed to assess past histories of drinking and, thus, must be supplemented with an additional clinical interview to identify patients with alcoholism in remission. Also, none of these instruments can be used to obtain psychiatric diagnostic classification, which requires a more sophisticated clinical interview (e.g., the SCID).

Urine Testing: Types of Tests Available

Those working in drug abuse treatment are fortunate to have a method of obtaining objective evidence of recent use versus abstinence for a variety of drugs with which patients may be involved. The two most common analytic methods available at commercial testing laboratories for urine testing are immunoassay tests (e.g., enzyme multiplied immunoassay test [EMIT]) and thin-layer chromatography (TLC). (See Verebey [1992] for a review of urine testing techniques.) TLC, one of the oldest technologies to be developed for drug testing, is based on the observation that molecules with differing sizes and properties will reliably migrate to a particular spot on a wet plate when appropriate solvents are applied. Thus, the presence of a particular drug molecule in urine can be reliably detected by comparing its migration with that of a known standard. TLC is a relatively inexpensive method of urine testing, but it is also somewhat insensitive. Thus, because TLC only detects relatively high urine drug concentrations, clinicians must realize that it may underestimate prevalence of use and give false negatives for individual patients. Immunoassay techniques, including the Abbot FPIA (fluorescence polarization immunoassay) and EMIT, are more sensitive methodologies. These methods are based on reactions in which the drug is used to form highly specific antigen-antibody complexes. Immunoassay tests provide a specific and sensitive assay for most common drugs of abuse and their metabolites. In fact, the ability to detect the abused drug's metabolites is one of the important features of these tests that makes them so useful in clinical practice.

Other convenient technologies have been developed for on-site drug testing. These methods, such as the Abuscreen ONTRAK test strips (Towt et al. 1995) and many other specific testing systems (see Table 6.4) are compact devices containing the reagents needed for drug detection in a small, lightweight plastic cup or strip. A small amount of urine is applied to the reagent, which changes in color or density within minutes, indicating the presence or absence of the specified drug. These on-site tests are available for all major drugs of abuse including cocaine, opiates, amphetamines, benzodiazepines, and marijuana. These new technologies have excellent sensitivity and specificity comparable to immunoassay tests and are reasonably cost-effective (e.g., on-track testing costs about $3.50 for each single drug test). In addition, they can be used to obtain immediate test results whenever clinically desirable. More information can be obtained by contacting the National On-site Testing Association, 203 N. Main Street, Flemington, NJ (telephone: 1-908-806-0008).

Hair testing is another technology for assessing drug exposure. How-

Table 6.4 **Methods for Detecting Abused Substances**

Method	Features
Self-Report Instruments	
Addiction Severity Index	Interview characterizing lifetime and current (past 30 days) use of all abused substances
Structured Clinical Interview DSM-III-R; IV (SCID)	Interview leading to psychiatric diagnosis of abuse or dependence; all possible abused substances reviewed
AUDIT	10-item self-report characterizing current excessive drinking
MAST	25-item self-report characterizing current excessive drinking
Urinalysis Testing	
TLC	Broad-spectrum testing; relatively low sensitivity
Immunoassay techniques EMIT[a] FPIA[b]	High specificity and sensitivity for most common drugs of abuse
On-site testing Abuscreen ONTRAK[c] Triage[d] EZ-SCREEN[e] AcuSign[f] Verdict[g] Micro Line[h]	Convenient, immediate results; sensitive and specific for most common drugs of abuse
Breath Alcohol Testing Alco-sensor[i] Intoximeter[j]	Provides accurate reflection of current blood alcohol levels; elevated levels indicate recent use

[a]Enzyme Multiplied Immunoassay Test (Behring Diagnostics; San Jose, CA).
[b]Fluorescence Polarization Immunoassay (Abbot Diagnostics; Abbot Park, IL).
[c]Roche Diagnostics, Sommerville, NJ.
[d]Bio Site, San Diego, CA.
[e]American Biomedica, Ancramdale, NY.
[f]Drug Test Resources International, Boca Raton, FL.
[g]MedTox, St. Paul, MN.
[h]Casco Standards, Yarmouth, ME.
[i]Alcopro, Knoxville, TN.
[j]Intoximeter Co., St. Louis, MO.

ever, to perform this method requires chemical testing expertise, and it is primarily used for determining, in a gross manner, whether a person used drugs over the past several months. It does not appear to have immediate utility in the methadone treatment program. Of more relevance to clinical practice is quantitative urine testing, which is now offered by some laboratories. A patient's "positive" urine (whose concentration exceeds the cutoff value used in qualitative testing) may simply represent carryover from a previous episode of drug use (Preston et al. 1997). However, by determining the actual concentration of drug in the urine and by tracking this over successive days, it is possible to determine whether a patient has in fact resumed drug use. Although potentially useful to the clinician, quantitative testing is currently rather expensive (about $10 or more per sample), and frequent samples are required; these cost factors make quantitative testing prohibitive for most clinics at the present time.

Urine Testing for Opiates and Cocaine

Immunoassay tests such as EMIT provide a highly sensitive and specific assay both for morphine, the metabolite of heroin, and for benzoylecgonine, the metabolite of cocaine; a cutoff of 300 ng/ml is used to determine positive versus negative samples for each. Both morphine and benzoylecgonine can generally be detected with the EMIT assay for one to three days following the use of either heroin or cocaine. The amount of time over which a drug can be detected will, however, depend significantly on the amount, recency, and duration of last use as well as individual differences in drug metabolism and elimination. Thus, individual patients may have positive urines for a longer time following cessation of drug use. Note, however, that EMIT will not reliably detect a variety of synthetic opioid compounds, including meperidine (Demerol), oxycodone (Percodan), dextromethorphan (used in cough syrup), propoxyphene (Darvocet), and fentanyl (an important drug to test for among impaired health care workers). TLC can detect some of these synthetic opioids but only in relatively high concentrations. Clinicians should check with individual laboratories to determine which opioid drugs are assayed and reported.

Urine Testing for Benzodiazepines

The EMIT method provides a specific assay for benzodiazepines, using oxazepam as the reference calibrator. Although not all benzodiazepines have oxazepam as a metabolite, the most commonly used benzodiazepines can be detected by EMIT. However, this test is less sensitive to clonazepam (Klonopin) than to other benzodiazepines and cannot detect lorazepam (Ativan) at all. Furthermore, it may fail to detect potent, short-acting benzodiazepines, such as triazolam (Halcion), which may not be present in sufficient concentrations at the commonly used doses. EMIT reagents are available for both 300 and 200 ng/ml cutoffs; the lower cutoff provides greater sensitivity and is recommended for clinical use with drug abusers. The duration of detection depends on the length of time that the benzodiazepine drug remains in the body. Drugs such as diazepam that are long acting, or have long-acting metabolites to which tests are sensitive, may be detected for up to two weeks after discontinuation of use. However, shorter-acting benzodiazepines (e.g., alprazolam or Xanax®) can generally be detected for only two to three days. Because of the large number of benzodiazepine drugs available and the limitations of EMIT, it may be necessary to conduct more extensive urinalysis testing to obtain a comprehensive picture of benzodiazepine use by methadone patients. TLC testing can provide additional information about the specific benzodiazepines patients may be abusing, including lorazepam, but sensitivity is low. Triage (see Table 6.4) is a newer on-site test system that has been specifically developed to detect benzodiazepine glucuronide metabolites, which are the most prevalent metabolites. This method could provide a more sensitive assay for the use of benzodiazepines by methadone patients, if desired.

Objective Monitoring for Alcohol

Recent drinking can be detected by analyzing blood, breath, urine, or saliva samples, all of which provide roughly the same information about the current concentration of alcohol in the body. Breath alcohol levels can be conveniently monitored at the clinic using a hand-held chemical sensor (Alcopro), and saliva tests have been developed as well. In addition, most immunoassay and on-site urine tests have specific reagents for alcohol testing. Because alcohol is metabolized at a steady rate, the duration over which it can be detected in body fluids depends significantly on the amount and recency of consumption. In general, however, alcohol levels will drop below those that can be detected within a few hours after consumption stops. Thus, these tests are useful only for the detection of recent drinking. On-site alcohol testing is primarily useful as a means of screening for current alcohol abuse, because it will verify recent drinking, particularly in patients who appear intoxicated when they come to the clinic.

Urine Testing for Other Drugs

Certification standards for urine testing laboratories differ from state to state, and available testing services differ from one laboratory to another. Because of this variability, it is essential that clinicians obtain detailed information about the capabilities and limitations of the laboratory they use for urine testing. Clinicians should understand which drugs are included and not included in routine screens as well as relative sensitivities of testing methods utilized. In general, routine screens provide information on opiates (heroin and some synthetic opioids such as Darvon and Demerol), cocaine, benzodiazepines, antidepressants, barbiturates and other nonbarbiturate sedatives (e.g., phenothiazines), as well as quinine, which is often used as a cutting agent for heroin and cocaine. Tests for alcohol and marijuana, although available, may not be routinely included in urine screens and may need to be specially requested. If cannabinoid testing is desired for marijuana screening, the clinician must remember that this drug is stored in body lipids and excreted slowly; therefore, it may be detected for a week or longer after just a single use, and for up to six weeks after cessation of chronic use. Certain drugs cannot be detected by either immunoassay or TLC, for example, clonidine, fentanyl, MDMA, and other designer drugs. If it becomes important to test for particular drugs owing to use patterns that develop in specific locales, other sophisticated testing methodologies can be utilized, but these are generally costly to implement. Overall, it is important to recognize the variability that can exist across laboratories and to learn about the capabilities and limitations of the laboratory selected to conduct urine testing for a given clinic.

Information Obtained from Urine Testing

A negative urine test provides extremely useful evidence of recent drug abstinence. By contrast, a positive urine test in fact gives little useful information about the amount or frequency of recent use. Thus, urine test results for a patient who uses heroin twice a week might appear identical to those for a patient who uses heroin several times a day. This insensitivity suggests that urine testing needs to be supplemented with self-report or quantitative testing if more detailed information is desired. The minimal information provided by a positive result also suggests that urine testing might be most usefully utilized in cases in which patients deny drug use or are involved in therapeutic procedures that require confirmation of abstinence. This strategy would conserve scarce urine testing resources for their most useful application.

Treatment and Clinical Recommendations

Heroin

Treatment

Raising the methadone dose is the primary therapeutic strategy available to deal with continued opiate use (usually heroin) during treatment, although other therapeutic strategies such as behavioral or counseling interventions can also be highly effective in treating continued opioid use. Although there is a clear inverse relationship between dose and opiate use, as discussed in Chapter 5, there is little systematic research about the reliability or time course of individual subject response to a dose increase. Beneficial effects may require several weeks to appear. Furthermore, it is clear that some patients will continue to use opiates even on methadone doses of 80–100 mg per day, which are generally considered to be at the high end of the acceptable range in current clinical practice. Because high-dose methadone is safe to administer to individuals who are already methadone tolerant, more research is warranted to determine whether the greater opioid blockade provided by doses higher than 100 mg per day might be clinically beneficial. Finally, the close association between cocaine and heroin use is notable and suggests that there may be a functional link between the use of the two drugs. Studies using interventions that have successfully reduced cocaine use have noted concurrent decreases in opiate use, suggesting that the problem of continued heroin use might be attacked indirectly via interventions designed to reduce the use of cocaine.

Clinical Recommendations

Methadone dose should be raised for those patients whose urine tests show continued heroin use. Dose increases should continue until heroin use is discontinued or the clinic's maximum dose is reached. Urine monitoring should continue to determine whether this strategy has been effective. If dose increases are insufficient, then the next step should be behavior therapy interventions designed to systematically place consequences on drug use. If the patient is also using cocaine, clinical intervention targeting both heroin and cocaine simultaneously is indicated.

Cocaine

Treatment

Cocaine has become the most prevalent supplemental drug of abuse among methadone maintenance patients and is therefore a dominant concern in the management of continued illicit drug use. Methadone as a medication does not directly address the problem of cocaine use, but the process of methadone treatment does bring cocaine abusers into daily contact with a therapeutic environment in which cocaine use can be addressed with additional therapies. It would be quite feasible to include a specific anticocaine pharmacotherapy in the treatment of methadone patients, for example, if such a medication existed. Unfortunately, although vigorous research is being conducted to identify useful pharmacologic treatments for cocaine addiction, there are no known effective treatments at the present time. Instead, programs must rely on counseling, structured contingencies, and other behavioral interventions in order to have an impact on the cocaine use of their patients. Research suggests that the combination of methadone maintenance and routine drug counseling may not be sufficient to control concurrent drug abuse for some patients (Kosten, Rounsaville, and Kleber 1987; Kosten et al. 1992). Thus, methadone programs must seek additional effective treatment strategies.

Increased counseling and surveillance is usually considered the first step in treating concurrent cocaine abuse, although these strategies may have little impact unless they are combined with motivational interventions specifically designed to promote cessation of cocaine use. One commonly used, though controversial, strategy is to gradually lower methadone doses and eventually discharge patients from treatment after they have had a succession of positive urine tests for cocaine. Because patients usually value methadone maintenance and want to continue in treatment, the possibility of being withdrawn from methadone because of continued cocaine or other drug abuse may motivate some patients to discontinue such use. Research suggests that this aversive control strategy may be effective with approximately one-half of the patients who receive it (e.g., Dolan et al. 1985). Even when the threat of methadone withdrawal does not successfully motivate a particular patient, adherence to this policy may have beneficial effects on the program overall, by discouraging other patients from beginning or continuing to use cocaine. It may also have a delayed impact on the patient who is discharged from the methadone program after submitting cocaine-positive urines; on subsequent readmission, the patient may be less likely to begin or to continue cocaine use for fear of being withdrawn from methadone.

Proponents of this approach believe that the failure to respond to patients' continued cocaine abuse with a series of progressively stringent consequences allows patients to ignore the negative impact of their ongoing drug abuse behavior. Opponents of this view argue that in this era of increasing HIV infection rates among injection drug users, there are strong public health reasons for retaining these individuals in treatment under any circumstances; indeed, the consequences of discharge, including the increased risk of premature death from a number of causes, can be great. Programs remain divided on both the policy in general and its application to specific patients. A new approach for motivating behavior change that incorporates treatment discharge as a final negative event (called behaviorally contingent pharmacotherapy) has proven effective for increasing patient compliance in stopping drug use. (For a description see Chapter 9.)

A rapid readmission policy allows noncompliant patients to be readmitted within 24 hours of release provided they agree to immediately pursue treatment goals, including the cessation of cocaine use. In addition to the behaviorally contingent pharmacotherapy approach, new behavioral interventions that utilize positive reinforcers to reward cocaine abstinence have also been developed and appear to be quite promising; these are described in Chapter 10.

Clinical Recommendations

Cocaine use is a serious problem among methadone patients because of its high prevalence and the harmful consequences associated with its use. Identifying those who use cocaine during treatment is an important priority, with urine testing being the preferred method for obtaining objective data. Cocaine use should also be addressed as part of the treatment plan. Intensified counseling treatment and urine surveillance may be a good first step, with more potent motivational interventions utilizing either positive or negative incentives for those patients who continue to use cocaine during treatment.

Program clinicians should remember that individuals injecting cocaine while on methadone remain at risk for HIV and should carefully consider whether discharging such patients is in the best interests of either the patient or the program. For many patients, engaging in methadone treatment can result in a decrease in cocaine use as well as in other risky behavior, even though complete abstinence is not initially achieved.

Benzodiazepines and Other Sedative-Hypnotics

Treatment

Benzodiazepines are unique from the other drugs discussed in this chapter because they have legitimate uses for treatment of both physical and psychologic complaints, especially anxiety. They are also among the most widely prescribed psychotropic medications in the world. However, there are disproportionately high rates of benzodiazepine use in methadone patients as compared to rates in the general population, and it appears that this use is usually a form of drug abuse rather than self-medication of an underlying psychiatric disorder. Research has also shown that patients who continue to use benzodiazepines while in treatment are more likely to engage in high-risk behaviors (i.e., injection of heroin, use of more amphetamines and cocaine, and sharing of needles) (Darke et al. 1993). Therefore, it is important to detect and address benzodiazepine use in methadone patients because of the increased potential of abuse in this population, dangerous patterns of use, and adverse consequences associated with chronic use of these drugs.

When a methadone patient has been taking one or more benzodiazepine drugs for a period of time and the use is no longer medically indicated, or when there are signs of abuse and dependence (such as a pattern of gradually increasing use, periods of intoxication, functional impairment, and unsuccessful attempts to decrease or discontinue use), detoxification may be indicated. The detoxification of someone who is dependent on sedative, hypnotic, or antianxiety tranquilizer substances requires careful supervision because of the serious and, at times, life-threatening withdrawal symptoms that may appear after abrupt cessation of these medications. The approaches to detoxifying someone from such medications are either a gradual step-by-step reduction of the medication itself or the substitution of a cross-tolerant, longer-acting medication that is gradually withdrawn over time (Alling 1992). Substitution of a long-acting substance is indicated when the abused drug has a short $t_{1/2}$, such as alprazolam (Xanax). A longer-acting barbiturate, such as phenobarbital, or a long-acting benzodiazepine, such as diazepam or clonazepam, permits a smoother and more comfortable withdrawal than that of short-acting drugs.

The preferred setting for sedative detoxification is a supervised inpatient unit. But inpatient treatment may not be feasible, acceptable, or warranted for a variety of reasons, in which case treatment may be conducted on an outpatient basis. However, outpatient detoxification is less desirable because patient compliance and withdrawal symptoms cannot be as readily monitored. Furthermore, studies investigating outpatient detoxification procedures with sedative-dependent methadone patients have reported low success rates. One study, for example, reported that only 55 percent of patients accepted and completed detoxification, with 17 percent of these patients still benzodiazepine positive at the end of treatment (McDuff et al. 1993). Another study reported an 86 percent completion rate, but 95 percent were still benzodiazepine positive long after the therapeutic benzodiazepine tapering dose would be expected to clear (DeMaria et al. 1996), indicating that patients had not stopped using these drugs. Thus, outpatient detoxification may be less effective for achieving abstinence from benzodiazepines.

Clinical Recommendations

There are some circumstances under which prescribed benzodiazepines may be medically appropriate, for example, for the treatment of anxiety or sleeplessness, symptoms that are often present in the methadone maintenance population. Given the relatively high abuse potential of benzodiazepines among opiate abusers, however, their prescription represents a problem for clinicians who must treat these symptoms of distress. One approach is to select benzodiazepines, such as chlordiazepoxide (Librium®) or oxazepam (Serax®), that have been shown to carry lower abuse liability, rather than short-acting or more potent compounds such as Xanax that may themselves be abused (Barnas et al. 1992; Iguchi et al. 1993). Other nonbenzodiazepine compounds, such as buspirone, may also be an alternative for treating symptoms of anxiety. As with the treatment of any symptoms in a drug-abusing population, the clinician must weigh the medical benefits against the risk of abuse. If a methadone patient has a history of benzodiazepine, sedative, or alcohol abuse, prescribed benzodiazepines should be administered only under highly regulated circumstances and for relatively short periods of time.

Using structured interviews, clinicians should routinely assess methadone patients for benzodiazepine abuse. In addition, current use should be evaluated through the use of urine testing. It is important to document all the different sedative compounds that a patient may be taking, including the amounts and frequencies. For those who are currently using benzodiazepines on a regular basis, discontinuation of use should be incorporated into the treatment plan. If possible, an inpatient detoxification should be arranged followed by an intensive aftercare plan designed to prevent relapse to any illicit drug use. A comprehensive reevaluation of psychiatric status is warranted once the patient is benzodiazepine free in order to detect any concurrent anxiety or depression that may have been masked by drug use. Since benzodiazepine abusers generally use other drugs as well and have a poor prognosis in treatment, they should be engaged in whatever forms of intensive treatment services are available at the clinic, including contingent incentive programs.

Alcohol

The high rates of alcohol dependence observed in methadone patients, combined with the substantial risk of death and disease associated with heavy alcohol use, suggest that it would be beneficial to vigorously treat alcoholism in this patient group. Alcoholic patients should be treated because heavy drinking poses a threat to recovery from other drug use and because drinking-related problems impact the operation of the methadone clinic. Heavy drinkers can be disruptive when they arrive intoxicated, and staff must deal with decisions about whether the daily methadone dose can be safely administered to an alcohol-intoxicated patient.

Psychosocial and Behavioral Treatment for Alcoholism

Daily contact with patients at the methadone clinic makes it convenient to deliver a variety of specific alcohol treatment interventions. One approach is to offer psychosocial treatment (individual or group) specifically targeted at the use of alcohol. However, one study's attempts to offer such treatment resulted in poor patient compliance and high rates of dropout among active alcoholics in methadone treatment (Stimmel et al. 1983). Thus, the utility of psychosocial interventions for addressing alcohol use among methadone patients has not yet been documented. Abstinence from alcohol could easily be incorporated into a behavioral incentive program at the clinic by using breath or urine tests as an objective measure of recent use. Note, however, that this option would address only the most extreme and flagrant misuse of alcohol, because a considerable amount of drinking could occur outside the clinic and therefore go undetected. Thus, additional interventions may be desired for patients whose excessive drinking poses a threat to their lifestyle and recovery but who do not generally arrive at the clinic intoxicated.

Medications for Alcoholism Treatment

Two medications are currently approved for the treatment of alcoholism: disulfiram (Antabuse®) and naltrexone (ReVia®). *Naltrexone cannot be used with methadone patients* because it is an opiate antagonist and thus would precipitate severe withdrawal symptoms in a methadone-dependent individual. However, disulfiram has been used successfully in methadone patients and is the recommended pharmacologic approach to treating alcoholism in this population.

Disulfiram

Disulfiram is a medication that blocks the normal metabolism of alcohol. For example, if a patient drinks alcohol after having taken disulfiram, there will be a toxic buildup in the body of acetaldehyde, a by-product of alcohol. Thus, disulfiram has an effect only if a patient drinks, in which case an extremely unpleasant acetaldehyde reaction occurs, consisting of sweating, flushing, palpitations, nausea, and blurred vision. Disulfiram can be a quite useful tool in the treatment of severe alcoholism, because patients will generally discontinue their drinking when they are using the medication regularly, to avoid the unpleasant acetaldehyde reaction. Furthermore, the methadone clinic provides a convenient location for delivering disulfiram treatment because medical screening and monitoring can be built into routine clinic operation.

Clinical Trials of Disulfiram

Results from clinical trials of disulfiram's efficacy have varied depending on the conditions under which the medication was prescribed. Ling et al. (1983), for example, conducted a placebo-controlled, multisite study of disulfiram treatment for severely alcoholic methadone patients and found no difference in outcomes between those assigned to receive 250 mg per day of disulfiram versus those who received placebo medication. In addition, there was substantial treatment dropout, with only 43 percent of patients completing 12 weeks of treatment. This double-blind study's observation of no difference in outcome is consistent with other data on disulfiram clinical trials (Fuller et al. 1986). One possible reason for a no difference outcome in a double-blind study of disulfiram is that all patients must be warned about the potential adverse consequences of drinking alcohol, and unless these patients are willing to take a chance and "test" their medication by drinking, those on placebo will be equally likely to avoid drinking because they are not certain which medication they are taking. Another possible reason for no difference outcomes is that some patients may not even be taking their prescribed medication.

Disulfiram Compliance

Several studies have concluded that the benefits of disulfiram are directly related to compliance with ingestion of the medication. One large study conducted with alcoholic veterans (Fuller et al. 1986) concluded that when alcoholic patients are simply given a disulfiram prescription, only about 20 percent can be expected to comply and actually take the medication. Thus, it appears that many alcoholics will not take disulfiram voluntarily if given a choice, but among those who do, drinking usually ceases immediately. This understanding about the importance of compliance has led to the development of monitored disulfiram strategies that can increase compliance.

It should be clear that the methadone clinic is an ideal place to dispense disulfiram under monitored conditions, because it can be given daily along with the methadone dose. A study by Liebson, Tommasello, and Bigelow (1978) showed that alcoholic methadone patients who were required to drink disulfiram (250 mg) mixed in with their methadone dose each day had substantially better outcomes than patients who were given weekly

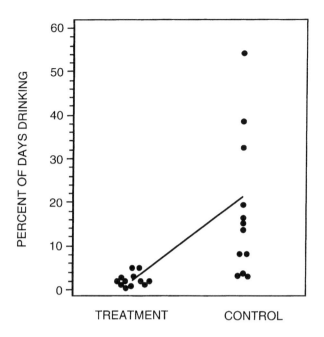

Figure 6.1. ● = a patient enrolled in the study and shows the percentage of days that patient drank alcohol while in the treatment condition (*left*) or the control condition (*right*). All patients were maintained on methadone. When in the treatment group, patients took disulfiram under supervision, whereas when in the control condition they took disulfiram on their own. *Source:* From Liebson, Tommasello, and Bigelow (1978).

disulfiram supplies and urged to take their daily dose each morning at home. (Those assigned to drink disulfiram at the clinic risked treatment termination if they refused.) Figure 6.1 shows the percentage of days of drinking for both groups of patients, but the difference between the two groups is actually understated because drinking in the control groups was substantial, both by clinical observation (intoxication, ataxia, belligerence) and by breath alcohol readings, whereas drinking in the treatment condition generally involved the patients' "cautious experimentation with the alcohol-disulfiram reaction." Improved outcomes were also reflected in arrest rates, which were substantially lower for disulfiram-treated versus control patients.

Disulfiram Treatment: Practical Issues

For patients with current alcohol dependence, some form of treatment intervention is indicated. The most certain method for ensuring immediate and sustained remission of alcohol problems is to place those patients on disulfiram, mixing it in with the daily methadone dose as part of their required treatment. Once patients stop drinking alcohol, alcohol-related disruptive behaviors usually end abruptly. In addition, psychologic problems such as depression frequently disappear. However, several practical issues surround the use of disulfiram.

Motivating participation. The Liebson, Tommasello, and Bigelow (1978) study shows that monitored disulfiram dispensed at the clinic can have substantial benefits for alcoholic methadone patients. Motivating acceptance of this procedure, however, remains a clinical challenge. Either positive or negative incentive procedures can be useful. Because alcohol drinking is often closely tied to the use of other illicit drugs, and may act as a trigger for drug use, some patients may be persuaded to stop drinking with the use of disulfiram if they are simultaneously offered the chance to earn incentives for discontinuing their other illicit drug use.

Detoxification. Because patients must stop alcohol use for at least 12 hours before beginning disulfiram treatment, there may be cases in which brief, medically supervised inpatient detoxification will be needed in order to ensure sobriety prior to the beginning of treatment. Medically supervised inpatient detoxification is recommended whenever there are medical complications or when a patient has a history of delirium or seizures during alcohol withdrawal. From a behavioral viewpoint, however, brief hospitalization may be needed simply to ensure that there is sufficient alcohol-free time in order to begin disulfiram treatment. Long-acting benzodiazepine drugs (e.g., chlordiazepoxide, diazepam, and oxazepam) are frequently administered during an alcohol detoxification (Sellers et al. 1983). These medications can effectively suppress withdrawal discomfort and symptoms and do not interfere with the start of disulfiram treatment.

Dosing regimens. Disulfiram's usual daily dose is 250 mg. However, patients are often started on a higher "loading" dose of 500 mg per day for the first few days. It may take several days before a full alcohol-disulfiram reaction is elicited with ingestion of alcohol, and sensitivity increases gradually over time during chronic ingestion. Once chronic administration has begun, single missed doses should not be a problem because disulfiram accumulates in the body. In fact, the medication can be effectively used with only a three-day per week dosing schedule (250 mg on Monday and Wednesday, 500 mg on Friday). Disulfiram administration can be continued indefinitely and should be discontinued only when clinical judgment suggests that adequate social stability has been established to support continued abstinence. However, this is a difficult judgment, and relapse is always a possibility, with the resultant need to reintroduce more intensive treatment. Once disulfiram is discontinued, patients should be advised not to drink alcohol for at least one week because it takes that long for the medication to be eliminated from the body.

Safety and side effects. Side effects associated with disulfiram can include skin eruptions, drowsiness, headache, impotence, and a metallic taste. These are most often reported during the first two weeks and typically disappear with longer-term treatment. Potentially more serious side effects include liver damage and neurotoxicity. Liver damage and hepatitis are relatively rare but potentially fatal reactions to disulfiram. Thus, patients on disulfiram should undergo periodic liver function tests. Because liver problems usually occur early in treatment, testing should be done every two weeks for the first two months, followed by testing at three- to six-month intervals thereafter (Wright, Vafier, and Lake 1988). Disulfiram has also been associated with serious neurotoxicity. Symptoms include fatigue, forgetfulness, and confusion and can progress to affective changes, ataxia, stupor, and frank psychosis. Because of daily interaction with staff, the methadone clinic is an ideal place to monitor patients for altered psychologic status. If problems with liver function or psychiatric status are noted during disulfiram therapy, the medication should be discontinued immediately. Note, however, that if a placebo can be substituted for an active drug without informing the patient, it is possible that the patient will continue to abstain indefinitely in order to avoid a potential disulfiram reaction.

Patients who have had previous toxic reactions with disulfiram or who have conditions that could be medically compromised by the disulfiram-alcohol interaction should not be placed on this therapy. Such conditions include ischemic heart disease, cardiomyopathy, cardiac arrhythmia, hepatic or pulmonary insufficiency, or renal failure (Wright and Moore 1990). Whether patients with impaired liver function owing to chronic alcohol use can receive disulfiram is controversial. There is obviously a catch-22 here, since these may be the very patients who could benefit the most from the medication. If possible, these patients should be hospitalized and observed during the start of therapy, thereby reducing the risk of liver problems. Otherwise, frequent liver function testing is advisable. In most cases, liver function should improve once drinking stops.

Drinking alcohol while on disulfiram. Patients must be adequately informed about the dangers of contact with any alcohol while on disulfiram. Contact can occur through medications with an alcohol base or even through externally applied alcohol, as in shaving lotions. Sensitization to the alcohol-disulfiram reaction increases over time, and, therefore, these warnings should be repeated periodically. Despite such warnings, there are reports, both anecdotal and published, of alcoholic or drug abuse patients who drink while on disulfiram. Presumably, this is accomplished by ingesting alcohol at a sufficiently slow rate as to make the acetaldehyde reaction tolerable. The first clinical response to such a report would be to make sure that compliance monitoring procedures are operating as expected and that the patient is actually taking the disulfiram. The next step would be to raise the disulfiram dose to 500 mg per day or more. Few additional steps can be taken. However, questioning the patient about the extent and frequency of alcohol use would provide helpful clinical insight and might reveal that alcohol intake is greatly reduced from predisulfiram amounts and that it is occurring at clinically acceptable levels.

Clinical Recommendations

Overall, research supports high rates of alcohol use and alcohol dependence among the methadone maintenance patient population. Thus, early identification of problem patients is essential, using self-report questionnaires and clinical interviews. The use of monitored disulfiram treatment can be a highly effective method to counteract the medical complications and behavioral problems associated with ongoing alcohol dependence among methadone patients and should be utilized whenever possible. Disulfiram treatment may be started after about 12 hours of abstinence, but inpatient detoxification may be necessary in some cases of highly alcohol-dependent patients. Typically, patients are maintained on a dose of 250 mg per day of disulfiram, which is administered at the clinic along with the daily methadone dose. Administration at the clinic addresses compliance problems typically associated with disulfiram and ensures that doses are taken. More research is needed, however, on which patients should be selected for disulfiram treatment (e.g., how much drinking is too much?) and on the most effective methods for convincing patients to participate in a disulfiram program (e.g., mandated versus voluntary).

Routine breath alcohol monitoring at the clinic may also be a useful strategy to prevent relapse or deter the escalation of alcohol drinking in patients with current or past alcohol dependence. It has been suggested that regular monitoring of breath alcohol readings, combined with contingencies based on these readings, could be the basis for a useful intervention with alcoholic methadone patients who will not agree to or cannot be given disulfiram for medical reasons (Bickel, Marion, and Lowinson 1987). Even though a breath monitoring intervention might not have an impact on the overall amounts of alcohol use, it could at least reduce the incidence of patients coming to the clinic while intoxicated. It is common in clinical practice to withhold a portion of the daily methadone dose as well as any scheduled take-home doses as a medical safety precaution for patients who come into the clinic with positive breath alcohol readings. This strategy can be recommended based on safety considerations; however, there has been no evaluation of this strategy or other contingent consequences based on breath alcohol readings as a therapeutic intervention.

Marijuana

The prevailing ideology in substance abuse treatment programs, including methadone programs, usually emphasizes abstinence from all drugs of abuse. This philosophy stems from clinical beliefs that use of any drug can have a domino effect leading to relapse to other drugs, that use of any drug can interfere with social functioning, and that medical and psychologic complications associated with drug use are harmful to patients. Despite this prevailing philosophy, marijuana use is often ignored or given only lip service, and testing for cannabinoids is frequently not included in routine urine screening assays—which may actually be a sensible approach. As previously noted, there does not, in fact, appear to be a clear relationship between the use of marijuana and the use of other drugs (heroin, cocaine, and benzodiazepines) during treatment, nor do any data support a relationship between marijuana use and poor treatment response in methadone programs. While clinics may not want to ignore marijuana use completely, these findings suggest that they should consider ranking its use relatively low in their priorities for clinical attention and resources. However, each clinic must make this choice because there can be excellent reasons related to health and well-being for methadone patients to discontinue their use of marijuana.

Tobacco

Treatment

The observation that cigarette smoking is nearly universal among methadone patients, combined with the associated risks of disease and premature death, suggests that treatment for tobacco dependence would be quite beneficial to the future health of the methadone maintenance population. Substance abuse treatment programs have historically not targeted tobacco smoking, however, because conventional wisdom has argued against addressing tobacco dependence in the context of treating other drug dependencies (Hughes 1993). However, both clinicians and researchers alike have begun to challenge this philosophy. Several survey studies have suggested that drug and alcohol abusers are interested in smoking cessation (e.g., Clemmey et al. 1997), and a growing number of substance abuse programs have begun offering some form of smoking cessation treatment. Only two studies, to date, have reported on smoking cessation treatment delivered to methadone patients. These studies, although preliminary, are encouraging; they suggest that some methadone patients are willing to try to quit smoking. The types of treatments that are best suited for this clinical subpopulation as well as the success rates that can be achieved, compared with those in the general population, remain to be determined.

Clinical Recommendations

Methadone clinics should offer smoking cessation programs to their patients. Based on a review of the scientific literature, clinical guidelines have been published that outline the elements of effective smoking cessation treatment (Hughes et al. 1996; USDHHS 1996). Cessation rates in the general population can be doubled with the use of nicotine replacement therapy, particularly with the nicotine patch. Furthermore, rates of cessation have been directly related to the amount of face-to-face therapy delivered as part of a smoking cessation program. Specifically, programs that involve four to seven hours of therapy spread over the first eight postcessation weeks have achieved the best results. Active elements of smoking cessation therapy include social support from the counselor and relapse prevention problem solving. Although these methods have not been specifically tested in methadone patients, there is every reason to believe that they will be effective. The methadone clinic provides a convenient setting in which to provide smoking cessation treatment. Patients can be frequently monitored for smoking status using breath carbon monoxide, which can be measured using a handheld device. Nicotine replacement products (patches or gum) can be dispensed along with methadone, and face-to-face counseling can be included as part of drug abuse treatment or provided as a special service. Drug abuse treatment staff are already familiar with the recommended therapy techniques, so little special training should be required. Furthermore, outlines of behavioral treatment programs for smoking cessation are readily available from the American Lung Association and the National Cancer Institute. Offering smoking cessation treatment in methadone clinics could be an important step in limiting the smoking-related death and disease among these patients.

Summary

Effective methadone treatment can produce substantial reductions in the use of illicit opioids and other drugs, and even if complete abstinence is not initially achieved, these decreases in drug use can result in marked improvements in health and in clinically significant decreases in risk of infections such as HIV and hepatitis. Thus, although continued drug use is found in some methadone patients, the relative decreases in drug use associated with methadone treatment can be substantial and clinically important.

When all drug classes are considered, other drug use can be quite common among methadone patients, with tobacco being the most prevalent drug used, followed by cocaine. Many methadone patients (up to 60%) continue to use heroin during treatment, and dependence on alcohol or sedatives (particularly benzodiazepines) occurs in a significant portion of the population (approximately 20–25%). Use of more than one drug is common, with an average of four to five lifetime drug dependencies found in methadone maintenance patients. The use of other drugs in methadone patients needs to be addressed, in part because of the adverse medical and psychologic consequences associated with other drug use, including continued risk of exposure to HIV infection.

Identifying secondary drug use in patients is the first step in treatment. Identification can be accomplished using a combination of interviews and self-reports, with urine testing being an essential tool to verify recent use. Once the type and pattern of other drug use is identified, targeted clinical interventions for each abused substance should be developed. These interventions can include initial detoxification (for alcohol and sedative-tranquilizers), medications (e.g., disulfiram for alcohol, the nicotine patch or gum for tobacco), intensive counseling services, and behavioral treatments. A more detailed discussion of appropriate behavioral treatment interventions, such as contingency management therapies, is provided in Chapters 9 and 10.

References

Alling F.A. 1992. Detoxification and treatment of acute sequelae. In: Lowinson J.H., Ruiz P., Millman R.B., Langrod J.G., eds. *Substance Abuse: A Comprehensive Textbook*. Williams & Wilkins, Baltimore, pp. 402–15.

Barnas C., Rossman M., Roessler H., Riemer Y., Fleischhacker W.W. 1992. Benzodiazepines and other psychotropic drugs abused by patients in a methadone maintenance program: familiarity and preference. *J. Clin. Psychopharmacol.* 12:397–402.

Benowitz N.L. 1993. Clinical pharmacology and toxicology of cocaine. *Pharmacol. Toxicol.* 72:3–12.

Bickel W.K., Amass L. 1992. The relationship of mean daily blood alcohol levels to admission MAST, clinic absenteeism and depression in alcoholic methadone patients. *Drug Alcohol Depend.* 32:113–18.

Bickel W.K., Marion I., Lowinson J.H. 1987. The treatment of alcoholic methadone patients: a review. *J. Subst. Abuse Treat.* 4:15–19.

Brooner R.K., King V.L., Kidorf M., Schmidt C.W., Bigelow G.E. 1997. Psychiatric and substance use comorbidity among treatment-seeking opioid abusers. *Arch. Gen. Psychiatry* 54:71–80.

Busto U., Sellers E.M., Naranjo C.A., Cappell H., Sanchez-Craig M., Sykora K. 1986. Withdrawal reaction after long-term therapeutic use of benzodiazepines. *N. Eng. J. Med.* 315:854–59.

Clemmey P., Brooner R., Chutuape M.A., Kidorf M., Stitzer M. 1997. Smoking habits and attitudes in a methadone maintenance treatment population. *Drug Alcohol Depend.* 44:123–32.

Curran H.V. 1991. Benzodiazepines, memory and mood: a review. *Psychopharmacology* 105:1–8.

Darke S., Swift W., Hall W., Ross M. 1993. Drug use, HIV risk-taking and psychosocial correlates of benzodiazepine use among methadone maintenance clients. *Drug Alcohol Depend.* 34:67–70.

DeMaria P.A., Gottheil E., Serota R., Sterling R.C. 1996. Phenobarbital vs. clonazepam in the outpatient sedative detoxification of methadone-maintained patients. *Am. J. Addictions* 5:167–73.

Dolan M.P., Black J.L., Penk W.E., Robinowitz R., DeFord H.A. 1985. Contracting for treatment termination to reduce illicit drug use among methadone maintenance treatment failures. *J. Consult. Clin. Psychol.* 53:549–51.

First M.B., Spitzer R.L., Gibbon M., Williams J.B.W. 1995. Structured Clinical Interview for DSM-IV Axis I Disorders. Biometrics Research Department, New York State Psychiatric Institute, New York, NY.

Fuller R.K., Branchey L., Brightwell D.R., Derman R.M., Emrick C.D., Iber F.L., James K.E., Lacoursiere R.B., Lee K.K., Lowenstam I., Maany I., Neiderhiser D., Nocks J.J., Shaw S. 1986. Disulfiram treatment of alcoholism: a Veterans Administration cooperative study. *JAMA* 256: 1449–55.

Hartel D.M., Schoenbaum E.E., Selwyn P.A., Kline J., Davenny K., Klein R.S., Friedland G.H. 1995. Heroin use during methadone maintenance treatment: the importance of methadone dose and cocaine use. *Am. J. Public Health* 85:83–88.

Hughes J.R. 1993. Treatment of smoking cessation in smokers with past alcohol/drug problems. *J. Subst. Abuse Treat.* 10:181–87.

Hughes J.R., Fiester S., Goldstein M., Resnick M., Rock N., Ziedonis D. 1996. Practice guideline for the treatment of patients with nicotine dependence. *Am. J. Psychiatry* 153(Suppl.):1–31.

Iguchi M.Y., Handelsman L., Bickel W.K., Griffiths R.R. 1993. Benzodiazepine and sedative use-abuse by methadone maintenance clients. *Drug Alcohol Depend.* 32:257–66.

Kosten T.R., Morgan C.H., Falcione J., Schottenfeld R.S. 1992. Pharmacotherapy for cocaine abusing methadone-maintained patients using amantadine or desipramine. *Arch. Gen. Psychiatry* 49:894–99.

Kosten T.R., Rounsaville B.J., Kleber H.D. 1987. A 2.5 year follow-up of cocaine use among treated opioid addicts: have our treatments helped? *Arch. Gen. Psychiatry* 44:281–84.

Liebson I.A., Tommasello A., Bigelow G.E. 1978. A behavioral treatment of alcoholic methadone patients. *Ann. Intern. Med.* 89:342–44.

Ling W., Weiss D.G., Charuvastra C., O'Brien C.P. 1983. Use of disulfiram for alcoholics in methadone maintenance programs. *Arch. Gen. Psychiatry* 40:851–54.

Maisto S.A., Connors G.J., Allen J.P. 1995. Contrasting self-report screens for alcohol problems: a review. *Alcohol Clin. Exp. Res.* 19:1510–16.

McDuff D.R., Schwartz R.P., Tommasello A., Tiegel S., Donovan T., Johnson J.L. 1993. Outpatient benzodiazepine detoxification procedure for methadone patients. *J. Subst. Abuse Treat.* 10:297–302.

McLellan A.T., Kushner H., Metzger D., Peters R., Smith L., Grissom G., Pettinati H., Argeriou M. 1992. The fifth edition of the Addiction Severity Index: historical critique and normative data. *J. Subst. Abuse Treat.* 9:199–213.

McLellan A.T., Luborsky L., Woody G.E., O'Brien C.P. 1980. An improved diagnostic evaluation instrument for substance abuse patients. *J. Nerv. Ment. Dis.* 168:26–33.

Nirenberg T.D., Cellucci T., Liepman M.R., Swift R.M., Sirota A.D. 1996. Cannabis versus other illicit drug use among methadone maintenance patients. *Psychology Addict. Behav.* 10:222–27.

Preston K.L., Griffiths R.R., Stitzer M.L., Bigelow G.E., Liebson I.A. 1984. Diazepam and methadone interactions in methadone maintenance. *Clin. Pharmacol. Ther.* 36:534–41.

Preston K.L., Silverman K., Schuster C.R., Cone E.J. 1997. Assessment of cocaine use with quantitative urinalysis and estimation of new uses. *Addiction* 92:717–27.

Preston K.L., Sullivan J.T., Strain E.C., Bigelow G.E. 1996. Enhancement of cocaine's abuse liability in methadone maintenance patients. *Psychopharmacology* 123:15–25.

Saxon A.J., Calsyn D.A., Greenberg D., Blaes P., Haver V.M., Stanton V. 1993. Urine screening for marijuana among methadone-maintained patients. *Am. J. Addictions* 2:207–11.

Sellers E.M., Naranjo C.A., Harrison M., Devenyi P., Roach C., Sykora K. 1983. Diazepam loading: simplified treatment of alcohol withdrawal. *Clin. Pharmacol. Ther.* 34:822–26.

Sells S.B., Simpson D.D. 1987. Role of alcohol use by narcotic addicts as revealed in the DARP research on evaluation of treatment for drug abuse. *Alcohol Clin. Exp. Res.* 11:437–39.

Selzer M.L. 1971. The Michigan Alcoholism Screening Test (MAST): the quest for a new diagnostic instrument. *Am. J. Psychiatry* 127:1653–58.

Skipsey K., Burleson J.A., Kranzler H.R. 1997. Utility of the AUDIT for identification of hazardous or harmful drinking in drug-dependent patients. *Drug Alcohol Depend.* 45:157–63.

Spitzer R.L., Williams J.B., Gibbon M., First M.B. 1992. The Structured Clinical Interview for DSM-III-R. *Arch. Gen. Psychiatry* 49:624–29.

Stimmel B., Cohen M., Sturiano V., Hanbury R., Korts D., Jackson G. 1983. Is treatment for alcoholism effective in persons on methadone maintenance? *Am. J. Psychiatry* 140:862–66.

Towt J., Tsai S.C., Hernandez M.R., Klimov A.D., Kravec C.V., Rouse S.L., Subuhi H.S., Twarowska B., Salamone S.J. 1995. ONTRAK TESTCUP: a novel, on-site, multi-analyte screen for the detection of abused drugs. *J. Analyt. Toxicol.* 19:504–10.

U.S. Department of Health and Human Services (USDHHS). 1996. *Smoking Cessation Clinical Practice Guideline #18.* AHCPR Publication No. 96–0692. U.S. Government Printing Office, Washington, DC.

Verebey K. 1992. Diagnostic laboratory: screening for drug abuse. In: Lowinson J.H., Ruiz P., Millman R.B., Langrod J.G., eds. *Substance Abuse: A Comprehensive Textbook.* Williams & Wilkins, Baltimore.

Wright C., Moore R.D. 1990. Disulfiram treatment of alcoholism. *Am. J. Med.* 88:647–55.

Wright C., Vafier J.A., Lake R. 1988. Disulfiram-induced fulminating hepatitis: guidelines for liver-panel monitoring. *J. Clin. Psychiatry* 49:430–34.

Comorbid Medical Disorders

Michael I. Fingerhood, M.D.

The provision of medical care to methadone patients depends on a trusting, caring relationship between care providers and patients. Especially because of the AIDS epidemic, medically ill addicts need lifetime medical care and associated support services. Historically, medical care for substance-abusing patients has been, at best, episodic and mostly lacking. Medical providers may avoid caring for patients with substance abuse, including those on methadone. Patients, in turn, sense this often unspoken displeasure and appear demanding or manipulative. A better understanding of the approach to patients taking methadone and knowledge of the comorbid medical conditions will benefit the doctor-patient relationship and ultimately lead to a change in attitude of both the physician and the patient. In a comfortable setting, methadone maintenance patients can be provided care with a high rate of visit compliance, comparable to that of any other type of patient.

Medical illness occurs frequently in patients with substance abuse. Although methadone maintenance treatment is associated with reduced risk for many medical complications, including acquisition of viruses spread by needle sharing (e.g., AIDS, hepatitis B and C), endocarditis, and soft tissue infections, many patients on methadone maintenance still present with the same complications seen in injecting-drug users. Often these complications are related to cocaine use, which is frequently injected by patients in methadone treatment. Additionally, by the time patients enter methadone treatment they often have already developed complications from their pre-treatment injecting-drug use. This chapter focuses on the provision of medical care to individuals on methadone, including issues related to the management of health maintenance and the myriad of health complications that can occur in this population.

Basic Primary Care

Opioid-dependent patients report high rates of physical problems upon entry to methadone treatment (Ryan and White 1996), and providing on-site primary medical care at the methadone clinic can result in better compliance when treating medical problems (Umbricht-Schneiter et al. 1994). However, on-site primary medical care is often unavailable at methadone clinics, and patients needing medical services are referred to other local medical clinics. Under these circumstances, close coordination with off-site medical providers can also be an effective means for providing necessary treatment for methadone-maintained patients.

The provision of primary care to patients on methadone maintenance focuses on screening and prevention. The medical history should include questions, discussion, and counseling related to HIV risk factors, including needle sharing (and, if available, the use of needle-exchange programs) and sexual practices (including the use of condoms). In a nonjudgmental fashion, histories of sexually transmitted diseases (STDs), domestic violence, and tuberculosis exposure should be explored. Focused questions should be asked regarding any history of medical complications of injecting-drug use outlined in this chapter, including endocarditis, HIV, skin infections, and liver disease.

The physical examination should always include a thorough examination of the skin (for signs of abscesses or cellulitis), pelvis (for signs of herpes, genital warts, or discharge), and nose (for septal perforation). The laboratory evaluation should be based on patients' histories. All individuals with a history of needle sharing or high-risk sexual activity should be encouraged to be HIV tested. For similar reasons, they should undergo screening for hepatitis B and C. Individuals with a history of hepatitis should undergo liver function tests (AST, ALT, GGT, alkaline phosphatase, and bilirubin). Syphilis screening, which is inexpensive, is also recommended. Screening for tuberculosis should be done annually, and all women should undergo Pap testing for cervical cancer at least annually. In addition, in general, routine immunization guidelines should be followed for all patients unless they are infected with HIV. Usually this means a tetanus booster every ten years; and, if individuals test negative for hepatitis B, they should be immunized with a series of three injections.

Methadone may have side effects even in individuals undergoing long-term maintenance. These effects include increased sweating, constipation, and menstrual abnormalities. Laboratory changes include lymphocytosis and increased prolactin levels. Constipation is by far the most commonly occurring side effect, and individuals on methadone maintenance should be encouraged to be on a high fiber diet. Chronic use of laxatives should be discouraged, but if constipation is severe, occasional doses of magnesium citrate, sorbitol, or lactulose can be prescribed.

GENERAL GUIDELINES FOR PRESCRIBING

Individuals on methadone maintenance are at high risk for abusing prescription drugs with abuse liability. Prescription drug abuse can be best avoided by careful and thoughtful prescribing of medications. Practitioners must not be "duped"—that is, acquiesce to demanding patients by prescribing medications inappropriately. To avoid possible abuse, medications should always be prescribed on a fixed schedule. Such scheduling improves symptom control, minimizes the development of symptoms (rather than reacting to symptoms after they occur), and keeps patients from focusing on immediate relief. Medications should be prescribed for short periods during treatment of acute symptoms. Individuals should be frequently seen for reassessment, and the practitioner should avoid refilling most medications by telephone.

Unfortunately, there is a risk that some patients will steal prescription blanks or alter their prescriptions. All prescription pads should be safeguarded and, ideally, marked "not for scheduled drugs." Prescriptions should be written clearly, and both the number of pills to be dispensed and the number of refills should be written out (not just a number). If no refills are to be given, "no refill" should be noted on the prescription. All prescribing of scheduled drugs should be documented clearly in the chart. Practitioners should beware of patients who lose prescriptions or medications, obtain prescriptions from multiple physicians, or repeatedly run out of medications earlier than expected.

Two classes of medications with abuse liability, barbiturates and benzodiazepines, generally should be avoided in patients taking methadone. Barbiturates are infrequently prescribed, and another reason, in addition to abuse potential, that the use of barbituates should be avoided in methadone patients is that they can induce methadone metabolism (see Chapter 5). Benzodiazepines also can interact with methadone, and they enhance methadone's effects (e.g., Preston et al. 1984). This interaction may account for the observation of substantial rates of illicit benzodiazepine use in some methadone patients. Thus, the physician working in a methadone clinic should be sensitive to the risk of inappropriate use of a prescribed benzodiazepine, or diversion of the prescription to the illicit market. It is common practice to recommend avoiding any use of prescription benzo-diazepines in a methadone-treated population.

Note, however, that given these cautions, some practitioners report successful use of prescribed benzodiazepines for selected methadone-maintained patients, such as those with a clear anxiety disorder. In such cases, benzodiazepines with high abuse potential, for example, diazepam (most commonly marketed as Valium®), lorazepam (Ativan®), and alprazolam (Xanax®), are typically avoided and instead low-abuse potential benzodiazepines such as oxazepam (Serax®) are prescribed. (For a review of the relative abuse potential of benzodiazepines, see Griffiths and Wolf [1990].)

Other potentially abusive medications that generally should be avoided in the methadone maintenance population include muscle relaxants, methylphenidate (Ritalin®), amphetamines, and clonidine. Clonidine use is not detected in routine urine screening, and consequently abuse of clonidine has been reported to be quite high in some areas and populations (e.g., Anderson et al. 1997). Because of this potential for clonidine abuse, or the diversion of a prescription to the illicit market (resulting in subsequent poor blood pressure control for the patient), clonidine should not be used in the management of hypertension in methadone-maintained patients. Other medications that need to be used cautiously in methadone-maintained patients include promethazine (Phenergan®), compazine, and cough syrups. In addition, oxaprozin (Daypro), a nonsteroidal anti-inflammatory drug (NSAID), should be avoided because it can give a false-positive result when testing a urine sample for benzodiazepines.

Pain Management

Pain management can be extremely difficult in methadone-maintained individuals. However, several general rules can help physicians in their approach to the management of acute pain in this population (Payte and Khuri 1993). First and most important, for patients experiencing acute pain, the physician should not discontinue the patient's daily methadone dose. If the patient is unable to take methadone orally, doses can be divided and delivered by intramuscular injection. No decrease in the daily maintenance dose should be made if the dose is given by injection. However, maintenance on methadone does not mean that a patient is in a chronic state of analgesia; experimental evidence indicates that pain perception adapts to a normal range for patients maintained on methadone (Schall et al. 1996).

Second, alternatives to pharmacologic therapy, such as relaxation techniques, exercise, acupuncture, biofeedback, and massage should be initially attempted, when possible. Third, if pharmacologic therapy is indicated, nonopiates such as NSAIDs should be used first. However, even these medications can cause adverse effects, such as hepatotoxicity and gastrointestinal effects (e.g., bleeding, ulceration) with chronic or high doses, so they should be used with caution.

Fourth, if an opioid is to be used for pain management, mixed agonist-antagonists such as pentazocine, butorphanol, nalbuphine, and buprenorphine generally should be avoided. Use of these compounds in a patient maintained on methadone could result in a precipitated withdrawal syndrome, further complicating the patient's management.

Fifth, when opiates are indicated, weaker opiates (codeine and propoxyphene) should be tried first, with a progression to stronger opiates (oxycodone and hydrocodone), and finally morphine. If morphine is to be used, MS contin, a long-acting formulation of morphine, may have lower abuse liability. Finally, it is important to communicate clearly to patients plans for controlling their pain, and to treat aggressively patients' pain.

Methadone can be used as an effective analgesic, but it is not recommended for the treatment of pain in methadone-maintained patients (i.e., as supplemental doses of methadone added to the daily dose). Acute doses of methadone in nonopioid-dependent patients provide analgesia for about six to eight hours. Thus, if methadone is used in pain management, three to four doses per day will be necessary.

Drug Interactions

Although there are no drugs that are absolutely contraindicated with methadone, some medications should be avoided (Table 7.1). For example, administration of an opiate antagonist would cause opiate withdrawal, so under routine clinical circumstances opiate antagonists such as naloxone, nalmefene, and naltrexone should be avoided.

A variety of drugs impact the metabolic clearance of methadone and may cause opiate withdrawal and opiate craving. For example, rifampin has been shown to have a clinically significant impact on methadone clearance, requiring an adjustment in the dosing of methadone maintenance (Kreek et al. 1976). Individuals under treatment for tuberculosis with rifampin need an upward adjustment of their methadone dose or split methadone dosing. Rifabutin, structurally similar to rifampin and used in HIV-positive patients for the prevention of mycobacterium avium-intracellular, does not appear to cause a similar effect on methadone blood levels (Brown et al. 1996).

Table 7.1 Medications That May Alter Methadone Blood Levels or Alter Methadone's Effects

Drugs Decreasing Blood Levels	Drugs Increasing Blood Levels	Drugs Acutely Producing Opioid Withdrawal Symptoms	Drugs Acutely Increasing Methadone's Effects
Barbiturates (e.g., phenobarbital)	Amitriptyline[a]	Metyrapone	Ethanol
Carbamezepine	Cimetidine		
Estrogens[a]	Fluconazole		
Phenytoin	Fluvoxamine		
Rifampin			
Spironolactone[a]			
Verapamil[a]			

[a]May influence methadone blood levels, although there is limited evidence of this effect.

Several anticonvulsants that induce liver enzymes can increase methadone metabolism, and patients have reported withdrawal symptoms later in the day after having received their dose of methadone (Tong et al. 1981; Bell et al. 1988). Anticonvulsants that can produce such effects include phenytoin, carbamazepine, and barbiturates (e.g., phenobarbital).

Several other medications may decrease methadone blood levels, although such evidence is more limited (Table 7.1; Plummer et al. 1988). In addition, some medications may increase methadone blood levels, or acutely potentiate the effects of methadone. Most notably, cimetidine and fluvoxamine can increase methadone blood levels, and alcohol can potentiate the effects of methadone (e.g., Donnelly et al. 1983; Bertschy et al. 1994).

In addition to interacting with other drugs, methadone can alter blood levels and the effects of other medications. For example, pharmacokinetic studies have found the concentration of zidovudine (AZT) to be elevated in some patients treated with methadone (Schwartz et al. 1992; Jatlow et al. 1997). It is unclear if this increase is clinically significant, but increased risk of AZT toxicity (lethargy, nausea, headache, and anemia) is possible, and therefore individuals on methadone should be followed closely. Similarly, methadone appears to increase blood levels of tricyclic antidepressants (e.g., desipramine; Maany et al. [1989]). Finally, methadone can delay alcohol elimination.

HIV INFECTION

Much data, direct and indirect, supports the use of methadone to deter the spread of HIV (Brickner et al. 1989). Nevertheless, many methadone patients are HIV positive, which is partially related to previous needle use but, especially for women, also to the heterosexual spread of HIV. In the United States, 50 percent of HIV-positive women contracted the virus through injecting-drug use, and another 25 percent through heterosexual activity with an injecting-drug user (Hahn et al. 1989).

The care of an HIV-positive patient taking methadone requires sensitivity to specific issues related to substance abuse as well as to those related to methadone. In studies of HIV-positive patients, comparing those who acquired HIV through injecting-drug use with those who acquired HIV through homosexual activity, there is little difference in disease progression or opportunistic infections (Selwyn et al. 1992). The major difference is in morbidity related to injecting-drug use—endocarditis, abscesses, and viral hepatitis. In addition, those who inject drugs have a higher rate of bacterial pneumonia and tuberculosis.

More than ever, the aim of HIV care is to attack the virus aggressively with triple therapy, in order to decrease the amount of circulating virus (viral load) to the lowest possible level. Such medical regimens can be complicated and are quite expensive. There is also the risk of viral resistance if the medications are not taken reliably. Therefore, complicated regimens consisting of multiple drugs should not be initiated until an HIV-positive patient has demonstrated compliance with medical visits. Linkage between the methadone maintenance program and HIV primary care can have a synergistic effect, benefiting patients in both areas and enhancing compliance (O'Connor et al. 1992).

The medical approach to providing care to HIV-infected individuals is given in Table 7.2. The initiation of therapy is based on viral load and CD4. The number of approved medications directed against HIV has increased, and therefore, only those individuals who are well versed in providing HIV care and up to date regarding therapies should initiate treatment.

Table 7.2 **HIV Standards of Care**

Baseline	Monitoring
Documentation of HIV serology	Viral load: every 3 to 4 months, or more often if indicated, to evaluate changes in therapy
Blood work: CBC (complete blood count), HIV viral load, CD4, chemistry panel, RPR, hepatitis serology	CD4: every 3 to 4 months CBC: every 3 to 4 months (if on AZT will need closer follow-up initially)
Screening: Pap smear, PPD	Pap smear: repeat in 6 months and then annually
Immunizations: pneumovax, tetanus if needed, hepatitis B if negative serology	

Skin and Soft Tissue Infections

Skin and soft tissue infections are the most common complications of injecting-drug use (Cherubin 1971; Haverkos and Lange 1990). These infections result from abusers using nonsterile techniques when injecting, and from their inability to inject properly into a vein. Although cultured samples of heroin have grown a wide range of organisms including staphylococcus, clostridium, and aspergillus, most likely the addict's skin is the primary source of the infection. Organisms isolated from abusers' works or paraphernalia are rarely found in the bloodstreams of infected users (Tuazon and Elin 1981).

The injection of cocaine causes blood vessels to spasm, which can result in the injection of drug and diluents (cutting agents) into soft tissue. Cocaine injection may also cause thrombus distant to the injection site. When veins in the arms are no longer available, drug users often turn to injecting in their legs, neck, and groin. Additionally, "skin popping" into subcutaneous tissue is common. Complications from these various forms of injecting drugs can include cellulitis, abscess, septic thrombophlebitis, pyomyositis, and pseudoaneurysms (Jacobson and Hirschman 1982; Orangio et al. 1984; Yeager et al. 1987; McIlroy et al. 1989). Furthermore, osteomyelitis or septic arthritis may occur, owing to bacterial spread from contiguous soft tissue, or from bacteremia (Chandrasekar and Narula 1986; Brancos et al. 1991). Other problems associated with the process of injecting drugs can include lymphatic obstruction and edema, which can result from chronic skin popping, and foreign body reactions from needle fragments that become lodged subcutaneously (which also can migrate centrally) (Angelos, Sheets, and Zych 1986; Galdun et al. 1987).

Staphylococcus aureus is the most likely microorganism to cause tissue infection, followed by streptococci, and Gram-negative rods. The initial management of tissue infections often requires incision and drainage. Infection may or may not be accompanied by fever and an elevated white blood cell count. Minor abscesses and infections can often be managed by an oral antibiotic (cephalexin or dicloxacillin) after incision and drainage. More severe infections require hospitalization for the administration of intravenous antibiotics. Resistant organisms, including methicillin-resistant staphylococcus, have been increasingly isolated in injecting-drug users who have attempted to treat their own infections by using antibiotics bought from the street market.

Cardiac Complications

The most common cardiac complication of injecting-drug use is endocarditis. Chronic injecting-drug use likely results in chronic low-grade bacteremia and creates endothelial valvular damage and platelet fibrin deposition. Some injecting-drug users are particularly prone to repeated bouts of endocarditis. The diagnosis of endocarditis is based on the presence of a murmur on examination, positive blood cultures, and echocardiographic evidence. At least four sets of blood cultures should be drawn from different sites and at different times in order to maximize the detection of the infectious agent. Although bacteremia is often indicative of endocarditis, 35–60 percent of bacteremias are unrelated to endocarditis and are most often related to soft tissue infections. If transthoracic echocardiogram is unable to detect a valvular vegetation and clinical suspicion for endocarditis is high, a transesophageal echocardiogram should be performed.

The incidence of bacterial endocarditis is estimated at 1.5 to 2 cases per 1,000 adults annually. Unlike endocarditis in individuals without a history of injecting-drug use, those with a history of injecting-drug use develop predominantly right-sided endocarditis, most often affecting the tricuspid valve. *Staphylococcus aureus* is the most frequently isolated organism. It is easily treatable, but large vegetations, greater than 1 cm, increase treatment failure. Methicillin-resistant *S. aureus* organisms are increasingly being seen.

Streptococcus typically causes left-sided, aortic, or mitral valve endocarditis. Left-sided infections have a higher medical failure rate and more commonly have subsequent morbidity and mortality. Complications include sequelae of emboli (e.g., stroke), conduction disturbance, and valve damage resulting in regurgitant flow and heart failure.

Less common causes of endocarditis include *Pseudomonas aeruginosa,* Serratia, Haemophilus, Neisseria, Enterobacteriaceae, and Candida. Pseudomonas infection may cause coexisting right- and left-sided endocarditis, with a poor prognosis. Candidal endocarditis has been found to be related to the presence of Candida in the diluents or cutting agents mixed with heroin (Podzamczer and Gudiol 1986; Collignon and Sorrell 1987). With rare exceptions, when treating endocarditis, intravenous antibiotics should be administered on an inpatient basis for the duration of therapy.

Most noninfection cardiac complications of drug abuse are attributed to cocaine. Cocaine has been reported to cause myocardial infarction, coronary artery spasm with angina, and cardiomyopathy (Levy and Kleinknecht 1980; Isner et al. 1986; Chokshi et al. 1989; Lange et al. 1989).

SEXUALLY TRANSMITTED DISEASES

All STDs are commonly seen in drug abusers, even those on methadone. Especially among women, sexual intercourse is often exchanged for drugs. Additionally, unprotected sexual intercourse is common in crack houses, putting noninjecting-drug users at risk for STDs and HIV. Guidelines for the treatment of STDs are given in Table 7.3.

Chlamydia is the most common STD in the United States. It is often asymptomatic, which makes transmission easy. Gonorrhea is also easily transmitted and can be seen as a cause of septic arthritis in drug users. The presence of genital herpes infection appears to increase the likelihood of sexual transmission of HIV infection. Additionally, HIV-infected individuals often shed herpes virus even when they do not have active disease.

The diagnosis of syphilis in a person with a history of injecting-drug use is confounded by an approximately 25 percent biologic false-positive rate for the standard serologic test for syphilis (STS or RPR). False-positive titers are rarely at greater than a 1:4 titer. Therefore, presentation of advanced syphilis can be seen among injecting-drug users. A person who presents with an erythematous rash affecting the palms and soles should be diagnosed as having secondary syphilis until proven otherwise. All positive STS or RPR titers should be tested for the more specific assay of free treponemal antibody (FTA). Syphilis screening should be performed yearly on all sexually active individuals, and all new positive results should be treated.

Individuals who test positive for syphilis with unknown previous testing and no history of symptomatic disease (a primary chancre) should be treated as if they have latent disease with three consecutive weekly injections of 2.4 million U of benzathene penicillin. Because penicillin is the most effective treatment, individuals who claim penicillin allergy, but who do not have a history of anaphylaxis, should be tested for penicillin allergy. The treatment of syphilis in HIV-infected individuals is identical, but there are reports of increased treatment failures in such individuals (Musher, Hamill, and Baughn 1990).

Scientific evidence has shown that human papillous virus, another STD, is the causative agent in the majority of cervical cancer cases. Sexual intercourse at an early age and higher numbers of sexual partners correlate as risk factors for cervical cancer. Women with a history of injecting-drug use, including those on methadone, have a high rate of abnormalities on Pap smears and all should undergo yearly testing. If a significant abnormality is found, referral should be made for colposcopy. Mild abnormalities should be followed up with a repeat smear in six months. HIV-positive women tend to have particularly aggressive forms of cervical cancer linked

Table 7.3 Treatment of STDs

Type of Disease	Drug of Choice	Dosage	Alternatives
Chlamydia Trachomatis			
Urethritis, cervicitis	Azithromycin	1 g oral once	Ofloxacin 300 mg oral bid × 7 days
	OR Doxycycline	100 mg oral bid × 7 days	Erythromycin 500 mg oral qid × 7 days
Gonorrhea			
Urethral, cervical, rectal, or pharyngeal	Ceftriaxone	125 mg IM once	Ciprofloxacin 500 mg oral once
			Ofloxacin 400 mg oral once
Syphilis			
Early[a]	Penicillin G benzathine	2.4 million U IM once	Doxycycline 100 mg oral bid × 14 days
Late[b]	Penicillin G benzathine	2.4 million U IM weekly × 3 weeks	Doxycycline 100 mg oral bid × 4 weeks
Chancroid	Erythromycin	500 mg oral qid × 7 days	Ciprofloxacin 500 mg oral bid × 3 days
	OR Ceftriaxone	250 mg IM once	
	OR Azithromycin	1 g oral once	
Herpes Simplex			
First episode genital	Acyclovir	400 mg oral tid × 7–10 days	Acyclovir 200 mg oral 5 times/day × 7–10 days
First episode proctitis	Acyclovir	800 mg oral tid × 7–10 days	Acyclovir 400 mg oral 5 times/day × 7–10 days
Recurrent	Acyclovir	400 mg oral tid × 5 days	
Severe (hospitalized patients)	Acyclovir	5 mg/kg IV q8h	
Prevention of recurrence	Acyclovir	400 mg oral bid	Acyclovir 200 mg oral 2–5 times a day
Vaginal Infection			
Trichomonas	Metronidazole	2 g oral once	Metronidazole 375 or 500 mg oral bid × 7 days
Bacterial vaginosis	Metronidazole gel 0.75%	5 g intravaginally bid × 5 days	Metronidazole 500 mg oral bid × 7 days
	Clindamycin 2% cream	5 g intravaginally qhs × 7 days	Clindamycin 300 mg oral bid × 7 days
Vulvovaginal candidiasis	Topical azole cream		Metronidazole 2 g oral once

Key: bid, twice daily; IM, intramuscularly; qid, four times daily; tid, three times daily.
[a]Primary, secondary, or latent less than one year.
[b]More than one year's duration, cardiovascular, gumma, late-latent.

to HPV, and invasive cervical cancer is an AIDS-defining illness. Hence, HIV-positive women should be screened every six months until they have two consecutive normal test readings. Thereafter, only yearly screening is necessary.

HEPATITIS

Despite the onslaught of AIDS, liver disease is the most prevalent medical problem among addicts, including those on methadone. Liver damage ranges from alcoholic-induced damage to viral hepatitis (B, C, and D) in injecting-drug users. It now appears that hepatitis C poses the greatest risk. In Baltimore, a study of individuals with a history of injecting-drug use presenting for detoxification found that 86 percent had hepatitis C (Fingerhood, Jasinski, and Sullivan 1993). These patients had elevated aminotransferase enzymes indicative of active hepatitis. It is estimated that 50 percent of individuals testing positive for hepatitis C develop chronic hepatitis, with 20 percent of those with chronic hepatitis later developing cirrhosis. Alcohol use probably increases the likelihood of disease progression. Hepatitis C tends to have an asymptomatic acute phase, with a slow progression of disease over many years. Presently, it is difficult to predict why in certain individuals the disease follows a more fulminant course. Transmission of the virus is through needle use, and the risk of sexual transmission is very low or nonexistent. Additionally, it is not understood why 25 percent of alcoholics without a history of injecting-drug use test positive for hepatitis C. Any injecting-drug user with elevated aminotransferases should be evaluated for chronic hepatitis C. Individuals who test positive for hepatitis C and who are symptomatic or have very elevated aminotransferase levels (greater than five times normal) should be considered for treatment with alpha-interferon. Prior to the initiation of treatment, these individuals should undergo a liver biopsy.

Chronic hepatitis B (carriers of HBSAg) is less common, affecting an estimated 5 percent of injecting-drug users (Fingerhood et al. 1993). Such individuals can transmit hepatitis B via needle sharing and sexual contact. The majority of individuals exposed to hepatitis B will develop immunity, as expressed by the development of hepatitis B surface antibody. During the acute phase of hepatitis B, all individuals are contagious but not all are symptomatic. Hepatitis B carriers may all be coinfected with delta virus (hepatitis D), increasing the risk of development of fulminant hepatitis (Shattock et al. 1985). A biphasic pattern of illness with relapse a few weeks after an initial episode of hepatitis B suggests delta infection. Several treatment modalities are now available, including interferon and lamundine, that appear effective at limiting the progression of active hepatitis from hepatitis B.

Methadone maintenance or the cessation of injection drug use does not stop or limit the progression of chronic viral hepatitis. However, cessation of alcohol use and the avoidance of hepatotoxic drugs is essential. More important, in individiuals who have chronic hepatitis or cirrhosis, isoniazid (INH) should not be used to treat tuberculosis; rifampin is a suitable alternative (see drug interactions). Additionally, disulfiram (Antabuse®) should be used with caution in these individuals. Alcoholic hepatitis typically improves with the cessation of drinking. Diagnosis and prognosis are truly based on the pathology present on biopsy, because individuals may present with severe jaundice and ascites, which is totally reversible with abstinence, or they may already have cirrhosis. Rapid improvement with abstinence makes hepatitis the more likely diagnosis, rather than cirrhosis.

When chronic acute hepatitis of any etiology progresses to liver failure, treatment becomes supportive. Unfortunately, many liver transplant programs will not consider individuals for transplant if they are taking methadone, although some transplant surgeons educated about methadone treatment will now consider methadone patients for liver transplantation. However, a decision as to whether the individual is sufficiently stable to wean off methadone must often be made prior to consideration for transplantation.

Pulmonary Complications

Most pulmonary complications seen in injecting-drug users are directly related to HIV-pneumocystis pneumonia and frequent bacterial pneumonias. Studies imply that HIV-negative drug users are also at greater risk for bacterial pneumonia. The fact that more than 90 percent of drug users smoke cigarettes may account for this higher risk. Additionally, aspiration pneumonia commonly occurs as a result of alcohol abuse or overdosing.

Secondary lung infections can occur in injecting-drug users as a result of septic emboli from endocarditis or thrombophlebitis. Chest X-rays of these patients will show wedge-shaped lesions. Septic emboli may cause an abscess, an empyema, or a pulmonary infarction. Antibiotics are targeted at the cause of infection and, in the case of empyema, a chest tube is indicated.

Tuberculosis must always be considered in an injecting-drug user with pulmonary symptoms, fever, and weight loss. A history of incarceration and HIV infection each add to the risk of tuberculosis. Chest X-ray may not show the typical upper lobe infiltrate. Any patient who is highly suspected of having tuberculosis should be hospitalized with respiratory isolation. If the diagnosis is confirmed, the use of direct observed therapy, the standard of care in many cities, adds dramatically to the success of completed treatment. All individuals on methadone maintenance should be screened for tuberculosis yearly, using the standard PPD; anergy testing is not necessary. In HIV-negative individuals, 10 mm of induration indicates a positive response, whereas in HIV-positive individuals, 5 mm of induration indicates a positive response. Newly positive responses should be strongly considered for treatment with INH (6 months of therapy in HIV-negative individuals and 12 months in HIV-positive individuals). Pyridoxine generally should be coadministered. Compliance with INH therapy is greatly enhanced when it is administered daily with methadone at the treatment program.

Additionally, drug users are at high risk for noninfectious pulmonary disease (Stern and Subbarao 1983; McCarroll and Roszler 1991). For example, heroin overdose may present with pulmonary edema (Frand, Shim, and Williams 1972), a complication that may be delayed for hours after the overdose. The occurrence of heroin-induced pulmonary edema is correlated with the purity or grade of heroin used. The chest X-ray of a patient with heroin-related pulmonary edema will show a widespread interstitial and alveolar pattern with a normal-sized heart, and heart function is normal in these patients. Treatment is supportive, and although patients are usually treated with intravenous naloxone, there is no good evidence that this has an impact on survival. Hypoventilation, although present, is not the cause of the pulmonary edema, and the mechanism of heroin-related pulmonary edema is likely related to capillary leak. Although the exact mechanism of this capillary leakage is not known, it has been postulated that opiate-induced histamine release is the cause.

Chronic lung disease can occur directly as a result of injecting drugs. Most likely it results from the injection of contaminants that are not fully dissolved and that cause emboli. Cotton and starch are often injected and cause granulomas. Pills that are ground and then injected (e.g., Ritalin®) may contain talc. Talc lung disease is progressive and causes reduced single-breath diffusing capacity (DL_{CO}) and expiratory obstruction (reduced FEV_1) (Overland, Nolan, and Hopewell 1980; Pare, Cote, and Fraser 1989). Chest X-ray in these patients will show increased interstitial markings, often with micronodules, bullae, and flattened diaphragms (Goldstein et al. 1986). Cigarette smoking can add to the progression of this disease, and pulmonary hypertension can develop as a result of hypoxia. Treatment for chronic lung disease includes steroids and bronchodilators, which provide symptomatic relief, and progression of the disease leads to the need for supplemental oxygen.

Bronchospasm is commonly seen in drug users after the smoking of heroin or cocaine. Local inflammation occurs and treatment with bronchodilators and steroids ameliorates symptoms. The smoking of freebase cocaine has also been reported to cause atelectasis, alveolar hemorrhage, pulmonary infarction, and bronchiolitis obliterans (Kissner et al. 1987).

Pneumothorax is an acute complication of injecting-drug use, which results from attempting to inject drugs into a neck vein (Douglass and Levison 1986). Hemothorax or a large hematoma in the neck may also be present. Symptoms of pneumothorax include sudden shortness of breath and pleuritic chest pain on the side of the attempted injection. Individuals with these symptoms require immediate medical attention and a chest X-ray. A pneumothorax is a medical emergency, most often requiring placement of a chest tube. Pneumothorax may also occur as a complication of *Pneumocystis carinii* pneumonia, but in this setting, individuals have a history of cough, fever, and progressive shortness of breath.

RENAL COMPLICATIONS

Kidney failure in injecting-drug users has been termed "heroin nephropathy" despite the lack of evidence to support heroin as the etiologic factor (Eknoyan et al. 1973; Rao, Nicastri, and Friedman 1974; Arruda, Kurtzman, and Pillay 1975; Cunningham et al. 1980; Cunningham, Zielezny, and Venuto 1983). Rather, the cutting agents used with heroin have been implicated as a contributing factor. Renal biopsy usually shows focal segmental to diffuse sclerosing glomerulonephritis. Seen almost exclusively in black men, often without a history of hypertension, the kidney failure begins with nephrotic syndrome and rapidly progresses to a stage that requires dialysis.

Renal amyloidosis can occur in addicts who skin-pop or have severe chronic abscesses from injecting-drug use and can lead to chronic renal failure requiring dialysis (Menchel et al. 1983; Neugarten et al. 1986). Renal biopsy reveals AA-protein amyloid, which can also be found in the skin, pleura, and liver. Progression to chronic renal failure is more gradual than for heroin nephropathy, often taking years.

The costs of maintaining drug users on dialysis for a lifetime are tremendous and complications are more likely if injecting-drug abuse continues. Dialysis access sites are likely to become infected and often require repeated surgery. The controlled setting of methadone maintenance is particularly important for injecting-drug users on dialysis because it may prevent further severe complications related to ongoing injecting-drug use.

Acute renal diseases that affect injecting drug users include myoglobinuria and glomerulonephritis related to endocarditis or infection with hepatitis B or C. Myoglobinuria related to injection of heroin and cocaine may occur without immobilization or limb compression (Richter et al. 1971; Herzlich et al. 1988; Pogue and Nurse 1989). Focal muscle tenderness may not be present, but blood tests reveal elevated levels of serum myoglobin and creatine phosphokinase associated with elevations in blood urea nitrogen and creatine; treatment with intravenous saline generally reverses the disorder. Methadone can be safely used in patients on dialysis; in such patients, methadone is not removed by dialysis, nor does the absence of renal function lead to methadone accumulation (Kreek et al. 1980).

Acute and chronic hepatitis B infection and chronic hepatitis C infection are associated with a variety of pathologic renal diseases (Levy and Kleinknecht 1980). Individuals may often have asymptomatic hepatitis, and chronic hepatitis may be present for years prior to the onset of renal dysfunction. Pathologic changes associated with hepatitis B and C include membranous, membranoproliferative, and minimal change diseases. The prognosis for glomerulonephritis associated with acute hepatitis is better than that with chronic hepatitis.

Neurologic Complications

Neurologic complications seen in drug-abusing patients can be infectious or noninfectious (Lowenstein et al. 1987). Changes in mental status suggest a wide range of possible diagnoses, especially in HIV-infected individuals, resulting in an often extensive workup that may include imaging (CT or MRI) and cerebrospinal fluid analysis (lumbar puncture). Delirium and hallucinations are most commonly related to alcohol but may also be related to the use of contaminated batches of heroin or cocaine from the street market. In 1996 scopolamine was sold as heroin on the Baltimore street market, and its use resulted in anticholinergic poisoning that presented as delirium. Individuals on methadone maintenance also commonly abuse benzodiazepines, which in large amounts can cause delirium.

Seizures are the most common noninfectious neurologic complication of drug abuse. Overdose-related seizures are usually related to hypoxia from respiratory depression and are usually of the grand mal type. Seizures may also occur as a result of cocaine-induced vasospasm, abscess, HIV-related infection, embolic or thrombotic stroke, meningitis, subdural hematoma, and alcohol withdrawal.

Traumatic mononeuropathies may occur directly at injection sites from hitting a nerve, or they may occur from persistent, direct pressure on a nerve after a change in mental status. Atraumatic mononeuropathies have been reported at a distance from the injection site, perhaps related to vasospasm. Additionally, Bell's palsy, a facial nerve palsy, is commonly seen in injecting-drug users who are HIV positive. Most mononeuropathies improve over time and do not require surgical intervention.

Infectious neurologic complications of intravenous drug use are most commonly related to bacteremia. Meningitis, brain abscess, subdural and epidural abscesses, and mycotic aneurysms have all been reported. Simple complaints of back pain or headache may deserve particular attention in the injecting-drug user. Fever or an elevated sedimentation rate accompanied by subacute back pain that has not resolved with conservative measures warrants imaging with a CT scan or MRI to pursue a diagnosis of epidural abscess or vertebral osteomyelitis (Sapico and Montgomerie 1980).

IMMUNOLOGY

Immunologic abnormalities are common in injecting-drug users, independent of HIV infection. Many of the abnormalities are of unclear clinical consequence. Most long-time addicts have hypergammaglobulinemia (attributed to chronic antigenic stimulation) with elevated total protein levels and normal or low albumin levels. Chronic liver disease may potentiate the abnormality. Serum protein electrophoresis will reveal a polyclonal gammopathy in such patients. These excess globulins contribute to the high rate of false-positive syphilis tests in injecting-drug users. Other false-positive tests found in addicts include Coombs, smooth muscle antibodies, monospot (heterophile antibody), and rheumatoid factor.

The most clinically relevant immunologic disorder in injecting-drug users is thrombocytopenic purpura (Ryan 1979). This disorder results from circulating immune complexes reacting with platelets. Quinine used as a cutting agent is the most commonly implicated causative agent. Despite very low platelet counts, severe bleeding is unusual. Platelets that are present are functional. Treatment with steroids (prednisone 15 mg every six hours) is indicated if the platelet count does not increase with observation (and if there is an absence of injecting-drug use), or if platelet counts are very low (less than 10,000 without bleeding or less than 30,000 with bleeding). Individuals who continue to inject drugs are at high risk for recurrence.

WOMEN AND DOMESTIC VIOLENCE

Women with a history of substance abuse, including those on methadone maintenance, have a high rate of domestic violence. Screening for domestic violence should be incorporated into the medical interview for all women on methadone maintenance. It is important to deal with the issue sensitively as the individual may be reluctant to disclose information because of shame, humiliation, and low self-esteem. Some women believe they deserve the abuse and therefore do not deserve help, or they may feel the need to protect a partner who is a source of support. Occasionally, the victim believes that medical providers will not find her claim of abuse to be plausible.

Complaints from veterans of domestic violence may range from obvious evidence of physical trauma to nonspecific complaints of fatigue, insomnia, or difficulty concentrating. Once a diagnosis of domestic violence is made, the medical provider must validate the seriousness of the situation to the patient. The immediate safety of the woman should be assessed. If safety is in question, the woman should be advised to stay with family or friends, or a shelter that provides special care for abused women. The National Domestic Violence Hotline (1–800–333-SAFE) is a 24-hour service that helps women find a safe place to stay in their community. However, women with ongoing substance abuse are often refused shelter at such places.

SUMMARY

It is highly common to find comorbid medical conditions in methadone patients. However, this is a population whose medical needs are often inadequately addressed. The methadone clinic provides a unique opportunity to intervene and provide the necessary medical care for opioid-dependent patients, and this care can decrease morbidity, mortality, and long-term health care costs. Some aspects of the provision of medical care to methadone-maintained patients can be unique (e.g., the selection of appropriate medications that will not interact with methadone), and many of the conditions seen in this patient population can be related to their drug use (e.g., diseases transmitted through drug injecting). However, central to the treatment of methadone-maintained patients is a staff familiar with substance abuse and willing to provide care that is responsive to patients' needs in a trusting and caring setting. In this respect the treatment of methadone-maintained patients is no different from the treatment that should be provided to all patients with medical needs.

References

Anderson F., Paluzzi P., Lee J., Huggins G., Svikis D. 1997. Illicit use of clonidine in opiate-abusing pregnant women. *Obstet. Gynecol.* 90:790–94.

Angelos M.G., Sheets C.A., Zych P.R. 1986. Needle emboli to lung following intravenous drug abuse. *J. Emerg. Med.* 4:391–96.

Arruda J.A., Kurtzman N.A., Pillay V.K. 1975. Prevalence of renal disease in asymptomatic heroin addicts. *Arch. Intern. Med.* 135:535–37.

Bell J., Seres V., Bowron P., Lewis J., Batey R. 1988. The use of serum methadone levels in patients receiving methadone maintenance. *Clin. Pharmacol. Ther.* 43:623–29.

Bertschy G., Baumann P., Eap C.B., Baettig D. 1994. Probable metabolic interaction between methadone and fluvoxamine in addict patients. *Ther. Drug Monitor.* 16:42–45.

Brancos M.A., Peris P., Miro J.M., Monegal A., Gatell J.M., Mallolas J., Mensa J., Garcia S., Munoz-Gomez J. 1991. Septic arthritis in heroin addicts. *Semin. Arthritis Rheum.* 21:81–87.

Brickner P.W., Torres R.A., Barnes M., Newman R.G., Des Jarlais D.C., Whalen D.P., Rogers D.E. 1989. Recommendations for control and prevention of human immunodeficiency virus (HIV) infection in intravenous drug users. *Ann. Intern. Med.* 110:833–37.

Brown L.S., Sawyer R.C., Li R., Cobb M.N., Colborn D.C., Narang P.K. 1996. Lack of a pharmacologic interaction between rifabutin and methadone in HIV-infected former injecting drug users. *Drug Alcohol Depend.* 43:71–77.

Chandrasekar P.H., Narula A.P. 1986. Bone and joint infections in intravenous drug abusers. *Rev. Infect. Dis.* 8:904–11.

Cherubin C.E. 1971. Infectious disease problems of narcotic addicts. *Arch. Intern. Med.* 128:309–13.

Chokshi S.K., Moore R., Pandia N.G., Isner J.M. 1989. Reversible cardiomyopathy associated with cocaine intoxication. *Ann. Intern. Med.* 111:1039–40.

Collignon P.J., Sorrell T. 1987. Candidiasis in heroin addicts. *J. Infect. Dis.* 155:595.

Cunningham E.E., Brentjens J.R., Zielezny M.A., Andres G.A., Venuto R.C. 1980. Heroin nephropathy: a clinicopathologic and epidemiologic study. *Am. J. Med.* 68:47–53.

Cunningham E.E., Zielezny M.A., Venuto R.C. 1983. Heroin-associated nephropathy: a nationwide problem. *JAMA* 250:2935–36.

Donnelly B., Balkon J., Lasher C., Lynch V., Bidanset J.H., Bianco J. 1983. Evaluation of the methadone-alcohol interaction. I. Alterations of plasma concentration kinetics. *J. Analytic Toxicol.* 7:246–48.

Douglass R.E., Levison M.A. 1986. Pneumothorax in drug abusers: an urban epidemic? *Am. Surg.* 52:377–80.

Eknoyan G., Gyorkey F., Dischoso C., Hyde S.E., Gyorkey P., Suki W.N., Martinez-Maldonado M. 1973. Renal involvement in drug abuse. *Arch. Intern. Med.* 132:801–6.

Fingerhood M.I., Jasinski D.R., Sullivan J.T. 1993. Prevalence of hepatitis C in a chemically dependent population. *Arch. Intern. Med.* 153:2025–30.

Frand U.I., Shim C.S., Williams M.H. 1972. Heroin-induced pulmonary edema: sequential studies of pulmonary function. *Ann. Intern. Med.* 77:29–35.

Galdun J.P., Paris P.M., Weiss L.D., Heller M.B. 1987. Central embolization of needle fragments: a complication of intravenous drug abuse. *Am. J. Emerg. Med.* 5:379–82.

Goldstein D.S., Karpel J.P., Appel D., Williams M.H. 1986. Bullous pulmonary damage in users of intravenous drugs. *Chest* 89:266–69.

Griffiths R.R., Wolf B. 1990. Relative abuse liability of different benzodiazepines in drug abusers. *J. Clin. Psychopharmacol.* 10:237–43.

Hahn R.A., Onorato I.M., Jones S., Dougherty J. 1989. Prevalence of HIV infection among intravenous drug users in the United States. *JAMA* 261:2677–84.

Haverkos H.W., Lange W.R. 1990. Serious infections other than human immunodeficiency virus among intravenous drug users. *J. Infect. Dis.* 161:894–902.

Herzlich B.C., Arsura E.L., Pagal M., Grob D. 1988. Rhabdomyolysis related to cocaine abuse. *Ann. Intern. Med.* 108:335–36.

Isner J.M., Estes N.A.M., Thompson P.D., Costanzo-Nordin M.R., Subramanian R., Miller G., Katsas G., Sweeney K., Sturner W.Q. 1986. Acute cardiac events temporally related to cocaine abuse. *N. Engl. J. Med.* 315:1438–43.

Jacobson J.M., Hirschman S.Z. 1982. Necrotizing fasciitis complicating intravenous drug abuse. *Arch. Intern. Med.* 142:634–35.

Jatlow P., McCance E.F., Rainey P.M., Kosten T., Friedland G. 1997. Methadone increases zidovudine exposure in HIV-infected injection drug users. In: Harris L.S., ed. Problems of Drug Dependence 1996: Proceedings of the 58th Annual Scientific Meeting, College on Problems of Drug Dependence, NIDA Research Monograph 174, Department of Health and Human Services, National Institute on Drug Abuse, Rockville, MD, p. 136.

Kissner D.G., Lawrence W.D., Selis J.E., Flint A. 1987. Crack lung: pulmonary disease caused by cocaine abuse. *Am. Rev. Respir. Dis.* 136:1250–52.

Kreek M.J., Garfield J.W., Gutjahr C.L., Giusti L.M. 1976. Rifampin-induced methadone withdrawal. *N. Engl. J. Med.* 294:1104–6.

Kreek M.J., Schecter A.J., Gutjahr C.L., Hecht M. 1980. Methadone use in patients with chronic renal disease. *Drug Alcohol Depend.* 5:197–205.

Lange R.A., Cigarroa R.G., Yancy C.W. Jr., Willard J.E., Popma J.J., Sills M.N., McBride W., Kim A.S., Hillis L.D. 1989. Cocaine-induced coronary artery vasoconstriction. *N. Engl. J. Med.* 321:1557–62.

Levy M., Kleinknecht C. 1980. Membranous glomerulonephritis and hepatitis B virus infection. *Nephron* 26:259–65.

Lowenstein D.H., Massa S.M., Rowbotham M.C., Collins S.D., McKinney H.E., Simon R.P. 1987. Acute neurologic and psychiatric complications associated with cocaine abuse. *Am. J. Med.* 83:841–46.

Maany I., Dhopesh V., Arndt I.O., Burke W., Woody G., O'Brien C.P. 1989. Increase in desipramine serum levels associated with methadone treatment. *Am. J. Psychiatry* 146:1611–13.

McCarroll K.A., Roszler M.H. 1991. Lung disorders due to drug abuse. *J. Thorac. Imaging* 6:30–35.

McIlroy M.A., Reddy D., Markowitz N., Saravolatz L.D. 1989. Infected false aneurysms of the femoral artery in intravenous drug addicts. *Rev. Infect. Dis.* 11:578–85.

Menchel S., Cohen D., Gross E., Frangione B., Gallo G. 1983. AA protein-related renal amyloidosis in drug addicts. *Am. J. Pathol.* 112:195–99.

Musher D.M., Hamill R.J., Baughn R.E. 1990. Effect of human immunodeficiency virus (HIV) infection on the course of syphilis and on the response to treatment. *Ann. Intern. Med.* 113:872–81.

Neugarten J., Gallo G.R., Buxbaum J., Katz L.A., Rubenstein J., Baldwin D.S. 1986. Amyloidosis in subcutaneous heroin abusers ("skin poppers' amyloidosis"). *Am. J. Med.* 81:635–40.

O'Connor P.G., Molde S., Henry S., Shockcor W.T., Schottenfeld R.S. 1992. Human immunodeficiency virus infection in intravenous drug users: a model for primary care. *Am. J. Med.* 93:382–86.

Orangio G.R., Pitlick S.D., Della Latta P., Mandel L.J., Marino C., Guarneri J.J., Giron J.A., Margolis I.B. 1984. Soft tissue infections in parenteral drug abusers. *Ann. Surg.* 199:97–100.

Overland E.S., Nolan A.J., Hopewell P.C. 1980. Alteration of pulmonary function in intravenous drug abusers: prevalence, severity, and characterization of gas exchange abnormalities. *Am. J. Med.* 68:231–37.

Pare J.P., Cote G., Fraser R.S. 1989. Long-term follow-up of drug abusers with intravenous talcosis. *Am. Rev. Respir. Dis.* 139:233–41.

Payte J.T., Khuri E.T. 1993. Principles of methadone dose determination. In: Parrino M.W., ed. *State Methadone Treatment Guidelines, Treatment Improvement Protocol (TIP) Series 1.* Substance Abuse and Mental Health Services Administration, Center for Substance Abuse Treatment, United States Department of Health and Human Services, Rockville, MD, pp. 47–58.

Plummer J.L., Gourlay G.K., Cherry D.A., Cousins M.J. 1988. Estimation of methadone clearance: application in the management of cancer pain. *Pain* 33:313–22.

Podzamczer D., Gudiol F. 1986. Systemic candidiasis in heroin addicts. *J. Infect. Dis.* 153:1182–83.

Pogue V.A., Nurse H.M. 1989. Cocaine-associated acute myoglobinuric renal failure. *Am. J. Med.* 86:183–86.

Preston K.L., Griffiths R.R., Stitzer M.L., Bigelow G.E., Liebson I.A. 1984. Diazepam and methadone interactions in methadone maintenance. *Clin. Pharmacol. Ther.* 36:534–41.

Rao T.K., Nicastri A.D., Friedman E.A. 1974. Natural history of heroin-associated nephropathy. *N. Engl. J. Med.* 290:19–23.

Richter R.W., Challenor Y.B., Pearson J., Kagen L.J., Hamilton L.L., Ramsey W.H. 1971. Acute myoglobinuria associated with heroin addiction. *JAMA* 216:1172–76.

Ryan C.F., White J.M. 1996. Health status at entry to methadone maintenance treatment using the SF-36 health survey questionnaire. *Addiction* 91:39–45.

Ryan D.H. 1979. Heroin and thrombocytopenia. *Ann. Intern. Med.* 90:852–53.

Sapico F.L., Montgomerie J.Z. 1980. Vertebral osteomyelitis in intravenous drug abusers: report of three cases and review of the literature. *Rev. Infect. Dis.* 2:196–206.

Schall U., Katta T., Pries E., Klöppel A., Gastpar M. 1996. Pain perception of intravenous heroin users on maintenance therapy with levomethadone. *Pharmacopsychiatry* 29:176–79.

Schwartz E.L., Brechbühl A.B., Kahl P., Miller M.A., Selwyn P.A., Friedland G.H. 1992. Pharmacokinetic interactions of zidovudine and methadone in intravenous drug-using patients with HIV infection. *J. Acq. Im. Def. Synd.* 5:619–26.

Selwyn P.A., Alcabes P., Hartel D., Buono D., Shoenbaum E.E., Klein R.S., Davenny K., Friedland G.H. 1992. Clinical manifestations and predictors of disease progression in drug users with human immunodeficiency virus infection. *N. Engl. J. Med.* 327:1697–1703.

Shattock A.G., Irwin F.M., Morgan B.M., Hillary I.B., Kelly M.G., Fielding J.F., Kelly D.A., Weir D.G. 1985. Increased severity and morbidity of acute hepatitis in drug abusers with simultaneously acquired hepatitis B and hepatitis D virus infections. *Br. Med. J.* 290:1377–80.

Stern W.Z., Subbarao K. 1983. Pulmonary complications of drug addiction. *Semin. Roentgenol.* 18:183–97.

Tong T.G., Pond S.M., Kreek M.J., Jaffery N.F., Benowitz N.L. 1981. Phenytoin-induced methadone withdrawal. *Ann. Intern. Med.* 94:349–51.

Tuazon C.U., Elin R.J. 1981. Endotoxin content of street heroin. *Arch. Intern. Med.* 141:1385–86.

Umbricht-Schneiter A., Ginn D.H., Pabst K.M., Bigelow G.E. 1994. Providing medical care to methadone clinic patients: referral vs on-site care. *Am. J. Public Health* 84:207–10.

Yeager R.A., Hobson R.W., Padberg F.T., Lynch T.G., Chakravarty M. 1987. Vascular complications related to drug abuse. *J. Trauma* 27:305–8.

8

Assessment and Treatment of Comorbid Psychiatric Disorders

Van L. King, M.D., and Robert K. Brooner, Ph.D.

Substantial psychiatric comorbidity exists among opioid abusers in the form of both other substance use disorders and other psychiatric disorders. This chapter focuses on nonsubstance use psychiatric disorders in methadone maintenance patients. A review of comorbid substance abuse disorders in methadone patients can be found in Chapter 6.

There are three sections to this chapter. The first section reviews the prevalence of comorbid psychiatric disorders in opioid abusers, and the second discusses mechanisms for screening, assessing, and diagnosing these comorbid conditions in methadone patients. Finally, the third section reviews treatment for these disorders. This chapter does not comprehensively review all aspects and treatments for psychiatric disorders, such as the relative strengths and weaknesses of different medications for the treatment of major depression. The interested reader can find a more detailed discussion of such topics in one of several excellent general psychiatric textbooks (e.g., Kaplan and Sadock 1999; Tasman, Kay, and Lieberman 1997). Rather, the purpose of this chapter is to provide information about those aspects of treating comorbid psychiatric disorders in methadone patients that are unique to this population.

Prevalence of Psychiatric Comorbidity in Opioid-Dependent Patients

Several studies have examined the rate of other psychiatric disorders in patients with opioid dependence (Table 8.1). Comparisons across studies can be difficult, because investigators use different interviews and cri-

Table 8.1 Studies of Prevalence of Comorbid Psychiatric Disorders in Opioid-Dependent Patients

Study	Number of Patients in Sample	Assessment[a]	Percentage of Patients with Psychiatric Disorder						
			Lifetime Psychiatric Disorder	Current Major Depression	Lifetime Major Depression	Current Anxiety Disorder	Lifetime Anxiety Disorder	Personality Disorder	APD[b]
Abbott, Weller, and Walker (1994)	144	SCID	84.7	7.6	25.0	16.7	27.1	45.8	31.3
Brooner et al. (1997)	716	SCID	47.5	3.2	15.8	5.0	8.2	34.8	25.1
Khantzian and Treece (1985)	133	Clinical	93.2	26.3	34.6	—	11.3	65	34.6
Kosten, Rounsaville, and Kleber (1982)	384	SADS	—	—	—	—	—	68	54.7
Rounsaville et al. (1982b)	533	SADS-L	86.9	23.8	53.9	—	16.1	—	26.5
Strain, Brooner, and Bigelow (1991)	66	ARC	47.0	0	19.7	—	—	—	30.3
Woody et al. (1983)	110	SADS-L	—	—	42.7	—	—	—	14.5

[a]SCID, Structured Clinical Interview for DSM-III-R; clinical, patients were assessed with a semistructured clinical interview and diagnosed using DSM-III criteria; SADS, Schedule for Affective Disorders and Schizophrenia—results are diagnoses using DSM-III; SADS-L, Schedule for Affective Disorders and Schizophrenia-Lifetime version—results are diagnoses using the Research Diagnostic Criteria (RDC); ARC, Alcohol Research Center Intake Interview—results are diagnoses using DSM-III-R criteria.
[b]APD, antisocial personality disorder.

teria to make diagnoses and because the population (community addicts versus patients in methadone treatment) and the length of time patients have been in treatment vary. This last point is illustrated in a study that examined self-reported depressive symptoms in patients on the day they began methadone treatment, and then at weekly intervals (Strain, Stitzer, and Bigelow 1991). Results showed that average scores on the Beck Depression Inventory (BDI) declined significantly from the day of admission versus the first week in treatment and that scores plateaued rapidly thereafter (Figure 8.1). These results suggest that rates of depression can appear elevated in patients evaluated at the time of treatment entry versus those who have been enrolled in methadone treatment for just a few days. Similarly, rates of major depression and depressive symptoms in opioid abusers entering treatment decrease after six months of methadone maintenance even though no specific intervention is used (Rounsaville et al. 1982a).

Although rates of particular disorders vary across studies, essentially all studies find high rates of comorbid conditions in this population, with particularly high rates of mood, anxiety, and personality disorders. The prevalence of these conditions, as well as other less common but particularly problematic disorders, are reviewed in this section.

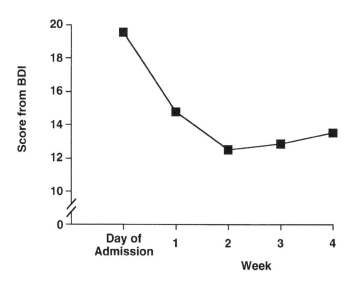

Figure 8.1.   Self-reported depressive symptoms in 58 opioid-dependent patients entering methadone treatment (day of admission) and at each subsequent week of treatment. BDI = Beck Depression Inventory. *Source:* Adapted from Strain, Stitzer, and Bigelow (1991).

Mood Disorders

Studies of mood disorders in opioid-dependent patients typically focus upon diagnoses of major depression, bipolar disorder, and dysthymic disorder. Major depression is the most common serious psychiatric condition in the general population, and across studies rates of major depression in opioid abusers clearly appear to be higher than rates found in the general population. For example, in a study conducted by Brooner et al. (1997) (see Table 8.1) the rate of major depression was three times higher than the Baltimore sample of the Epidemiological Catchment Area (ECA) survey, a study that evaluated psychiatric disorder in the general population (Robins et al. 1985). There is considerable variability across studies in reported rates of both lifetime and current major depression in opioid-dependent patients, with the prevalence of a lifetime diagnosis of major depression as low as 15.8 percent and as high as 53.9 percent (Table 8.1). Similarly, the prevalence of current major depression can be as low as 0 percent and as high as 26.3 percent. The lower rates of depression found in some studies may be owing in part to a longer stabilization period in treatment before diagnostic evaluation (e.g., Strain, Stitzer, and Bigelow 1991; Brooner et al. 1997), as well as to the evaluation of patients both in and out of methadone treatment in some studies, and to the absence of a standard time frame for evaluation (e.g., Rounsaville et al. 1982b; Khantzian and Treece 1985).

Most studies reporting on the prevalence of bipolar disorder in opioid-dependent patients have found low rates (both lifetime and current rates of about 1%), which are consistent with rates found in the general population (APA 1994). On the other hand, the prevalence of dysthymic disorder in opioid-dependent patients is somewhat higher—at least 3 to 4 percent (Brooner et al. 1997), and some studies have found rates around 15 percent (Abbott, Weller, and Walker 1994; Khantzian and Treece 1985).

Anxiety Disorders

Studies examining the rates of anxiety disorders in opioid-dependent patients have typically reported the diagnoses of four conditions: panic disorder, generalized anxiety disorder (GAD), obsessive-compulsive disorder (OCD), and the phobias. As in the general population, the most commonly found anxiety disorders in opioid abusers are the phobias. Lifetime rates of phobias range between 2.3 percent and 9.6 percent (Khantzian and Treece 1985 and Rounsaville et al. 1982b, respectively). Rates for a current diagnosis of a phobia are probably lower, although at least one study found rates as high as 9.2 percent (Rounsaville et al. 1982b).

The second most common anxiety disorder is GAD, with lifetime rates ranging as high as 5.4 percent (Rounsaville et al. 1982b). However, current rates of GAD appear to be closer to 1 percent. Similarly, lifetime rates of panic disorder can be as high as 2 percent (Brooner et al. 1997), but current rates are less than 1 percent. Finally, OCD is also relatively rare, with most studies finding lifetime rates of less than 2 percent and current rates of 1 percent or less (e.g., Rounsaville et al. 1982b; Woody et al. 1983; Brooner et al. 1997).

Personality Disorders

Personality disorders are highly prevalent comorbid conditions found in opioid-dependent patients, and the overall rates of personality disorder across studies range from 34.8 percent to 68 percent. Antisocial personality disorder (APD) (either with or without another personality disorder diagnosis) is the most common personality disorder (Table 8.1). Although rates of APD vary across studies, from 14.5 percent (Woody et al. 1983) to as high as 54.7 percent (Kosten et al. 1982), in general, it appears that about one-quarter to one-third of patients can be diagnosed with APD. For example, Brooner et al. (1997) documented a 25.1 percent rate of APD in their study of treatment-seeking opioid abusers, which is eight times the rate of APD in the general population, as measured in the ECA study (Robins et al. 1985). The lower rates of APD in some studies reflect the higher proportion of females in those studies (e.g., Strain, Brooner, and Bigelow 1991; Brooner et al. 1997). The most common other personality disorders in the Brooner et al. (1997) study were borderline (5%), avoidant (5%), passive-aggressive (4%), and paranoid (3%). The other studies listed in Table 8.1 reported rates of borderline personality between 3.7 percent and 12.1 percent (Khantzian and Treece 1985 and Kosten, Rounsaville, and Kleber 1982, respectively), and rates for other personality disorders are less than 5 percent.

Other Psychiatric Disorders

Although relatively uncommon, opioid-dependent patients in methadone treatment can have evidence of other comorbid psychiatric disorders. Some of these, such as schizophrenia, are relatively rare (i.e., a current prevalence of 1 to 2%). Others, such as eating disorders, can have a higher lifetime prevalence (i.e., greater than 1% in women), but are rarely found as a current diagnosis (Abbott, Weller, and Walker 1994; Brooner et al. 1997). Posttraumatic stress disorder (PTSD) has not been routinely assessed in studies of opioid abusers. However, using data from the ECA study, Cottler et al. (1992) reported a lifetime rate of 8.3 percent for PTSD among cocaine/opiate abusers compared with 0.3 percent in the general population, which suggests that PTSD may be a significant problem in methadone maintenance patients.

The diagnosis of attention-deficit hyperactivity disorder (ADHD) has historically received little attention in opioid-dependent patients, although it may be a relatively common disorder in this population (Eyre, Rounsaville, and Kleber 1982). For example, a study of 125 new admissions to our methadone clinic found that one-fifth had a retrospective childhood history of ADHD, though only 12 percent had three or more significant current symptoms warranting specific treatment for ADHD. These patients were also more likely to have a history of comorbid anxiety and mood disorders and APD (King et al. 1998). The detection of this condition can be important because impulsivity and poor attention may affect a patient's ability to engage in treatment.

DETECTION AND ASSESSMENT OF COMORBID PSYCHIATRIC DISORDERS

Several standardized instruments can be used to screen and diagnose psychiatric disorders in methadone maintenance patients. In general, these instruments fall into two categories: self-rating questionnaires (i.e., the patient completes a form), and interviewer-based instruments (i.e., the patient answers questions presented by a trained interviewer). The former require less work on the part of staff, who simply need to review a form and score it. However, self-rating questionnaires do not provide diagnoses; rather, they provide assessments of symptoms. On the other hand, interviews can provide diagnoses and the patients' responses can be checked, thereby increasing the probability that the interview results are valid. However, interviews take time and effort on the part of staff, and therefore can be expensive. Examples of commonly used questionnaires and interviews are summarized in this section.

Questionnaires

Beck Depression Inventory

The BDI is a rapidly administered questionnaire that rates significant depressive features over the previous week (Beck, Ward, and Mendelson 1961). It is a useful screening tool for identifying patients with possible depression, but it does not provide a diagnosis of depression. The BDI contains 21 items and a patient can typically complete the form in less than 10 minutes.

Symptom Checklist-90-R (SCL-90-R)

The SCL-90-R is a standardized self-report that measures psychologic distress along nine primary symptom dimensions and three summary indices (Derogatis 1983). Like other self-report measures, it does not produce a diagnosis, but it does provide valuable information about self-reported psychologic distress (and the particular areas of such distress, such as depression, anxiety, etc.).

Interviews

Addiction Severity Index (ASI)

The ASI is a structured interview assessing seven life domains relevant to patients with substance use disorder (alcohol use, drug use, family/social, psychiatric, legal, medical, employment; McLellan et al. [1980]). Although the ASI does not diagnose psychiatric disorders, it does provide quantitative responses in areas of interest to drug abuse treatment programs. Patients are assessed using a 30-day interval, and sequential administrations of the ASI (e.g., at 1-month intervals) can be used to track changes over time. The ASI takes 45 minutes to administer and can be very helpful in identifying problem areas in treatment as well as to monitor progress in treatment.

Structured Clinical Interview for DSM-IV (SCID)

The SCID is a semistructured interview that yields Axis I and Axis II disorders based on DSM criteria (First et al. 1995). It covers a broad range of diagnoses, including substance abuse and dependence, mood, psychotic, anxiety, and eating disorders. The SCID requires extensive training and is best administered by clinicians with experience in evaluating patients in the diagnostic categories covered, because its use requires the ability to make clinical judgments.

Diagnostic Interview Schedule (DIS)

The DIS is a structured interview that provides diagnoses of psychiatric disorders based on DSM criteria (Robins et al. 1995). However, unlike the SCID, the DIS requires less training and may be helpful in case identification for referral to professional staff for further diagnostic evaluation. Staff without clinical training can learn to use the DIS. Whereas the SCID is a semistructured interview (interviewers must ask questions in the interview, but then can reword and ask their own questions if needed to clarify the diagnosis), the DIS is a structured interview (specific instructions are given for questions and how they are to be asked).

Clinical Evaluation

Although standard assessments for screening and evaluating patients are useful, many clinicians evaluate patients without using these tools. Such an approach can be used efficiently and provide a comprehensive review of psychiatric conditions commonly found in patients with opioid dependence. However, when using such an approach, the clinician should still depend on standardized diagnostic criteria such as those found in DSM-IV (APA 1994) for determining diagnoses. In addition, it is important that the clinician probe for those conditions most commonly found in opioid-dependent patients (e.g., major depression, dysthymic disorder, APD and other personality disorders, anxiety disorders, ADHD, as well as other substance use disorders). Furthermore, it is also recommended that patients be briefly assessed for conditions with high morbidity such as psychotic disorders and bipolar disorder, although such disorders are uncommon in opioid abusers entering methadone treatment.

Rarely, if ever, does treatment of a comorbid condition obviate the need for extensive substance abuse and rehabilitative treatment in methadone maintenance patients. Once patients abstain from drug use, dysphoria often subsides, and they feel more encouraged and less in need of additional support. Thus, it is important for staff to emphasize to the dysphoric patient the need to become abstinent since depressive symptoms improve with abstinence. The support of a drug counselor is often sufficient to help the patient through the early stages of drug treatment and the achievement of abstinence. However, if a patient continues to have significant psychiatric complaints after two or more weeks of abstinence, referral for psychiatric evaluation is certainly indicated.

When initially evaluating a patient who has complaints of psychiatric symptomatology, the most relevant factor in the initial history is whether the patient is abstinent from abused drugs. Unfortunately, patients typically have scant drug-free history as adults and, consequently, have never had an adequate psychiatric evaluation. A thorough history with reference to recent physical examination and laboratory work will determine whether a patient is able to receive outpatient treatment for his or her psychiatric complaints or whether a drug abuse treatment residential unit or inpatient psychiatric unit is needed. If a patient is intoxicated in the clinic on a daily basis or is using large amounts of substances daily, the probability of outpatient treatment producing a drug-free state quickly enough to evaluate serious psychiatric complaints (e.g., suicidal tendencies, prominent neurovegetative complaints, paranoia) will be small. Similarly, if a patient is continually positive for abused drugs on urine toxicology screens but does not claim to use large amounts of substances, the patient's feelings of hopelessness about his or her situation may necessitate an inpatient stay. The judicious use of a residential unit for several days to two weeks can greatly aid the process of sorting out substance-induced symptoms from independent depression or bipolar disorder.

If a patient is to be managed as an outpatient, a minimal period of abstinence (one to two consecutive weeks of negative urine toxicology screens) is required. Often, however, a patient is not able to accomplish this goal without being substantially pressured by the staff of the treatment program. It is often a mistake to prescribe psychotropic medications unless a patient is abstinent for at least one to two weeks. Exceptions to this rule would be patients who have a definite independent psychotic disorder that requires neuroleptics, or patients who have been previously diagnosed with a mood or anxiety disorder when abstinent, who had subsequently stopped taking medication. Requiring intensive work on drug rehabilitation allows time for a thorough evaluation, and the anticipation of pharmacotherapy (e.g., antidepressant medication) can act as a significant positive reinforcement for drug abstinence. The dysphoria associated with continued drug use is associated not only with the chemical effects of the drug or its withdrawal, but also with the discouragement and guilt that a patient feels in connection with continued drug use. Mood may often improve remarkably within days of successful drug abstinence, even if a patient's use was less frequent than daily and the patient had no appreciable physical withdrawal state. More frequent supportive psychotherapy or counseling contact is often needed to encourage patients during the first few days of abstinence. Short, weekly visits to a psychiatrist can serve as a powerful motivator for drug abstinence in some patients.

The alternative to abstinence prior to medication treatment for a psychiatric disorder is problematic at best. If a patient is still abusing drugs, the clinician must rely heavily on a previous history of specific symptoms as well as on the patient's response to specific medication or treatments. Sometimes a reliable (preferably drug-free) friend or family member can provide valuable information about the patient's previous psychiatric and family history. Records from psychiatric hospitalizations or from significant episodes of outpatient treatment can be helpful, although patients are usually not observed long enough in an abstinent state to determine independent psychiatric symptoms reliably. In addition, physicians who are inexperienced in treating severely drug-dependent patients may have started patients on medication regimens during previous treatment episodes without good rationale. It is not uncommon for patients to be put on antidepressants or mood stabilizers on the day of admission to a psychiatric hospital or rehabilitation unit even though they were still using drugs heavily and on a daily basis. Rapidly treating these patients with such medications is more likely to confuse them as well as jeopardize their future care. It can be argued that starting a medication treatment for mood or anxiety symptoms without several days of abstinence may help the patient become abstinent if a mood or anxiety disorder is complicating their drug or alcohol use problems. However, rapid changes in mood are common during early abstinence, and the patient may take medication unnecessarily. An even greater risk is that patients will view medication as the easy route to alleviating their misery, and believe they do not need to engage in the more difficult work of rehabilitation. In certain instances, patients come to believe that the "depression" or "anxiety" needs to be medicated first, before they can become abstinent, because they are "only self-medicating" this distressing condition. A clear message regarding the separate nature of the patients' substance use disorder and the comorbid psychiatric condition is vital from the outset of treatment.

Substance-Induced versus Independent Comorbid Disorders

Determining whether the initiation or continuation of comorbid psychiatric disorder is in some way related to concurrent substance use disorder can be challenging (Miller 1993; Brooner et al. 1997). Some authors describe the disorders as *primary* or *secondary* to elucidate this relationship. These terms often refer to the condition that was first apparent (primary), which, in some way, determines either the initiation or course of the secondary diagnosis. For example, if alcohol abuse temporally precedes a depressive disorder, then the alcohol use disorder would be primary. Because of the early onset of substance use in methadone patients, however, virtually all other psychiatric conditions will occur after the onset of substance use disorder. Although it is especially apparent in methadone maintenance patients, this oversimplified approach generally has limited heuristic value. In addition, these designations have not been consistently used in the literature, thus further limiting their clinical and teaching value.

Other authors use the designations *major* and *minor*. Again, few conditions would be more impairing than chronic narcotic dependence, and one could imagine various situations in which the "minor" condition (e.g., dysthymic disorder) might be the "major" focus of treatment for a patient who was abstinent yet still on methadone maintenance. These designations suffer from many of the same problems as the primary and secondary designations.

Another, more satisfactory approach is the use of the designations *substance-induced* versus *independent* psychiatric disorder. With this classification, emphasis is placed on the temporal relationship between changes in drug use (either increases or decreases) and the symptoms being evaluated. It is also important to know whether a patient had similar symptoms during times of significant drug abstinence (preferably of several weeks or months of duration). Substance-induced disorders are self-limiting if the appropriate steps are taken to abstain from abused drugs and if the appropriate drug abuse treatment is undertaken. Using this classification, the naturalistic history of the onset of a psychiatric disorder (e.g., major depression) can be determined in relation to the pattern of substance use in order to best determine whether the condition's initiation, continuation, or offset was connected to the substance use. For example, using this approach, Brooner et al. (1997) reported that 77 percent of treatment-seeking opioid abusers who met criteria for lifetime major depression had a substance-induced rather than an independent disorder.

The presence of untreated or poorly controlled medical disorders (e.g., HIV disease, hepatitis, diabetes mellitus, chronic obstructive pulmonary disease [COPD], thyroid disease) or treatment for medical conditions (e.g., interferon treatment for chronic active hepatitis; steroid treatment for asthma, COPD, or rheumatologic disease) are other important factors to consider. These conditions and treatments can substantially impact mood and neurovegetative symptoms and can be confused with an independent psychiatric disorder. It is vital to rule out medical or substance-induced mood changes and to treat any independent psychiatric disorder in order to improve a patient's ability to engage in drug abuse treatment via counseling, medication treatments, and medical management.

Treatment of Comorbid Psychiatric Conditions

Comorbid disorders are associated with the increased risk of drug use while patients are in treatment. For example, depression was associated with continued drug use in a six-month treatment follow-up of opioid-dependent subjects (Rounsaville et al. 1986). In addition, Kosten, Rounsaville, and Kleber (1986b) found that depression was associated with continued drug use in a 2.5-year follow-up of opiate abusers. Methadone patients who have a comorbid psychiatric disorder have higher lifetime rates of other substance abuse disorders (in addition to their opioid dependence) when compared with methadone patients who do not have a comorbid psychiatric disorder (Strain, Brooner, and Bigelow 1991; Rutherford, Cacciola, and Alterman 1994; Brooner et al. 1997). Personality disorder is associated with higher rates of substance abuse (Rutherford, Cacciola, and Alterman 1994; Brooner et al. 1997; Kidorf et al. 1998) as well as poorer treatment outcome (Woody et al. 1985; Reich and Green 1991). APD may convey more risk than other personality disorders (Brooner et al. 1997), although not all studies find this relationship (Rutherford, Cacciola, and Alterman 1994). Thus, the identification of comorbid psychiatric conditions can serve as a useful indicator for patients who may be at increased risk for poor treatment performance. These patients may need further treatment resources targeting these vulnerabilities. In addition, they may need treatment for their comorbid psychiatric conditions, both to improve compliance with treatment goals and to decrease morbidity associated with these conditions.

Coordination of Treatment Services

The methadone clinic can play a key role in the coordination of various treatment services, including psychiatric treatments. To this end, the structure of the methadone treatment program can be of great benefit in and of itself in helping patients in the process of rehabilitation. Regular daily attendance, with clear contingencies and expectancies, can provide a stabilizing environment for patients with unstable personalities. Personality characteristics of avoidance, argumentativeness, manipulation, and poor organization and untimeliness can be addressed in a straightforward, therapeutic manner. Psychiatric medications can be given at the medication window to ensure that patients are receiving treatment for their psychotic or mood disorders. Patients can be required to make appropriate appointments for psychiatric or medical evaluation if clinic staff believe (or the patient would have the staff believe) that a condition is interfering with their substance abuse treatment. Intensive and continuing efforts to integrate the care of patients in the program can mean the difference between treatment retention or dropout.

Many patients in methadone treatment have health care providers outside the clinic, psychiatric and otherwise. Such patients can be required to submit prescriptions, written by outside health care providers, to the medical director of the methadone clinic for approval, in order to avoid problems with drug interactions and abuse. The methadone clinic should consider having a policy that reserves the right to require an independent evaluation in the clinic if staff are concerned about a patient's outside care, or are concerned that a patient is not telling his or her complete history to an outside provider (e.g., being in a methadone program or actively abusing drugs; it is common for a patient not to tell his or her private physician about being in a methadone program). If a patient is doing poorly in treatment and abusing drugs, the clinic should consider requiring that the patient allow clinic staff to speak with outside providers to discuss and coordinate the patient's substance abuse and other treatments.

Adequate medical care is an essential part of the rehabilitation process and, when relevant, can be incorporated as a required element of the treatment plan. Our clinic uses a general philosophical approach that allows patients the maximum latitude in their treatment involvement as long as they are doing well. Thus, the clinic requires gradually increasing amounts of accountability and coordination of services both inside and outside of the clinic if a patient is doing poorly in substance abuse treatment (see Chapter 9). However, some patients have an adversarial relationship with the treatment program because of contingencies on drug use and may not be entirely honest with program staff. For these patients off-site psychologic counseling or psychiatric care can be helpful; this approach, however, prevents patients from receiving the most comprehensive care because of constraints on coordination with outside providers.

Counseling and Psychotherapy

Once a diagnosis is made, an appropriate treatment plan must be formulated. Unfortunately, many methadone patients have scant financial means or psychological-mindedness to access and benefit from sophisticated psychotherapy. If medication is not warranted, counseling from the methadone clinic counselor with support from a supervisor or doctoral staff may be adequate. At times, referral to the local community mental health center may be necessary for more expert regular psychotherapy. Several studies have shown the efficacy of psychotherapy for improving general psychiatric symptoms and drug abuse treatment outcome (see Chapter 9), but unfortunately, in the methadone clinic, patient needs often exceed the availability of funds to pay for such resources as psychotherapy.

An important aspect of treatment for many psychiatric conditions is work activity, either paid or volunteer. Work activity builds confidence and self-attitude and can substantially improve psychiatric symptoms in chronically unproductive patients. In addition, it can provide structure and pro-social behavior, which can greatly aid the process of drug abuse rehabilitation. If a patient with a comorbid psychiatric disability is not able to participate in work, a psychiatric psychosocial rehabilitation program may be appropriate. Participation in such a program can make evident any incompletely treated disorders and promote further psychosocial rehabilitation (e.g., an undetected social phobia or extensive negative symptoms of schizophrenia in an otherwise minimally symptomatic person). Clinic staff need to monitor compliance with this aspect of treatment, however, because it can be a difficult commitment for many patients.

Treatment of Depression

Substance-Induced Depressive Disorder

A substantial proportion of depressive disorders in methadone maintenance patients are substance-induced. For example, one study found that 77 percent of treatment-seeking opioid abusers who met criteria for lifetime major depression had a substance-induced rather than independent disorder (Brooner et al. 1997). It is worthwhile to review the propensity for various abused drugs to cause depression, concentrating on those drugs most commonly abused in methadone clinics: alcohol, cocaine, and benzodiazepines.

Alcohol. Alcohol use is often associated with dysphoria and complaints of both depression and anxiety (Schuckit and Monteiro 1988). Numerous studies have shown high rates of alcohol dependence in methadone patients (see Chapter 6), and some evidence suggests that alcohol use may increase over time among patients in a methadone maintenance program (Kosten, Rounsaville, and Kleber 1986a). However, patients often fail to appreciate that chronic alcohol use can dramatically impact mood.

Unfortunately, covert alcohol use is difficult to detect with routine urine toxicology screens and breathalyzers if a patient drinks in the afternoons and evenings, after attending the clinic. Obtaining serum liver function tests (AST, ALT, GTT) can be quite helpful in this regard, as these test results are often elevated if the patient is using alcohol regularly. The use of disulfiram administered daily with the methadone dose is an effective deterrent and is well tolerated in most patients (see Chapter 6). Depressive symptoms are not uncommon in alcoholics, but abstinence improves these complaints in the majority of patients within two to four weeks (Brown and Schuckit 1988). Nevertheless, alcohol-induced mood symptoms can linger for weeks after initial abstinence; therefore, it can be difficult to determine whether they are symptomatic of an independent mood disorder.

Benzodiazepines and other sedative/hypnotics. Patients with chronic benzodiazepine abuse can present with a lethargic, unmotivated, anhedonic, and tearful depression. Alternately, patients can present with delirium, or in agitated, disinhibited states of intoxication or withdrawal that can mimic manic states. Popular benzodiazepines currently abused in methadone clinics include alprazolam (Xanax®) and clonazepam (Klonopin®). Clonazepam is favored most, primarily because of prominent sedative effects. It is also difficult to detect on standard benzodiazepine urine screens, except at very high levels (at times over 5 mg daily, which is a very high dose), but this threshold for detection varies among individuals. Some laboratories have specific urine tests available for the detection of clonazepam; however, these tests may not detect the drug in patients taking as little as 1 mg daily. A clonazepam serum level is a more sensitive method of detecting covert, daily clonazepam use. This test is quite expensive, so it should be used judiciously.

Concern about low-dose benzodiazepine abuse may seem misguided to clinicians who are simply glad to reduce injecting-drug abuse in these patients. However, the effects of these "low" doses of benzodiazepines are clinically obvious and can make an individual lethargic, dopey, and impair the rehabilitation process. Along with undetected alcoholics, patients using low doses of benzodiazepines may present to a psychiatrist with treatment refractory mood symptoms. The therapeutic process is undermined both psychologically and psychopharmacologically if clinicians do not address continuing drug use, even if the drug use is "low dose" or difficult to detect. Many patients have little appreciation for a healthy mental state and will be satisfied with a new, less impaired baseline if staff are willing to collaborate with them. In addition, it is important not to ignore low-dose benzodiazepine use because rarely does a patient on methadone maintenance abuse any drug at "low" doses for more than a short period of time.

Other sedating drugs commonly abused include clonidine, promethazine (Phenergan®), and antihistamines in over-the-counter sleeping and cold remedy preparations. Although there are the obvious problems of toxicity, tolerance, and hemodynamic instability associated with the abuse of these medications at high doses, the incidence of substance-induced depressive symptoms with chronic use does not seem as great as with the benzodiazepines. Patients typically will be sedated, so abuse of these substances is reasonably easy to monitor on a clinical basis. One must remember that some methadone maintenance patients have a high toleration of (or even preference for) sedation, and even frank mental impairment, if they do not need to work or be around others.

Cocaine and other stimulants. Cocaine use can also present as a mood disorder. For example, a patient may describe a severe depressive syndrome after binging on cocaine for several days. This condition can take several days to remit. Cocaine intoxication can present with agitation, hallucinations, paranoia, repetitive behavior patterns, and formication. Again, these symptoms typically remit rapidly after cessation of drug use. The mood effects of other stimulants such as amphetamines can be similar to cocaine's effects.

Other drugs and medications. Psychiatric symptoms in patients on methadone may be related to their methadone dose. For example, complaints of sleeplessness, irritability, and general dysphoria are common if patients are not maintained on an adequate methadone dose, or if they are rapidly metabolizing methadone (e.g., concurrent use of certain medications that alter methadone's metabolism; see Chapter 7). If such symptoms are caused by inadequate dosing, they can be rapidly dissipated with an increase in the methadone dose. This is also an important consideration in patients who are tapering their dose; significant increases in depressive symptoms occur in patients as their methadone dose is tapered (Kanof, Aronson, and Ness 1993). Paradoxically, some patients complain of sleeplessness if they are dosed with methadone too late in the day. In this case, switching to a morning methadone dosing schedule can be helpful.

Marijuana use is common in this patient population, and studies show that mood and anxiety symptoms can be secondary to marijuana use. From a clinical standpoint, we are not aware of significant mood or anxiety disturbances owing to marijuana use in our clinic. This is an area that could benefit from further investigation.

Ongoing complaints of sleeplessness and lethargy, but only mild or inconsistently present mood disturbance, can sometimes be attributed to caffeinism or excessive smoking at night. Often patients do not view these substances as drugs and are sincerely surprised to learn of their potent effects. Caffeine and nicotine can also interfere with the management of depressive or manic symptoms. At times patients need to taper off over-the-counter sleep remedies they believe to be "non-addicting" yet have grown habituated to taking.

Antidepressant Medication Treatment

Studies of the use of antidepressants for the treatment of depression in methadone maintenance patients show outcomes for methadone patients that are no different than those found with the general population. Tricyclic antidepressants (TCAs) are the best studied antidepressant medications in methadone-maintained patients, and methadone maintained patients who have major depression respond well to TCAs (Woody, O'Brien, and Rickels 1975; Nunes et al. 1991, 1998). Adverse effects of TCAs can be problematic, however, especially in conjunction with the effects of methadone. For example, both methadone and TCAs can cause constipation, and adequate bowel hygiene including a high-fiber diet and sometimes a stool softener are important. Dry mouth can be a common side effect with TCAs, and patients need to be counseled to brush their teeth regularly and to avoid sugary snacks and soft drinks to prevent dental caries. Dental problems are quite common in many opioid-dependent patients, and, curiously, some patients believe that methadone causes dental problems (rather than years of personal neglect). (Possibly the analgesic effects of chronic methadone administration may impair early detection of dental problems by patients.)

Increased serum levels of the TCA desipramine when methadone was added to a stable dosing regimen have been reported (Maany et al. 1989). These increases are probably related to methadone's ability to impair the metabolism of TCAs (Kosten et al. 1990). Thus, somewhat lower doses of TCAs may be needed in methadone-maintained patients. A patient who is being stabilized on a TCA should undergo regular testing for TCA blood levels.

Serotonin-specific reuptake inhibitors (fluoxetine, sertraline, paroxetine, fluvoxamine) and other newer antidepressants (bupropion, mirtazapine, venlafaxine, nefazadone) are generally as well tolerated in methadone patients as in the general population. Fluvoxamine can increase methadone blood levels (Table 7.1). Monoamine oxidase inhibitors (MAOIs) are not recommended for use in methadone-maintained patients, and severe and even fatal adverse interactions can occur with the combination of an MAOI and opioids. Furthermore, MAOIs are contraindicated in patients with cocaine and alcohol use disorders.

Methadone itself has mood-altering effects. Many patients feel a mild euphoria one to two hours after methadone dosing and may feel sedated during that time. Patients tapering off methadone maintenance often describe feeling more "alive" and "feeling emotions more intensely" once their methadone dose is in the range of 10–20 mg daily. Conversely, some patients experience a mild dysthymia with chronic low-dose opioids (methadone or other opioids), although higher doses produce the expected euphoric effect.

On the other hand, methadone appears to blunt the emotional pain of depression and may have antidepressant effects in some patients. Opioids have been used for the treatment of refractory depressive disorders. For example, in a study of 10 patients with chronic refractory major depression who were treated with low-dose buprenorphine (a mixed opioid agonist-antagonist also useful in the treatment of opioid dependence), 4 had marked benefit that lasted at least through the end of a six-week trial (Bodkin et al. 1995).

Treatment of Anxiety Disorders

Like depression, complaints of anxiety are common in substance-dependent patients. This complaint is especially common in alcoholics and benzodiazepine-dependent patients, and is also heard in cocaine/stimulant users and users of psychedelics and marijuana. Complaints are usually general, but panic anxiety is sometimes described. Symptoms reminiscent of OCD can be seen with cocaine or stimulant intoxication, although specific anxiety disorders are not usually substance-induced. The same general approach applies to the evaluation of substance-induced anxiety as to the evaluation of substance-induced depression. A period of abstinence is essential; because of the long $t_{1/2}$ of many benzodiazepines, detoxification and then observation on a residential unit for one to two weeks is invaluable for proper assessment. Anxiety symptoms from alcohol use can also have a protracted course, so time in a protected setting can be beneficial for diagnostic purposes.

Once substance-induced symptoms are ruled out, the evaluation and treatment of anxiety should be approached similarly to any nondrug-dependent patient. Using an approach that parallels the one described for depression is useful. Medical causes and drug side effects should be ruled out. The patient's history should be thoroughly examined to determine psychosocial problems that are contributing to anxiety, and cognitive-behavioral strategies should be utilized. If the anxiety is accompanied by a depressive syndrome that is responsive to medication, the depression should be treated aggressively. GAD, panic, or other anxiety disorders are better treated with specific cognitive-behavioral therapy combined with antidepressant or buspirone treatment. Even if good quality cognitive-behavioral therapy is not available, the majority of patients will respond well with medication and supportive counseling. Methadone can have mild, nonspecific anxiolytic effects, but it is not effective for specific anxiety disorders. Benzodiazepines are virtually unusable in the treatment of methadone patients, because in this population, the risk for abuse is far greater than the potential benefit. If the clinician wishes to try a trial of a benzodiazepine in a methadone-maintained patient with a clear anxiety disorder who has no concurrent drug or alcohol use, a benzodiazepine with low abuse potential (e.g., oxazepam) should be used. Benzodiazepines with high abuse potential (e.g., alprazolam, clonazepam) should be avoided, and any use of benzodiazepines in methadone-maintained patients should be considered only under special circumstances.

Treatment of Personality Disorders, Especially APD

Personality disorder (primarily antisocial personality) is the most frequent comorbid disorder in methadone maintenance patients. Various studies have shown that patients with personality disorder respond more poorly to treatment of Axis I disorders, including substance use disorders (Rounsaville et al. 1987; Reich and Green, 1991; Kidorf et al. 1998). Woody et al. (1985) compared methadone maintenance patients with and without APD under two conditions: standard drug counseling and professional psychotherapy. As expected, APD patients did not respond as well to treatment as non-APD patients. However, APD patients with an additional comorbid Axis I disorder improved as much as non-APD patients. This finding suggests that patients with APD may be more likely to benefit from treatment under certain circumstances (e.g., when distressed) than at other times.

Other investigators (Vaillant 1975) have recommended highly structured behavioral programs to improve the effectiveness of treatment for APD patients. Preliminary evidence from a behavioral study that targets patients with APD gives some encouragement in this regard (Brooner et al. 1998). The experimental and control groups were treated using two different, highly structured, behaviorally contingent approaches. Patients improved significantly in both conditions, but there was no significant difference between groups. Management and treatment of patients with severe personality disorder is challenging, but cautious optimism may be warranted in certain subgroups of APD patients or with certain highly structured behavioral interventions.

Treatment of Schizophrenia and Bipolar Disorder

As mentioned, few schizophrenic patients apply for methadone treatment, and rates of schizophrenia in the clinic are similar to rates in the community at large. Several factors may account for these low observed rates, including the need to be timely and to behave properly in the clinic, which can be difficult for many schizophrenic patients. In addition, patients with schizophrenia may not use illicit opioids because the lifestyle of a person dependent on opioids is beyond their capability, given their psychotic symptoms. If they do use illicit opioids, this use may only be sporadic.

Diagnosing psychotic disorder is often more straightforward than diagnosing mood or anxiety disorder. The mean age of patients in methadone treatment is the midthirties, whereas schizophrenia typically has a younger age of onset. Thus, patients with schizophrenia who apply for methadone treatment have typically had a long history of psychiatric treatment to support the diagnosis of schizophrenia. Also, patients with schizophrenia frequently request neuroleptic treatment or find that neuroleptics quickly improve their symptoms. Patients with substance-induced symptoms, on the other hand, are often unwilling to endure routine neuroleptic treatment. Close psychiatric follow-up is needed when a patient with schizophrenia is symptomatic, and therefore, treatment by an on-site psychiatrist or closely involved mental health center is essential.

Although there may be additive sedative effects from concurrent methadone and neuroleptic treatment, in practice, antipsychotics are effective and tolerated at doses similar to those prescribed for patients who are not taking methadone. Clinically, methadone does not appear to decrease the incidence of extrapyramidal adverse effects or akathisia from neuroleptic treatment. However, the general calming effect of chronic methadone may help to stabilize the affective state of the chronically psychotic patient. Interestingly, Schmauss, Yassouridis, and Emrich (1987) found marked antipsychotic effects of buprenorphine, a mixed opioid agonist-antagonist, in schizophrenic patients, so some individuals may benefit from possible antipsychotic effects of other opioids, including methadone. In addition, the regular clinic attendance and routine contact can be stabilizing for these patients. Neuroleptics can also be given at the medication window with methadone if a patient is noncompliant, thereby further integrating care. Not surprisingly, psychotic patients may have additional substance abuse problems, including alcohol dependence. Disulfiram can be used in conjunction with neuroleptic treatment for alcohol-dependent schizophrenic patients if they are judged to comprehend the aversive nature of the disulfiram treatment. Patients need to be monitored for sedation and possible exacerbation of psychosis when initiating disulfiram, and consequently, the risk-to-benefit ratio needs to be carefully weighed (Banys 1988).

Severe bipolar disorder is not common in the methadone clinic, for reasons similar to those for schizophrenia. However, bipolar II disorder (hypomania and major depression) may be seen in the methadone clinic. Typically, bipolar II patients are initially seen with either a depressive, mixed depressive/anxious, or hypomanic presentation. Frequently they have limited or no appreciation of the hypomanic condition, and substance use often escalates during this time. If the abused substance is cocaine, hypomania may go undetected if a patient is not seen by an experienced clinician who will consider a primary psychiatric illness in the differential diagnosis.

Appropriate medication treatment for bipolar disorder begins with mood stabilizers, in particular lithium carbonate and divalproex sodium (Depakote®). Carbamazepine (Tegretol®) is best avoided because of hepatic induction. If carbamazepine is used in a methadone-maintained patient, the patient's methadone dose may need to be raised almost twofold, or the patient may need dosing on a more frequent basis (i.e., twice per day). Neuroleptic medications are needed at times on an adjunctive basis for the treatment of bipolar disorder. Methadone may be of some help in the manic patient, through its general calming effect. Benzodiazepines are contraindicated, including clonazepam (which has not shown specific antimanic activity in any case).

Attention-Deficit Hyperactivity Disorder

Although some reports suggest that rates of ADHD in substance-abusing patients may be high, there is limited information about rates of ADHD among methadone maintenance patients. Not infrequently, patients may self-diagnose ADHD either as a way of explaining their erratic behaviors to themselves or in a clear attempt to seek drugs. When establishing the diagnosis of ADHD in a methadone patient, it is important to determine the necessary childhood behaviors, using corroborating informants (such as the patient's parents, or old school or medical records, if possible). Because most adult patients with childhood histories of ADHD do not require specific, ongoing psychiatric care (particularly the use of medications), it is important to observe the patient free of abused drugs for some time to assess any impairment before considering the use of medications.

For significant, impairing symptoms of ADHD (prominent distractibility or hyperactivity), the first pharmacologic intervention should be either a TCA, bupropion (Wellbutrin®), or venlafaxine (Effexor®). If a patient fails to respond to one of these medications, then pemoline (Cylert®) should be considered. And finally, if pemoline is unsuccessful a course of either methylphenidate (Ritalin®) or amphetamine may be effective. Amphetamine abuse is on the rise, so use of a stimulant to treat ADHD in methadone patients should be reserved for the most symptomatic patients who are resistant to nonabusable medications and who are otherwise doing well in treatment.

Summary

Psychiatric diagnosis and treatment of patients with severe substance use disorder is extremely challenging. Studies indicate high rates of co-morbid psychiatric disorder in these patients, particularly personality disorders. In addition, high rates of HIV risk behavior and poor outcome are more common in patients with comorbid disorders. Because of the intensive needs of these patients, a structured, consistent treatment setting is essential. Psychiatric, substance abuse, and medical treatment must be integrated for optimal outcome. Careful assessment of psychiatric symptoms when in a drug-free state is also important so that appropriate additional therapy can be offered to maximize the opportunity for rehabilitation. Patients with independent comorbid psychiatric disorders need access to psychiatric services combined with appropriate, individualized treatment planning for optimal response to substance abuse treatment.

References

Abbott P.J., Weller S.B., Walker S.R. 1994. Psychiatric disorders of opioid addicts entering treatment: preliminary data. *J. Addict. Dis.* 13:1–11.

American Psychiatric Association (APA). 1994. *Diagnostic and Statistical Manual of Mental Disorders, Fourth Edition.* American Psychiatric Association, Washington, DC.

Banys P.J. 1988. The clinical use of disulfiram (Antabuse): a review. *Psychoactive Drugs* 20:243–61.

Beck A.T., Ward C.H., Mendelson M. 1961. An inventory for measuring depression. *Arch. Gen. Psychiatry* 4:53–63.

Bodkin J.A., Zornberg G.L., Lukas S.E., Cole J.O. 1995. Buprenorphine treatment of refractory depression. *J. Clin. Psychopharmacol.* 15:49–57.

Brooner R.K., Kidorf M.S., King V.L., Stoller K.B. 1998. Preliminary evidence of improved treatment response in antisocial drug abusers. *Drug Alcohol Depend.* 49:249–60.

Brooner R.K., King V.L., Kidorf M., Schmidt C.W. Jr., Bigelow G.E. 1997. Psychiatric and substance use comorbidity among treatment-seeking opioid abusers. *Arch. Gen. Psychiatry* 54:71–80.

Brown S.A., Schuckit M.A. 1988. Changes in depression in abstinent alcoholics. *J. Stud. Alcohol* 49:412–17.

Cottler L.B., Compton W.M., Mager D., Spitznagel E.L., Janca A. 1992. Post-traumatic stress disorder among substance users from the general population. *Am J. Psychiatry* 149:664–70.

Derogatis L.R. 1983. SCL-90-R. *Administration, Scoring and Procedures Manual II,* 2nd ed. Clinical Psychometric Research, Baltimore.

Eyre S.L., Rounsaville B.J., Kleber H.D. 1982. History of childhood hyperactivity in a clinic population of opiate addicts. *J. Nerv. Ment. Dis.* 170:522–29.

First M.B., Spitzer R.L., Gibbon M., Williams J.B.W. 1995. Structured Clinical Interview for DSM-IV Axis I Disorders. Biometrics Research Department, New York State Psychiatric Institute, New York, NY.

Kanof P.D., Aronson M.J., Ness R. 1993. Organic mood syndrome associated with detoxification from methadone maintenance. *Am. J. Psychiatry* 150:423–28.

Kaplan H.I., Sadock B.J. 1999. *Comprehensive Textbook of Psychiatry/VII,* 7th ed. Williams & Wilkins, Baltimore.

Khantzian E.J., Treece C. 1985. DSM-III psychiatric diagnosis of narcotic addicts. *Arch. Gen. Psychiatry* 42:1067–71.

Kidorf M.S., Brooner R.K., King V.L., Stoller K.B. 1998. Antisocial personality disorder and treatment outcome in opioid dependent outpatients. Paper presented at the 60th Annual Scientific Meeting of College on Problems of Drug Dependence, Phoenix, AZ, June 13–18.

King V.L., Mirsky A.F., Kidorf M.S., Brooner R.K. 1998. Psychiatric comorbidity and substance abuse treatment outcome in methadone maintenance patients with a history of ADHD. In: Harris L.S., ed. Problems of Drug Dependence, 1997, Proceedings of the 59th Annual Scientific Meeting of College on Problems of Drug Dependence, National Institute on Drug Abuse Research Monograph, vol. 178. U.S. Government Printing Office, Washington, DC, p. 129.

Kosten T.R., Gawin F.H., Morgan C., Nelson J.C., Jatlow P. 1990. Evidence for altered desipramine disposition in methadone-maintained patients treated for cocaine abuse. *Am. J. Drug Alcohol Abuse* 16:329–36.

Kosten T.R., Rounsaville B.J., Kleber H.D. 1982. DSM-III personality disorders in opiate addicts. *Comprehen. Psychiatry* 23:572–81.

———. 1986a. A 2.5 year follow-up of treatment retention and reentry among opioid addicts. *J. Subst. Abuse Treat.* 3:181–89.

———. 1986b. A 2.5-year follow-up of depression, life crises, and treatment effects on abstinence among opioid addicts. *Arch. Gen. Psychiatry* 43:733–38.

Maany I., Dhopesh V., Arndt I.O., Burke W., Woody G., O'Brien C.P. 1989. Increase in desipramine serum levels associated with methadone treatment. *Am. J. Psychiatry* 146:1611–13.

McLellan A.T., Luborsky L., Woody G.E., O'Brien C.P. 1980. An improved diagnostic evaluation instrument for substance abuse patients: the Addiction Severity Index. *J. Nerv. Ment. Dis.* 168:26–33.

Miller N.S. 1993. Comorbidity of psychiatric and alcohol/drug disorders: interactions and independent status. *J. Addict. Dis.* 12:5–16.

Nunes E.V., Quitkin F.M., Brady R., Stewart J.W. 1991. Imipramine treatment of methadone maintenance patients with affective disorder and illicit drug use. *Am. J. Psychiatry* 148:667–69.

Nunes E.V., Quitkin F.M., Donovan S.J., Deliyannides D., Ocepek-Welikson K., Koenig T., Brady R., McGrath P.J., Woody G. 1998. Imipramine treatment of opiate-dependent patients with depressive disorders. *Arch. Gen. Psychiatry* 55:153–60.

Reich J.H., Green A.I. 1991. Effect of personality disorders on outcome of treatment. *J. Nerv. Ment. Dis.* 179:74–82.

Robins L.N., Cottler L.B., Bucholz K., Compton W.M. 1995. *Diagnostic Interview Schedule (DIS) for DSM-IV.* Washington University School of Medicine, St. Louis, MO.

Robins L.N., Helzer J.E., Weissman M.M., Orvaschel H., Gruenbert E., Burke J.D. Jr., Regier D.A. 1985. Lifetime prevalence of specific psychiatric disorders in three sites. *Arch. Gen. Psychiatry* 41:949–58.

Rounsaville B.J., Dolinsky Z.S., Babor T.F., Meyer R.E. 1987. Psychopathology as a predictor of treatment outcome in alcoholics. *Arch. Gen. Psychiatry* 44:505–13.

Rounsaville B.J., Kosten T.R., Weissman M.M., Kleber H.D. 1986. Prognostic significance of psychopathology in treated opiate addicts. *Arch. Gen. Psychiatry* 43:739–45.

Rounsaville B.J., Weissman M.M., Crits-Christoph K., Wilber C., Kleber H.D. 1982a. Diagnosis and symptoms of depression in opiate addicts. *Arch. Gen. Psychiatry* 39:151–56.

Rounsaville B.J., Weissman M.M., Kleber H.D., Wilber C. 1982b. Heterogeneity of psychiatric diagnosis in treated opiate addicts. *Arch. Gen. Psychiatry* 39:161–66.

Rutherford M.J., Cacciola J.S., Alterman A.I. 1994. Relationships of personality disorders with problem severity in methadone patients. *Drug Alcohol Depend.* 35:69–76.

Schmauss C., Yassouridis A., Emrich H.M. 1987. Antipsychotic effect of buprenorphine in schizophrenia. *Am. J. Psychiatry* 144:1340–42.

Schuckit M.A., Monteiro M.G. 1988. Alcoholism, anxiety and depression. *Br. J. Addictions* 83:1373–80.

Strain E.C., Brooner R.K., Bigelow G.E. 1991. Clustering of multiple substance use and psychiatric diagnoses in opiate addicts. *Drug Alcohol Depend.* 27:127–34.

Strain E.C., Stitzer M.L., Bigelow G.E. 1991. Early treatment time course of depressive symptoms in opiate addicts. *J. Nerv. Ment. Dis.* 179:215–21.

Tasman A., Kay J., Lieberman J. 1997. *Psychiatry.* W.B. Saunders, Philadelphia.

Vaillant G.E. 1975. Sociopathy as a human process: a viewpoint. *Arch. Gen. Psychiatry* 32:178–83.

Woody G.E., Luborsky L., McLellan A.T., O'Brien C.P., Beck A.T., Blaine J., Herman I., Hole A. 1983. Psychotherapy for opiate addicts: does it help? *Arch. Gen. Psychiatry* 40:639–45.

Woody G.E., McLellan A.T., Luborsky L., O'Brien C.P. 1985. Sociopathy and psychotherapy outcome. *Arch. Gen. Psychiatry* 42:1081–86.

Woody G.E., O'Brien C.P., Rickels K. 1975. Depression and anxiety in heroin addicts: a placebo-controlled study of doxepin in combination with methadone. *Am. J. Psychiatry* 132:447–50.

9

INTEGRATING PSYCHOSOCIAL SERVICES WITH METHADONE TREATMENT

Behaviorally Contingent Pharmacotherapy

Michael Kidorf, Ph.D., Van L. King, M.D.,
and Robert K. Brooner, Ph.D.

Drug abuse treatment programs offering methadone or LAAM are ideal settings in which to incorporate counseling and other psychosocial services that can maximize the effectiveness of medication treatments. In addition, they are valuable sites for evaluating methods by which these nonpharmacologic services can maximize the effectiveness of medication. The typical structure of methadone treatment, which involves long-term intervention with frequent clinic attendance, supports the feasibility of implementing nonpharmacologic treatments. Indeed, the necessity of counseling to address the complex problems of drug abusers was recognized by the founders of methadone treatment, and counseling has been a standard part of this treatment modality since its inception. Nevertheless, the availability of counseling does not guarantee that it will be regularly or effectively used by patients, and patient compliance with counseling is a highly pertinent service-delivery issue in methadone treatment.

Psychosocial treatments are useful for addressing the myriad of problems that drug abusers may bring with them to treatment. Most treatment-seeking opioid abusers engage in extensive use of nonopioid drugs, most have severe family and social problems including employment difficulties, and many have comorbid psychiatric disorders (e.g., Havassy, Hall, and Wasserman 1991; Brooner et al. 1997). These are problems that can respond to supplemental, nonpharmacologic interventions, and the structure of methadone treatment provides an opportunity to expose patients to various psychosocial interventions, to assess intensively response, and to monitor this response over prolonged periods of time.

However, psychosocial services are surprisingly underutilized in methadone treatment. Although poor funding often limits a program's services, many patients fail to attend even once-per-week counseling sessions. The failure of patients to receive adequate counseling is costly to both patients and treatment programs. Inadequately treated patients often continue to use drugs during treatment, and in some programs, this leads to eventual discharge (e.g., Gill, Nolimal, and Crowley 1992). Staff can become highly demoralized when surrounded by patients who continue using drugs, and both patients and staff may come to the mistaken conclusion that treatment is ineffective.

These issues associated with the nonpharmacologic aspects of methadone treatment are addressed in this chapter. Specifically, the purpose of this chapter is twofold. It begins with a review of evidence that counseling and group therapies are effective treatments for methadone patients. Although these treatments *are* effective, they are only effective if patients comply with such treatments. This issue of compliance with the nonpharmacologic aspects of methadone treatment is a prominent, common difficulty in methadone programs. Thus, the second aim of this chapter is to describe a service-delivery model designed to encourage patients to attend scheduled counseling sessions consistently. This model, Behaviorally Contingent Pharmacotherapy (BCP), involves the structured integration of pharmacologic treatments (i.e., methadone), verbal-expressive forms of therapy, and simple behavioral interventions to enhance attendance at counseling sessions. It conceptualizes drug use as a highly specific, goal-directed behavior motivated by the expected positive consequences of use (McHugh and Slavney 1998), such as temporary feelings of tranquillity or euphoria, heightened pleasure from social activities, and cognitive dampening of self-doubts and ruminations over life problems. Drug use is then a decision on the part of the individual—positive consequences outweighing negative consequences—rather than simply a behavior driven by uncontrollable "cravings" or symptoms of physical dependence. Methadone targets symptoms associated with physical dependence (i.e., withdrawal) and reduces the reinforcing effects of heroin use through cross tolerance, whereas BCP concurrently focuses on helping patients recognize the results from their decision to continue using drugs and aids the patient and staff by providing a clear set of consequences associated with continued drug use. This approach emphasizes the patient as the central agent capable and responsible for continued drug use or abstinence and is a highly effective service-delivery model that can be implemented within the usual budgetary constraints of existing programs (Brooner et al. 1996).

INDIVIDUAL COUNSELING

Individual counseling has long been a routine component of opioid substitution treatment, although many programs describe these interventions as ancillary to the dispensing of methadone or LAAM. Ball and Ross (1991) provide normative data on the counseling practices of six methadone programs. They found that about 50 percent of the patients in these programs received at least one 20- to 60-minute counseling session per week. In addition, patient-to-counselor caseloads ranged from 25:1, which can enhance meaningful integration of pharmacologic and psychosocial treatments, to 70:1, which shifts the primary focus of treatment onto the medication. Ten types of individual counseling services were identified in the Ball and Ross study, ranging from initial intake sessions to brief (often unscheduled) counseling contacts and more specialized psychologic and vocational services.

More than a cursory outline of the responsibilities of individual counselors is beyond the scope of this chapter. The reader is referred to a manual published by the CSAT (Kauffman and Woody 1995) that provides a useful and comprehensive approach for counselors involved in the treatment of opioid abusers receiving methadone treatment. Briefly, counselors at the start of treatment should assess patients for patterns of polydrug use and identify problems in other life areas, such as housing, social, family, legal, and occupational functioning. The assessment should also lead to a good appreciation of the individuality of patients and the historical and cultural influences reflected in the logic and purpose of their behavior. Effective counseling also requires frequent review of the treatment plan and any associated contingencies. This work is powerfully enhanced by repeated education about the rationale and purpose for the treatment plan and any changes in it during the course of therapy. Careful education about the treatment plan can reduce patients' conception of treatment as a mysterious force beyond their control or influence.

Counselors should work with patients to identify problem areas and prioritize them in the treatment plan in order to establish a rational and orderly approach to their resolution. Cessation of all drug use should be the primary treatment goal; other problem areas (e.g., employment, familial) may be most successfully addressed following abstinence. Nevertheless, problems presenting significant barriers to recovery (e.g., excessive idle time resulting from unemployment) might be addressed concurrently with the initial goal of complete abstinence. Many patients attempt to find single solutions to multiple overlapping problems, which often leads to failure and demoralization, and yields further "evidence" to the patient that counseling is useless. Counselors should limit this problem by helping patients separate complex overlapping problems into smaller units, which increases the likelihood of success. These recommendations are supported by available literature indicating that counselors are most effective when they engage patients in regular counseling early in the treatment process (Simpson et al. 1995), establish good therapeutic rapport (Allison and Hubbard 1985), and remain organized and consistent in their clinical approach to problem identification and resolution (McLellan et al. 1988).

A present-oriented counseling focus using cognitive-behavioral and problem-solving strategies is a useful framework for administering individual counseling. Counselors should utilize nonconfrontational and supportive techniques with patients struggling to meet the demands of the treatment program. Several good models for this orientation are available, but the overall approach is best summarized in the book *Motivational Interviewing* (Miller and Rollnick 1991). This book outlines a number of motivational principles that provide an excellent context for behavior change. Equally important is the need for counselors to express empathy through reflective listening and to communicate respect for the suffering endured by patients and the conflict over continued use evident among those seeking treatment. It is not difficult to express appropriate respect to patients. Respect is easily communicated by listening closely to all concerns, by providing timely responses to questions, and by keeping all scheduled appointments or contacting patients in advance when scheduling changes are required.

How effective is individual counseling for opioid abusers receiving methadone therapy? This question was addressed in a study by McLellan et al. (1993) at the University of Pennsylvania. Opioid abusers entering treatment ($N = 92$), all of whom received a steady methadone dose of 60–90 mg over a six-month study period, were randomly assigned to one of three counseling conditions: methadone only (low intensity), methadone plus standard counseling (medium intensity), and methadone plus standard counseling enhanced by other clinical services (high intensity). Counselors of low-intensity patients had minimal contact with patients and neither the counselor nor the patients received weekly urinalysis results. In the medium-intensity condition, counselors scheduled one session per week for patients over the first month, and increased or decreased the rate of counseling based on weekly urinalysis results. They could also award take-home privileges to those who were drug free and employed. Counselors of high-intensity patients not only scheduled individual counseling sessions in a manner similar to those providing medium intensity but also referred patients to other professional services available within the clinic, including sessions with a psychiatrist, employment counseling, and family therapy.

Data were not presented on the number of scheduled or attended counseling sessions by patients in each group. Instead, a brief interview measure called the Treatment Services Review (McLellan et al. 1992) was used to assess the number of times various content areas (e.g., drug use, employment, psychiatric, legal) were discussed with staff. The counseling manipulation was delivered as intended; that is, high-intensity patients discussed both drug use and psychiatric issues with staff more frequently than medium-intensity patients, and medium-intensity patients discussed these issues with staff more frequently than low-intensity patients. Results showed that counseling produced significant differences in treatment outcome. For example, patients receiving high-intensity services had greater rates of consecutive weeks of opioid and cocaine abstinence, as determined from urine testing (Table 9.1). Some patients in the low-intensity condition (30%) performed well without counseling. However, most performed poorly, and needed to be therapeutically transferred to the medium-intensity condition after three months. Patients transferred to the medium-intensity condition showed significant reductions in both cocaine and opiate use after only four weeks of more-intensive counseling.

The results of this study show that counseling can dramatically improve the outcome of methadone treatment. Note, however, that reductions in drug use observed in the study were attained even though the number of

Table 9.1 **Effect of Psychosocial Services in Methadone Treatment on Patient Abstinence**

Group[a]	Percentage of Patients with Opiate Abstinence[b]			Percentage of Patients with Cocaine Abstinence[b]		
	8 weeks	12 weeks	16 weeks	8 weeks	12 weeks	16 weeks
Low intensity	31	22	0	31	25	22
Medium intensity	100	59	28	89	59	34
High intensity	94	74	55	94	74	45

Source: Adapted from McLellan et al. (1993).
[a]Refers to the level of nonpharmacologic treatment services provided; see text for details.
[b]Consecutive weeks of abstinence, as determined by urine testing.

counseling sessions received by patients in the medium- and high-intensity groups seemed modest. High-intensity patients had an average of only nine drug use discussions per month, and discussion of other important topic areas (e.g., vocational, social, psychiatric) was even less frequent. Because patients were not required to attend the additional counseling services, the continued drug use in both the medium- and high-intensity groups may have resulted partly from failure to access the additional services offered in the study. It is therefore possible that the favorable outcomes achieved in this study could be improved if patients were to attend extra counseling sessions each week.

GROUP COUNSELING AND SKILLS TRAINING

Many methadone programs offer group counseling services. Groups are useful for educating patients about drug abuse and the associated risk of HIV infection, about 12-step programming, and for providing general support and the opportunity for discussion. Furthermore, group therapy is an ideal way to deliver skills training material efficiently and effectively. Well-written manuals are available on many group therapy topics and can be used by counselors to improve the quality and consistency of material presented in group formats. Traditionally, optimal group size is 5–10 patients (e.g., Yalom 1975), but this number can be increased to about 14 when groups are structured and skills oriented and the counselor is experienced in group-based interventions. Group counseling is an extremely cost-effective intervention that allows many patients to receive treatment at one time. When possible, group patients heterogeneously in order to increase interest and patient involvement, for example, male and female patients who are still using drugs with those who are recently abstinent. It is important that basic group rules (e.g., arriving on time, listening to others, giving constructive feedback) are routinely reviewed and consistently followed in order to maximize the effectiveness of group counseling. Despite the general popularity of this intervention, relatively few data exist on the efficacy of group counseling for patients in opioid substitution treatment. There is sufficient evidence in work with alcohol-dependent patients, however, to warrant the general view that group-based interventions are effective conduits to behavior change, especially groups that enhance skills for abstinence and coping with stressful life events (see Chaney 1989). In fact, group-based coping-skills training may be particularly effective with patients exhibiting high levels of psychiatric severity and antisocial behaviors (Cooney et al. 1991).

Relapse Prevention and Coping-Skills Training

Coping-skills training is perhaps best conducted in a group setting. The group leader asks participants to identify a number of "high-risk" occasions, especially those that focus on interpersonal stressors (e.g., interpersonal conflict, pressures to drink) and helps the group generate potential responses to these situations. After an appropriate coping response has been identified, the group leader teaches the new skill via role playing. Patients model the group leader's behavior and subsequently receive feedback from the leader and other group participants. The use of videotaping is particularly helpful for providing feedback and maintaining patient interest. We have found it useful to use situations that naturally occur in the clinic setting as the content for role playing. For instance, patients might role-play situations in which they are informed that their urine test was drug positive or that their clinic privileges were temporarily withdrawn. After the patients have completed the group training, the group leader and other staff are in a position to observe directly the patients' performance of the new skills in the face of conflicts naturally occurring in the clinic.

The primary aim of coping-skills groups is to provide patients with the cognitive and social tools essential to abstain from drug use. Recently, there has been interest in the development of groups that teach relapse prevention, thereby targeting individuals either who are abstinent on a stable or decreasing methadone dose or who have successfully detoxified from methadone and are drug free. Implicit to this approach is the consideration of opioid dependence as a chronic relapsing disorder that requires proactive and ongoing treatment. In fact, it could be argued that many patients make maximal use of the group content when they are drug free and have achieved some stability, though often at this time patients believe that their work is done and "reward" themselves by leaving the group. This problem is often reinforced by staff who further withdraw support once the patient is drug free. Continued staff encouragement of patients to pursue treatment even during periods of abstinence is consistent with the original intention of relapse-prevention models (Marlatt and Gordon 1985), which was to help break the cycle of relapse by identifying and changing internal and external factors contributing to the decision to use drugs.

Khantzian et al. (1992), for instance, describe a type of group therapy (i.e., Modified Group Therapy for Substance Abusers) that utilizes a psychodynamic approach to help patients understand how their psychologic vulnerabilities and emotional reactions affect the probability of relapse. Group leaders communicate empathy and encourage the sharing of experiences to help patients manage feelings of isolation and low self-worth.

Four major areas of group focus include self-care, relationship conflicts, self-esteem, and affect regulation. Using a more behavioral approach, McAuliffe (1990) developed a relapse-prevention group based on a conditioning model of addiction. Patients in this group learn alternative responses to environmental stimuli that trigger decisions to use opioids. Group members also attend self-help meetings and participate in social activities with group members and former drug abusers who are currently abstinent. McAuliffe (1990) published evidence for the effectiveness of this group in the United States and in Hong Kong, although a host of methodological confounds (including the lack of appropriate control groups) makes the results difficult to interpret. Finally, a recently developed program (Rawson et al. 1990) that combines coping skills and relapse-control training and provides guided instruction on the neuropsychologic consequences of recovery (e.g., withdrawal, craving) has shown some efficacy (Magura et al. 1994).

Job-Skills Training

In addition to modifying directly drug use behavior, an important goal for any type of drug abuse treatment is to help patients initiate lifestyle changes consistent with abstinence. Although this could be accomplished indirectly through coping-skills and relapse-prevention training, a more direct route is to convey the skills necessary to pursue treatment goals that have been traditionally associated with drug abstinence and stability. One of the more important lifestyle changes for many opioid abusers is to find and maintain employment. Full-time employment provides necessary structure and responsibility and, not surprisingly, is associated with good drug abuse treatment outcome (McLellan et al. 1981; Kidorf, Stitzer, and Brooner 1994). Opioid abusers represent a particularly good population for teaching job-seeking skills. In a study of opioid-dependent outpatients, not knowing how to look for work was a primary factor differentiating patients who did and did not secure employment within a three-year period (Hermalin et al. 1990). Furthermore, the criminal and drug use history of opioid abusers tends to render them relatively unattractive to potential employers, and their occupational interests often fall notably short of their academic skills or employment experience (Silverman et al. 1995). These factors probably cause these individuals considerable frustration in their pursuit of employment and might further serve to reduce the likelihood of their continuing to search for jobs on their own.

Hall et al. (1981) showed that drug abusers could be taught skills that led to successful employment. They developed a job-seekers workshop that was tested in two groups of heroin addicts. In this study, methadone maintenance patients ($N = 60$) were assigned either to a job-seekers skills training group or to a job-seeking information control group. Patients were recruited from four different drug abuse clinics and had expressed interest in attaining employment. Patients in the job-seekers skills training group attended group workshops that taught skills for networking and using the telephone, completing applications, and responding to questions during job interviews. The primary dependent measure was employment, which was generally verified through paycheck or time clock stubs. The results showed that more experimental subjects (52%) than control subjects (30%) were employed at the three-month follow-up. This difference was not significant owing to the small sample but nevertheless demonstrates that a behavioral skills program can help many motivated patients attain employment. The data do not indicate, however, the impact of this treatment on patients who might be more ambivalent about pursuing employment. That only 60 patients were identified across four treatment programs suggests that the majority of unemployed patients were uninterested in pursuing enhanced support for attaining work.

In sum, group counseling can be highly effective and easily applied in community treatment clinics. Many patients can be treated at the same time, which is especially helpful because most community clinics have limited resources and large patient-to-staff ratios. Group counseling with drug abusers is perhaps most effective when it is structured (i.e., manualized) and skills oriented, two features that make groups relatively easy for counselors to administer. Although the emphasis on skills training is based on the more established alcoholism literature, recent studies (e.g., Hall et al. 1981; Magura et al. 1994) provide support for its effectiveness with opioid abusers. Compliance with group counseling can be a problem; however, several studies have shown that attendance can be dramatically improved by offering limited methadone take-home privileges specifically based on counseling attendance. It is also important to note that high-intensity group counseling has been tolerated as well as less intensive care. Thus, it appears that methadone patients will meet the treatment expectations established by the clinic.

INDIVIDUAL PSYCHOTHERAPY

We describe psychotherapy here as a form of verbal-expressive therapy in which a trained individual develops a professional relationship with a patient and uses psychologic principles to modify or remove problematic thoughts, feelings, and behaviors. In many respects, opioid abusers are good candidates for psychotherapy. Virtually all patients entering treatment are highly conflicted and demoralized by their continued use of drugs despite compelling reasons to stop. They respond to treatment staff with considerable trepidation, often avoiding the very treatments that can provide explanations for their continued motivations to use drugs. These problems are not unique to drug abusers. Patients with other psychiatric problems (e.g., eating disorders) present with similar clinical features. The psychotherapeutic techniques used to help those patients can also be helpful to patients struggling with drug dependence (e.g., Andersen 1984).

Yet there has been little systematic study of the effectiveness of psychotherapy with drug abusers. The reasons for this may be attributed to both the patients and the treatment providers. First, opioid abusers are usually uninterested in pursuing psychotherapy. This is apparently a long-standing problem; almost four decades ago Nyswander et al. (1958) commented on the small percentage of drug abusers in the New York City area who responded to the availability of professional psychotherapy. Second, opioid abusers, by definition, engage in behaviors such as drug use and drug seeking that strongly compete with therapy attendance and subsequent development of a therapeutic relationship. Many also exhibit cognitive impairment and other deficits that limit the processing of therapeutic content. Third, many opioid abusers lack the financial resources necessary to complete successfully a course of psychotherapy. Finally, psychologists, psychiatrists, and other mental health professionals typically do not receive the necessary training required to conduct psychotherapy with this population.

In the late 1970s NIDA funded two large-scale studies to evaluate the effects of psychotherapy on the treatment outcome of opioid abusers receiving methadone treatment. These studies were conducted at the University of Pennsylvania (Woody et al. 1983) and at Yale University (Rounsaville et al. 1983). In the Woody et al. (1983) study, 110 patients were recruited and randomly assigned to one of three treatment groups: supportive-expressive therapy plus standard drug counseling (SE), cognitive-behavioral therapy plus standard drug counseling (CB), and standard drug counseling alone (DC). Supportive-expressive therapy (e.g., Luborsky 1984) is an analytically oriented psychotherapy that uses patient-therapist interactions to identify relationship themes. Cognitive-behavioral therapy (e.g., Beck 1976) is a directive psychotherapeutic technique in which the therapist helps a patient identify and modify those thought processes and decisions that result in the continuation of problem behaviors.

These researchers were careful to integrate the delivery of psychotherapy within the normal routine of methadone delivery and counseling services typically offered at the clinic. For instance, therapists worked in offices located at the clinic, remained in communication with the study patients' counselors, and promptly contacted patients who missed scheduled appointments. The overall attendance rates to the specialized therapy sessions were modest despite efforts by the staff to make them easily accessible. Across conditions, patients attended approximately 57 percent of the scheduled counseling sessions.

The results showed that, on average, patients in all treatment groups improved in most outcome measures over time. The psychotherapy conditions appeared to be particularly effective in modifying nonsubstance-related treatment outcome variables. Patients in both the SE and CB conditions, for example, reported significant alleviation of psychologic symptoms; patients in the SE condition also showed improvement in employment status. Many of these gains were maintained throughout the six-month follow-up, but the magnitude of these effects clearly diminished over time. Small reductions in self-reported drug use were observed in each treatment condition, although any between-group differences were not sustained by the six-month follow-up.

The researchers conducted a number of additional analyses with this data set to evaluate the effect of individual difference variables on treatment outcome. In one subanalysis, patients were grouped according to severity of psychiatric symptoms (high or low) based on severity scores derived from symptom report checklists administered at baseline. Low-severity patients benefited whether or not they were referred to supplemental psychotherapy. Those with the highest psychiatric severity, however, achieved significantly better outcome only when counseling was enhanced by professional psychotherapy. In another reanalysis of this study, patients were grouped according to psychiatric diagnosis (Woody et al. 1985): (1) opioid dependence only ($N = 16$); (2) opioid dependence and depression ($N = 16$); (3) opioid dependence and depression and antisocial personality disorder ($N = 17$); and (4) opioid dependence and antisocial personality disorder ($N = 13$). Patients in the first three groups demonstrated improvement in areas of substance use and psychiatric functioning, whereas those with "pure" APD evidenced only minimal gains from psychotherapy.

One confound in this study is that patients in the psychotherapy conditions were exposed to more counseling (i.e., specialized therapy plus routine counseling) than those in the comparison condition (i.e., routine counseling alone). Woody et al. (1995) remedied this problem by designing a follow-up study in which patients were randomized into two different groups: standard counseling plus supportive-expressive psychotherapy

($N = 57$) or standard counseling plus supplemental drug counseling ($N = 27$). Both groups evidenced improvement in a number of outcome variables, and the experimental group exhibited less cocaine use via random urinalysis results. Furthermore, treatment gains in the psychotherapy group were maintained over six months, whereas positive outcomes achieved in the control condition diminished over time.

In the psychotherapy study conducted by Rounsaville et al. (1983), enrollment was limited to male opioid abusers with another Axis I psychiatric disorder, excluding schizophrenia and bipolar disorder. These researchers experienced considerably more difficulty than Woody et al. (1983) in attracting patients to the study; only about 5 percent of eligible patients agreed to participate. Those who consented were randomly assigned to short-term interpersonal therapy ([IPT]; $N = 37$) or to a comparison condition ($N = 35$). The primary goal of IPT (Klerman et al. 1984) is to help patients develop more effective strategies for dealing with interpersonal problems. Patients assigned to the comparison condition were referred to a once-per-month meeting with a psychiatrist. Patients in both conditions attended other scheduled individual and group counseling sessions; however, overall compliance rates were not reported.

In contrast to the Woody et al. (1983) study, the specialized psychotherapy was not well integrated into the usual procedures of the clinic. The settings in which the routine methadone treatment and specialized psychotherapy was provided were physically separated. This separation may have affected both recruitment into the study and psychotherapy attendance rates for those who chose to participate. Indeed, an extremely high study dropout rate was observed: only 38 percent of the IPT group and 54 percent of the comparison group completed the six-month study. Most of the treatment outcome data followed suit and compared unfavorably to the results of the Woody et al. (1983) clinical trial. Although patients in both study conditions demonstrated clinical improvement over time, only a few meaningful between-group differences emerged. In addition, unlike the reanalysis done by Woody et al. (1985), in which differences by psychiatric diagnosis were found, this study found no evidence of individual differences in response to the treatment interventions.

Several tentative conclusions can be drawn from these studies. The results offer mixed support for the efficacy of psychotherapy in the treatment of opioid abusers. Both of the Woody et al. (1983, 1995) studies demonstrate that the inclusion of psychotherapy is associated with reductions in drug use and psychiatric symptom reporting, and that treatment gains are often sustained after discontinuing the service. This latter result supports the findings of studies with other populations of substance abusers that have shown the long-term benefits of specialized psychotherapy (e.g., Carroll et al. 1994). Although similar results were not obtained in the Rounsaville et al. (1983) study, the specialized therapy services were offered outside of the routine methadone treatment clinic, and results may have been confounded by this procedure. Finally, it must be noted that the effects of specialized therapy will likely be proportional to the rate of exposure to the treatment. The positive outcomes in the Woody et al. (1983, 1995) studies were obtained despite poor overall compliance with the psychotherapy intervention. The patients in the Rounsaville et al. (1983) study received even less of the planned psychotherapy. These facts suggest that improvement from specialized psychotherapies could be enhanced by ensuring that patients receive a larger "dose" of the treatment.

FAMILY-BASED THERAPIES

The families of opioid abusers are rarely included in the treatment process in any meaningful or structured way. This is particularly unfortunate because both the family of origin and the immediate family may provide powerful environmental incentives for reduction in drug use. Many of the reasons for underutilization of family-based therapies are similar to those responsible for the limited use of professional individual psychotherapy. Drug abuse counselors are rarely trained to provide marital or family interventions, and professionally trained therapists are costly, making their services unattainable under the existing budgets of most programs. It is likewise difficult to refer patients to other settings routinely offering family services because relatively few patients have adequate insurance or money to pay for such treatment. The general reluctance of both patients and family members to become involved in family-based treatments (Stanton and Todd 1982) is an additional disincentive for implementing these interventions with opioid abusers; it is not feasible to expend the financial resources of a program in order to offer family therapy if no one will participate. This is an unfortunate situation because available research shows that including family members in drug abuse treatment has many potential benefits.

The goal of family therapy is to improve the psychologic functioning of the family system (or couple), thereby positively influencing other treatment outcome variables such as drug use and treatment retention. In this section, we first present the two most widely used family-based interventions: family therapy and conjoint (marital) therapy. We conclude by presenting a third option that involves bringing drug-free significant others (including family members) into treatment to act as "community monitors" of patient compliance with the treatment plan.

Family Therapy

Kauffman (1989) presents four models of family psychotherapy: (1) structural-strategic therapy (Minuchin 1974); (2) behavior therapy; (3) systems therapy (Bowen 1971); and (4) psychodynamic therapy. Of these models, structural-strategic therapy has received the most empirical support among opioid abusers (Stanton and Todd 1982). Structural-strategic therapy is a short-term, goal-oriented, nonconfrontational intervention that helps families develop new adaptive strategies for dealing with recurrent problems. The therapist is responsible for devising a treatment plan that includes objective outcome criteria, including reducing drug use and enhancing participation in constructive activity. Kauffman (1989) describes several other structural strategies that might be used by the therapist to enhance the effectiveness of family treatment, including affiliating with the family system, transforming complicated problems into workable goals, encouraging patients to speak directly to each other (and not about each other), and respecting patients' feelings and family boundaries.

In a study of the efficacy of a structural-strategic approach, Stanton and Todd (1982) randomly assigned young male opioid abusers (less than 36 years old) receiving methadone substitution to one of four treatment groups. In the paid family therapy condition ($N = 21$), each family member received $5 for attending therapy sessions and received extra money if the patient submitted drug-negative urine samples. In the unpaid family therapy condition ($N = 25$), family members were encouraged to participate, but monetary incentives were not given for attendance or abstinence. Two additional comparison conditions were used: a family movie treatment condition ($N = 19$), in which movies of family interactions across different cultures were viewed on a weekly basis, and a no treatment control condition ($N = 53$). Treatment was delivered once per week for 10 weeks, but additional sessions could be scheduled in crisis situations. All patients were scheduled for weekly counseling independent of group therapy sessions.

Study results supported the efficacy of the therapy. Patients in the paid and unpaid therapy conditions reported a higher proportion of opioid-free days (81% and 76%, respectively) than those in the family movie and non-family control conditions (66% and 62%, respectively). This was true as well when days free of nonopioid drugs were considered (88% and 85% for paid and unpaid family therapy groups vs. 79% and 75% for family movie and nonfamily groups). These promising results for drug use were seen despite striking differences in compliance rates of patients participating in these two conditions. All family members in the paid family therapy condition, for example, attended at least 4 sessions of treatment, and most (81%) completed the scheduled 10 sessions. In the unpaid condition, however, almost one-half (48%) did not even attend 4 sessions, and only 40 percent completed the 10 sessions. In fact, the compliance rate of patients in the unpaid family therapy condition was less than that of patients in the family movie condition, in which 94 percent of the patients attended at least 6 sessions and 56 percent of the patients completed 10 sessions. Differences in drug use observed immediately following treatment were maintained over the one-year follow-up period, although there were no between-group differences in attainment of more constructive drug-free social activity at any point during the study.

These results demonstrate that family therapy can reduce the drug use of opioid-dependent outpatients receiving methadone substitution. Although the Stanton and Todd (1982) study tested the efficacy of structural-strategic therapy, it seems reasonable to hypothesize that other professionally delivered family treatments (e.g., behavioral, psychodynamic) would also have positive effects. What is not as clear, however, is how family therapy might affect the treatment outcome of older drug abusers who are likely to be more estranged from their families of origin. The investigators also do not present strategies for dealing with ongoing cocaine use, which is much more prevalent now than when the study was conducted. The comparison between paid and unpaid therapy conditions demonstrated that the intervention of paying patients and family members to attend sessions produced significant increases in rates of compliance, although surprisingly marginal differences in rates of drug use. Again, the poor attendance of patients in the unpaid family therapy condition points to the difficulties in attracting patients and family members to this type of treatment. In fact, the investigators describe a large subset of eligible patients who were never included in the study because they did not permit family contact.

Conjoint Therapy

Although there have been relatively few systematic studies of the effects of conjoint therapy for opioid abusers, work accomplished in the area of alcohol abuse and dependence demonstrate the benefits of this approach. O'Farrell, Cutter, and Floyd (1985), for example, describe a standard manualized behavioral marital therapy (BMT) package that includes disulfiram (Antabuse®) contracting, communication skills training, and shared recreational activity. The goal is to reduce problem drinking and facilitate positive and mutually reinforcing social interaction. An important component of BMT is the utilization of the nonalcoholic spouse to monitor treatment and reinforce positive behaviors. For instance, the spouse might monitor disulfiram ingestion, attendance to self-help meetings, and performance of other behaviors conducive to maintaining abstinence from alcohol. In addition, the spouse might provide reinforcement (reciprocal verbal praise, intimate behavior, cooking meals, etc.) contingent on observable changes of behavior. Controlled studies with alcohol-dependent patients have demonstrated that spousal involvement enhances compliance with disulfiram treatment (Azrin et al. 1982), reduces total alcohol consumption (O'Farrell, Cutter, and Floyd 1985; McCrady et al. 1986), enhances treatment retention (Zweben, Pearlman, and Li 1983), and helps maintain treatment gains over time (O'Farrell et al. 1993).

However, important differences between opioid and alcohol abusers may limit the generalizability of these findings. Perhaps most problematic is that the majority of drug abusers entering treatment are not involved in stable romantic relationships (e.g., Kidorf, Brooner, and King 1997), thus limiting this intervention to a smaller number of patients with steady partners. But even this group is often involved with partners who are actively drug dependent or significantly impaired by other psychiatric problems (Kauffman 1985). It is likely that such partners would have difficulty complying with the many requirements of intensive BMT. Probably the most generalizable aspect of BMT to the treatment of opioid abusers is its use of stable significant others to monitor and support actively the treatment behavior of patients. The manner in which such an intervention might be implemented in a methadone substitution program is described next.

Involvement of Significant Others

The previously described family-based interventions are applicable for patients who either have an intact family or who are involved in a stable romantic relationship. These interventions focus on improving family functioning as a means to impact important areas of treatment outcome such as drug use and retention. The problem, of course, is that the skills needed to deliver family-based interventions are highly specialized and require considerable training and supervision, which is rarely available to staff in drug abuse treatment programs. Yet, family members might alternatively be utilized to monitor and support the patient's efforts to meet goals that have been established in his or her treatment plan. In this way, family involvement more closely resembles a community reinforcement approach (Azrin 1976; Azrin et al. 1994; Hunt and Azrin 1973), which emphasizes control of external reinforcers as a means of modifying drug use. Studies using this approach with alcohol abusers have utilized spousal support to enhance compliance with disulfiram therapy, provide social and other reinforcement contingent on abstinence, and help patients become involved in social activities that compete with alcohol use (Hunt and Azrin 1973; Azrin et al. 1982; Sisson and Azrin 1986; Azrin et al. 1994). This model has also been successfully applied to the treatment of drug and alcohol abusers in an approach called network therapy (Galanter 1993; Galanter, Keller, and Dermatis 1997). In this therapy, selected drug-free family members or friends are enlisted into the therapy process to provide ongoing support and to promote attitude and behavior change in the drug-abusing patient.

A treatment model that involves support from the social network can also be adapted to opioid abusers receiving methadone substitution by utilizing drug-free family members or friends to support community-based treatment goals. One particularly important goal is for patients to become more involved in drug-free activities and to develop more extensive drug-free social support outside of the clinic. Research showing a strong association between positive social support and reduced risk for relapse to opioid use and many other substances (e.g., Havassy, Hall, and Wasserman 1991) supports the aggressive pursuit of this goal. Enhancing social support can be pursued by having drug-free significant others lead patients into drug-free activities and then monitoring their involvement in these settings. In fact, simply including a drug-free individual as part of the treatment functions is an important step in instituting more regular involvement with drug-free social support. An advantage to this approach is that it does not require the same degree of experience necessary to conduct traditional family or marital therapy, and can therefore be more easily implemented in drug abuse treatment clinics.

One might think that the biggest stumbling block to this approach is that patients do not have any drug-free individuals in their lives to bring into treatment. Although this is a common belief among the treatment staff, it appears to be a misconception strongly encouraged by the patients. Kidorf, Brooner, and King (1997) showed that 85 percent of the patients targeted for this intervention both identified drug-free significant others and involved them in the treatment plan when doing so ensured continued treatment in the program. Patients and their significant others were required to attend a significant-other group for six weeks that focused on strategies for enhancing social support outside of the clinic; almost 80 percent of all scheduled sessions were attended. Although other treatment outcome data were not presented in this study, the results clearly show that opioid abusers will bring significant others into treatment *if* the program is committed to the intervention.

IMPLICATIONS OF THE COUNSELING AND THERAPY LITERATURE

The previous review has important practical implications for staff working in opioid substitution programs. Individual counseling was found to add significantly to the effects of methadone substitution alone. In addition, patients exposed to more counseling achieved better outcomes than those receiving less counseling. We believe that counselors should rely primarily on a nonconfrontational interaction style that conveys support, builds rapport, and motivates patients to identify the reasons for maintaining their drug use, and how they will change the process of deciding to use drugs. Group counseling appears to be most effective when it is structured and skills oriented and represents a cost-sensitive method for increasing counseling intensity. Skills developed in the group setting can be evaluated in a patient's natural interactions with staff and other patients in the treatment setting. Patients who continue to use drugs despite increased counseling intensity, and those with high levels of psychiatric distress and familial problems, will likely achieve additional therapeutic benefit from attending specialized individual or group-based psychotherapies and family therapy. And finally, compliance with community-based treatment goals established within the program can be optimized for all patients with the help of significant-other monitoring.

This chapter has also pointed to the limited interest and poor attendance of patients to the individual and group-based treatments reviewed. Many of the major clinical trials described previously either failed to report actual rates of counseling attendance or provided data showing modest to poor rates of compliance (see Table 9.2). It is likely that many patients and some program staff perceived these interventions, from individual and group counseling to the specialized therapies, as ancillary to the methadone (Kidorf, Stitzer, and Griffiths 1995). This detail was explicitly revealed in studies evaluating the effectiveness of specialized psychotherapies. Attendance rates were higher when the therapy was offered within the methadone treatment program (Woody et al. 1983, 1985) than when similar services were offered outside the methadone treatment setting (Rounsaville et al. 1983). Yet in the Woody et al. (1983, 1985) stud-

Table 9.2 Rates of Compliance with Scheduled Counseling and Therapy Sessions across Selected Studies

Study	Type of Therapy	Length of Therapy (weeks)	Number of Scheduled Sessions	Number of Attended Sessions	Compliance Rate (%)
Stanton and Todd (1982)	Family (paid)	10	10	4–10	Unknown
	Family (unpaid)	10	10	0–10	Unknown
Woody et al. (1983)	Individual counseling	24	24	17	71
	Individual counseling + supplementary psychotherapy	24	48	24	50
Rounsaville et al. (1983)	Individual/group counseling	24	Unknown	Unknown	Unknown
	Individual/group counseling + supplementary psychotherapy	24	Unknown	Unknown	Unknown
McLellan et al. (1993)	Individual counseling	24	14–44	Unknown	Unknown
Magura et al. (1994)	Individual counseling + group counseling	24	120–144	Unknown	Unknown
Woody et al. (1995)	Individual counseling + supplementary counseling	24	48	23	48
	Individual counseling + supplementary psychotherapy	24	48	26	54
Iguchi et al. (1996)	Group counseling (with incentives)	12	8	4.8	60
	Group counseling (without incentives)	12	8	0	0

ies, only 50 percent of the patients attended scheduled psychotherapy sessions. The low rates of attendance reported in most studies make it almost impossible to evaluate the true impact of routine counseling and specialized psychotherapies on rehabilitation when the interventions are delivered on an intermittent schedule in an unpredictable manner. This body of literature further suggests that verbal persuasion is insufficient to enhance initial compliance with these interventions, especially among patients with severe problem profiles characterized by multiple drug use disorders and serious psychiatric and social problems. Even though considerable attention is being directed toward studies attempting to match patients to specific verbal and behavioral therapies, the larger problem facing programs is how to get patients to attend regularly even routine counseling much less enhanced or specialized forms of treatment. The magnitude of this problem is profound and severely limits the effectiveness of available psychosocial and medication treatment for drug abuse. The remainder of this chapter reviews a new treatment service-delivery approach that is capable of significantly enhancing counseling attendance in opioid substitution programs.

BEHAVIORALLY CONTINGENT PHARMACOTHERAPY (BCP)

A new service-delivery model, which was instituted in our opioid substitution program several years ago, links the continued delivery of methadone with attendance at scheduled counseling sessions (Brooner et al. 1996). Patients who consistently choose to miss their individual and group counseling sessions are eventually discharged from the program following a brief (21- to 30-day) methadone detoxification. However, to minimize the potential adverse effects of treatment discharge, all are provided rapid readmission if they subsequently agree to attend the scheduled counseling. This treatment delivery approach was instituted based on empirical data and clinical impression suggesting that patients might be motivated to reduce drug use and engage more fully in psychosocial treatments if by doing so they could continue to receive medication (Dolan et al. 1985; McCarthy and Borders 1985; Kidorf and Stitzer 1993). This program is described here because we believe that it exemplifies a rational, structured approach for fully integrating the pharmacologic and psychosocial treatment elements of a drug abuse rehabilitation program (Onken, Blaine, and Boren 1995).

BCP utilizes behavioral principles of avoidance in which a low-frequency behavior (counseling attendance) may increase if such behavior results in avoiding an undesirable consequence (treatment discharge). Note, however, that the use of BCP does not simply punish patients failing in treatment (e.g., using drugs), by discharging them from the program. Patients are discharged every day from substitution programs without any apparent clinical benefit. BCP was designed primarily to improve treatment performance with the intent of retaining patients in treatment. The approach borrows heavily from the contingency management literature (see Chapter 10), from the psychosocial literature of effective treatments for drug abuse and other motivated disorders, and from aspects of the community reinforcement model that incorporate drug-abstinent family members as community monitors and reinforcers of therapeutic progress.

BCP utilizes a stepped-care approach with three aspects of methadone treatment used as incentives to increase counseling attendance and reduce drug use: (1) medication dosing time, (2) amount of counseling required, and (3) continued availability of methadone. Because many patients favor early methadone dosing hours, progressively later medication hours are given to patients who repeatedly miss scheduled counseling sessions. If patients continue to use drugs or miss sessions, their counseling requirements are increased. This penalty enhances the potential impact of counseling on patient behavior and provides another avoidance opportunity (i.e., if a patient's behavior improves, added counseling requirements can be avoided). Finally, if noncompliance persists, a gradual detoxification from methadone is implemented. Thus, the treatment model was designed to extend retention while enhancing contact with psychosocial treatment components that can improve outcome. The treatment approach might technically be viewed as an avoidance schedule, but the goal is to produce a motivating set of behavioral contingencies that promote more positive clinical outcomes.

The Structured Levels of Care

The BCP program offers a progression of counseling services in which both the quantity or "dose" of individual and group counseling and the clinical specialization of the treatment provider is enhanced for patients who are consistently drug positive or who consistently miss scheduled counseling sessions, and reduced for patients who are drug negative and regularly attend counseling sessions. All patients are educated about the structured levels of care when they initially apply for treatment and again on the day of admission; the treatment model is then regularly reviewed with patients by the treatment staff. The careful attention paid to educating and reeducating the patient about the treatment methods used in the program ensures that they remain aware of the consequences of continued drug use and failure to attend scheduled counseling sessions. The structural and dynamic aspects of this "levels of treatment" approach produce a predictable response to the changing clinical status of patients and therefore enhances individualized care. It is also cost-effective because the most intense and specialized psychosocial treatments are required only for those doing poorly at lower levels of care. In addition, the escalating intensities of weekly counseling have the added value of improving the daily structure of drug-using patients whose day-to-day lives are often disorganized and chaotic.

The program uses three distinct levels of weekly counseling based on the patient's most recent clinical status. These levels of care as well as the movement from one to another of these levels are described subsequently. All changes in counseling levels are based on highly objective behaviors (i.e., rates of positive urine specimens and rates of counseling attendance) and are monitored weekly by senior clinical staff.

All new admissions to the program begin treatment in Level 1 (standard care), where they are required to attend one individual counseling session per week (30 minutes) and an eight-session drug education group. Patients at this level are therefore required to attend approximately 1.5 hours of counseling per week during the first eight weeks of care and about 30 minutes of individual counseling thereafter. Patients who remain stable at this level for several months (i.e., drug free, counseling compliant, and engaged in productive occupational, educational, or community activities) may be referred to case management status, which represents a limited version of medical maintenance in that patients are required to come to the program once or twice per week for medication and to attend one counseling session per month.

Patients in Level 1 who are drug positive or miss their counseling session in any two of three weeks are referred to Level 2 (enhanced care), where they are scheduled to attend one individual counseling session and three to four group sessions per week for a minimum of five weeks (i.e., 3.5 to 4.5 hours of counseling per week). The counseling groups are primarily skills oriented and manualized, including relapse control, job-skills training, stress management, role recovery, coping skills, and time management. These group treatments are delivered by senior clinical staff in the program, which is a cost-effective method for offering enhanced care and one that directly supports the efforts of primary counselors to improve the patients' functioning. The primary counselor, in consultation with his or her supervisor and with input from the patient, selects from the list of available groups those that have the greatest apparent relevance to the patients' continued drug use. Patients who are attending all scheduled counseling and who are drug negative during the final two weeks in Level 2 are referred back to Level 1 (standard care) for continuing care.

Patients in Level 2 who continue to use drugs and miss counseling sessions are referred to Level 3 (intensive care) for six weeks. At this point, patients are scheduled for two individual counseling sessions (30 minutes each) per week and between six and eight group counseling sessions, including twice weekly cognitive-behavioral therapy and a mandatory significant-other group. In total, patients in Level 3 are required to attend approximately seven hours of counseling per week. As mentioned earlier, the significant-other involvement is incorporated to monitor a patient's involvement in specific aspects of the treatment plan outside the clinic in order to improve the extent of drug-free social supports. Patients who are drug free and attending all counseling sessions in the last two weeks of Level 3 are referred back to Level 2 enroute for return to Level 1 (standard care). Patients in Level 3 who choose to continue missing scheduled counseling and use drugs are discharged from the program after detoxification from methadone or LAAM, which is usually completed within 30 days.

Contingent Reinstatement Intervention

The contingent discharge from the program resulting in detoxification from methadone or LAAM follows considerable evidence from a patient of his or her unwillingness to follow the clearly articulated and predictable plan of care. Although it is always tempting to maintain these patients in treatment despite their obvious noncompliance with the treatment plan, doing so hinders treatment success by letting patients avoid those services most likely to impact positively on their ongoing decisions to use drugs. Patients who choose detoxification from methadone or LAAM in preparation for discharge from the program are encouraged to begin attending their counseling sessions during this preparation for discharge in the hopes that the reality of being detoxified from the treatment medications will motivate them to follow the treatment plan. Many patients begin attending their counseling sessions during this period and therefore discontinue the medication detoxification. The medication dose in these patients is returned to the predetoxification maintenance level after achieving one full week of counseling attendance. Those who elect to complete detoxification from the medication are guaranteed rapid (i.e., 24-hour) readmission to the program if they agree to reenter at Level 3 and attend all scheduled counseling. Discharge from the program is therefore utilized as a discrete, reversible therapeutic intervention whose goal is to encourage patients to participate fully in the aspects of their treatment plan that they previously ignored. This discharge procedure should reduce the likelihood of patients cycling through one after another methadone treatment program with little apparent benefit.

Overall, there are several important advantages of this service-delivery system:

1. It systematically lays out treatment expectations for patients and staff, which are uniform for all patients;
2. It focuses on improving individual and group therapy attendance, elements of treatment that have the best chance of identifying and altering the patient's decisions that result in high rates of drug use and other life problems;
3. It ensures that poorly performing patients receive additional and more specialized services (i.e., twice weekly cognitive-behavioral therapy); and
4. It provides all patients the opportunity for rapid readmission simply by agreeing to follow the well-articulated plan of care.

Preliminary results from a six-month clinical trial (Brooner et al. 1996) evaluating the efficacy of BCP support these claims. One hundred fifty-four patients were randomly assigned to either the BCP or standard-care condition. Patients in both conditions were referred to higher levels of counseling based on drug use and counseling compliance, as detailed previously. However, the detoxification contingency during Level 3 was introduced only for patients in the BCP condition; control patients could remain in treatment independent of their counseling compliance and drug use. Data for the first 73 patients over the initial three months of treatment show that patients in the BCP condition were much more likely to comply with psychosocial treatments (85% vs. 35%, $p < .01$) and to submit drug-negative urine samples (57% vs. 33%, $p < .05$) than those assigned to the control condition. More important, the six-month retention rate among patients in both study conditions was excellent and showed no between-group differences (contingent, 90% vs. noncontingent, 81%) and, if anything, favors patients treated in the contingent condition. These preliminary results support the efficacy of a stepped-care approach that integrates methadone pharmacotherapy with enhanced psychosocial treatments and that uses continued treatment availability as an ongoing motivator to improve treatment outcome gradually over time. The BCP approach has several advantages over the more traditional use of abrupt program discharge as a punishment for patients who are difficult and recalcitrant. More data are needed, however, to support fully the efficacy of this approach and also to address concerns about the relative adverse effects associated with a patient's discharge from treatment (i.e., increased drug use, risk of infectious disease exposure).

SUMMARY

Drug abusers entering opioid substitution programs present with many drug use disorders, comorbid psychiatric diagnoses, and other medical and psychosocial difficulties that methadone and LAAM were never intended to treat. A number of psychosocial interventions have shown promise in treating these problems and thereby add substantially to the benefits of methadone or LAAM. Individual drug abuse counseling, in particular, has been shown to actively promote less drug use and overall better outcomes. Group therapy represents an efficient and potentially effective method for delivering education and skills-training interventions. Specialized psychotherapies may be beneficial for some patients if offered under conditions that maximize utilization. Family therapy and significant-other monitoring also appear to be promising interventions for drug abusers and deserve more attention. However, patients often lack interest in these services and frequently miss counseling sessions when offered them. Compliance can be improved by implementing a new service-delivery model (i.e., BCP) that escalates counseling requirements for poor performers and imposes detoxification from methadone as an ultimate motivator to change patient behavior.

Together, the approaches described represent a mixture of techniques designed to improve motivation for behavior change, to teach coping and decision-making skills needed to initiate and sustain abstinence, and to enhance nondrug-using sources of support and reinforcement. Although a minimal level of counseling service is mandated by federal regulations, clinics should select the additional services that they will offer based on resources and patient needs, keeping in mind that procedures to motivate attendance may be needed when working with methadone-maintained drug abusers in order to realize potential benefits and make implementation of these services worthwhile.

References

Allison M., Hubbard R.L. 1985. Drug abuse treatment process: a review of the literature. *Int. J. Addictions* 20:1321–45.

Andersen A.E. 1984. Anorexia nervosa and bulimia: biological, psychological, and sociocultural aspects. In: Galler J.R., ed. *Nutrition and Behavior,* Plenum, New York.

Azrin N.H. 1976. Improvements in the community reinforcement approach to alcoholism. *Behav. Res. Ther.* 14:339–48.

Azrin N.H., McMahon P.T., Donohue B., Besalel V.A., Lapinski K.J., Kogan E.S., Acierno R.E., Galloway E. 1994. Behavior therapy for drug abuse: a controlled treatment outcome study. *Behav. Res. Ther.* 32:857–66.

Azrin N.H., Sisson R.W., Meyers R., Godley M. 1982. Alcoholism treatment by disulfiram and community reinforcement therapy. *J. Behav. Ther. Exp. Psychiatry* 13:105–12.

Ball J.C., Ross A. 1991. *The Effectiveness of Methadone Maintenance Treatment.* Springer-Verlag, New York.

Beck A.T. 1976. *Cognitive Therapy and the Emotional Disorders.* International University Press, New York.

Bowen M. 1971. Family therapy and family group therapy. In: Kaplan H., Sadock B. eds. *Comprehensive Group Psychotherapy.* Williams & Wilkins, Baltimore.

Brooner R.K., Kidorf M., King V.L., Bigelow G.E. 1996. Using behaviorally contingent pharmacotherapy in opioid abusers enhances treatment outcome. In: Harris L.S., ed. Problems of Drug Dependence 1996, Proceedings of the 58th Annual Scientific Meeting, College on Problems of Drug Dependence. National Institute on Drug Abuse Research Monograph, Department of Health and Human Services, National Institute on Drug Abuse, Rockville, MD, vol. 174, p. 305.

Brooner R.K., King V.L., Kidorf M., Schmidt C.W. Jr., Bigelow G.E. 1997. Psychiatric and substance use comorbidity among treatment-seeking opioid abusers. *Arch. Gen. Psychiatry* 54:71–80.

Carroll K.M., Rounsaville B.J., Nich C., Gordon L.T., Wirtz P.W., Gawin F. 1994. One-year follow-up of psychotherapy and pharmacotherapy for cocaine dependence. *Arch. Gen. Psychiatry* 51:989–97.

Chaney E.F. 1989. Social skills training. In: Hester R.K., Miller W.R., eds. *Handbook of Alcoholism Treatment Approaches: Effective Alternatives.* Pergamon, New York, pp. 206–21.

Cooney N.L., Kadden R.M., Litt M.D., Getter H. 1991. Matching alcoholics to coping skills or interactional therapies: two-year follow-up results. *J. Consult. Clin. Psychol.* 59:598–601.

Dolan M.P., Black J.L., Penk W.E., Robinowitz R., DeFord H.A. 1985. Contracting for treatment termination to reduce illicit drug use among methadone maintenance treatment failures. *J. Consult. Clin. Psychol.* 53:549–51.

Galanter M. 1993. *Network Therapy for Drug and Alcohol Abuse.* Guilford Press, New York.

Galanter M., Keller D.S., Dermatis H. 1997. Network therapy for addiction: assessment of the clinical outcome of training. *Am. J. Drug Alcohol Abuse* 23:355–67.

Gill K., Nolimal D., Crowley T. 1992. Antisocial personality disorder, HIV risk behavior and retention in methadone maintenance therapy. *Drug Alcohol Depend.* 30:247–52.

Hall S.M., Loeb P., LeVois M., Cooper J. 1981. Increasing employment in ex-heroin addicts II: methadone maintenance sample. *Behav. Ther.* 12:453–60.

Havassy B.E., Hall S.M., Wasserman D.A. 1991. Social support and relapse: commonalities among alcoholics, opiate users, and cigarette smokers. *Addictive Behav.* 16:235–46.

Hermalin J.A., Steer R.A., Platt J.J., Metzger D.S. 1990. Risk characteristics associated with chronic unemployment in methadone clients. *Drug Alcohol Depend.* 26:117–25.

Hunt G.M., Azrin N.H. 1973. A community-reinforcement approach to alcoholism. *Behav. Res. Ther.* 11:91–104.

Iguchi M.Y., Lamb R.J., Belding M.A., Platt J.J., Husband S.D., Morral A.R. 1996. Contingent reinforcement of group participation versus abstinence in a methadone maintenance program. *Exp. Clin. Psychopharmacol.* 4:315–21.

Kauffman E. 1985. Family systems and family therapy of substance abuse: an overview of two decades of research and clinical experience. *Int. J. Addictions* 20:897–916.

Kauffman E.F. 1989. Family therapy in substance abuse treatment. In: *Treatment of Psychiatric Disorders: Volume 2.* American Psychiatric Association, Washington, DC.

Kauffman J.F., Woody G.E. 1995. *Matching Treatment to Patient Needs in Opioid Substitution Therapy.* DHHS Publication No. SMA 95–3049. Center for Substance Abuse Treatment, Rockville, MD.

Khantzian E.J., Halliday K.S., Golden S., McAuliffe W.E. 1992. Modified group therapy for substance abusers: a psychodynamic approach to relapse prevention. *Am. J. Addictions* 1:67–76.

Kidorf M., Brooner R.K., King V.L. 1997. Motivating methadone patients to include drug-free significant others in treatment: a behavioral intervention. *J. Subst. Abuse Treat.* 14:23–28.

Kidorf M., Stitzer M.L. 1993. Contingent access to methadone maintenance treatment: effects of cocaine use of mixed opiate-cocaine abusers. *Exp. Clin. Psychopharmacol.* 1:200–206.

Kidorf M., Stitzer M.L., Brooner R.K. 1994. Characteristics of methadone patients responding to take-home incentives. *Behav. Ther.* 25: 109–21.

Kidorf M., Stitzer M.L., Griffiths R.R. 1995. Evaluating the reinforcement value of clinic-based privileges through a multiple choice procedure. *Drug Alcohol Depend.* 39:167–72.

Klerman G.L., Weissman M.M., Rounsaville B.J., Chevron E.S. 1984. *Interpersonal Psychotherapy of Depression.* Basic Books, New York.

Luborsky L. 1984. *Principles of Psychoanalytic Psychotherapy: A Manual for Supportive-Expressive (SE) Treatment.* Basic Books, New York.

Magura S., Rosenblum A., Lovejoy M., Handelsman L., Foote J., Stimmel B. 1994. Neurobehavioral treatment for cocaine-using methadone patients: a preliminary report. *J. Addict. Dis.* 4:143–60.

Marlatt G.A., Gordon J.R. 1985. *Relapse Prevention.* Guilford Press, New York.

McAuliffe W.E. 1990. A randomized controlled trial of recovery training and self-help for opioid addicts in New England and Hong Kong. *J. Psychoactive Drugs* 22:197–209.

McCarthy J.J., Borders O.T. 1985. Limit setting on drug abuse in methadone maintenance patients. *Am. J. Psychiatry* 142:1419–23.

McCrady B.S., Noel N.E., Abrams D.B., Stout R.L., Nelson H.F., Hay W.M. 1986. Comparative effectiveness of three types of spouse involvement in outpatient behavioral alcoholism treatment. *J. Stud. Alcohol* 47: 459–67.

McHugh P.R., Slavney P.R. 1998. *The Perspectives of Psychiatry.* Johns Hopkins University Press, Baltimore.

McLellan A.T., Alterman A.I., Woody G.E., Metzger D. 1992. A quantitative measure of substance abuse treatment: the treatment services review. *J. Nerv. Ment. Dis.* 180:100–109.

McLellan A.T., Arndt I.O., Metzger D.S., Woody G.E., O'Brien C.P. 1993. The effects of psychosocial services in substance abuse treatment. *JAMA* 269:1953–59.

McLellan A.T., Ball J.C., Rosen L., O'Brien C.P. 1981. Pretreatment source of income and response to methadone maintenance: a follow-up study. *Am. J. Psychiatry* 138:785–89.

McLellan A.T., Woody G.E., Luborsky L., Goehl L. 1988. Is the counselor an active ingredient in substance abuse rehabilitation? An examination of treatment success among four counselors. *J. Nerv. Ment. Dis.* 176:423–29.

Miller W.R., Rollnick S. 1991. *Motivational Interviewing.* Guilford Press, New York.

Minuchin S. 1974. *Families and Family Therapy*. Harvard University Press, Cambridge, MA.

Nyswander M., Winick C., Bernstein A., Brill L., Kaufer G. 1958. The treatment of drug addicts as voluntary outpatients: a progress report. *Am. J. Orthopsychiatry* 28:714–29.

O'Farrell T.J., Chaquette K.A., Cutter H.S., Brown E.D., McCourt W.F. 1993. Behavioral marital therapy with and without addictive couples relapse prevention sessions for alcoholics and their wives. *J. Stud. Alcohol* 54:652–66.

O'Farrell T.J., Cutter H.G., Floyd F.J. 1985. Evaluating behavioral marital therapy for male alcoholics: effects on marital adjustment and communication from before to after treatment. *Behav. Ther.* 16:147–67.

Onken L.S., Blaine J.D., Boren J.J., eds. 1995. *Integrating Behavioral Therapies with Medications in the Treatment of Drug Dependence*. National Institute on Drug Abuse Research Monograph 150, Department of Health and Human Services, National Institute on Drug Abuse, Rockville, MD.

Rawson R.R., Obert J.L., McCann M.J., Smith D.P., Ling W. 1990. Neurobehavioral treatment for cocaine dependence. *J. Psychoactive Drugs* 22:159–71.

Rounsaville B.J., Glazer W., Wilber C.H., Weissman M.M., Kleber H.D. 1983. Short-term interpersonal psychotherapy in methadone-maintained opiate addicts. *Arch. Gen. Psychiatry* 40:629–36.

Silverman K., Chutuape M.A., Svikis D.S., Bigelow G.E., Stitzer M.L. 1995. Incongruity between occupational interests and academic skills in drug abusing women. *Drug Alcohol Depend.* 40:115–23.

Simpson D.D., Joe G.W., Rowan-Szal G.R., Greener J. 1995. Client engagement and change during drug abuse treatment. *J. Subst. Abuse* 7:117–34.

Sisson R.W., Azrin N.G. 1986. Family-member involvement to initiate and promote treatment of problem drinkers. *J. Behav. Ther. Exp. Psychiatry* 17:15–21.

Stanton M.D., Todd T.C. 1982. *The Family Therapy of Drug Abuse and Addiction*. Guilford Press, New York.

Woody G.E., Luborsky L., McLellan A.T., O'Brien C.P., Beck A.T., Blaine J., Herman I., Hole A. 1983. Psychotherapy for opiate addicts: does it help? *Arch. Gen. Psychiatry* 40:639–45.

Woody G.E., McLellan A.T., Luborsky L., O'Brien C.P. 1985. Sociopathy and psychotherapy outcome. *Arch. Gen. Psychiatry* 42:1081–86.

———. 1995. Psychotherapy in community methadone programs: a validation study. *Am. J. Psychiatry* 152:1302–8.

Yalom I.D. 1975. *The Theory and Practice of Group Psychotherapy.* Basic Books, New York.

Zweben A., Pearlman S., Li S. 1983. Reducing attrition from conjoint therapy with alcoholic couples. *Drug Alcohol Depend.* 11:321–31.

10

Contingency Management Therapies

Elias Robles, Ph.D., Kenneth Silverman, Ph.D.,
and Maxine L. Stitzer, Ph.D.

Methadone is an effective but incomplete treatment for opiate dependence. Even if heroin use is brought under control, numerous problems remain to be addressed in the methadone maintenance population, not the least of which is the use of other drugs of abuse, such as cocaine. To address these psychosocial and drug use problems, counseling has always been included as a part of methadone treatment. Chapter 9 reviews the various types of counseling and psychosocial treatments that have been utilized and evaluated.

Within this panoply of therapy interventions, contingency management is one of the most effective and generally useful. Contingency management procedures may be loosely considered motivational interventions designed to promote a clinically desirable change in behavior. Under these procedures, patients are offered some attractive options (e.g., a clinic privilege) contingent on performing a clinically desired target behavior (e.g., drug abstinence as verified by drug-free urinalysis results). This type of contingency often increases the frequency of the therapeutically desired behavior, thereby accomplishing an important goal of treatment. In addition to their proven effectiveness, contingency management procedures are considerably versatile because they can be used to increase a wide range of desirable behaviors, from counseling attendance, to compliance with medication regimens (e.g., daily ingestion of disulfiram for treatment of chronic alcohol abuse), to drug abstinence.

Contingency management procedures are firmly rooted in an extensive body of basic and applied research in learning and conditioning. This body of research has not only guided the development of these procedures but, if the underlying principles are understood, can also be useful to practitioners in applying contingency management procedures to novel clinical situations and problems. This chapter briefly discusses the underlying rationale of contingency management procedures and then presents a review of controlled studies that have assessed the effectiveness of contingency management techniques in the treatment of methadone patients. The final section of the chapter contains clinical recommendations for designing and implementing contingency management programs in the treatment of methadone patients.

Rationale for Contingency Management Interventions

The approach taken in the treatment of any disorder reflects, at least in part, the way the therapist views the underlying causes of the disorder. For example, the 12-step approach to treatment is based on the concept that drug abuse is a disease over which the individual has little or no control. This concept implies that the drug abuser must seek outside help (i.e., from a higher power) in order to overcome the ravages of the disease. Contingency management approaches stem from a quite different view of the origins of drug abuse. In particular, drug abuse is viewed as a learned behavior, supported by the biologic reinforcing effects of drugs. This behavior can be counteracted by applying principles of behavior management, including reward and punishment.

The term *operant* refers to behavior that changes the environment by operating or acting on it. In a behavioral approach to drug abuse, the behaviors involved in drug-seeking are viewed as operant behaviors that result in the ingestion of a drug. The consequences of an operant behavior determine whether or not the behavior will occur under similar circumstances in the future. In the terminology of operant conditioning, consequences are classified as *reinforcing,* if they increase the likelihood that a behavior will occur in the future, and *punishing,* if they decrease the likelihood that the behavior will occur again. In the research laboratory, where these principles were first recognized, the dispensing of food pellets following a rat's lever press usually results in more lever pressing. Many humans escalate their drug use over time after initial exposure, which indicates that drugs can act as reinforcers for humans. However, not all humans who try drugs become abusers because modifying predispositions and circumstances determine who will and will not become a drug abuser after exposure to the reinforcing effects of drugs. In fact, humans may differ on just how reinforcing they find drug effects both initially and with repeated use over time.

The reinforcing power of drugs is not restricted to humans; it can be clearly demonstrated in other animal species including monkeys, dogs, rodents, and even birds. Much research has shown that laboratory animals, given the opportunity, will self-administer the same drugs that are abused by humans (Griffiths, Bigelow, and Henningfield 1980). This evidence supports a biologic basis for drug reinforcement. In support of this concept of biologic reinforcement, we also know that drugs act on certain regions of the brain, which are the same regions that control pleasurable sensations derived from biologic reinforcers including food, water, and sexual activity (Koob and Bloom 1988; Koob and Le Moal 1997). The biologic basis of drug reinforcement is what makes use of drugs such a compelling option for some people, and it also underlies much of the difficulty people have when trying to stop using drugs. In addition, research has shown that behaviors maintained by drug reinforcement are similar to those maintained by other reinforcers such as food, water, and social contact. Specifically, the frequency of the behavior will change (i.e., increase or decrease in frequency) if its consequences change. For example, drug self-administration can be decreased by decreasing the dose available to a dose that is too low to be reinforcing (Heyman 1983), by presenting a punishment contingent on drug-seeking or drug-taking responses, or if using drugs results in immediate loss of other valued reinforcers.

The identification of drug use as an operant behavior and drugs as biologic reinforcers has affected our understanding and the clinical treatment of drug abuse. Most important, with respect to this chapter, these views have led to systematic efforts to decrease drug use by manipulating the consequences of drug use versus abstinence. Over the past 20 years, treatment researchers and providers have designed and studied the arrangement of different consequences of drug use and related behaviors, in efforts to decrease drug use and increase more productive activity. Such programs are called *contingency management* programs.

CONTINGENCY MANAGEMENT INTERVENTIONS IN METHADONE TREATMENT

The methadone clinic is a place well suited for the implementation of therapeutic contingency management programs, in part because methadone tends to retain patients in treatment for extended periods of time, allowing sufficient time to implement and fully evaluate contingency management interventions. Equally important, methadone itself or features of its delivery (dose size, dosing frequency, take-home doses) can be used as reinforcers in contingency management programs to promote a desirable change in behavior. As a result of these circumstances, much of what we know about contingency management interventions in drug treatment has been learned from methadone patients.

Contingency management interventions can be specified by defining four major dimensions:

1. The *target behavior*, which is the behavior the therapist wants to change (e.g., attend counseling sessions);
2. The *conditions* (antecedents) under which the target behaviors are to occur (e.g., every Monday at 2:00 P.M. with no reminders from program staff);
3. The *reinforcer* (e.g., one bus token); and
4. The *contingency*, which specifies the rules according to which reinforcers can be earned for producing the target behavior (e.g., one bus token for each counseling session attended).

Contingency management interventions conducted in methadone programs have varied in all of these main dimensions. For the purpose of this chapter, we have grouped contingency management procedures by the reinforcers utilized in order to emphasize the therapeutic resources available to clinicians for use in changing the behavior of methadone patients.

Contingent Methadone

The continued opportunity to receive methadone can function as a reinforcer, and this opportunity can be incorporated into contingency management procedures. For example, in an early study of this type (described in Chapter 6), Liebson, Tomasello, and Bigelow (1978) required chronic alcoholic patients to take disulfiram as a condition of continuing methadone maintenance treatment and showed that in a controlled design study, this could be an effective intervention for managing alcoholic patients.

McCarthy and Borders (1985) studied a "structured" methadone-delivery system versus a usual care control treatment in 69 patients. The goal was to prevent excessive drug use during treatment. Thus, if patients in the structured group delivered a drug-positive urine sample during 4 or more consecutive months, they were placed on an irreversible methadone detoxification and forced to leave the program. Patients in the unstructured treatment condition continued to receive methadone treatment regardless of their drug use. After 12 months, the structured group achieved significantly more drug-free months (63%) than the unstructured group (49%). A comparison between the first and last month urines showed greater treatment improvement by patients in the structured treatment (14 vs. 3 patients improved). The structured treatment also retained more patients (53%) during the full 12 months than the unstructured treatment (30%). Thus, the study showed that placing even modest expectations on patients and backing these up with contingencies had a beneficial effect on treatment outcome.

More recently, Kidorf and Stitzer (1993) used continued treatment access to motivate new methadone intake patients to stop their drug use at the beginning of treatment. Study patients ($N = 44$) were enrolled in a 90-day premaintenance probationary program. Those randomly assigned to contingent treatment were required to submit two consecutive weeks of cocaine-free urines during their first seven weeks of treatment to gain entry into a two-year maintenance program. Noncontingent patients gained access to the program independent of urinalysis results. Fifty percent of patients in the contingent group versus 14 percent in the noncontingent group submitted two consecutive weeks of drug-free urines during the seven-week probationary period.

These and other studies (e.g., Dolan et al. 1985) have shown that the threat of treatment termination can effectively motivate a therapeutic behavioral change in methadone patients. (A more refined version of this approach—BCP—is described in Chapter 9.) One shortcoming of these studies, however, is that they did not evaluate the status of terminated patients. Although these avoidance procedures clearly provide a structure and motivation that is helpful to some patients, those who leave the program may be worse off than if they had continued in methadone treatment even as poor performers. Potential adverse effects in terminated patients need more study, particularly since such effects can have serious consequences, including HIV infection and premature death.

Methadone Dose Changes

Methadone's reinforcing effects can also be harnessed by providing short-term methadone dose increases or decreases contingent on the occurrence or nonoccurrence, respectively, of target responses. Two studies that used this approach have shown that methadone dose changes can be effective for motivating behavior change.

In a methadone detoxification study by Higgins et al. (1986), 39 participants were randomly assigned to either contingent, noncontingent, or control treatment groups. After having been stabilized on 30 mg per day in the first three weeks, all participants received identical gradual methadone dose reductions (detoxification) during the eight-week study intervention phase. As their methadone dose decreased, members of the contingent and noncontingent groups could obtain daily methadone dose supplements up to 20 mg, but patients in the contingent group qualified for the dose supplements only if they provided an opiate-free urine sample. During the second half of the evaluation phase, the percentage of opiate-positive urine samples was significantly lower for the contingent group (14%) than for either the noncontingent (38%) or control (50%) groups. Thus, the study showed that the opportunity to receive extra methadone during a detoxification could prevent relapse to opiate use, but this was true only if the extra dose was given contingent on submitting opiate-free urines. This study provides a powerful demonstration that the contingency (not the dose increase per se) is the critical element for an effective intervention.

Another study (Stitzer et al. 1986) used dose change as either a reward (patients could receive dose increases for providing drug-free urines) or a punishment (patients received dose decreases for submitting drug-positive urines) in order to determine whether one system might work better than the other. After a 10-week baseline, study patients ($N = 20$) were randomly assigned to the increase or decrease procedure. Doses were adjusted weekly (by 5–15 mg) based on urine test results and could fluctuate up and down for both groups. The dose increase group could go as high as 160 percent of their starting dose but never went below their baseline dose, whereas the dose decrease group could go as low as 40 percent of their starting dose but never went above that original dose. Both dose change procedures resulted in significantly more negative urines during the contingent phase (42%) than during the baseline phase (13%). This study showed that contingencies involving small methadone dose changes (5–15 mg/week) could be effective for some patients in motivating abstinence from supplemental drug use when incorporated into a structured contingency plan. The specific nature of the dose change procedure did not seem to matter. Note, however, that there were more study dropouts when the dose decrease procedure was used. Therefore, the precaution about the potential adverse effects of treatment termination procedures that were discussed previously applies as well to interventions that involve methadone dose reductions.

Methadone Split Dosing

A final variation on the theme of dose alteration contingencies is split dosing. This is a procedure in which participants receive half of their daily dose during the clinic's morning hours, and the other half during the clinic's evening hours. Split dosing is inconvenient and mildly aversive for patients; thus, they may be willing to change behavior in order to avoid the procedure. Kidorf and Stitzer (1996) investigated the procedure in 16 polydrug-abusing patients who had not responded previously to contingent take-home interventions. Study patients participated in both experimental and control procedures at different times. In the control condition, treatment was as usual. In the experimental condition, urine samples were collected on Mondays and Thursdays. Patients testing positive on Mondays were placed on split dosing Mondays, Tuesdays, and Wednesdays. Patients testing positive on Thursdays were placed on split dosing Thursdays and Fridays. Split dosing was not in effect during the weekends. Study patients could also earn a take-home dose for each drug-negative urine sample submitted during the study. While in the experimental condition, patients submitted significantly more drug-free urines (29%) than during the baseline (12%) or control (9%) conditions. However, patients were often not fully compliant with the split-dosing procedure and ended up taking only half their dose.

Dose Change Summary

This section has shown that contingent dose changes, both increases and decreases, can be an effective method to motivate behavior change in methadone patients. This information must be counterbalanced, however, against the known importance of maintaining patients on an adequate stable methadone dose in order to achieve successful outcomes (see Chapter 5) and the potential adverse effects of treatment termination. Hence, clinicians should be aware of the potential disadvantages of any contingencies that involve methadone dose reduction, because these can lead to increased drug use or treatment dropout. This caution would also apply to the split-dose procedure because patients frequently did not take both halves of their dose, even though both were available. On the other hand, contingent dose increases could be a useful clinical strategy to motivate targeted changes in behavior.

Take-Home Methadone Doses

The requirement for daily ingestion of methadone imposes a burden on patients who must travel to the clinic seven days a week to obtain their dose. To ease this burden, patients can be given one or more "take-home" doses of methadone so that they can ingest some of their doses in the convenience of their home. Survey research on methadone patients (e.g., Stitzer et al. 1977; Chutuape, Silverman, and Stitzer 1998) has indicated that take-home dosing is the most highly desired privilege available at the methadone clinic. Furthermore, take-home doses are an ideal reinforcer for use in contingency management procedures, because they are a discrete commodity that can be delivered to the patient following each instance of the desired target behavior. In addition, there is no evidence that take-home doses lose potency as a reinforcer with repeated use in contingency programs; on the contrary, patients may find them more desirable after experiencing their benefits. Overall, take-home doses are a potent positive reinforcer available within the routine operation of the methadone treatment clinic.

A New Way to Use Take-Home Doses

In the operation of a typical methadone treatment program, take-home privileges are reserved for patients who have been drug free for a prolonged period of time (e.g., 90 days or more), and employment may also be required. Take-home doses have been used differently in the research described in this chapter, in which they are used as reinforcers to promote behavior change in patients who would not typically be awarded take-home privileges because of their ongoing drug use. To enhance the ability of the take-home to function as a reinforcer, these studies have typically required a relatively small amount of behavior change (e.g., attendance at a single counseling session, two-week periods of abstinence) prior to awarding a take-home dose. The studies outlined next, then, describe a different way of utilizing take-home privileges to promote behavior change and evaluate their ability to promote desired behavior change effectively.

Clinic Behavior Targets

Contingent take-home privileges can be used to enhance participation in drug treatment activities. For example, one study showed that patients were more likely to keep their clinic fees up-to-date by paying their clinic fees weekly on Wednesday in order to receive a Thursday take-home dose (Stitzer and Bigelow 1984a). Several other studies have shown that contingent take-homes can increase attendance of regularly scheduled drug abuse counseling (Stitzer et al. 1977) or supplemental counseling sessions (Kidorf et al. 1994; Iguchi et al. 1996). The study by Kidorf et al. (1994) is especially noteworthy because patients did not have to attend the extra therapy sessions, and when no reinforcers were offered, only 7 percent of the sessions were attended. However, when a take-home dose could be earned for attendance, there was a 10-fold increase in compliance, with 75 percent of the scheduled sessions attended. Similarly, Iguchi et al. (1996) demonstrated that a take-home incentive program dramatically impacted the attendance rate of methadone patients at a special group therapy program. Subjects in the contingent take-home group attended 60 percent of the scheduled group therapy sessions on average, whereas only a single session was attended by any member of the control group that did not receive take-homes for attendance.

Drug Use Targets

Take-home doses can also be used to promote abstinence from cocaine, benzodiazepines, and other supplemental drugs that patients use during treatment. Two similar studies have investigated the effectiveness of contingent take-home privileges in methadone maintenance patients (Stitzer, Iguchi, and Felch 1992; Iguchi et al. 1996). After a stabilization and baseline evaluation period, study patients were randomly assigned to begin receiving take-homes contingent on drug-free urines or to a control/comparison condition. In the Stitzer, Iguchi, and Felch (1992) study, control patients received a noncontingent procedure in which take-homes were delivered independently of any behavior; in the Iguchi et al. (1996) study, comparison patients received take-homes for attending special group therapy sessions. In both studies, under the contingent protocol, the first take-home dose was earned after patients submitted urine samples free of all common drugs of abuse that could be detected (except alcohol and marijuana) for two weeks, and an additional take-home was authorized after each successive two-week drug-free period up to a maximum of three (Stitzer, Iguchi, and Felch) or four (Iguchi et al.) take-homes per week. One take-home was forfeited for each drug-positive urine sample, and two more drug-free weeks were required to regain lost take-home privileges.

Both of the studies showed that take-home doses effectively promoted abstinence among a portion of methadone maintenance patients (Table 10.1). Specifically, about one-third of the patients (30–40%) showed clinical improvement on measures of drug use when exposed to the contingent take-home procedures. More important, patients who received take-homes under noncontingent procedures tended to worsen on measures of drug use during the study. Therefore, it is possible that a contingent take-home procedure, in addition to promoting clinical improvement in some patients, can prevent deterioration of treatment performance in other patients who do not have an obvious positive response to the intervention.

Another small sample study by Iguchi et al. (1988) showed that the ef-

Table 10.1 **Outcomes of Two Contingent Take-Home Studies**

| | Percentage of Patients | |
	Contingent	Noncontingent
Improved[a]	32	8
	42	15
No change	33	30
	27	17
Worsened[b]	35	62
	31	68

Source: Top two data points in each outcome category are from Stitzer et al. (1992); bottom points are from Iguchi et al. (1996).
[a] Ten percent or greater increase in drug-free urines during intervention as compared to baseline and four or more consecutive weeks of drug-free urines during intervention.
[b] Ten percent or larger decrease in drug-free urines during intervention as compared to baseline.

ficacy of take-home reinforcers was not enhanced by combining these with an aversive dose decrease procedure in which daily methadone dose was decreased by 10 mg each week for patients who provided more than one drug-positive urine; 38 percent of the subjects in each group (take-home dose versus take-home and dose decrease) remained in treatment and discontinued drug use for at least five weeks. There were more treatment dropouts in the dose decrease than in the take-home alone group. This was an important study because it suggests that there is no benefit, and some risk (i.e., treatment dropout), to imposing additional aversive consequences when a take-home incentive program is in place.

These findings point out that not all patients will respond to contingent take-home interventions with clinically meaningful improvement; overall, these studies suggest that only about one-third of patients will make behavior changes large enough to be clinically noticeable. However, the use of contingency management programs may be an important step in the prevention of treatment performance deterioration among those patients who do not dramatically improve their drug use behavior. Therefore, having such programs in place to sustain overall performance of a clinic population can have important benefits. This conclusion is derived from research studies using intensive urine surveillance schedules (thrice weekly testing) and offering rapid initiation of take-home privileges for evidence of recent abstinence. Whether or not the same conclusion applies to the more usual clinical situations in which urine surveillance is less frequent and in which more prolonged periods of drug-free time may be required to earn take-home doses needs to be determined through additional research.

Research has therefore shown that take-home privileges can be quite effective for motivating specific instances of desired behavior such as counseling attendance. In addition, some (approximately one-third) maintenance patients will also stop supplemental drug use (including opiates, cocaine, and benzodiazepines) in order to earn take-home privileges.

Monetary Reinforcers

In many ways, monetary reinforcers are ideal for use in contingency management procedures: money is a reinforcer that can be exchanged for an infinite variety of goods and services and it has universal appeal. Unlike take-home privileges, the magnitude of a monetary reinforcer (i.e., amount of money offered) can be varied continuously over an almost limitless range of values without risking satiation. The one disadvantage of money is its limited availability to treatment programs for use in contingency management procedures. The studies reviewed in the following sections have evaluated the efficacy of money as a reinforcer. If money were shown to be more effective than other reinforcers, it would be worthwhile for treatment systems to attempt the removal of barriers to its use.

Cash Payments

Several early studies showed the benefits of offering cash payments to patients who submitted drug-free urine samples (between $4 and $15 per sample) during methadone detoxification (Hall et al. 1979; McCaul et al. 1984) or maintenance (Stitzer et al. 1982) treatment. All these studies showed better outcomes on measures of drug use for patients who could receive cash benefits for providing drug-free urines. For example, the study by Stitzer et al. (1982) targeted benzodiazepine use in patients who exhibited chronic illicit use of these drugs, which were popular among methadone patients prior to the cocaine epidemic. During the intervention, patients were given a choice of reinforcers for providing benzodiazepine-free urines. Choices were (1) $15 in cash, (2) two methadone take-home doses, or (3) two opportunities to self-regulate their methadone dose by up to ±20 percent. Reinforcers were available twice weekly and were delivered immediately after the urinalysis test was completed. The group as a whole had a significantly higher rate of benzodiazepine-negative urines during the intervention (43%) than during the pre- (4%) or postbaseline (8%) periods. Five of the 10 participants were abstinent throughout most of the three-month intervention. Patients chose money on 63 percent of the occasions when reinforcers were earned and take-homes on the remaining occasions.

Overall, these studies point to the utility of money as an effective reinforcer to promote and sustain abstinence in drug abusers during both detoxification and maintenance treatment. Because the studies were conducted some time ago, however, they provide little guidance about the amount of cash that might be necessary to sustain clinically meaningful improvement in contemporary addicts. Furthermore, providing cash for abstinence could have an unwanted adverse impact on drug use if patients decide to use the cash to purchase drugs. Whether this concern is warranted is not clear, but it is not without some basis. It is widely assumed among clinicians that having money in hand frequently leads to drug use in many drug abusers. Both reports from drug abusers themselves (Kirby et al. 1995) and correlations observed between access to money and drug use (Shaner et al. 1995) provide support for this assumption. To circumvent this potential unwanted side effect of cash payments, more recent studies using monetary reinforcement have turned to a system of voucher incentives, which is described next.

Voucher Incentive Programs

In voucher incentive programs, patients are offered the chance to earn money for providing drug-free urine samples. However, money is not paid as cash; rather, patients can use the money to purchase goods or services, with the only restriction being that the items selected must be consistent with the basic necessities of living or with the treatment plan. These purchases can include payment of rent or utility bills, payment of clinic fees, and the purchase of a wide variety of retail items. Clinic staff make the actual purchases and arrange delivery. Thus, the procedure, although used with appropriate caution, is somewhat labor-intensive for staff.

Higgins et al. (1991) developed the voucher-based reinforcement procedure that has been most widely utilized to date. The population for which the program was initially developed were cocaine abusers applying for outpatient treatment at a clinic in Burlington, Vermont. There are two notable features of this procedure. First, the payment schedule (based on thrice weekly urine testing) was specifically designed to promote sustained abstinence. The initial cocaine-free urine was worth a relatively small sum of money ($2.50), but each successive drug-free urine was worth progressively more. Thus, the longer patients remained continuously abstinent, the more valuable their abstinence became. Furthermore, should a patient relapse, the money schedule was reset to its original low value and the patient had to begin the procedure again in order to accumulate drug-free time and the associated cash value of abstinence. Second, it was possible to earn a substantial total amount—$1,155—for continuous abstinence during the three-month program. This total was arrived at somewhat arbitrarily but embodies the concept that the amount offered should be sufficiently large that drug-abusing patients perceive it as a worthwhile alternative to the drug they are foregoing.

Silverman et al. (1996a–1996c) have shown that this voucher reinforcement program is highly effective for eliminating the use of cocaine and opiates in methadone patients who use these drugs during treatment, and they have also shown that the same voucher-based reinforcement concept could support attendance of unemployed methadone patients at an on-site job-skills training program. In the Silverman et al. (1996a) study, which targeted cocaine use, patients ($N = 37$) were randomly assigned either to the previously described abstinence reinforcement procedures or to a control group that received vouchers on a noncontingent basis independent of their drug use. Overall rates of cocaine-free urines during the 12-week intervention averaged 50 percent for the contingent reinforcement group during most study weeks, compared with about 10 percent for the control group (Figure 10.1). Patients receiving vouchers for cocaine-free urine samples maintained impressive durations of cocaine abstinence; these patients were continuously abstinent for five weeks, on average, compared with one week for control subjects, and 47 percent achieved six or more weeks of sustained cocaine abstinence.

Another study (Silverman et al. 1996b) examined the ability of voucher reinforcers to suppress ongoing opiate use in a smaller number of patients ($N = 13$) who continued to use only heroin during treatment. These subjects were studied before, during, and after the 12-week intervention. Results from this study showed that the overall rate of opiate-positive urines was 78 percent during a prestudy baseline compared with 22 percent during the 12-week intervention and 35 percent afterward. Ten of 13 study patients engaged in sustained periods of opiate abstinence during the voucher intervention.

These two studies show that vouchers can exert a powerful influence on the use of a single drug—cocaine or heroin—and can promote sustained abstinence in half, or more, of those patients who chronically abuse these drugs during treatment. Voucher reinforcers may be more potent in their ability to suppress ongoing drug use compared with other clinic-based reinforcers (e.g., take-home doses, dose changes), as discussed previously. However, studies of vouchers versus other contingencies, such as methadone take-home dose, have not been conducted. More

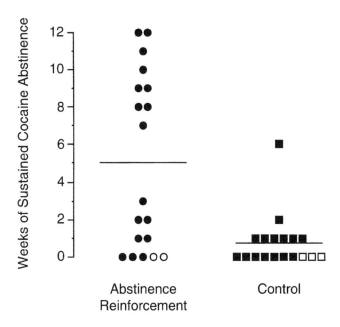

Figure 10.1.   Longest duration of sustained abstinence achieved during a 12-week voucher condition. Each circle and square represents data for an individual patient in the study. The horizontal lines indicate group means. Nineteen abstinent reinforcement patients received vouchers for cocaine-free urine samples, and their results are shown on the left (circles). The results of the eighteen control subjects are shown on the right (squares). Open symbols represent patients who dropped out of the study early. *Source:* From Silverman et al. (1996a).

research is needed to determine the comparative efficacy of various reinforcers for suppressing ongoing drug use when used in contingency management procedures. Nevertheless, voucher-based reinforcers appear highly promising.

Clinical Recommendations

We have reviewed a range of contingency management interventions developed and tested in clinical research settings, most of which have been effective in addressing clinical problems in methadone programs. Table 10.2 summarizes these studies' methodological characteristics and major results. A variety of reinforcers including contingent availability of methadone treatment, short-term methadone dose alterations, methadone take-home privileges, cash payments, and monetary-based voucher incentives

Table 10.2 Experimentally Controlled Evaluations of Behavioral Treatments in Methadone Patients

Intervention	Study	N	Number of Groups	Design	Experimental Conditions	Duration	Target	Effect*
Take-Homes or Split Dosing								
Take-homes	Milby et al. (1978)[a]	69	2	Random assignment; parallel groups	Weekly take-home vs. control	21 weeks	Polydrug use / Productivity	Decreased / Increased
Take-homes	Stitzer et al. (1992)	53	2	Random assignment; partial crossover	Contingent vs. noncontingent take-homes	Variable	Polydrug use	Decreased
Take-homes	Iguchi et al. (1996)	66	2	Random assignment; parallel groups	Take-homes contingent on clean urines vs. take-homes contingent on Training in Interpersonal Problem Solving (TIPS) attendance	36 weeks	Polydrug use / Clinical improvement	No difference / Increased
Take-homes and split dosing	Kidorf and Stitzer (1996)	16	2	Random assignment; crossover	Contingent take-homes + split doses vs. control	24 weeks	Polydrug use	Decreased
Take-homes	Kidorf et al. (1994) expt. #1	10	2	Within subjects reversal	Contingent take-homes vs. control	12 weeks	Attendance to counseling	Increased
Take-homes	Kidorf et al. (1994) expt. #2	15	2	Within subjects reversal	Contingent take-homes after 1 vs. 2 sessions attended	9 weeks	Attendance to counseling	Unclear
Take-homes	Stitzer et al. (1977)	16	1	Within subjects reversal	Contingent weekend take-homes vs. control	40 weeks	Attendance to counseling	Increased
Take-homes	Stitzer and Bigelow (1984a)	5	1	Counterbalanced order	Baseline vs. rebates vs. take-homes	24 weeks	Compliance with fee payment	Increased
Methadone Dosing								
Dose supplements	Higgins et al. (1986)	39	3	Random assignment; parallel groups	Contingent vs. noncontingent supplementary doses vs. control	13 weeks	Opiate use during detoxification	Decreased
Dose changes	Stitzer et al. (1986)	20	2	Random assignment; partial crossover	Contingent dose increase vs. contingent dose decrease	18 weeks	Polydrug use	Decreased from baseline in both groups
Take-homes and dose changes	Iguchi et al. (1988)	16	2	Random assignment; parallel groups	Contingent take-homes vs. take-homes + dose reduction	32 weeks	Polydrug use	Decreased from baseline in both groups
Methadone treatment	Liebson, Tomasello, and Bigelow (1978)[b]	25	2	Random assignment; parallel groups	Contingent vs. noncontingent methadone doses, on disulfiram intake	6 months	Drinking days / Number of arrests / Number of days employed	Decreased / Decreased / No difference

Treatment	Study	N		Design	Comparison	Duration	Outcome	Result
Methadone treatment	Dolan et al. (1985)[a]	21	1	Within subject reversal	Contingency vs. no contingency contracting	5 months	Polydrug use	Decreased
Methadone treatment	McCarthy and Borders (1985)	69	2	Random assignment; parallel groups	Structured vs. unstructured treatment	52 weeks	Polydrug use	Decreased
Methadone treatment	Kidorf and Stitzer (1993)	44	2	Matched yoked	Contingent vs. noncontingent access to treatment	7 weeks	Cocaine use	Decreased
Monetary-based Reinforcers								
Cash	Hall et al. (1979)	81	2	Random assignment; parallel groups	Contingent cash vs. control	16 days	Polydrug use during detoxification	Decreased
Cash	Stanton, Steier, and Todd (1982)[c]	64	3	Random assignment; parallel groups	Contingent $5 for attendance of each family member vs. contingent $5 per family member + movie vs. control	10 weeks	Attendance / Attendance to counseling	Decreased / Increased
Cash	McCaul et al. (1984)	20	2	Random assignment; parallel groups	Noncontingent $5 vs. contingent $10 + take-homes	13 weeks	Opiate use during detoxification	Decreased
Vouchers	Silverman et al. (1996a)	37	2	Random assignment; parallel groups	Contingent vouchers vs. no	12 weeks	Cocaine use	Decreased
Vouchers	Silverman et al. (1996b)	13	1	Within subjects reversal	Contingent vs. noncontingent vouchers	25 weeks	Opiate use	Decreased
Vouchers	Silverman et al. (1996c)	7	1	Within subjects reversal	Contingent vouchers of increasing value vs. those of decreasing value	16 weeks	Attendance to job-skills training	Increased
Menu of Reinforcers								
Cash, take-homes, dose increases	Stitzer et al. (1982)	10	1	Within subjects reversal	Contingent choice of 2 take-homes, or $15, or methadone dose ± 20 mg vs. control	36 weeks	Benzodiazepine use	Decreased
Contingency Management + Other Treatment								
Cash + prenatal care + relapse prevention + therapeutic child care	Carroll et al. (1995)[a]	14	2	Random assignment; parallel groups	Group counseling vs. $15 + prenatal care + relapse prevention groups + child care	Variable	Polydrug use	No differences

Note: In an attempt to maintain uniformity in the quality of the evidence reported here, only articles describing controlled studies that were published in peer-reviewed journals are included.
[a]Not described in the text.
[b]See Chapter 6.
[c]See Chapter 9.
*$p < .05$.

have been shown to promote behavior change effectively. The reviewed studies lead to the following clinical recommendations.

Take-Home Privileges

A contingent methadone take-home program based on urinalysis results can be a useful addition in the operation of a methadone clinic. Take-home doses can also be offered to patients for achieving specific therapeutic target behaviors, such as counseling attendance, when appropriate. Figure 10.2 is an example of a contingency agreement written for a patient who could earn take-home doses of methadone.

Dose Alterations

Methadone dose alterations should be approached with caution, particularly in the case of decreases, because of the demonstrated need for adequate doses to maintain good treatment response and because of the danger of enhanced treatment dropout for patients taking low doses. However, more refined methods for making continued treatment contingent on improved performance have been recently developed (see Chapter 9 for an example of such a treatment program), and these methods may ultimately prove to be useful. In addition, contingent dose increases may be effectively used to promote behavior change.

Money-Based Incentives

Reinforcers that involve monetary payments are clearly effective and should be used according to a clinic's resources. However, it would behoove practitioners to identify other nonmonetary reinforcers such as food vouchers, bus tokens, and movie passes that could be awarded to patients who achieve targeted therapeutic goals. If such reinforcers are beyond the financial means of a clinic, donations can sometimes be obtained through community sources.

OTHER ISSUES IN THE CLINICAL USE OF CONTINGENCIES

Individual Contingency Contracting

One of the issues that clinic directors and staff must decide is whether to offer contingent incentive programs to all patients or to specific, target-

Sample Contingency Contract

I, _____ agree to the following treatment plan:

My goal and that of my counselor is for me to stop using cocaine.

Verification of cocaine abstinence will be through regular urine testing under the following conditions:

    - Collection of urine samples twice per week on randomly selected days

    - Collection of samples under staff supervision prior to receiving methadone

    - Notification of urine collection prior to receiving methadone

I will be able to earn take-home privileges based on cocaine-free urines under the following rules:

    - One take-home per week awarded after two weeks of cocaine-free urines

    - Second take-home awarded after four weeks of cocaine-free urines

    - Third take-home awarded after six weeks of cocaine-free urines

    - One take-home privilege lost for each cocaine-positive urine

    - Lost take-homes reinstated after two weeks of cocaine-free urines

    - Day of the week for take-home awards to be negotiated

Special requirements:

    A take-home scheduled for the following day will be canceled if I am intoxicated at the clinic (alcohol or drugs).

    I am expected to cooperate with take-home recall procedures:

    - Be at home 8 A.M.–9 A.M. on all take-home days to receive phone calls

    - Return unopened take-home to the clinic if called in the morning

    - Lose all take-home privileges (for two weeks) if unopened bottle is not returned upon request

Patient _____   Date_____

Counselor _____   Date_____

Figure 10.2. Sample contingency contract for patient earning take-home doses of methadone.

ed patients, in the form of individual contingency contracts. Standardized clinicwide procedures have the advantage of being easier to implement while treating all patients equally. However, considering that patients vary widely in their baseline performance on a number of outcome dimensions, and thus have different treatment needs and goals, some individualized contracting is recommended as a useful strategy. But, note that even in the previously discussed research in this chapter, the patients selected for study were often those who exhibited poor performance on the target behavior of interest in the study and, therefore, were in need of the therapy interventions being tested.

Factors to Consider in Devising Contingent Interventions

The examples derived from the research studies presented in this chapter should be useful guides in designing contingency management programs for clinical practice. The effectiveness of interventions can depend importantly on the detailed methods used in implementation. Therefore, practitioners who are interested in trying the procedures described here should discuss such details with other clinicians who have successfully used contingency interventions, consult with researchers who develop such interventions, and read further about using contingency procedures (e.g., DeRisi and Butz 1975; Sulzer-Azfoff and Meyer 1991), in order to understand fully the nuances of the procedures. Even with these precautions, experience shows that programs modeled after previously effective interventions will not always be effective when applied in new situations. In general, when a contingency management intervention fails to achieve the desired change in behavior, manipulations can be made in any or all of the procedure's four key elements: (1) the *target behavior*; (2) the *antecedent stimuli,* which are intended to set the occasion for the target behavior; (3) the *reinforcer*; and (4) the *contingency* or rules according to which reinforcers can be earned for emitting the target behavior (Table 10.3). In the following sections, we discuss some of the common pitfalls encountered in designing contingency management interventions and suggest strategies that can be utilized to improve the chances of success.

Target Behaviors

One advantage of contingency management interventions is that they set clear expectations for behavior change. Thus, it is important that target behaviors be clearly specified, objectively defined, easily observed, and

Table 10.3 **Elements of a Contingency Management Intervention**

Element	Definition	Examples
Target behavior	Specific behavior that can be observed and measured	Attend counseling sessions; pay clinic fee; abstain from drugs
Antecedents	Specifies when, where, and how target behavior is to be performed	Attend group sessions Mondays at 4:00 P.M.; pay $30 each Wednesday; submit drug-free urine on randomly selected weekday
Consequences	Reward delivered if target behavior is observed	Earn one take-home dose; earn $10 fee rebate; earn 10-mg dose increase; earn $10 food coupon
Contingency	Rules for earning rewards	One reinforcer for each instance of target behavior; one reinforcer for each fourth instance of target behavior; one reinforcer for randomly selected instance of target behavior (one out of six)

readily quantified in order to avoid any confusion about what is expected. One potential pitfall in implementing these procedures, however, is that the specified target behavior may be one that a patient has never performed, or is not even capable of performing. In this case, the therapist may be setting the patient up for failure. For example, a counselor may arrange a contingency in which a patient earns a take-home methadone dose for every 10 job applications the patient completes. However, this intervention may fail if the patient lacks the necessary reading skills to identify potential jobs in the newspaper, or the reading, spelling, and writing skills needed to complete an application. Alternately, a patient may fail to demonstrate the target behavior (e.g., complete 10 job applications) if another incompatible behavior occurs at very high frequencies and precludes the occurrence of the target behavior. For example, if a patient is using drugs at very high rates and consequently spends a substantial proportion of each day seeking drugs, there may be little time left for job hunting. Thus, the target behavior (i.e., treatment goal) must be realistic and obtainable for the patient.

If a patient fails to earn rewards because the patient never performs the target behavior, remedial strategies should be used to address the underlying problem. If a patient lacks the prerequisite skills needed to complete job applications (i.e., reading, writing, and spelling), the target behavior may be changed to something within the patient's abilities. For example, the patient could be directed to jobs that do not require these skills, either in the application process or on the job. Alternatively, the target behavior could be changed completely, for example, to focus on concrete steps leading toward enrolling in a literacy program.

Antecedent Stimuli

To be reinforced, a response may have to be emitted in a particular place, at a particular time, and under a specified set of circumstances. For example, patients may need to provide a drug-free urine under the supervision of a laboratory technician every Monday, Wednesday, and Friday at the clinic site, between 8:00 A.M. and 12:00 noon to receive a methadone take-home. In other words, only under some specific circumstances would a drug-free laboratory report be reinforced. For this contingency to have reliable effects, it is essential that the conditions under which a particular behavior does (or does not) lead to reinforcement be clearly understood by the patients. These so-called antecedent stimuli are sometimes specified as instructions to the patients that are presented orally or in written format such as in the clinic procedures outline or treatment consent form. Because at times the conditions may be complex, giving patients brief tests on the rules they must follow in order to earn reinforcers and providing additional explanation and examples as needed will ensure that patients clearly understand the conditions.

Reinforcers

What serves as a reinforcer may vary from one person to another, or even across time and circumstances in the same person. A take-home methadone dose, for example, may not have the same reinforcing value for someone who owns a car as for someone who does not, for someone who holds a job as for someone who does not, and so on. Although contingency management interventions may utilize consequences that appear desirable, such as take-home methadone doses or monetary vouchers, the ability of those consequences to serve as reinforcers cannot be assumed. Contingency management interventions may fail if the consequences provided for emitting the target behavior do not serve as reinforcers for the treated individuals or if they do not maintain their reinforcing effectiveness over time.

Identifying Reinforcers

It can be useful to identify events that will serve as reinforcers for many patients by surveying the methadone clinic population. During these surveys, patients are asked to rate their interest in different potential reinforcers that the clinic might provide, to rank order their interest in a list of potential reinforcers, or to make specific choices between pairs of reinforcers (Stitzer and Bigelow 1978; Kidorf, Stitzer, and Griffiths 1995). Take-home methadone doses have been consistently rated as the top priority in previous surveys of this type. In cases in which counselors want to develop individual contracts, it may also be useful to ask an individual patient what rewards he or she would like to work for and to negotiate from a starting point suggested by the patient.

Reinforcer Magnitude

It is clear from previous research in animals and in humans that magnitude is an important determinant of reinforcer efficacy (e.g., Hodos 1963; Pliskoff and Hawkins 1967; Stitzer and Bigelow 1983, 1984b). Once a potentially effective reinforcer is identified, it is important to deliver it in an amount sufficient to motivate behavior change. For example, a 2-mg methadone dose increase may be ineffective, whereas a 10- or 20-mg increase would prompt a behavioral response. Negotiating the magnitude as well as the type of reinforcer with the patient is probably the best way to proceed. Alternatively, the therapist may offer the maximum size reward that is considered clinically feasible.

Rules of the Contingency

The *contingency* in a contingency management intervention is the rule specifying that the reinforcer will be delivered only if the target behavior occurs, and will not be available if the behavior does not occur. Contingency rules can vary along several dimensions, but two dimensions seem particularly critical—the immediacy and the schedule of reinforcement.

Immediacy of Reinforcement

It is essential that reinforcers closely follow behavior in time. Research in animals and in humans has shown that reinforcing effectiveness decreases as the delay between the occurrence of the behavior and presentation of the reinforcer increases (Gonzalez and Newlin 1976). Therefore, in contingency management programs, it is important to ensure that patients receive reinforcers as soon as possible after the target behavior. If a contingency management program fails, a clinician may consider whether there are substantial delays in reinforcement that could be reduced.

Schedule of Reinforcement

Most studies described in this chapter delivered a reward every time the target behavior occurred (e.g., every drug-free urine delivered, every counseling session attended). Another way to deliver rewards is with a schedule of intermittent reinforcement (i.e., when only some instances of the behavior are reinforced). For example, rather than reinforcing each drug-free urine, a contingency management program could require that a patient provide six drug-free urines collected over two to three consecutive weeks, one of which would be randomly selected to earn a take-home methadone dose. Although such a schedule has not actually been tested in drug abuse interventions, it should be effective based on principles of learning and conditioning, which show that large amounts of behavior can be maintained with intermittent reinforcement (e.g., Kazdin 1973; Koegel and Rincover 1977; McLeod and Griffiths 1983). Intermittent schedules of reinforcement also make more efficient use of resources. Remember, though, that they could fail if a patient makes the target response too infrequently to receive reinforcement. To address this problem, patients could be started on a frequent reinforcement schedule with each drug-free urine earning the reinforcer, then shifted to an intermittent schedule after the behavior (abstinence) is established. Ideally, the requirement for reinforcement could be gradually increased over time, thereby reinforcing longer and longer periods of abstinence.

SUMMARY

Evidence from laboratory and clinical research supports the idea that drug use is an operant behavior, maintained in large part by the biologically reinforcing effects produced by drugs of abuse. Drug seeking and drug taking, however, can also be influenced by other consequences that are imposed in a therapeutic context. Contingency management treatment programs are designed to alter the consequences of drug-related behaviors. In most cases, reinforcing consequences are programmed for objectively defined and clinically desirable target behaviors. The studies reported in this chapter demonstrate the clinical efficacy and utility of contingency management procedures in the treatment of drug abuse problems. Taken together, the results clearly show that drug use can be reduced when positive consequences (take-home privileges, dose increases, money) are offered for abstinence or when aversive consequences (dose decreases, treatment termination) are made contingent on continued drug use; however, aversive procedures may cause treatment dropout and associated adverse outcomes. These examples should be useful guides in designing contingency management programs for clinical practice—either clinicwide contingency programs or contracts with individual patients designed to promote attainment of tailored treatment goals. Furthermore, if clinicians understand the principles underlying these contingency management examples, they may be able to make alterations in the target behavior, antecedent conditions, nature or magnitude of the reinforcer, or contingency relationship in order to maximize the efficacy of their own clinical interventions.

References

Carroll K.M., Chang G., Behr H., Clinton B., Kosten T.R. 1995. Improving treatment outcome in pregnant, methadone-maintained women. *Am. J. Addictions* 4:56–59.

Chutuape M.A., Silverman K., Stitzer M.L. 1998. Survey assessment of methadone treatment services as reinforcers. *Am. J. Drug Alcohol Abuse* 24:1–16.

DeRisi W.J., Butz G. 1975. *Writing Behavioral Contracts: A Case Simulation Practice Manual.* Research Press, Champaign, IL.

Dolan M.P., Black J.L., Penk W.E., Robinowitz R., DeFord H.A. 1985. Contracting for treatment termination to reduce illicit drug use among methadone maintenance treatment failures. *J. Consult. Clin. Psychol.* 53:549–51.

Gonzalez F., Newlin R. 1976. Effects of delayed-reinforcement on performance under IRT > t schedules. *J. Exp. Analysis Behav.* 26:221–35.

Griffiths R.R, Bigelow G.E., Henningfield J.E. 1980. Similarities in animal and human drug-taking behavior. In: Mello N.K., ed. *Advances in Substance Abuse.* JAI Press, Greenwich, CT, pp. 1–90.

Hall S.M., Bass A., Hargreaves W.A., Loeb P. 1979. Contingency management and information feedback in outpatient heroin detoxification. *Behav. Ther.* 10:443–51.

Heyman G.M. 1983. A parametric evaluation of the hedonic and motor effects of drugs: pimozide and amphetamine. *J. Exp. Analysis Behav.* 40:113–22.

Higgins S.T., Delaney D.D., Budney A.J., Bickel W.K., Hughes J.R., Foerg F., Fenwick J.W. 1991. A behavioral approach to achieving initial cocaine abstinence. *Am. J. Psychiatry* 148:1218–24.

Higgins S.T., Stitzer M.L., Bigelow G.E., Liebson I.A. 1986. Contingent methadone delivery: effects on illicit opiate use. *Drug Alcohol Depend.* 17:311–22.

Hodos W. 1963. Effects of increment size and reinforcer volume on progressive ratio performance. *J. Exp. Analysis Behav.* 6:387–92.

Iguchi M.Y., Lamb R.J., Belding M.A., Platt J.J., Husband S.D., Morral A.R. 1996. Contingent reinforcement of group participation versus abstinence in a methadone maintenance program. *Exp. Clin. Pharmacol.* 4:315–21.

Iguchi M.Y., Stitzer M.L., Bigelow G.E., Liebson I.A. 1988. Contingency management in methadone maintenance: effects of reinforcing and aversive consequences on illicit polydrug use. *Drug Alcohol Depend.* 22:1–7.

Kazdin A.E. 1973. Intermittent token reinforcement and response maintenance in extinction. *Behav. Ther.* 4:386–91.

Kidorf M., Stitzer M.L. 1993. Contingent access to methadone maintenance treatment: effects on cocaine use of mixed opiate-cocaine abusers. *Exp. Clin. Pharmacol.* 1:200–206.

———. 1996. Contingent use of take-homes and split-dosing to reduce illicit drug use of methadone patients. *Behav. Ther.* 27:41–51.

Kidorf M., Stitzer M.L., Brooner R.K., Goldberg J. 1994. Contingent methadone take-home doses reinforce adjunct therapy attendance of methadone maintenance patients. *Drug Alcohol Depend.* 36:221–26.

Kidorf M., Stitzer M.L., Griffiths R.R. 1995. Evaluating the reinforcement value of clinic-based privileges through a multiple choice procedure. *Drug Alcohol Depend.* 39:167–72.

Kirby K.C., Lamb R.J., Iguchi M.Y., Husband S.D., Platt J.J. 1995. Situations occasioning cocaine use and cocaine abstinence strategies. *Addiction* 90:1241–52.

Koegel R.L., Rincover A. 1977. Research on the difference between generalization and maintenance in extra-therapy responding. *J. App. Behav. Analysis* 10:1–12.

Koob G.F., Bloom J.E. 1988. Cellular and molecular mechanisms of drug dependence. *Science* 242:715–23.

Koob G.F., Le Moal M. 1997. Drug abuse: hedonic homeostatic dysregulation. *Science* 278:52–58.

Liebson I.A., Tomassello A., Bigelow G.E. 1978. A behavioral treatment of alcoholic methadone patients. *Ann. Intern. Med.* 89:342–44.

McCarthy J.J., Borders O.T. 1985. Limit setting on drug abuse in methadone maintenance patients. *Am. J. Psychiatry* 142:1419–23.

McCaul M.E., Stitzer M.L., Bigelow G.E., Liebson I.A. 1984. Contingency management interventions: effects on treatment outcome during methadone detoxification. *J. Appl. Behav. Analysis* 17:35–43.

McLeod D.R., Griffiths R.R. 1983. Human progressive ratio performance: maintenance by pentobarbital. *Psychopharmacology* 79:4–9.

Milby J.B., Garrett C., English C., Fritschi O., Clarke C. 1978. Take-home methadone: contingency effects on drug-seeking and productivity of narcotic addicts. *Addictive Behav.* 3:215–20.

Pliskoff S.S., Hawkins T.D. 1967. A method for increasing the reinforcement magnitude of intracranial stimulation. *J. Exp. Analysis Behav.* 10:281–89.

Shaner A.E., Eckman T.T., Roberts L.J., Wilkens J.N., Tucker D.E., Tsuang J.W., Mintz J. 1995. Disability income, cocaine use, and repeated hospitalization among schizophrenic cocaine abusers. *N. Engl. J. Med.* 333:777–83.

Silverman K., Higgins S.T., Brooner R.K., Montoya I.D., Cone E.J., Schuster C.R., Preston K.L. 1996a. Sustained cocaine abstinence in methadone patients through voucher-based reinforcement therapy. *Arch. Gen. Psychiatry* 53:409–15.

Silverman K., Wong C.J., Higgins S.T., Brooner R.K., Montoya I.D., Contoreggi C., Umbricht-Schneiter A., Schuster C.R., Preston K.L. 1996b. Increasing opiate abstinence through voucher-based reinforcement therapy. *Drug Alcohol Depend.* 41:157–65.

Silverman K., Chutuape M.A., Bigelow G.E., Stitzer M.L. 1996c. Voucher-based reinforcement of attendance by unemployed methadone patients in a job skills training program. *Drug Alcohol Depend.* 41:197–207.

Stanton M.D., Steier F., Todd T.C. 1982. Paying families for attending sessions: counteracting the dropout problem. *J. Marital Family Ther.* 8:371–73.

Stitzer M.L., Bickel W.K., Bigelow G.E., Liebson I.A. 1986. Effect of methadone dose contingencies on urinalysis test results of polydrug-abusing methadone-maintenance patients. *Drug Alcohol Depend.* 18:341–48.

Stitzer M.L., Bigelow G.E. 1978. Contingency management in a methadone maintenance program: availability of reinforcers. *Int. J. Addictions* 13:737–46.

———. 1983. Contingent payment for carbon monoxide reduction: effects of pay amount. *Behav. Ther.* 14:647–56.

———. 1984a. Contingent methadone take-home privileges: effects on compliance with fee payment schedules. *Drug Alcohol Depend.* 13:395–99.

———. 1984b. Contingent reinforcement for carbon monoxide reduction: within-subject effects of pay amount. *J. Appl. Behav. Analysis* 17:477–83.

Stitzer M.L., Bigelow G.E., Lawrence C., Cohen J., D'Lugoff B., Hawthorne J. 1977. Medication take-home as a reinforcer in a methadone maintenance program. *Addictive Behav.* 2:9–14.

Stitzer M.L., Bigelow G.E., Liebson I.A., Hawthorne J.W. 1982. Contingent reinforcement for benzodiazepine-free urines: evaluation of a drug abuse treatment intervention. *J. Appl. Analysis Behav.* 15:493–503.

Stitzer M.L., Iguchi M.Y., Felch L.J. 1992. Contingent take-home incentive: effects on drug use of methadone maintenance patients. *J. Consult. Clin. Psychology* 60:927–34.

Sulzer-Azfoff B., Meyer G.R. 1991. *Behavior Analysis for Lasting Change.* Holt, Rinehart, and Winston, New York.

Practical Issues of Program Organization and Operation

Louise A. Glezen, M.S., and Connie A. Lowery, R.N., C.A.R.N.

This chapter addresses a number of issues linked to the topic of practical issues encountered in the organization and operation of a methadone clinic. These topics include a discussion of the physical organization of the clinic, clinic staffing, assessing a patient's eligibility for treatment, managing specific behavior problems, and programmatic and community issues associated with the operation of a methadone clinic. Although initially it may seem unusual to bring these topics together, they are often related. For example, treatment eligibility and the management of special behavioral problems are closely related, because a key element in managing problems such as loitering, drug dealing, and inappropriate behavior within the clinic (all of which are addressed in this chapter) is the proactive addressing of these potential problems at the time a patient enters treatment. The first step in the management of behavioral problems occurs at the time of assessment and initiation of treatment. Thus, the purpose of this chapter is to provide a summary of these topics related to organization and operation, keeping in mind that they often are interrelated.

Practical Issues Regarding the Organization of a Methadone Clinic

Although this section focuses on methadone treatment, several of the points made here are applicable to clinics providing other forms of substance abuse treatment (both pharmacologic, such as LAAM, and medication-free counseling).

Location of the Clinic and Community Concerns

Although drug abuse crosses cultural, racial, ethnic, and socioeconomic groups, many communities are averse to treatment programs being established in their neighborhood. They fear increased crime, as well as inappropriate behavior such as drug dealing, prostitution, and intoxication. In addition, discarded syringes can raise community concerns about the risk of HIV infection. Although many people express high levels of concern about drug abuse, and identify drug use as a problem in or around where they work, shop, or live, they are often opposed to a treatment program in their neighborhood. This attitude, sometimes referred to as the "not in my backyard," or NIMBY, syndrome, often makes it difficult to open new or expand existing substance abuse treatment programs. Communities often oppose the presence of an existing treatment program, or the opening of a new methadone program.

Even though considerable research has demonstrated reductions in the number of days of criminal activity following enrollment in methadone treatment, a community's perception of substance abusers and substance abuse treatment at times fails to appreciate the overall good accomplished by treatment clinics (Ball et al. 1975; Nurco et al. 1984; Ball and Ross 1991). These community attitudes present a challenge to treatment providers and, in many cases, overcoming such a challenge becomes the responsibility of the director of the facility. In such situations, the program director should actively work with the community to address concerns and resolve problems to the mutual satisfaction of everyone concerned. Specifically, the program director should work with community members, informing and teaching them about the effectiveness of treatment. In addition, some communities may believe that clinics provide services to patients drawn from other regions, and it can be helpful for the program director and staff to provide information demonstrating the extent to which the clinic provides services to members of the local community. Finally, and most important, clinics should attempt to be responsive to community concerns. Patients who are not engaged and responding to treatment should be considered for discharge, as should those who are found to be loitering, dealing drugs, prostituting, or engaging in other criminal activity. Serious problems with the surrounding community typically lead to increased time and effort spent by the program in resolving these concerns.

Since treatment with methadone requires a patient to come to a clinic daily for medication, it is important that programs be accessible by public transportation so that patients can easily comply with daily attendance requirements. In a review of six programs, all were located in nonresidential areas although several were within a business area in a metropolitan city (Ball and Ross 1991). Opiate-dependent patients residing in very rural areas may be better served by a mobile program that dispenses methadone and provides access to medical and counseling staff; however, such programs are not routinely available and have primarily been pilot programs (e.g., Brady 1996; Wiebe and Huebert 1996). In some urban areas, this type of mobile treatment program may be the solution to zoning problems and community objections.

The Facility

The needs of both patients and staff should be taken into consideration in the physical layout of a methadone clinic. Entry from the street to the clinic should provide easy accessibility for the physically disabled patient or staff member. If the program is not at street level, provisions should be made for elevator access. Ramps and wide hallways are necessary for patients who require a wheelchair. The importance of facilitating a smooth flow of patient traffic throughout the building should be given thoughtful consideration when designing a clinic (Lowinson and Millman 1979).

Clinic staff need to be provided with a well-lit, secured parking area located in close proximity to the facility. If this is not possible, staff should have the option to request security transport to their vehicles, particularly if the facility is located in an isolated area or program hours extend into the night.

It is equally important for patients to be provided with convenient parking accommodations, but patient and staff parking should be in separate locations. Parking areas should be monitored by security staff, and some facilities may even be equipped with 24-hour video monitoring. If this is not feasible, parking areas should be patrolled frequently by security personnel, to ensure that patients are not loitering, stealing, or engaging in other illegal activities.

Within the clinic, restricted areas such as a medical records storage room, supply storage area, and administrative offices should be positioned away from the entrance to the clinic and from the mainstream of traffic. More frequently used rooms such as counselors' offices, laboratories, and the fee payment office should be located so that they may be easily accessed by patients.

The space of the clinic itself should be well appointed and spacious enough to serve the needs of the patients while providing an environment conducive to a therapeutic, counseling relationship. Fire extinguishers and smoke or fire detectors should be placed throughout the clinic according to fire codes. Adequate space should be provided to conduct medical evaluations, dispense medication, and provide private counseling. Regulations regarding the storage of methadone vary among countries; in the United States the DEA has final authority over methadone dispensing, and the DEA will provide consultation regarding a program's security policies, procedures, and equipment in order to guarantee compliance with regulations.

Consideration should be given during the designing phase of the methadone clinic to enable adequate observation of patient traffic and security (Lowinson and Millman 1979). Some programs employ the services of security personnel to monitor patient behavior in the program. The use of security mirrors to prevent blind spots within the building can be helpful in providing staff with an easy view of patients waiting for an appointment or to complete a clinic activity, such as submitting a urine specimen or paying clinic fees (Ball and Ross 1991). Security may be augmented by video monitoring.

Finally, it is extremely important that physical facilities be well maintained and present a professional atmosphere. Thus, areas both inside and outside the clinic should be kept clean, damage from vandalism, such as graffiti, should be promptly repaired, and the facility should undergo regular maintenance and painting. The image presented by the clinic delivers an important message to patients, staff, and the community: that the clinic is operated in a professional manner, that the people who work there and receive treatment there take pride in the operation, and that the attitude of professionalism, as exemplified by the care of the physical facilities, extends to the delivery of care provided to the patients.

Organization of Space within the Clinic

The Waiting Area

The waiting area should provide patients with educational materials. Pamphlets and booklets may be obtained inexpensively or sometimes may be obtained free of charge from local or state health departments or other associations, such as the American Cancer Society or local domestic violence centers. Patients should be provided such information to familiarize themselves with community resources. If the clinic is affiliated with a hospital, patients also should be made aware of hospital services available to them. Clinic staff may prepare their own educational or inspirational reading material for patients and present materials on bulletin boards near areas of congregation, such as the dispensing windows. In addition, patients may be given the opportunity to participate in the creation of bulletin board displays.

Counseling Space

The optimal design for a methadone clinic allocates a private office for each counselor. Offices should be sufficiently insulated so that conversations cannot be overheard in a neighboring office or the hallway. The counselor's office should be comfortable, well lit, and provide adequate space for a desk, a chair for the counselor, and at least one other chair. Storage space such as a filing cabinet or computer terminal is desirable. Some programs provide a large community area for clinical staff with private counseling offices that are used when patients arrive for appointments (Lowinson and Millman 1979).

When space is a concern, a group counseling room may also serve as the clinic's conference room. This room should be large enough to accommodate staff meetings and training events, as well as group therapy sessions attended by at least 10 patients. Resources such as a television and videotape recorder can be kept in this room, as videos can be effectively used for both staff training and didactic group meetings of patients. In addition, videotaping counseling sessions can be highly useful for subsequent supervision and training with counseling staff.

Dispensing Area

Methadone is typically administered to patients through a dispensing window, which resembles a bank teller window. Many methadone programs will administer medication from two windows to facilitate a smoother flow of traffic and decrease waiting time. The dimensions and placement of the window can be an aid in reducing the risk of methadone diversion. The window should be positioned to provide nursing staff a clear and complete view of patients as they ingest medication. The dimensions of the opened window should allow patients to be visible from the waist up. The ideal window size is a square approximately three feet high and three feet wide.

Because the dispensing window is a large opening, a safety barrier such as bars or Plexiglas can be used to cover part of the space (although Plexiglas may impede the detection of breath alcohol, clear communication, and the use of breath alcohol tests). Although less aesthetically pleasing, bars provide a strong physical barrier that can decrease accessibility to the staff. The windows must be capable of being secured with a locking mechanism that is approved by the DEA or other, non-U.S. regulatory agencies.

The area directly in front of the medication window should be relatively open so that staff can have a full view of patients at all times. An unobstructed view by the nursing staff of patient activities is recommended to provide some regulation of patient movement within the clinic. If this is not possible because of preexisting features of the building design, security mirrors can be strategically placed to aid staff in observing patients as they wait in a dispensing line.

In addition, there should be a means for immediately alerting security personnel if a potential, or actual, problem arises. Some programs are staffed with security personnel who are present and visible throughout the clinic. It is not uncommon for dispensing windows to be equipped with panic buttons to alert directly security officers or the local police department. These buttons should be easily accessible to the dispensing staff but not visible to patients (e.g., under a ledge at the window).

Medical Area

The examination/treatment room should be well lit and provide privacy for the patient to discuss issues freely with medical staff. The room should be large enough to include an examination table and storage space for medical supplies, including equipment such as an ECG machine, microscope, otoscope/opthalmoscope, thermometer, scale, and centrifuge. The room also should have adequate countertop space and a sink for proper hand washing. Materials contaminated with body fluids should be disposed according to exposure control plans set forth by the clinic to prevent transmission of blood-borne pathogens (i.e., Universal Precautions). Discarded needles and any other items that could cause injury ("sharps") should be disposed of in leakproof, puncture-resistant, labeled containers. Other waste contaminated with blood or body fluids should be placed in bags that are easily closed, designed to prevent leakage during transport, and labeled with a biohazard symbol.

Hours of Operation

The hours of operation for a methadone clinic are an important aspect of the overall administration of the clinic and should be selected after allowing for several considerations, including the needs of the patient population, community concerns, the hours of operation of local transportation systems, and the level of personnel available to provide staffing of the clinic. To enable and encourage patients to obtain or maintain meaningful employment, the program should provide hours for medication and other treatments that permit the working patient to receive the full complement of services provided by the program. Some state and local jurisdictions encourage methadone programs to provide hours before and after the normal work day.

Community concerns should also be considered when designing the clinic's hours of operation. For example, hours may be selected that do not conflict with local church services, or with school dismissal. Similarly, hours should be selected to complement times when local public transportation services are in operation. Finally, hours of operation must allow adequate staffing of the clinic, especially at times when some staff members may be on vacation or out of the clinic because of illness.

Most programs provide all treatment-related activities during the same times medication is dispensed. Thus, access to medical services and group and individual counseling are usually available at times of medication administration. Intake applications may be conducted during routine dispensing times or may be scheduled during nondispensing hours to allow the medical staff time to assess applicants without interruption from patients currently in treatment at the clinic.

Many clinics follow a schedule of being open (e.g., early morning), then closed (e.g., lunch), and then open again later in the same day (e.g., late afternoon and/or evening) in order to exert some control over patient flow; with this operating system, patients can be given specific time periods when they should attend the clinic. Access to the earliest medication times is sometimes viewed as a privilege and may be selectively given to employed or drug-abstinent patients (Ball and Ross 1991).

For programs carrying a large census, it may be necessary to give patients time intervals to report to the clinic or limit the number of patients permitted in the clinic at a given time, so as to minimize large numbers of patients reporting for dosing at one time (which can become a strain on clinic staff). If employed patients are assigned a specified reporting time during the day, every effort should be made to schedule these patients according to their work hours. Also, some clinics with a large census and a small facility may detain patients before they enter the building, if there is suddenly a large number of patients reporting to the clinic. If patients are held outside, for example, in a line at the door, security and other staff should be on-site monitoring patients and maintaining order. Outdoor lines, although sometimes necessary, often provoke community concerns and generally should be avoided.

Staffing of A Methadone Clinic

Overview

Methadone treatment clinics typically are staffed by a physician, a program director (who in some cases is the physician), nurses, counselors, and support staff. This group of staff members should operate as a team and provide expertise consistent with the wide variety of services that are delivered on-site.

Physician

Every program needs to have a physician who functions as the medical director for the clinic. The medical director should coordinate all medical aspects of care provided through the clinic, including medical evaluations of new patients, orders for medications (both methadone and other medications that may be prescribed through the clinic), assessments of patients who develop any new medical problems, and referral and coordination with outside medical providers when patients are treated at other sites. In some clinics day-to-day management of minor medical problems is provided by a nurse practitioner or physician's assistant.

Program Director

The program director provides overall administrative coordination for the clinic. In some cases the program director is also the medical director for the clinic. The program director acts as the primary liaison with outside agencies, including accreditation organizations, professional groups, and the local community. In addition, the program director is responsible for the policies and procedures of the clinic, personnel-related matters such as hiring, reviews, and disciplinary actions, facility maintenance, compliance with regulatory, funding, or accreditation requirements, and budgetary matters.

Nursing Staff

Nursing staff are necessary for the administration of medication. However, they also provide a wide range of other services to the patients. Nurses are often the only clinic staff to interact with patients every day, because they provide daily medication administration. This interaction allows nurses an opportunity to make daily assessments of a patient's health and emotional status and evaluate the necessity of medical or counseling interventions. Patients may present with a variety of physical or emotional concerns, which must be evaluated on an individual basis. Nursing staff can be the first to notice even a slight change in behavioral or emotional status that may be pertinent to the patient's well-being. In this circumstance, the nurse must utilize appropriate clinic resources to ensure patient safety and well-being.

In addition to these daily responsibilities, nurses are essential during the intake or admission procedure. Their responsibilities can include collecting blood for laboratory testing, obtaining ECGs, completing a patient history, HIV counseling (which may include informing patients of their HIV results), and administering intradermal skin tests for tuberculosis.

Finally, nursing staff are instrumental in providing education in a methadone clinic. They should be well versed in teaching in group settings as well as one-on-one instruction. Some examples of possible topics of nursing groups include nutrition, tuberculosis, women's (or men's) issues, parenting, breast self-examination, and HIV or other STDs. In addition to these patient-related groups, nursing staff may be called upon to provide staff training as needed.

Counselors

Counseling staff should be charged with guiding a patient through the rehabilitative process by first engaging the patient in the treatment process, assessing the patient's strengths and weaknesses, and developing a plan of action toward abstinence from illicit opiates and then generalizing to other substances of abuse (McCann et al. 1994). The counselor and the patient may work through individual or group interactions. Family members and significant others may be included in the treatment process (Hagman 1994).

Support Staff

Support staff can include clerical, laboratory, financial, facilities management, security, technical, and administration members of the clinic staff. The size and affiliation of the program dictates the size of the support staff. These staff, although often not directly involved in the treatment process, should be aware of the program's mission and goals.

All Staff

Because opiate dependence is a chronic condition and because treatment is plagued with relapses and problems that reach far beyond actual drug use itself, it is important for staff to be aware of their own thoughts and feelings about drug use and addiction. All staff involved with the program must accept that drug addiction is a chronic problem that is not easily resolved. Progress in treatment can be slow and requires limited and realistic goals for patients and staff. Relapse to drug use is not uncommon, and staff that acknowledge and understand that relapse can occur are better prepared to manage patients during drug-using episodes and to deal with the resulting crises. All clinic staff need to maintain objectivity, patience, a rational perspective on drug addiction, and a firm understanding of what can reasonably be accomplished in treatment, especially when patients challenge staff and test limits. Understanding individual and family dynamics is important, because staff come to learn of arrangements between family members and the patient's role in his or her family's operations. The need for clear and frequent communication among staff is extremely important both in the day-to-day operation of the clinic and in the periodic assessments of the mission, goals, and objectives of the clinic. For a new staff member at a methadone clinic, supervision can be key to that member's success in working with this patient population. For all staff at a methadone clinic, supervision is a valuable mechanism for addressing staff members' responses to a patient's behavior.

Staff Training

Staff training is an essential component of a treatment program. Training upon hiring is customary, but ongoing training of staff is essential to maintain an understanding of current updates in the field of substance abuse and methadone treatment. This training can be achieved through in-service instruction, seminars, workshops, and academic courses. Methadone clinic personnel are composed of various disciplines, and training requirements may be mandated by either the program itself, state and federal regulatory agencies, or professional organizations. Some staff may have more intensive and individualized educational/training requirements to maintain licensure or professional certification (Brill 1991).

ASSESSING PATIENT ELIGIBILITY AND APPROPRIATENESS FOR METHADONE TREATMENT

Under most circumstances, persons applying for methadone treatment must have a current diagnosis of opioid dependence in order to be eligible for methadone treatment. However, there can be exceptions under certain circumstances, as described in more detail subsequently. In the United States, federal regulations stipulate the conditions under which a person can be admitted to methadone treatment (as well as the operation of a methadone clinic in general). Since these regulations are periodically revised, it is recommended that the staff of a methadone clinic maintain up-to-date copies of the federal regulations and be familiar with their contents.

Determining Whether a Patient is Currently Opioid Dependent

Before discussing the determination that a person is currently opioid dependent, it is useful to consider the word *dependence* and how it can be used. *Dependence* is often applied in two different ways by clinicians and researchers. The first way is to speak of "physical" or "physiologic dependence," which is usually indicated by a person showing a withdrawal syndrome when he or she stops using a psychoactive substance. The second way is to speak of a "syndrome of dependence," using criteria such as those found in the *Diagnostic and Statistical Manual of Mental Disorders, Fourth Edition* (APA 1994) (DSM-IV; see Figure 11.1). Included in these criteria are features of physiologic dependence, such as evidence of withdrawal when a person stops using the substance.

However, physiologic dependence is not the only feature of a syndrome of dependence, it is not the defining feature, and it is not even a necessary feature in the diagnosis of a syndrome of dependence. Patients with terminal cancer can be prescribed daily opioids to help control their pain, and thus be physiologically dependent on opioids (i.e., a withdrawal syndrome would present if patients' opioid medication were suddenly stopped). Nevertheless, patients would not fulfill the criteria for a syndrome of dependence (Figure 11.1). On the other hand, a person could use illicit opioids only on the weekends, develop problems because of such opioid use, but not show evidence of withdrawal—that person is not physiologically dependent.

In the United States, federal regulations state that a physician must determine whether a person is currently physiologically dependent on opioids in order for that person to be admitted to a methadone program. The person can be admitted to methadone *maintenance* treatment only if he or she has evidence of a physiologic dependence for at least one year prior to admission, or for most of that year. The physician can make a reasonable judgment, given that it is often difficult to determine just when a person has become physiologically dependent on opioids.

Persons also can be admitted for methadone *detoxification* treatment. In the United States, federal regulations describe two forms of detoxification: short term (i.e., a detoxification that lasts 30 days or less), and long term (i.e., a detoxification that lasts more than 30 days but no more than 180 days). For both forms of detoxification, a history of one year of physiologic dependence is not needed (although a physician must document

A maladaptive pattern of substance use, leading to clinically significant impairment or distress, as manifested by 3 (or more) of the following, occurring at any time in the same 12-month period:

(1) tolerance, as defined by either of the following:

    (a) a need for markedly increased amounts of the substance to achieve intoxication or desired effect

    (b) markedly diminished effect with continued use of the same amount of the substance

(2) withdrawal, as manifested by either of the following:

    (a) the characteristic withdrawal syndrome for the substance (refer to Criteria A and B of the criteria sets for Withdrawal from the specific substances)

    (b) the same (or a closely related) substance is taken to relieve or avoid withdrawal symptoms

(3) the substance is often taken in larger amounts or over a longer period than was intended

(4) there is a persistent desire or unsuccessful efforts to cut down or control substance use

(5) a great deal of time is spent in activities necessary to obtain the substance (e.g., visiting multiple doctors or driving long distances), use the substance (e.g., chain-smoking), or recover from its effects

(6) important social, occupational, or recreational activities are given up or reduced because of substance use

(7) the substance use is continued despite knowledge of having a persistent or recurrent physical or psychological problem that is likely to have been caused or exacerbated by the substance (e.g., current cocaine use despite recognition of cocaine-induced depression, or continued drinking despite recognition that an ulcer was made worse by alcohol consumption)

Figure 11.1. DSM-IV criteria for substance dependence. *Source:* Reprinted with permission from the *Diagnostic and Statistical Manual of Mental Disorders, Fourth Edition.* Copyright 1994 American Psychiatric Association.

that they believe the person is currently physiologically dependent on opioids).

Although the clearest method of determining whether a person is currently physiologically dependent on opioids is to monitor that person for several days while he or she is not taking opioids, and to assess for signs of withdrawal, this approach is obviously unrealistic under most circumstances. However, several means can be used to determine indirectly whether a patient is physiologically dependent on opioids. These can include the person's self-reports of opioid use, documentation supporting opioid dependence (such as past methadone treatment episodes, or legal problems because of opioid use), evidence on physical examination of drug use (e.g., needle tracking), and one or several opioid-positive urine samples. In some cases, it may be useful to use a naloxone challenge to determine physiologic dependence (see Chapter 13 for a description of naloxone challenges).

Exceptions: Patients Who Are Not Currently Opioid Dependent

Under certain circumstances, a clinician may decide to admit a person who is not currently opioid dependent into methadone treatment. In the United States, federal regulations recognize that there are three populations who may be admitted to methadone treatment even though they are not currently opioid dependent. In all three cases, these patients must have previous evidence of being physiologically dependent on opioids.

The first such population are persons who have been incarcerated and either are going to be released from jail within the next 14 days or have been released in the past six months. Such patients must have documented evidence that they would have qualified for methadone treatment prior to their incarceration, and a physician must believe that methadone treatment is now medically justified. Under such special circumstances, a person can be admitted to methadone treatment even if he or she does not have evidence of current opioid dependence.

The second group that can be admitted to methadone treatment is women who are pregnant and are at risk for relapse to opioid use (i.e., they have a documented history of opioid dependence). Again, a physician must determine that there is medical justification for starting methadone treatment. Note that this is typically methadone maintenance, because patients will be receiving methadone for more than 180 days (the longest period of detoxification possible).

Finally, previously treated patients who have voluntarily been detoxified from maintenance can be admitted for up to two years following their discharge from treatment, even if they are not currently dependent on opioids. Such readmission can occur only if there is medical justification.

Preadmission Assessment

In addition to the previously described determination of eligibility, persons who are applying to methadone treatment should undergo further assessments before their actual admission to treatment. These can include laboratory tests, history and physical examination (including vital signs), a medical assessment by the program physician or their designee (e.g., a nurse practitioner), urine testing for drugs of abuse, a breath check for evidence of recent alcohol use, and a meeting with counseling staff to prepare these individuals for methadone treatment. Results from these preadmission assessments can be used to guide both the admission to treatment and early treatment goals and plans.

ADMISSION AND INITIATION TO METHADONE TREATMENT

Once it has been determined that a patient is eligible for methadone treatment, he or she typically is given a date to begin clinic attendance. On the first day of treatment the patient should sign a consent for methadone treatment, undergo any remaining assessments that were not completed during the preadmission assessment period, and receive the first dose of methadone.

Dose Induction

A full description of the procedure for methadone dose induction can be found in Chapter 4. In the United States, federal regulations stipulate that the first dose of methadone cannot be greater than 30 mg and that the total dose the first day should not be greater than 40 mg (unless the treating physician documents the reason for giving a higher dose on the first day).

Ongoing Medical and Nursing Assessments and Treatments

Once a patient has entered methadone treatment, continuing evaluation and treatment for medical and other psychiatric disorders is necessary (see Chapters 7 and 8). Early after treatment entry, it is important that patients be screened for tuberculosis through the administration of a PPD skin test. Patients entering methadone treatment represent a population at high risk for tuberculosis, and the methadone clinic is an excellent site for screening and treating patients who have a positive PPD.

Issues Associated with the Daily Operation of a Methadone Clinic

Rules and Regulations for the Clinic

The rules and regulations for a methadone clinic can provide a clear set of guidelines and expectations for patients, help staff come to agreement among themselves regarding the operation of their program, and also give staff a mechanism for confronting patients about problematic behaviors in the clinic. Properly thought out and communicated, the rules and regulations for a program can ensure a safe and effective treatment and work environment for both patients and staff.

The primary means of informing patients about the rules and regulations of the clinic is to give patients a written copy of the rules and regulations at the time of their admission to the clinic (or at the time of their application for admission). These rules should be written in a clear, simple, and easily understandable format. When given to a patient, a member of the staff should determine if the patient can read and then *verbally* review the rules with the patient; the importance of this interaction cannot be emphasized too strongly. This review communicates several messages to the patient: that staff are serious about the rules, that staff care about patients and their understanding of the rules, and that the clinic is a well-run operation that is a clean, safe, and professional site for the delivery of treatment. This meeting can include topics such as the clinic's expectations regarding compliance with the medication reporting schedule, attendance at individual or group counseling, payment of clinic fees, compliance with submission of urine samples, maintenance of confidentiality, and an agreement to participate actively in the treatment process. In addition, rules regarding loitering, invalid urine samples, illicit drug and alcohol use, possession of drugs or weapons, drug transactions, verbal or physical aggression toward staff or other patients, and theft or destruction of staff, patient, or program property should be included (Deitch 1979; Elk 1993).

Staff members meeting with patients and reviewing the rules and regulations also serves two additional useful purposes: first, it communicates to the patient that staff know the rules, and second, it functions as a useful reminder so that staff *do* know the rules. In addition to explaining the rules to patients, staff need to explain clearly the consequences of those rules.

A clinic's rules also should express the program's philosophy, the general goals of treatment, the mechanisms used by the clinic to achieve those goals, and the services available. Included in the rules and regulations should be an explanation of a patient's rights and responsibilities. In addition, the rules should address issues of grievance. A patient may grieve a program policy or a program decision such as termination. There should be a clear and concise route for the patient to follow. Typically, the patient's counselor will assist the patient through the grievance procedure unless the counselor is the source of the grievance (in which case the counselor's supervisor should manage the grievance).

Finally, although there is a tendency for staff to focus on the clinic's expectations of a patient while engaged in treatment, it is also important for staff to discuss with the patient what he or she can expect from the clinic. The clinic should provide treatment in a safe, clean environment; there should be strict maintenance of confidentiality; and the patient should expect to be treated with compassion, respect, and without discrimination or prejudice.

Attending the Clinic for Medication and Take-Home Dosing

Methadone must be ingested daily, and it is not unusual for patients to attend a methadone clinic each day early in the course of their treatment. However, as patients stabilize and achieve a significant period of sustained abstinence, it is reasonable to consider giving take-home doses of methadone. A take-home dose is often a highly desirous privilege, because it relieves patients from making the daily trip to the clinic. Instead, they receive a dose to ingest at the clinic as well as another dose to be taken at home the following day.

Patients treated in the United States who are admitted to a short-term (30-day or less) methadone detoxification are required to attend the clinic each day—no take-home doses are allowed. If the patient is admitted to a long-term detoxification (more than 30 days but not more than 180 days), they must attend the clinic six days per week (i.e., they can have a take-home dose one day per week). However, patients do not have to get a take-home dose; it is left to the clinic's discretion.

Patients who are in methadone maintenance treatment can be given several take-home doses if they have been doing well in treatment for a sustained period. The use of take-home doses as incentives to achieve treatment goals in maintenance patients can be quite powerful (see Chapter 10 for a detailed description of their use). In the United States, federal regulations stipulate that maintenance patients must attend the clinic six days per week for at least the first three months, but thereafter they can attend the clinic three times per week (with the maximum number of take-home doses being two; i.e., they cannot take home more than two doses at one time). However, they must have good treatment performance in order to receive take-home doses (e.g., adherence to clinic rules, abstinence from drug and alcohol use, not engaging in criminal activity). After two years in treatment and continuing good progress in rehabilitation, patients can attend the clinic twice per week (with the maximum number of take-home doses being three), and after three years of continuing good treatment performance, they can attend once per week (with the maximum number of take-home doses being six). The federal regulations for once weekly dosing contain other provisions (e.g., having to do with employment of the patient), and the program and physician must be extremely familiar with these requirements if a patient is to receive six take-home doses. If a patient is maintained on a daily dose of methadone greater than 100 mg, the patient must attend the clinic at least six days per week for dosing. Exceptions to this rule can be made, but only after the program has received approval from the FDA, as well as local state authorities.

Whereas take-home doses can also relieve pressures on the clinic by decreasing traffic and the number of interactions with patients, daily attendance at the clinic can be advantageous because it allows the clinic to monitor the patient closely and respond quickly if the patient is not doing well. In addition, daily attendance provides a routine for patients who often have had poor structure in their daily schedules and lives. Finally, it decreases the risk of diversion of take-home doses. Thus, although a clinic may have reasons for decreasing a patient's attendance to a less than daily schedule, it is probably best if this is done only with patients who are well engaged in treatment with clear objective evidence of success (e.g., urines negative for illicit drugs, documented evidence of employment).

Staff Issues in the Treatment of Methadone Patients

Boundaries in Staff-Patient Interactions

Issues of boundaries in interactions among all levels of staff and patients often arise in the methadone clinic. Patients interact with numerous staff and are dependent on them for different aspects of their treatment. Blurring of boundaries can be as subtle as accepting candy from a patient, which may be construed by the patient as a nicety to be repaid with a small favor. A boundary invasion also can take the form of staff members disclosing personal information about themselves or other staff to a patient.

Seemingly harmless information can be misconstrued and used as a detriment to staff. A good rule of thumb is to consider carefully the therapeutic value of each interaction with a patient. Staff should be encouraged to ask themselves how a statement or action would be helpful to a patient's successful treatment.

Many professional groups, such as the American Psychological Association and the American Psychiatric Association, strictly prohibit non-professional relationships with patients. Professionals may face legal ramifications from both the patient and the professional organization for violations of their code of conduct. An awareness of these professional guidelines may aid new staff in appreciating the importance of maintaining appropriate boundaries in the clinic.

Confidentiality

In the United States, identifying information for individuals applying to or in treatment for a substance abuse problem is protected under the Federal Confidentiality Regulations (42 CFR Part 2) (Parrino 1993). These regulations prohibit disclosing any information that may identify an individual as having, at any time, a problem with drugs or alcohol, and require that individuals give their permission, in writing, before the treatment provider shares any such information (e.g., to a police officer, outside physician, or family member). If the patient has released the information to someone, the regulations prohibit the recipient of that information from forwarding those records to someone else. Violation of these regulations is punishable by increasingly higher fines and in some cases imprisonment.

Because the Federal Confidentiality Regulations are written in complex and sometimes confusing verbiage, some states now require that an abbreviated and more reader-friendly summary of the regulations be given to patients. The regulations indicate how and when information may be disclosed and also specify situations in which information may be disclosed without a patient's permission, such as in medical emergencies or in the case of state or regulatory agency reviews. In addition, the regulations compel staff to report any indication or acknowledgment of abuse/neglect of a child or an elderly dependent. Reports of child abuse/neglect can be made anonymously to the child welfare bureau or the local department of protective services, without staff members divulging their affiliation with a methadone program. Certainly, staff of programs operating within a larger institution, such as a hospital, may simply identify themselves as being employed through the larger institution.

Counseling and Group Therapy

Issues related to counseling and group therapy in the context of the methadone treatment clinic are addressed in detail in Chapters 9 and 10. In the United States, federal regulations require that programs provide a range of services including medical evaluations, counseling, and other treatments such as vocational and educational programs.

Each patient should be assigned a primary counselor who is responsible for conducting an initial evaluation of the patient, generating a treatment plan based on this assessment, meeting with the patient regularly, and coordinating treatments for the patient both within the clinic and with outside agencies (e.g., vocational rehabilitation, social services). A clinic's caseload for each counselor depends on the severity of problems for that clinic's particular patient population. Maintenance patients who are well engaged in treatment, employed, and have had no illicit drug or problematic alcohol use for years will require little effort beyond the provision of medication, periodic urine testing, and occasional check-ins with a counselor. New patients who have multiple drug problems and who are ambivalent about entering treatment and giving up their drug use may require considerable efforts on the part of staff. No single counselor in a clinic should have all new patients or all highly stable patients, but rather a mix of patients. Typical caseloads for counselors in methadone clinics are between 30 and 50 patients, although a caseload of 50 can be too high under some circumstances. Unfortunately, managed care initiatives and cost-cutting efforts in some clinics have resulted in even higher counselor caseloads, a less than optimal and desirable means for clinics to operate.

Although the primary point of treatment and coordination of care in the clinic is a one-on-one interaction between patient and counselor, group therapy can be a cost-effective means of providing treatment that produces excellent clinical outcomes. In the methadone clinic, group treatment can take several forms, including didactic sessions (e.g., related to health issues such as HIV infection), special group issues (e.g., women's issues), topics related directly to achieving and maintaining abstinence (e.g., senior patients discussing with new patients how to avoid using drugs), and groups on issues related only indirectly to drug use (e.g., problems in familial interactions).

Nursing-Related Issues in the Methadone Clinic

Dispensing of Methadone

Although methadone hydrochloride is available in liquid, tablet, or injectable form, according to the Code of Federal Regulations (Title 21, Section 291.505) approved methadone programs may dispense methadone only in an oral form (Parrino 1993). When in liquid form, it is commonly mixed with cherry juice or an orange-flavored drink to make it more palatable. The dose is gaged using a manual pipet pump. Treatment programs equipped with computers may use an automated dispensing pump controlled by dedicated software. Most of these systems are equipped with or can be adapted to maintain dosage records.

Standard Precautions

In the United States, the Occupational Safety and Health Administration (OSHA) has set forth a standard requiring the implementation of provisions to protect all personnel who may come in contact with blood or other potentially infectious materials. In compliance with this standard, a policy and procedure should be formulated and strictly enforced to minimize exposure to infectious materials. If an exposure does occur, the policy should provide a plan of action. This plan should be reviewed and updated annually, or more often if necessary, in keeping with OSHA standards. Potentially infectious materials include semen, vaginal secretions, cerebrospinal, synovial, pleural, pericardial, peritoneal, and amniotic fluids, saliva (dental procedures), any body fluid that is visibly contaminated with blood, and all body fluids in situations in which it is difficult or impossible to differentiate between body fluids. Aside from fluids, care must be taken to protect against other possible infectious materials.

Practicing common sense is the basis for Standard Precautions. Staff should wash their hands regularly and directly following contact with blood or potentially infectious materials. Hands should also be washed before and after the application of gloves. In the case of a water outage, an antiseptic hand cleanser should be available for immediate use. Food, drink, and cosmetics are not permitted to be handled or stored in areas where there is a likelihood of contact with blood or other potentially infectious material.

The clinic must provide staff with specialized personal protective equipment consisting of devices that prevent exposure of skin, mucous membranes, eyes, or street clothes to potentially infectious materials. The type of personal protective equipment worn should be appropriate to the nature of the anticipated contamination. Typical protective equipment found in a methadone clinic are gloves, gowns, masks, goggles, and face shields. Disposable gloves should be replaced if they become torn or punctured, and gowns should be impervious. Masks, eye goggles, or face shields may be worn in combination when there is potential for splashes, sprays, or droplets of blood or potentially infectious material. The use of personal protective equipment is mandatory and should be enforced. These items should be easily accessible and the supply constantly maintained.

Urine Collection and Testing

In the United States, federal regulations for methadone treatment require that a urine test for drugs of abuse be obtained prior to the onset of treatment, and then at least eight times on a random schedule over the subsequent year. After the first year, random testing must be done at least once per three-month period. However, if a patient is receiving six take-home doses each week, the patient must be randomly tested once each month. Urine samples are to be collected in a way that minimizes the chance of falsification, tests are to be done at a laboratory that meets federal and state requirements, and drugs to be screened must include opiates, methadone, amphetamines, cocaine, and barbiturates.

However, in actuality, clinics may operate using more specific procedures for collecting urine samples, follow a more frequent schedule for collecting and testing samples, and test for a broader range of drugs. The method of collecting urine samples from patients can vary, but most programs utilize some type of monitored or observed specimen collection procedure to ensure the authenticity of the specimen. Before providing urine samples, patients may be required to leave their coats and bags outside the bathroom where the specimen is collected. Many programs then utilize a same sex staff member who observes the patient through a one-way mirror, often with a toilet strategically placed to minimize the chance that the patient is providing a fraudulent specimen. Other programs have developed alternate methods of observing patients, such as videotaping and temperature monitoring, as a means of meeting the objective of collecting valid specimens while remaining sensitive to staffing and patient concerns for privacy.

Testing for drugs more frequently than eight times per year increases the chance of detecting illicit drug use, but the associated cost can make it difficult for clinics to conduct frequent testing. Some clinics collect urines frequently, such as once a week, but test samples only monthly (and do not inform patients which week samples are being tested). Intensive urine testing in the first weeks of treatment has been shown to be highly predictive of subsequent in-treatment drug use.

Finally, although federal regulations do not stipulate testing for other drugs such as benzodiazepines and cannabis, several studies have shown substantial rates of use of these other drugs in methadone patients (and relatively low rates of barbiturate use). Thus, programs should consider broadening the array of drugs tested, especially taking into account local use patterns of particular drug classes.

MANAGEMENT OF SPECIFIC BEHAVIORAL PROBLEMS

The population of people with opioid dependence attending the methadone clinic can represent a wide spectrum of patients, presenting with variable levels of motivation for treatment, needs for treatment of comorbid psychiatric and other medical disorders, and compliance with the program rules and regulations. Even the most well-run methadone clinic periodically encounters patients who are not prepared to engage fully in treatment and who present with behavioral problems that require special attention. Although it can be tempting to simply discharge a patient who has shown problematic behavior, this may not be the optimal long-term solution for the patient, the community, or the clinic. However, it is also important for clinics to spell out clearly specific circumstances that will lead to discharge from the clinic (e.g., selling drugs, bringing a weapon on to the grounds, threatening to harm other patients or staff, diverting methadone). This section reviews several of these specific behavioral problems and techniques that may be helpful in managing patients who exhibit such problematic behaviors.

The Aggressive Patient

A patient may become agitated or aggressive over the enforcement of program policy, especially when that policy prevents the patient from receiving medication or continuing in treatment. On the other hand, a patient may be confronted by other patients with whom he or she has an unresolved conflict. A patient may be particularly susceptible to become agitated if he or she is intoxicated from alcohol or drugs. In such circumstances, preparedness is the key component to defuse such situations quickly and without incident. So how should staff react when a patient becomes hostile or threatening?

One member of the staff should become the spokesperson for the program. It may be the counselor, or a supervisor if the patient demands a staff member with more authority. The first consideration is the safety of the patient, the staff, and other patients. Because the patient may be in possession of a weapon or an item that could be used as a weapon—a penknife, steak knife, cane, keys, or pepper spray—staff should maintain a safe distance from the patient and remove any articles of clothing or jewelry from around their necks. The appointed staff member should try to calm the patient (without engaging in physical contact). The patient should be moved to a less public area that provides an easy exit for the spokesperson or the patient. If that is not possible, other patients should be removed from the immediate area for their safety as well as to discourage any fueling from an audience. Other patients may encourage the already agitated patient by pressuring them to "go for it," with no concern for the patient's future at the program.

Staff who are not involved in the actual confrontation should contact security personnel (if available) and make themselves visible so that the patient knows staff are present and supportive of the program. Security officers should also make their presence known and remain nearby as long as the spokesperson is in control. There should never be any physical contact with the patient unless he or she physically threatens to harm someone. It is important to assess quickly if patients are intoxicated and, if so, their level of intoxication and, if possible, the substance involved. For example, alcohol can produce angry and aggressive behavior in patients, PCP can trigger aggression and at times psychotic behavior, and cocaine can produce paranoia or agitation. If the patient is not de-escalating, staff should consider escorting him or her to a local emergency room for further evaluation and acute treatment.

Drug Dealing in the Vicinity of the Clinic

The potential for drug transactions is increased in the vicinity of the clinic. Programs that have a stable patient population may experience less drug dealing owing to a small number of new enrollees. The long-term patient has been medically stabilized and is usually fully engaged in the treatment process. In programs composed of long-term patients, the patients are less likely to supplement insufficient methadone doses with other drug use; have higher rates of employment, enrollment in school, or involvement in other constructive and rewarding activities; and are less frequently exposed to individuals new to the treatment process who may still be using illicit drugs.

Suspicions of drug dealing may arise when there is a change in the frequency of drug-positive urine tests. Increased loitering in and around the clinic may be indicative of active drug dealing. In addition, exchanges of money among patients or conflicts among patients may indicate that drugs are being purchased. Program policy should clearly detail what actions may be taken. Some programs warn that a search of person and property is permitted for cause, with illicit drugs being confiscated and destroyed and the patient being discharged from the clinic.

Diversion of Methadone

Methadone can be diverted at the window in the clinic or outside the clinic as a take-home dose. The proper ingestion of medication at the window is the responsibility of the patient and the nursing staff, but all staff members should be alert and aware of possible diversion. Measures can be implemented to improve compliance with ingestion and greatly reduce the opportunity for diversion. Such measures can include the following:

1. Having photographs of patients for nurses to reference quickly when a new patient comes to the window;
2. Requiring that patients speak to the nurse before leaving the window so that staff know that patients have swallowed their methadone;
3. Requiring that medication be kept in the nurse's line of vision at the window; and
4. Requiring that patients drink water following methadone ingestion and undergo mouth checks.

To ensure that patients take their methadone take-home doses, the program can require patients to return empty take-home bottles. Although this procedure does not eliminate diversion, it decreases the likelihood of the sale of methadone on the street market. Aversive consequences can be implemented upon failure to comply, such as denying the next take-home dose (Lowinson and Millman 1979; Elk 1993), or discharging patients from treatment for repeated failures to comply with take-home dose rules. Another method to decrease the chance of diversion is to dispense take-home doses in sealed tamperproof bottles, then to call patients and inform them that the bottles must be returned with the seals intact.

Patients Who Present at the Clinic Intoxicated

It is inevitable that staff will encounter patients impaired because of the use of alcohol or drugs. A thorough knowledge of the physiologic and behavioral indications of intoxication is crucial for the safety of the patient and staff. Staff should be well trained to assess and intervene in the case of an impaired patient, particularly because the intoxicated patient may present a risk to himself or herself, other patients, and staff. Depending on the substance used, the patient's behavior may include aggression, requiring intervention by security. If the patient is driving, there is danger of injury to the patient or others on the road. Therefore, staff should assess the patient's level of intoxication and determine whether he or she drove to the clinic. If the patient did drive to the clinic, staff should attempt to call a cab or family member to pick up the patient. If the patient is unwilling to accept assistance and leaves the clinic area, a staff member may call the police and give information describing the patient's impaired status, vehicle license tag number, and any other information, as long as such information complies with the clinic's regulations regarding confidentiality.

A combination of alcohol, methadone, and other substances may precipitate serious medical complications, and a program should have specific guidelines and policies for alternate methadone dosing of patients who are intoxicated. Alternate doses for impaired patients may be easily determined when utilizing objective data as a measurement. One example is the breath alcohol level, which is easily ascertained with commercially available equipment. Determining an alternate methadone dose can be more challenging when staff must rely on subjective measures. It is important to keep in mind that a patient may have a very low breath alcohol level but appear extremely intoxicated; therefore, a policy should allow for clinical judgment.

Loitering in the Vicinity of the Clinic

The issue of loitering is often a source of contention between the community and the program. A program may prohibit loitering in a variety of ways, but the most common method is the use of written rules and regulations. In such a written document, a clinic specifically indicates when and for how long a patient may be in or around the program. Some programs access local zoning laws that legally prohibit loitering within a specific distance of the program. The responsibility of enforcing a no loitering policy is often given to program staff or hired security. Programs located on the grounds of a hospital may have access to security personnel and equipment that will discourage loitering based on the guidelines of the institution. Some programs employ the services of security personnel to monitor patient behavior inside and outside the program, whereas other programs require that staff patrol the area immediately surrounding the clinic each day.

Patients Who Express Suicidal or Homicidal Statements

It is not unusual for patients abusing drugs to report suicidal thoughts. Drug abuse and the lifestyle associated with drug use can often lead to demoralization. Furthermore, suicidal ideation can be associated with affective disorders such as major depression, and some studies have reported high rates of such disorders in patients with opioid dependence.

When evaluating a patient who reports suicidal thoughts, it is important to make a determination about the degree of *intention* the patient is experiencing, and to determine the *reason* for his or her suicidal thoughts. It is not uncommon for persons seeking methadone treatment to report suicidal ideation, for example, on a self-report questionnaire, but when evaluated in a clinical interview they describe low intention to actually harm themselves. However, some patients will report a moderate or even high intention to harm themselves when evaluated.

For all patients with suicidal ideation, it is important to determine the reason for their suicidal thoughts. Many patients applying for methadone treatment report thoughts of harming themselves because they are tired and want to end their drug use. Such patients appear demoralized with their life situation and often report that they would not have such thoughts or concerns if they knew they were entering treatment. However, other patients may report that their suicidal ideation is one of several features suggestive of a major depression. While it would be premature to treat such a patient for major depression before his or her drug use is under control, a high index of suspicion should be maintained if there is strong supportive evidence of a vulnerability to major depression (e.g., a family history of affective disorders or a past history of major depression while not using drugs). Yet other patients may express suicidal ideation as one component of a personality disorder.

When evaluating a patient with suicidal ideation, it also is important to assess him or her for other factors that may increase risk of a suicide attempt. A patient may report suicidal thoughts but have low intentions because of familial responsibilities or strong religious convictions. Conversely, the loss of a spouse or significant other, a diagnosis of a significant medical problem, the loss of a job, or other significant psychosocial stressors can be indicators that a patient is at increased risk for acting on his or her thoughts of self-harm. In addition, a past suicide attempt, or writing a goodbye note can indicate that a patient is at high risk for making a suicide attempt.

If there is evidence suggesting a high risk for a suicide attempt, it is imperative that staff be observant, alert, and responsive. If the patient is at the clinic, and a psychiatrist is not available on-site, then staff should arrange to transport the patient to an emergency room for psychiatric evaluation. If the patient is not at the clinic, there should be a mechanism for contacting family or police and having the patient escorted to an emergency room for evaluation. Consultation with a local community mental health center or hospital emergency room or having a psychiatrist on-call for such situations provides the clinic staff with additional support.

Patients in the methadone clinic may also express a desire to harm someone else. A patient at times may make a nonspecific statement that reflects his or her momentary frustration—a comment such as "I'm going to get someone." Such remarks should not be ignored; often an intervention by a trusted member of the staff can help calm the patient, thereby decreasing his or her frustration.

However, some patients report a desire to harm a specific person such as another patient in the clinic, a staff member, or someone in their family. These threats must be taken seriously. Staff should assess the patient and his or her motivation for the comments and consider their duty as health care professionals to warn the person threatened. Staff should also consider consulting with a lawyer or risk management representative at their institution about the situation, should inform the administrative and medical directors of the clinic, and consider the need to warn other local authorities such as the police. If appropriate, the patient should be transported to an emergency room for further evaluation by a psychiatrist if one is not available on-site.

Summary

A well-operating methadone clinic recognizes the importance of the facility's location, its internal design and organization, as well as its role in the surrounding community. The clinic must operate under local and federal guidelines, and staff need to be familiar with the regulations that may govern methadone treatment in the clinic's area. In addition, the clinic itself should have its own set of rules and regulations that are well known to both staff and patients. These rules and regulations aid in the smooth and professional operation of the clinic, by making clear expectations and consequences of behavior for patients who attend the clinic. However, despite the best efforts and organization of a methadone clinic, patients can present with behavior problems such as loitering, drug dealing, and diversion of methadone. Clinics operate optimally when a plan for response to these special behavioral problems is in place as part of the organization of the program.

References and Suggested Further Reading

American Psychiatric Association (APA). 1994. *Diagnostic and Statistical Manual of Mental Disorders, Fourth Edition.* American Psychiatric Association, Washington, DC.

Ball J.C., Levine B.K., Dearee R.G., Newman J.F. 1975. Pretreatment criminality of male and female drug abuse patients in the United States. *Addict. Dis.* 1:481–89.

Ball J.C., Ross A. 1991. *The Effectiveness of Methadone Maintenance Treatment.* Springer-Verlag, New York.

Brady J.V. 1996. *Enhancing Drug Abuse Treatment by Mobile Health Services; Final Report to the National Institute on Drug Abuse.* Substance Abuse Center, Institutes for Behavior Resources, Baltimore.

Brill L. 1991. *The Clinical Treatment of Substance Abusers.* Free Press, New York.

Deitch, D.A. 1979. Program management: magical expectations and harsh realities. In: Dupont R.L., Goldstein A., O'Donnell J., eds. *Handbook on Drug Abuse.* U.S. Government Printing Office, Washington, DC.

Elk R. 1993. A substance abuse research treatment clinic: effective procedures and systems. *J. Subst. Abuse Treat.* 10:459–71.

Hagman, G. 1994. Methadone maintenance counseling. *J. Subst. Abuse Treat.* 11:405–13.

Lowinson J.H., Millman R.B. 1979. Clinical aspects of methadone maintenance treatment. In: Dupont R.L., Goldstein A., O'Donnell J., eds. *Handbook on Drug Abuse.* U.S. Government Printing Office, Washington, DC.

McCann M.J., Rawson R.A., Obert J.L., Hasson A.J. 1994. *Treatment of Opiate Addiction with Methadone: A Counselor Manual; Technical Assistance Publication Series 7.* Substance Abuse and Mental Health Services Administration, Center for Substance Abuse Treatment, Rockville, MD.

Nurco D.N., Shaffer J.W., Ball J.C., Kinlock T.W. 1984. Trends in the commission of crime among narcotic addicts over successive periods of addiction and nonaddiction. *Am. J. Drug Alcohol Abuse* 10:481–89.

Parrino M.W. 1993. *State Methadone Treatment Guidelines; Treatment Improvement Protocol (TIP) Series 1.* Substance Abuse and Mental Health Services Administration, Center for Substance Abuse Treatment, Rockville, MD.

Wiebe J., Huebert K.M. 1996. Community mobile treatment: what it is and how it works. *J. Subst. Abuse Treat.* 13:23–31.

12

Special Treatment Issues for Women

Hendrée E. Jones, Ph.D., Martha L. Velez, M.D., Mary E. McCaul, Ph.D., and Dace S. Svikis, Ph.D.

Heroin use is reported by a relatively small percentage of the U.S. population. In the 1996 National Household Survey on Drug Abuse, it was estimated that 1.1 percent of the U.S. population had used heroin and that 0.2 percent had used heroin in the past year (SAMHSA 1997a). Among those people who had used heroin, rates of lifetime use for women were lower than for men (0.6% and 1.7%, respectively), and this pattern of difference between the sexes persisted for use in the past year (0.1% and 0.3% for females and males, respectively; SAMHSA [1997a]). Differences between sexes also were observed in rates of intravenous drug use, with males being twice as likely as females to report injecting drugs intravenously (1.6% vs. 0.8%), although there was no difference between sexes in rates of injecting-drug use in the past year (0.1% for females and males; SAMHSA [1997a]). Although these overall rates of heroin and injecting-drug use for women may appear to be low, it is notable that these percentages translate to over 700,000 women who had used heroin in their lifetime, over 850,000 women who had injected drugs in their lifetime, and nearly 150,000 women who used heroin during 1996. Thus, drug use, including heroin use, represents a significant problem for a large number of women in the United States.

This use is especially of concern because a substantial proportion of women who use drugs are of childbearing age. For example, in 1996, 7.3 percent of women between the ages of 15 and 44 years reported illicit drug use during the past month (SAMHSA 1997b). When patterns of recent drug use are examined as a function of pregnancy status, nonpregnant women are found to be more than twice as likely to report recent illicit drug use (7.2%) as pregnant women (3.2%), despite comparable rates of lifetime illicit drug use (45.2% vs. 41.5%, respectively; SAMHSA [1997b]). In a national survey of women delivering live births in the United States in 1992, 5.5 percent or 221,000 women were estimated to have used an illicit drug at least once during their pregnancy (NIDA 1992). Taken together, these findings suggest that some women reduce drug use during pregnancy, although clearly a significant number of women continue drug use despite their pregnancy. Because of differing hospital screening and assessment policies and the stigma associated with substance abuse during pregnancy, it is likely that these self-report data provide a conservative estimate of the true prevalence of substance abuse in women (McCaul, Svikis, and Feng 1991).

This chapter provides a review of special treatment issues for opioid-dependent women. It begins with a discussion of pertinent and unique issues associated with drug use and treatment for women. It then reviews the use of methadone in the treatment of the pregnant opioid-dependent woman and finishes with a review of outcomes in neonates of mothers who have been maintained on methadone during their pregnancy.

SPECIAL ISSUES ASSOCIATED WITH DRUG USE AND TREATMENT AMONG WOMEN

Women can have different risk factors and reasons for initiating drug use relative to men (Stein and Cyr 1997). Compared to males, female drug abusers have poorer functioning in many aspects of life including physical health, psychologic well-being, relationships, social functioning, and economic stability. In addition, barriers to care may further hinder women from entering substance abuse treatment. This section reviews these special needs and treatment issues of addicted women.

Medical Issues

Drug-abusing women have more severe medical problems relative to their male counterparts (Kosten, Rounsaville, and Kleber 1985). Many of these medical problems are related to gynecologic problems and STDs (e.g., Schoenbaum et al. 1989; Solomon et al. 1993). Compared with nonsubstance-abusing women, women who use drugs are at increased risk for gynecologic problems and reproductive complications, including amenorrhea, anovulation, ovarian atrophy, luteal phase dysfunction, spontaneous abortion, and premature menopause (Lex 1991). Women who abuse drugs are also at increased risk for contracting infectious diseases. Drug use is the largest risk factor for contracting HIV infection among women, with approximately 50 percent of AIDS cases in women from intravenous drug use by the woman herself and an additional 20 percent from intravenous drug use by her sexual partner(s) (CDC 1994). Compared to men, drug-abusing women are at greater risk for HIV infection because the virus is more easily transmitted by sexual intercourse from men to women, women are likely to have unprotected sexual intercourse to finance their addiction, and women's sexual partners are more often individuals who engage in high-risk behaviors (McCaul and Svikis in press).

Most other medical complications associated with opiate abuse are the consequences of needle use (Stein 1990). Although women have lower overall rates of injecting-drug use compared to men, there are no known differences in the complications of needle use in women compared to men. These complications are well known and include diseases such as hepatitis leading to acute and chronic liver disease, endocarditis, talc granulomatosis, and skin abscesses (Stein and Cyr 1997).

Psychological Issues

Women with substance abuse disorders are at increased risk for several psychologic problems, including affective disorders (Helzer and Pryzbeck 1988), suicide attempts (Gomberg 1989), psychopathology (Marsh and Simpson 1986), low self-esteem, anxiety, and depression (Cuskey, Berger, and Densen-Gerber 1977; Colten 1979; Bartholomew et al. 1994), low levels of coping skills for everyday life events (Luthar et al. 1993), and high levels of overall psychologic distress (Kosten, Rounsaville, and Kleber 1985; Luthar, Cushing, and Rounsaville 1996). Although it is not always clear if such psychologic issues precede or are a consequence of drug use, their high prevalence in women suggests the need for targeted treatment services addressing these issues in this population.

Family and Social Issues

In addition to the greater risk of psychologic problems drug-abusing women face, they also have more difficulty in their relationships and social functioning. Drug-abusing women, compared to their male counterparts, tend to lack confidence in their communication skills (Colten 1979), be more passive in their relationships with partners, and are more likely to be divorced or separated. They also are more likely to report feelings of loneliness (Tucker 1979), smaller networks of social support, and a higher frequency of unresolved sexual issues (Cuskey, Berger, and Densen-Gerber 1977; Colten 1979; Bartholomew et al. 1994). In general, female substance abusers are more socially isolated, with fewer friends and fewer romantic relationships, and have more difficulty socializing than male substance abusers (Wallen 1992).

Substance-abusing women report higher rates of alcohol and drug dependence in their family of origin (Wallen 1992; Haller et al. 1993; Beckwith, Espinosa, and Howard 1994). Among patients enrolled in methadone maintenance treatment, 70 percent of women reported a history of illicit drug use by at least one sibling (Pivnick et al. 1994).

High rates of reported childhood sexual abuse are present in the female drug-abusing population. In one study of alcoholic women, 66 percent reported childhood sexual abuse, compared with 35 percent of the general population of women (Miller, Downs, and Gondoli 1989). For many women, these patterns of childhood exposure to substance-abusing family members and physical/mental/sexual abuse continue into adulthood. One-third to one-half of substance-abusing women live with a substance-abusing man (Kosten, Rounsaville, and Kleber 1985; Griffin et al. 1989). In fact, women who experience severe violence are twice as likely to report that their partners had been intoxicated and six times as likely to report that their partners had been high on drugs at some point during the past year (Kaufman-Kantor and Straus 1989). Substance use by the woman herself places her at increased risk of becoming a victim of violence (e.g., Downs, Miller, and Panek 1993). Women are three times as likely to experience violence if intoxicated and six times as likely if they have used drugs in the past year (Kaufman-Kantor and Straus 1989).

Economic and Legal Issues

Drug-abusing women tend to be at an economic disadvantage to men in that they have poorer occupational functioning (Ellinwood, Smith, and Vaillant 1966) and can be dependent on men for economic support, often via prostitution or exchanging sex for drugs or daily needs (e.g., food and shelter). They tend to report low levels of vocational training and job skills and high rates of unemployment (e.g., Allen 1995). Drug-abusing women display a large incongruity between the types of jobs they rate as most interesting and their current skills levels, overestimating their job capabilities relative to their education, job training, and work experience (Silverman et al. 1995).

Although these women have many problems, they are less likely than drug-abusing men to display socially deviant behaviors such as those involving the legal system (Kosten, Rounsaville, and Kleber 1985; Luthar et al. 1993; Luthar, Cushing, and Rounsaville 1996). However, a majority of women have had at least one legal conviction (Stevens and Arbiter 1995). Interestingly, there is evidence that legal involvement can improve enrollment and retention in substance abuse services (Knisley et al. 1993).

Barriers to Care for Women Entering Drug Treatment

It has been estimated that women enrolled in drug treatment are only 30 percent of the estimated 1.5 million women needing drug abuse treatment (IOM 1989). Minority women may be even less represented in substance abuse services. In a survey of drug-abusing women enrolled in methadone treatment programs and street settings in low-income communities, black women were less likely to be currently enrolled or have a history of drug treatment relative to white women (Lewis and Waters 1989). Quite often women seeking treatment are not able to receive it immediately because of a lack of drug treatment slots. Women may be hindered not only from a lack of financial resources but also from a number of specific barriers. These barriers include insufficient outreach focused on women who are not highly motivated to enter treatment; gender and cultural insensitivity in program composition; the fear of legal consequences such as loss of child custody; the lack of child care, transportation, and health insurance coverage; the inability to find another person to care for other dependent family members; the ineligibility for treatment medications if pregnant or not using reliable birth control; and the social stigmatization of female drug users (Chasnoff 1991).

In typical drug abuse treatment, the addiction itself is the focus. The treatment program attempts to extinguish drug-seeking and drug-taking behavior by focusing on relapse prevention and providing counseling that targets abstinence. This type of approach has limited effectiveness if drug using is targeted exclusively and other psychosocial challenges are given little attention (Carroll and Rounsaville 1995).

Because women appear to have unique treatment needs, researchers have recommended comprehensive gender-specific models for drug treatment services (Finnegan 1988; Finnegan, Davenny, and Hartel 1993). Table 12.1 shows typical areas that a woman's drug abuse treatment program should address. Outreach to increase women's access to care should include utilizing workers from the community, developing liaisons with community-based organizations, and providing transportation. Furthermore, women-only groups are an effective way for treatment programs to

Table 12.1   **Specific Treatment Needs of Drug-Abusing Women**

Medical	Relationships and Social Functioning	Special Considerations	Psychologic	Economic
General health care	Parenting skills	Child care during treatment	Depression and anxiety	Interview and job-skills training
Obstetric and gynecologic care	Communication skills	Transportation	Sexual abuse	Employment
HIV prevention	Conflict resolution	Housing	Sexuality	Maintaining a job
Nutritional counseling	Developing a support network	Literacy	Issues of loss	Money management
Family planning			Self-esteem	

Source: Based on Finnegan (1988); Finnegan (1991); Jansson et al. (1996); and McCaul and Svikis (in press).

deal with sensitive issues such as self-esteem, anxiety, depression, sexuality, communication skills, and personal health (Blume 1990). This specialized women's programming appears to increase knowledge and self-esteem and provide social support, which may lead to decreased anxiety (Bartholomew et al. 1994). Additionally, screening for partner violence is necessary because women who return to violent relationships tend to relapse into drug use (Miller, Downs, and Gondoli 1989). All interventions should also address HIV intervention and work on vocational training and skills needed to acquire and maintain a job. As long as women remain economically dependent on men, they will continue to be at high risk for relapse.

Methadone Treatment and the Pregnant Woman

Medical and Obstetrical Complications Associated with Use of Opiates during Pregnancy

The majority of drug-abusing women who are pregnant do not seek prenatal care early in their pregnancy and are therefore more vulnerable to medical and obstetrical complications (Table 12.2). A complete and comprehensive medical and drug abuse history, especially with regard to polysubstance abuse, is critically important in the treatment of the drug-dependent woman. Heavy drug use is associated with low weight gain during pregnancy (Edelin et al. 1988). Although studies suggest a link between drug abuse and serious prenatal consequences such as preeclampsia, stillbirths, abruptio placentae, premature labor, and fetal distress, to what ex-

Table 12.2 **Medical Problems Associated with Maternal Opioid Use**

General Medical Problems	Infections and Viruses	Sexually Transmitted Diseases
Opioid intoxication, overdose, withdrawal	Endocarditis	Syphilis
	Septicemia	Condyloma acuminatum
Poor dental hygiene	Pneumonia	Herpes
Anemia	Cellulitis and abscesses	Gonorrhea
Thrombophlebitis	Tuberculosis	Chlamydia
Edema	Urinary tract infections	
Tetanus	Hepatitis	
Hypertension	HIV infection	
Diabetes mellitus	AIDS and AIDS-related complex	
Nutritional deficiencies		

Source: Based on Ostrea and Chavez (1979); Fitzsimmons et al. (1986); Keith et al. (1986); Cox et al. (1988); Regan, Leifer, and Finnegan (1988); Selwyn et al. (1989); Finnegan (1991); Hoegerman and Schnoll (1991); and Martin, Payte, and Zweben (1991).

tent these complications are a direct result of the drugs or the effects of a lack of prenatal care, poor nutrition, and lifestyle are as yet unknown (Robins and Mills 1993).

Regardless of the drug used, all pregnant substance abusers are at high risk for pregnancy complications. The medical complications may vary owing to the drug or combination of drugs, the time during pregnancy when the drug was used, the route of drug administration, possible withdrawal or cycling between intoxication and withdrawal, lack of prenatal care, or failure to identify and treat drug-related problems.

The History of Methadone Treatment during Pregnancy

The occurrence of neonatal drug withdrawal associated with maternal opiate abuse was acknowledged in the late 1800s; however, the upward trend of heroin use in the 1950s and 1960s among women of childbearing age sparked concern about the in utero effects of opiates on the developing child. In 1973 the FDA declared that all women with confirmed pregnancies would undergo detoxification within 21 days after acceptance into a methadone program. This decision was then reversed following reports of adverse consequences, including death to the fetus related to opioid withdrawal (Zuspan, Gumpel, and Mejia-Zelaya 1975). The initiation of methadone maintenance for pregnant opiate-dependent women in the early 1970s led researchers to question the effects of this pharmacotherapy on pre- and postnatal development.

As a result of studies conducted in the late 1960s and early 1970s, methadone became the standard of care for pregnant opioid addicts and is the only medication currently approved for their treatment. The maternal and fetal benefits of methadone maintenance during pregnancy have been demonstrated by clinicians and researchers (Wilson, Desmond, and Wait 1981; Kaltenbach and Finnegan 1989a; Finnegan 1991). Compared to heroin abuse, methadone maintenance treatment during pregnancy has been associated with better prenatal care, increased fetal growth, reduced fetal mortality, decreased risk of HIV infection, decreased cases of preeclampsia and neonatal withdrawal, increased likelihood that the infant will be discharged to his or her parents (Kandall et al. 1977; Finnegan 1978, 1991), and increased retention in treatment (Svikis et al. 1997b). Because the majority of this work was performed in comprehensive care settings where women had access to obstetrical/medical services, psychiatric care, social workers, and counseling services, conclusions that can be made about the benefits of methadone itself in producing improved birth outcomes are limited.

The use of methadone in the treatment of pregnant drug abusers is not without controversy. Concerns surrounding methadone are based on several factors. First, debate still continues over the use of opioid replacement therapy in general in the treatment of drug abuse. Second, many critics of methadone maintenance assume that denying access to methadone would increase a pregnant woman's motivation to become abstinent. However, in practice, attempts at abstinence are not usually successful, and the choice for the pregnant drug user is usually between abuse of street drugs and treatment program participation. Third, inaccurate dissemination and amplification by the media regarding the morbidity of children born to methadone-treated mothers, based sometimes on data from small or ill-defined groups of children born to heroin abusers or methadone-maintained mothers, fuels methadone treatment fears (Hans 1996).

Entry to Treatment

The subpopulation of substance-abusing pregnant women is unique and has specific needs that must be addressed to facilitate better access and utilization of both obstetric and substance abuse treatments. The maternal and infant complications associated with substance abuse can be mitigated only with appropriate care and treatment. It has been shown that comprehensive care of the opiate-addicted mother has a positive impact on the outcome of her pregnancy (Kandall et al. 1977; Ellwood et al. 1987; Svikis et al. 1997a). Guidelines for comprehensive prenatal care have been established (Figure 12.1) (Finnegan 1991; Jansson et al. 1996). They include intensive perinatal management for high-risk pregnancy, psychosocial

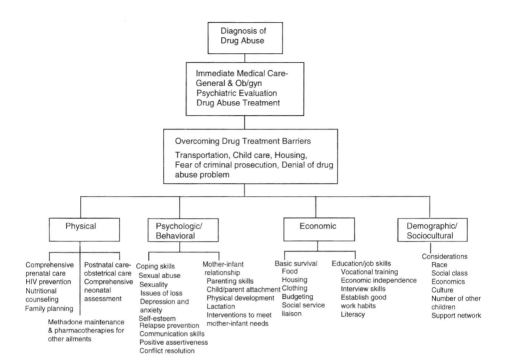

Figure 12.1.   Guidelines for comprehensive prenatal care of the opioid-dependent mother. *Source:* Data from Finnegan (1991); Jansson et al. (1996).

counseling, prenatal/parenting education classes, psychiatric therapy, and methadone maintenance when needed. A residential component is also valuable for assisting pregnant women in abstaining from drugs and giving the developing fetus the best chance of a healthy birth. However, getting women involved in these types of comprehensive care settings is often difficult because there are many inhibiting factors. Primary barriers to care for pregnant, drug-abusing women can include a fear of criminal prosecution and removal of their children by the legal system, a lack of transportation services, an absence of child care resources for existing children, poor access to obstetrical care, social stigmatization by the medical community, and a lack of treatment services addressing women's issues (Jansson et al. 1996).

The most effective treatment for pregnant addicts is delivered in the context of well-organized and comprehensive services. In addition to methadone and psychologic services for the treatment of addiction, general medical care and obstetrical care are needed. These latter features of a comprehensive treatment program for pregnant, opioid-dependent patients should include both routine medical testing, as found in the typical community-based methadone clinic and tests appropriate for the special needs of this population. Thus, for example, ECGs should be performed owing to the cardiac toxicity associated with the abused drugs. Screening for infectious illnesses is important because they comprise a high percentage of medical complications in drug-abusing individuals and can cause harm to mother and child if not properly treated. The treatment and management of HIV is sometimes required not only for the mother but also for the infant (Finnegan 1991). Drug-abusing women should also be tested for liver function because they may have an active or postviral hepatitis disorder. Frequent urine cultures should be conducted in order to rule out urinary tract infections. Tuberculin tests should be conducted because this population is at higher risk for tuberculosis. Skin and venous access sites for infection and cellulitis should be inspected because pregnancy can result in expanded injection sites, such as the breast. In addition to medical complications, there are also possible obstetrical complications in drug-dependent women (Table 12.3). Patients should undergo a sonogram because intrauterine growth retardation is seen in this population. In summary, the woman's health status should be carefully and thoroughly evaluated.

In addition to the physical consequences of drug use, depression is common in pregnant addicts. Thus, careful psychiatric assessment, including a comprehensive mental status examination, should be conducted. The most common psychiatric conditions found in pregnant addicts are personality disorders. These can frequently interfere with treatment and lead to conflicts with health care staff (Hoegerman and Schnoll 1991). Many pregnant, drug-abusing women have been disenfranchised by their community and society and need education about nutrition, parenting, and money management. In addition, they may have unstable living situations,

Table 12.3 **Obstetric Problems Associated with Opioid Abuse**

Spontaneous abortion	Gestational diabetes
Intrauterine death	Postpartum hemorrhage
Abruptio placentae	Eclampsia
Amnionitis	Increased hospitalization
Chorioamnionitis	Preeclampsia
Septic thrombophlebitis	Stillbirth
Placental insufficiency	Intrauterine growth retardation
Premature rupture of membranes	Premature labor

Source: Based on Connaughton et al. (1975); Ostrea and Chavez (1979); Fitzsimmons et al. (1986); Keith et al. (1986); Finnegan (1991); Hoegerman and Schnoll (1991); and Martin, Payte, and Zweben (1991).

be unemployed, and have poor or nonexistent literacy skills; thus, social services advocates are critical.

Methadone Dosing

Opioid-dependent women who are in methadone maintenance treatment before becoming pregnant can be maintained on their pre-pregnancy methadone dose after conception. However, a majority of women do not seek treatment until they are already pregnant; therefore, they should be admitted to a treatment program for medical and psychologic evaluation as well as the determination of an adequate methadone dose. The opioid-dependent patient should initially be evaluated for signs and symptoms of withdrawal including lacrimation, irritability, rhinorrhea, nausea, vomiting, abdominal cramping, uterine irritability, increased fetal activity, and hypotension. If evidence of withdrawal is present, the initial dose can be determined in one of several ways. For inpatients, one option is to give an initial dose of 10 mg of methadone, with additional 5-mg doses given every 4–6 hours if withdrawal symptoms continue for the first 24 hours. On the next day, the previous day's total dose is administered as the maintenance dose. The patient is then evaluated for withdrawal over the next 24 hours, and additional doses are given as needed (Finnegan and Wapner 1987).

Another procedure that can be used with inpatients involves evaluating the patient every 6 hours for the strength of 10 withdrawal signs on a 0- to 2-point scale. The 10 signs are pupillary dilation, rhinorrhea, lacrimation, piloerection, nausea or vomiting, diarrhea, yawning, cramps, restlessness, and subjective evaluation. A total withdrawal score (range 0–20) is calculated for the time of evaluation, and if the withdrawal score is greater than 5, the patient is medicated on a milligram per point basis. For example, if a patient scores a 6 on her first assessment, she would be given 6 mg of methadone. At the next assessment, if she scores a 4 she would not be dosed. If she scores a 12 on the third assessment, she would receive a 12-mg dose of methadone. The total dose required for the first 24 hours is then given as one or two doses the next day (Hoegerman and Schnoll 1991).

If the patient is being treated as an outpatient, an initial dose of 15 mg should be given on the morning of the first day, followed by close observation for intoxication or withdrawal and possible medication in the afternoon. If withdrawal signs persist, her total daily dosage can be increased by 10 mg; however, it may need to be increased 10 mg per day until she is stabilized (Smith, Wesson, and Tusel 1989). Once the patient is stabilized, she can begin once daily dosing. However, methadone-maintained women frequently complain of increasing withdrawal symptoms as pregnancy progresses, and they frequently need elevations of their dose in order to maintain the same plasma level and to remain withdrawal free. Methadone metabolism increases during the third trimester of pregnancy, so for a given dose of methadone, plasma levels can be significantly lower and withdrawal symptoms increased during the final months of pregnancy (Kreek, Schecter, and Gutjahr 1974; Kreek 1979, 1986; Pond et al. 1985; Gazaway, Bigelow, and Brooner 1993).

One factor to consider when dosing with methadone during pregnancy is whether to dose once versus twice per day (split dosing). It has been found that a single daily dose of methadone significantly affects the behavior of the fetus, whereas a more stable pattern of fetal behavior is noted with split dosing (Wittmann and Segal 1991). Split dosing may be especially relevant in the third trimester of pregnancy. During this time, steady-state methadone levels decline, in part owing to increased progestin in the mother (which leads to increased metabolism of methadone and an overall increase in clearance; Cooper et al. [1983]).

Although there is evidence to suggest that a maternal methadone dose of less than 20 mg per day at the time of birth reduces the presence of neonatal withdrawal signs and symptoms (Kreek, Schecter, and Gutjahr 1974; Strauss et al. 1976a; Madden et al. 1977; Schnoll 1986), it is important to place the mother on an effective dose of methadone to reduce illicit drug use and eliminate withdrawal signs. Many data suggest that higher methadone doses are more efficacious than lower doses in reducing illicit drug and needle use, which are important considerations for the overall health of the mother and infant (Jarvis and Schnoll 1994).

Detoxification during Pregnancy

In addition to the debate over the use of methadone as a pharmacotherapy for pregnant heroin addicts, opinions also differ about the efficacy of detoxifying a pregnant woman from methadone. Detoxification during the last trimester of pregnancy is associated with increased fetal adrenal response and increased levels of epinephrine and norepinephrine in the amniotic fluid. These elevated levels of epinephrine and norepinephrine are reduced when methadone dose is readministered, suggesting that detoxification late in pregnancy should not be recommended unless the fetus can be monitored for stress (Zuspan, Gumpel, and Mejia-Zelaya 1975).

A majority of treatment practitioners in the area of perinatal addiction hold the belief that methadone should be maintained for the duration of a pregnancy to reduce the possibility of illicit drug use, and to minimize the risk of HIV infection. The necessity of daily methadone treatment also gives the treatment provider an opportunity to maintain close contact with the pregnant woman, which might not occur if she was not on methadone. Although the prevailing opinion of treatment providers supports the continuation of methadone throughout pregnancy, there may be occasions when this is not possible. Jarvis and Schnoll (1995) highlighted several reasons that may necessitate the withdrawal of methadone from a pregnant woman. First, owing to unforeseen reasons, she may need to move to an area where methadone treatment is not available. Second, she may request a methadone detoxification before delivery. Third, she may be too disruptive in the treatment environment, necessitating removal from the clinic. If a pregnant patient has a circumstance requiring methadone detoxification, the risks of withdrawal should be clearly explained before it is initiated. It is important to inform the patient that cycling on and off methadone places her fetus at greater risk for fetal stress than maintaining a constant level of methadone. If she elects to go through with the detoxification, it is recommended that intensive psychosocial support be provided.

Studies of methadone withdrawal in nonpregnant methadone patients suggest that patients have better outcomes when they are aware of their dose. However, the literature on the use of methadone in pregnant women suggests that withdrawal from methadone should be done without informing the patient about the dose and speed of the detoxification. The medication should be placed in a fixed volume of liquid, preferably with a flavor mask so that the patient receives the same volume of liquid and so that it tastes the same throughout the withdrawal period. The dose should not decrease at a rate greater than 10 mg per week (Jarvis and Schnoll 1995); 5 mg every two weeks has been recommended (Finnegan 1991). No matter how slowly the dose is decreased, the mother and fetus should undergo intensive physiologic monitoring. If detoxification is necessary, it is not advised prior to the fourteenth week of gestation because of the potential risk of inducing abortion, and it should not be done after the thirty-second week of pregnancy because of possible withdrawal-induced fetal stress (Finnegan 1991).

EFFECTS OF METHADONE ON PRE-
AND POSTNATAL DEVELOPMENT

Before an adequate review of the current knowledge about the birth and long-term outcomes of prenatal methadone exposure can be addressed, the methodological challenges and limitations of the data must be acknowledged. It is well known that women who are in methadone treatment programs during pregnancy often continue to use other psychoactive drugs, both illicit and licit (e.g., alcohol and nicotine) (Oleske 1977; Wilson, Desmond, and Wait 1981; Rosen and Johnson 1982; Rosen and Johnson 1985; Edelin et al. 1988; Robins and Mills 1993). Comorbid drug abuse makes it difficult to disassociate the negative effects of one drug from another. Methadone treatment itself (i.e., the dose, dosing regimen, and period of gestation when initiated) varies greatly among programs and patients, thus limiting conclusions across studies about dose-effect relationships. Furthermore, there are numerous confounding variables both prenatally (e.g., inadequate maternal nutrition, amount of prenatal care, exposure to other drugs, obstetrical complications, etc.) (Hans 1992) and postnatally (e.g., delivery complications, toxin exposure, caretaking practices, exposure to violence) (Strauss et al. 1976a; Hans 1992). The assessment and treatment approach to neonatal abstinence syndrome also varies across studies and treatment settings (Kaltenbach 1996), thereby making it difficult to make a causal link between methadone exposure and abstinence severity. Children who are followed up in longitudinal studies are a select sample, which may impact studies significantly. For instance, they may be the offspring of mothers who remain in service systems and, therefore, have a better outcome because their parents are motivated (or alternately, a worse outcome because their parents are overwhelmed by substance abuse problems). Alternatively, the children may appear less affected because the offspring with the greatest problems were lost to follow-up assessment (Robins and Mills 1993). Moreover, some studies lack a proper comparison group; in such studies, it is important that groups are matched for race, socioeconomic status, sex, birth weight, gestational age, neonatal complications, rearing practices, and other environmental factors. Data are also frequently gathered using unstructured interviews or nonstandardized instruments (Wilson, Desmond, and Wait 1981; Hans 1989; Robins and Mills 1993).

The mother and child's socioeconomic status is also an issue. Most drug-exposed infants are from impoverished segments of society. The developmental consequences of poverty have only recently been examined, and controlling for socioeconomic status in such studies would strengthen conclusions about the effect of drug use itself on birth and development. Beyond the obvious problems of nutrition and health, children from low socioeconomic groups are likely to face an increased risk of homelessness or transient housing, and exposure to violence and crime. Finally, it is important to stress that not all drug-using women are comparable in their parenting skills. Protective factors such as quality parenting or other caretaking factors should be examined to determine how they impact long-term child outcome.

Neonatal Abstinence Syndrome

In utero exposure to all of the commonly used opioids with subsequent withdrawal can result in a neonatal abstinence syndrome. Neonatal abstinence syndrome is highly prevalent in infants born to opioid-dependent mothers, including women maintained on methadone. It has been estimated that 60 percent of infants prenatally exposed to methadone will have significant withdrawal symptoms (Finnegan 1988). The neonatal abstinence syndrome is characterized by a constellation of signs and symptoms (Table 12.4), including CNS hyperirritability, gastrointestinal dysfunction, respiratory distress, yawning, sneezing, skin discoloration, and fever. Neonates experiencing abstinence often attempt to suck frantically on their fists or thumbs, yet their sucking reflex may be uncoordinated and ineffectual. Infants undergoing abstinence frequently develop mild tremors that occur only when the infant is disturbed; however, tremors can progress to a point at which they occur spontaneously without stimulation. High-pitched crying, increased muscle tone, greater irritability, decreases in cud-

Table 12.4 **Withdrawal Symptoms in Infants Prenatally Exposed to Opiates**

Autonomic	Central Nervous System	Respiratory	Gastrointestinal
Yawning	Coarse tremors	Rhinorrhea	Salivation
Wakefulness	Seizures (myoclonic	Stuffy nose	Hiccups
Lacrimation	jerks)	Sneezing	Vomiting
Fever	Twitching	Respiratory	Diarrhea
Rub or scratch	Hyperactivity	distress	Weight loss or
marks	Hypertonicity	Respiratory	inadequate weight
Diaphoresis	High-pitched crying	alkalosis	gain
Skin mottling	Hyperreflexia		
Voracious sucking	Hyperacusis		
Unpatterned	Photophobia		
sucking	Apneic spells		
Hypothermia	Irritability		
Poor sleep pattern	Tremulousness		
Sneezing			

Source: Based on Glass (1974); Harper, Solish, and Purow (1974); Desmond and Wilson (1975); Finnegan et al. (1975); Harper et al. (1977); Kandall et al. (1977); Madden et al. (1977); Dinges, Davis, and Glass (1980); Finnegan (1988); and Hoegerman and Schnoll (1991).

dliness, and decrements in responsivity to visual stimulation also may develop (Kaplan et al. 1976; Strauss et al. 1976b, 1979; Chasnoff et al. 1984; Jeremy and Hans 1985; Finnegan and Kaltenbach 1992). In addition, methadone-exposed infants have been observed to be deficient in their ability to interact with the environment, with a reduced capacity for attention and less social responsiveness immediately after birth (Kaltenbach and Finnegan 1988). Deficits in interaction are present until infants are free from other withdrawal symptoms and completely detoxified. If abstinence is appropriately recognized, assessed, and adequately treated, the risk of severe consequences such as dehydration, seizures, and death can be minimized (Martin, Payte, and Zweben 1991; Jarvis and Schnoll 1995).

Although the onset of withdrawal symptoms can vary from minutes to hours after birth, the majority of symptoms are present within 72 hours of delivery. Many factors influence the onset of withdrawal in infants, including the timing of the last methadone dose relative to parturition, the character of the labor, the type and amount of anesthesia or analgesic administered during labor, and the gestational age, nutrition, and health of the infant (Finnegan 1991). Premature, methadone-exposed infants have a less severe abstinence syndrome relative to full-term infants. This may be owing to the immaturity of the infant, which may either mitigate the expression of abstinence or delay methadone metabolism, thus delaying or preventing manifestations of abstinence (Doberczak, Kandall, and Wilets 1991). Alternatively, the reduction in total methadone exposure may result in less severe expression of withdrawal.

A relationship between maternal methadone dose and the presence or severity of infant withdrawal has been difficult to establish. Several studies have reported a significant positive relationship between severity of withdrawal and methadone dose during pregnancy (Ostrea, Chavez, and Strauss 1976; Harper et al. 1977; Madden et al. 1977; Doberczak, Kandall, and Friedman 1993). By contrast, other studies have observed no relationship between severity of withdrawal and maternal methadone dose (Blinick, Jerez, and Wallach 1975; Rosen and Pippenger 1976; Stimmel et al. 1982–83; Mack et al. 1991). In fact, one study separated 147 women into low-, moderate-, and high-methadone dose groups during pregnancy and reported no differences among the groups on gestational age, birth weight or number of days infants required medication (Kaltenbach and Finnegan 1989a).

One possible reason for the discrepancy among studies of methadone dose and infant outcome is that the assessment of clinical severity of neonatal narcotic withdrawal is often based on individual hospital guidelines. Although standardized withdrawal assessment tools have been developed to address this problem (e.g., Finnegan et al. 1975), many hospitals adopt their own version of scales, thus reducing the ability to compare study results across different settings.

In summary, although data are conflicting, it appears that a majority of studies suggest no relationship between maternal methadone dose and withdrawal severity. Furthermore, when weighing the risk-to-benefit ratio for both mother and child, it is important to remember the benefits of administering adequate methadone doses as a means for eliminating or greatly reducing illicit opioid use (and consequently decreasing other risks, including HIV infection and hepatitis). Administration of an adequate methadone dose appears to be a safer alternative for both the fetus and mother than inadequate or no doses of methadone.

Therapy for Neonatal Abstinence Syndrome

The first step in evaluating an infant who has been exposed to methadone or other opioids in utero is to use a standard scoring system for the neonatal abstinence syndrome (Finnegan 1986). A decision to medicate the infant for withdrawal then can be based on the score, and the infant's response to treatment interventions can be tracked over time with repeated standardized evaluations.

As with all forms of therapy, the use of a medication for the treatment of neonatal withdrawal from opioids represents a balance of the risks and benefits that can be derived. Unfortunately, outcomes from studies of the treatment of neonatal withdrawal do not provide clear and consistent results and clinical recommendations. A review that analyzed and summarized published reports on the pharmacologic treatment of the neonatal abstinence syndrome found that most studies compared the use of either phenobarbital, paregoric, or diazepam in the treatment of neonatal opioid abstinence (Theis et al. 1997). Although methodological flaws (e.g., nonrandomization, lack of double blinding) and varied outcome measures limited the conclusions that could be drawn from these studies, it was concluded that diazepam appeared less efficacious than phenobarbital or paregoric and that the efficacy of phenobarbital depended on the extent of prenatal exposure and outcome examined.

When selecting a pharmacotherapy for the treatment of neonatal abstinence, the drug presumed responsible for the abstinence syndrome should also be considered (e.g., opiates for opiate withdrawal). Diluted opium tincture appears to be the preferred medication for opioid withdrawal because it contains narcotics without the undesirable constituents contained in paregoric (e.g., camphor, benzoic acid). As of yet, neither the dosage nor the therapeutic level necessary to control withdrawal symptoms has been systematically investigated. However, it has been recommended to use 0.2 ml of a 0.4 mg/ml formulation every 3 hours (with increases in dose if indicated; Levy and Spino [1993]). The use of methadone to treat neonatal opioid withdrawal is controversial. Some researchers state that it should not be used because its prolonged half-life (26 hours) makes dosage adjustment difficult (Rosen and Pippenger 1975). However, others believe methadone is a useful compound for alleviating opioid withdrawal in newborns and suggest an initial dose of 1 to 2 mg twice per day (Hoegerman and Schnoll 1991).

In addition to using pharmacotherapy to treat neonatal opioid abstinence, a supportive environment can be helpful in alleviating an infant's symptoms of withdrawal. For instance, the infant's environment should be calm, quiet, and warm. Gentle handling, swaddling to decrease sensory stimulation and help the infant regulate body temperature, using a pacifier to relieve irritability and increased sucking urge, and providing frequent, small feedings also help the infant maintain homeostasis. These interventions, combined with pharmacotherapy when appropriate, can optimize the management of neonatal abstinence.

Birth Outcomes

Birth Weight

Numerous studies have reported higher birth weights in newborns of methadone-maintained women compared with newborns of heroin-dependent women not receiving methadone maintenance treatment (Zelson 1973; Connaughton et al. 1975; Kandall et al. 1976, 1977). Furthermore, women who are in methadone programs and who continue using heroin during pregnancy have newborns of lower weight than those born to women on methadone who stop using heroin (Kandall et al. 1976). Similarly, mothers who are enrolled in a methadone maintenance program have newborns with increased birth weight and experience fewer birth complications relative to infants whose mothers use illicit methadone, as well as to infants whose mothers abuse street heroin either alone or in combination with other drugs (Stimmel et al. 1982–83). Higher methadone doses during the first trimester have been shown to be associated with higher birth weights (Kandall et al. 1976), although the relationship between methadone dose during later trimesters and birth weight has not been systematically examined.

Although methadone maintenance treatment is associated with improved birth outcome relative to illicit opioid use, methadone-exposed infants still have lower birth weights relative to nondrug-exposed infants (Chasnoff, Hatcher, and Burns 1982; Kaltenbach and Finnegan 1987; Hans 1989). However, note that although methadone-exposed infants weigh less at birth and have smaller head sizes relative to nondrug-exposed infants, methadone-exposed infants do not appear to be growth retarded (Kaltenbach and Finnegan 1987).

Head Circumference

Children who are prenatally exposed to methadone have small head circumference at birth, suggesting a potential structural effect on the brain and a predictor of poor neurobehavioral outcome later in life (Chasnoff, Hatcher, and Burns 1982; Rosen and Johnson 1982; Lifschitz et al. 1985; Kaltenbach and Finnegan 1987; Hans 1989). In follow-up studies of methadone-exposed children born with small head circumference, findings have been inconsistent. Head circumference has been observed to be smaller in methadone-exposed children at 2 and 3 years of age compared with non-exposed children (Rosen and Johnson 1985; Hans 1989). However, by the time children enter preschool this difference between groups disappears (Lifschitz et al. 1985).

Long-Term Consequences in Older Children

Cognitive Functioning

Exposure to methadone in utero does not appear to affect early cognitive functioning in infants. For example, when methadone-exposed children are compared with nondrug-exposed children at 3, 6, and 12 months of age, no differences are found using the Bayley Mental Development Index (BMDI) (Strauss et al. 1976b; Kaltenbach and Finnegan 1987). Similarly, infants exposed in utero to methadone demonstrate cognitive functioning within the normal range for the first 2 years of life.

A comparison of two groups of opioid-exposed children with differing severities of neonatal withdrawal syndrome at the time of birth also demonstrated no statistically significant difference in cognitive functioning at six months of age using the BMDI (Kaltenbach and Finnegan 1986). However, at two years of age children with more severe neonatal withdrawal syndrome at birth were smaller, more tense, and had less psychomotor development. These results remained significant even after maternal intelligence quotient scores, socioeconomic status, and obstetrical/medical complications were statistically controlled (Hans 1989). However, if there are differences in cognitive development as a function of withdrawal severity at birth, these differences may not persist beyond the first year or two of life. For example, using the McCarthy Scales of Children's Abilities (MSCA) (McCarthy 1972) no differences were observed between methadone-exposed and comparison children aged three to six years (Strauss et al. 1979; Lifschitz et al. 1985; Kaltenbach and Finnegan 1989b).

Although methadone-exposed children appear normal when tested on the BMDI and the MSCA, researchers have often described poorer performance of methadone-exposed children in areas such as fine and gross motor coordination, attention, and language when they are compared with control groups (Strauss et al. 1976b; Wilson, Desmond, and Wait 1981; Chasnoff et al. 1984; Rosen and Johnson 1985). Thus, the relationship between methadone exposure and early childhood cognitive functioning remains somewhat ambiguous.

In school age children and adolescents, little information exists about the possible consequences of prenatal drug exposure in general, let alone prenatal *opioid* exposure. Wilson et al. (1979) were the first to report on a sample group of children ages 6–11 years with documented prenatal *drug* abuse histories compared with a matched control group. Both groups had a high prevalence of academic problems, with no significant differences between the groups. A study that specifically examined the consequences of prenatal methadone exposure, and that compared such children to unexposed children, found that methadone-exposed children were more likely to meet the criteria for attention deficit hyperactivity and disruptive behavior diagnoses, but were not at higher risk for affective disorders (Hans 1996).

In summary, information on the relationship between prenatal methadone exposure and cognitive functioning is severely lacking, especially for older children. However, results from the limited studies available suggest that prenatally drug-exposed children are at high risk for behavioral and academic problems. However, that risk may not be greater when methadone-exposed children are compared with control groups that are appropriately matched on sociodemographic characteristics.

Brain Growth

Concerns about infant brain growth were stimulated by a longitudinal study examining cerebral sonographic characteristics of methadone-exposed infants and comparison infants at birth, one month, six months, and one year of age (Kaltenbach and Finnegan 1989b). At birth and at one month of age, intracranial hemidiameters were smaller and were slower to resolve in methadone-exposed children, suggesting slower brain growth for these children. However, thalamic and temporal lobe measurements were not different between the two groups. Interestingly, by six months of age there was evidence that the brain size of the methadone-exposed children was catching up to that of the comparison group. In addition, development at six months, as assessed by the BMDI, was in the normal range for the methadone-exposed group (Pasto et al. 1989).

Parenting and Social Environment

Few long-term investigations have examined the impact of the mothers' lifestyle on the long-term development of prenatally drug-exposed children. One study comparing methadone-maintained mothers with drug-free control mothers reported that methadone-maintained mothers were lacking in parenting skills and had greater difficulty meeting child-rearing demands (Fiks, Johnson, and Rosen 1985). Another study compared mothers enrolled in methadone maintenance and their preschool children to a control sample of nondrug-using mothers and their preschoolers recruited from the same area. Results indicated that relative to the control group, methadone-maintained mothers performed less adaptively on personality and parenting measures. The methadone-maintained mothers were less goal oriented and more impulsive, irresponsible, immature, and self-centered. In addition, methadone-maintained mothers exhibited a more threatening and disciplinarian approach to parenting, and their children were more hyperactive and disruptive compared with the control mothers and their children, both of whom displayed socially adaptive behaviors (Bauman and Daughtery 1983).

SUMMARY

Important medical, psychologic, and social differences exist between male and female drug abusers. These differences have implications for the content and delivery of therapeutic services to drug-abusing women. The importance of comprehensive and coordinated services is highlighted for pregnant women. Methadone maintenance should be provided in a comprehensive-care setting that meets a pregnant woman's unique requirements and addresses not only substance abuse problems but also many problem areas such as personal health, psychologic stressors, relationships, and daily life requirements. The dose of methadone should be carefully monitored throughout the gestation and adjustments made in the dose or the dosing regimen as needed, with particular attention given to the third trimester, at which time methadone metabolism is increased. Only under the most dire circumstances should a patient undergo detoxification during pregnancy. Overall it appears that when the physical, psychologic, and economic issues of the pregnant opioid abuser are addressed concurrently with methadone treatment, the benefits far outweigh the risks for the mother, the fetus, and the infant.

References

Allen K. 1995. Barriers to treatment for addicted African-American women. *J. Nat. Med. Assoc.* 87:751–56.

Bartholomew N.G., Rowan-Szal G.A., Chatham L.R., Simpson D.D. 1994. Effectiveness of a specialized intervention for women in a methadone program. *J. Psychoactive Drugs* 26:249–55.

Bauman P.S., Daughtery F.E. 1983. Drug-addicted mothers' parenting and their children's development. *Int. J. Addict.* 18:291–302.

Beckwith L., Espinosa M., Howard J. 1994. Psychological profile of pregnant women who abuse cocaine, alcohol and other drugs. NIDA Research Monograph, vol. 144, Department of Health and Human Services, National Institute on Drug Abuse, Rockville, MD, p. 116.

Blinick G., Jerez E., Wallach R.C. 1975. Methadone maintenance, pregnancy and progeny. *JAMA* 225:477–79.

Blume S.B. 1990. Chemical dependency in women: important issues. *Am. J. Drug Alcohol Abuse* 16:297–307.

Carroll K.M., Rounsaville B.J. 1995. Psychosocial treatments for substance dependence. In: Oldham J.M., Riba M.B., eds. *American Psychiatric Press Review of Psychiatry.* American Psychiatric Association, Washington, DC, vol. 14, 127–49.

Centers for Disease Control (CDC). 1994. *HIV/AIDS Surveillance Report 6.* CDC, Atlanta, GA.

Chasnoff I.J. 1991. Drugs, alcohol, pregnancy and the neonate: pay now or pay later. *JAMA* 226:1567–68.

Chasnoff I.J., Hatcher R., Burns W.J. 1982. Polydrug- and methadone addicted newborns: a continuum of impairment? *Pediatrics* 70:210–13.

Chasnoff I.J., Schnoll S.H., Burns W.J., Burns K. 1984. Maternal non-narcotic substance abuse during pregnancy: effects on infant development. *Neurobehav. Toxicol. Teratol.* 6:277–80.

Colten M.E. 1979. A descriptive and comparative analysis of self perceptions and attitudes of heroin-addicted women. In: *Addicted Women: Family Dynamics, Self-Perceptions and Support Systems.* DHHS: U.S. Government Printing Office, Washington, DC.

Connaughton J.F. Jr., Finnegan L.P., Schut J., Emich J.P. 1975. Current concepts in the management of the pregnant opiate addict. *Addict. Dis.* 2:21–35.

Cooper J.R., Altman F., Brown B.S., Czechowicz D. 1983. Research on the treatment of narcotic addiction—state of the art. NIDA Research Monograph. U.S. Department of Health and Human Services, Rockville, MD.

Cox S.M., Hankins G.V.D., Leveno K.J., Cunningham F.G. 1988. Bacterial endocarditis—a serious pregnancy complication. *J. Reprod. Med.* 33: 671–74.

Cuskey W.R., Berger L.H., Densen-Gerber J. 1977. Issues in the treatment of female addiction: a review and critique of the literature. *Contemp. Drug Problems* 7:307–71.

Desmond M.M., Wilson G.S. 1975. Neonatal abstinence syndrome: recognition and diagnosis. *Addict. Dis.* 2:113–21.

Dinges D.F., Davis M.M., Glass P. 1980. Fetal exposure to narcotics: neonatal sleep as a measure of nervous system disturbance. *Science* 209:619–21.

Doberczak T.M., Kandall S.R., Friedman P. 1993. Relationships between maternal methadone dosage, maternal-neonatal methadone levels and neonatal withdrawal. *Obstet. Gynecol.* 81:936–40.

Doberczak T.M., Kandall S.R., Wilets I. 1991. Neonatal opiate abstinence syndrome in term and preterm infants. *J. Pediatrics* 118:933–37.

Downs W.R., Miller B.A., Panek D.D. 1993. Differential patterns of partner-to-woman violence: a comparison of samples of community, alcohol abusing and battered women. *J. Fam. Violence* 8:113–35.

Edelin K.C., Gurganious L., Golbar K., Oellerich D., Kyei-Aboagye K., Adel Hamid M. 1988. Methadone maintenance in pregnancy: consequences to care and outcome. *Obstet. Gynecol.* 71:399–404.

Ellinwood E.H., Smith W.G., Vaillant G.E. 1966. Narcotic addiction in males and females: a comparison. *Int. J. Addict.* 1:33–45.

Ellwood D., Sutherland P., Kent C., O'Connor M. 1987. Maternal narcotic addiction: pregnancy outcome in patients managed by a specialized drug dependency antenatal clinic. *Aust./N.Z. J. Obstet. Gynecol.* 27:92–98.

Fiks K.B., Johnson H.L., Rosen T.S. 1985. Methadone-maintained mothers: 3-year follow-up of parental functioning. *Int. J. Addict.* 20:651–60.

Finnegan L.P. 1978. Management of pregnant drug-dependent women. *Ann. N.Y. Acad. Sci.* 311:135–46.

———. 1986. Neonatal abstinence syndrome: assessment and pharmacotherapy. In: Rubatelli F.F., Granati B., eds. *Neonatal Therapy: an Update.* Exerpta Medica, New York.

———. 1988. Influence of maternal drug dependence on the newborn. In:

Kacew S., Lock S., eds. *Toxicologic and Pharmacologic Principles in Pediatrics.* Hemisphere, Washington, D.C.

———. 1991. Treatment issues for opioid dependent women during the perinatal period. *J. Psychoactive Drugs* 23:191–201.

Finnegan L.P., Connaughton J.F. Jr., Kron R.E., Emich J.P. 1975. Neonatal abstinence syndrome: assessment and management. *Addict. Dis.* 2:141–58.

Finnegan L.P., Davenny K., Hartel D. 1993. Drug use in HIV-infected women. In: Johnstone F., Johnson M., eds. *HIV Infection in Women.* Churchill Livingstone, Edinburgh, pp. 133–55.

Finnegan L.P., Kaltenbach K. 1992. Neonatal abstinence syndrome. In: Hoekelman R.A., Nelson N.M., eds. *Primary Pediatric Care,* 2nd ed. Mosby Yearbook, St. Louis, MO.

Finnegan L.P., Wapner R.J. 1987. Drug use in pregnancy. In: Neibyl J.R., ed. *Narcotic Addiction in Pregnancy.* Lea & Febiger, Philadelphia.

Fitzsimmons J., Tunis S., Webster D., Izes J., Wapner R., Finnegan L. 1986. Pregnancy in a drug abusing population. *Am. J. Drug Alcohol Abuse* 12:247–55.

Gazaway P.M., Bigelow G.E., Brooner R.K. 1993. The influence of pregnancy upon trough plasma levels of methadone and its opioid effects. In: Harris L., ed. Problems of Drug Dependence 1992. Proceedings of the 54th Annual Scientific Meeting, College on Problems of Drug Dependence. National Institute on Drug Abuse Research Monograph, vol. 132, Department of Health and Human Services, National Institute on Drug Abuse, Rockville, MD, p. 112.

Glass L. 1974. Narcotic withdrawal in the newborn infant. *J. Nat. Med. Assoc.* 66:117–20.

Gomberg E. 1989. Suicide risk among women with alcohol problems. *Am. J. Public Health* 79:1363–65.

Griffin M.L., Weiss R.D., Mirin S.M., Lange U. 1989. A comparison of male and female cocaine abusers. *Arch. Gen. Psychiatry* 46:122–26.

Haller D.L., Knisley J.S., Dawson K.S., Schnoll S.H. 1993. Perinatal substance abusers: psychological and social characteristics. *J. Nerv. Mental Dis.* 181:509–13.

Hans S.L. 1989. Developmental consequences of prenatal exposure to methadone. *Ann. N.Y. Acad. Sci.* 562:195–207.

———. 1992. Maternal opioid drug use and child development. In: Zagon I., Slotkin T.S., eds. *Maternal Substance Abuse and the Developing Nervous System.* Academic, New York.

———. 1996. Prenatal drug exposure: behavioral functioning in late childhood and adolescence. In: Wetherington C.L., Smeriglio V.L., Finnegan

L.P., eds. *Behavioral Studies of Drug-Exposed Offspring: Methodological Issues in Human and Animal Research.* National Institute on Drug Abuse Research Monograph, vol. 164, Department of Health and Human Services, National Institute on Drug Abuse, Rockville, MD, pp. 261–76.

Harper R.G., Solish G., Feingold E., Gersten-Woolf N.B., Sokal M.M. 1977. Maternal ingested methadone, body fluid methadone, and the neonatal withdrawal syndrome. *Am. J. Obstet. Gynecol.* 129:417–24.

Harper R.G., Solish G., Purow H.M. 1974. The effect of a methadone treatment program upon pregnant heroin addicts and their newborn infants. *Pediatrics* 54:300–305.

Helzer J., Pryzbeck T. 1988. The co-occurrence of alcoholism with other psychiatric disorders in the general population and its impact on treatment. *J. Studies Alcohol* 49:219–24.

Hoegerman G., Schnoll S. 1991. Narcotic use in pregnancy. *Clin. Perinatol.* 18:51–76.

Institute of Medicine (IOM). 1989. *Prevention and Treatment of Alcohol Problems: Research Opportunities.* National Academy Press, Washington, DC.

Jansson L.M., Svikis D., Lee J., Paluzzi P., Rutigliano P., Hackerman F. 1996. Pregnancy and addiction: a comprehensive care model. *J. Subst. Abuse Treat.* 13:321–29.

Jarvis M.A., Schnoll S.H. 1994. Methadone treatment during pregnancy. *J. Psychoactive Drugs* 26:155–61.

———. 1995. Methadone use during pregnancy. In: Chiang C.N., Finnegan L.P., eds. *Medications Development for the Treatment of Pregnant Addicts and Their Infants.* National Institute on Drug Abuse Research Monograph, vol. 149, Department of Health and Human Services, National Institute on Drug Abuse, Rockville, MD, pp. 58–77.

Jeremy R.J., Hans S.L. 1985. Behavior of neonates exposed in utero to methadone as assessed on the Brazelton Scale. *Infant Behav. Dev.* 8:323–36.

Kaltenbach K. 1996. Exposure to opiates: behavioral outcomes in preschool and school-age children. In: Wetherington C.L., Smeriglio V.L., Finnegan L.P., eds. *Behavioral Studies of Drug-Exposed Offspring: Methodological Issues in Human and Animal Research.* National Institute on Drug Abuse Research Monograph, vol. 164, Department of Health and Human Services, National Institute on Drug Abuse, Rockville, MD, pp. 230–41.

Kaltenbach K., Finnegan L.P. 1986. Neonatal abstinence syndrome, pharmacotherapy and developmental outcome. *Neurobehav. Toxicol. Teratol.* 8:353–55.

———. 1987. Perinatal and developmental outcome of infants exposed to methadone in utero. *Neurotoxicol. Teratol.* 9:311–13.

———. 1988. The influence of neonatal abstinence syndrome and mother infant interaction. In: Anthony E.J., Chiland C., eds. *The Child in His Family. Perilous Development: Child Raising and Identity Formation under Stress.* J. Wiley, New York.

———. 1989a. Children exposed to methadone in-utero: assessment of developmental and cognitive ability. *Ann. N.Y. Acad. Sci.* 562:360–62.

———. 1989b. Prenatal narcotic exposure: perinatal and developmental effects. *Neurotoxicology* 10:597–604.

Kandall S.R., Albin S., Gartner L.M., Lee K.S., Eidelman A., Lowinson J. 1977. The narcotic dependent mother: fetal and neonatal consequences. *Early Human Dev.* 1:159–69.

Kandall S.R., Albin S., Lowinson J., Berle B., Eidelman A.I., Gartner L.M. 1976. Differential effects of maternal heroin and methadone use on birth weight. *Pediatrics* 58:681–85.

Kaplan S.L., Kron R.E., Phoenix M.D., Finnegan L.P. 1976. Brazelton neonatal assessment at three and twenty-eight days of age: a study of passively addicted infants, high risk infants and normal infants. In: Alksne H., Kaufman E., eds. *Critical Concerns in the Field of Drug Abuse.* Marcel Dekker, New York.

Kaufman-Kantor G., Straus M.A. 1989. Substance abuse as a precipitant of wife victimizations. *Am. J. Drug Alcohol Abuse* 15:173–89.

Keith L.G., Donald W., Rosner M.A., Mitchelle M., Bianchi J. 1986. Obstetric aspects of perinatal addiction. In: Chasnoff I.J., ed. *Drug Use in Pregnancy, Mother and Child.* MTP Press, Boston, pp. 23–41.

Knisley J.S., Christmas J.T., Dinsmoore M., Spear E., Schnoll S.H. 1993. The impact of intensive prenatal and substance abuse care on pregnancy outcome. In: Harris L., ed. Problems of Drug Dependence 1992. Proceedings of the 54th Annual Scientific Meeting, College on Problems of Drug Dependence. National Institute on Drug Abuse Research Monograph, vol. 132, Rockville, MD, p. 300.

Kosten T.R., Rounsaville B.J., Kleber H.D. 1985. Ethnic and gender differences among opiate addicts. *Int. J. Addict.* 20:1143–62.

Kreek M. 1986. Drug interactions with methadone in humans. In: Braude M.C., Ginzburg H.M., eds. *Strategies for Research on the Interactions of Drugs of Abuse.* National Institute on Drug Abuse Research Monograph, vol. 68, Department of Health and Human Services, National Institute on Drug Abuse, Rockville, MD, pp. 193–225.

———. 1979. Methadone disposition during the perinatal periods in humans. *Pharmacol. Biochem. Behav.* 11(Suppl.):7–13.

Kreek M., Schecter A., Gutjahr C. 1974. Analyses of methadone and other drugs in maternal and neonatal body fluids: use in evaluation of symptoms in a neonate of mother maintained on methadone. *Am. J. Drug Alcohol Abuse* 1:409–19.

Levy M., Spino M. 1993. Neonatal withdrawal syndrome: associated drugs and pharmacological management. *Pharmacotherapy* 13:202–11.

Lewis D., Waters J. 1989. Human immunodeficiency virus seroprevalence in female intravenous drug users: the puzzle of black women's risk. *Social Sci. Med.* 29:1071–76.

Lex B. 1991. Some gender differences in alcohol and polysubstance users. *Health Psychol.* 10:121–32.

Lifschitz M.H., Wilson G.S., Smith E.O., Desmond M.M. 1985. Factors affecting head growth and intellectual function in children of drug addicts. *Pediatrics* 75:269–74.

Luthar S.S., Cushing G., Rounsaville B.J. 1996. Gender differences among opioid abusers: pathways to disorder and profiles of psychopathology. *Drug Alcohol Depend.* 43:179–89.

Luthar S.S., Glick M., Zigler E., Rounsaville B.J. 1993. Social competence among cocaine abusers: moderating effects of comorbid diagnosis and gender. *Am. J. Drug Alcohol Abuse* 19:283–98.

Mack G., Thomas D., Giles W., Buchanan N. 1991. Methadone levels and neonatal withdrawal. *J. Pediatr. Child Health* 27:96–100.

Madden J.D., Chappel J.N., Zuspan F., Gumpel J., Mejia A., Davis R. 1977. Observation and treatment of neonatal narcotic withdrawal. *Am. J. Obstet. Gynecol.* 127:199–201.

Marsh K.L., Simpson D.D. 1986. Sex differences in opioid addiction careers. *Am. J. Drug Alcohol Abuse* 12:309–29.

Martin J., Payte J.T., Zweben J.E. 1991. Methadone maintenance treatment: a primer for physicians. *J. Psychoactive Drugs* 23:165–76.

McCarthy D.A. 1972. *Manual for the McCarthy Scales of Children's Abilities.* Psychological Corporation, San Antonio.

McCaul M., Svikis D., Feng T. 1991. Pregnancy and addiction: outcomes and interventions. *Maryland Med. J.* 40:995–1001.

McCaul M.E., Svikis D.S. 1999. Intervention issues for women. In: Ott P., Tarter R., Ammerman R.T., eds. *Sourcebook on Substance Abuse: Etiology, Epidemiology, Assessment and Treatment.* Allyn & Bacon, Needham Heights, MA.

Miller B.A., Downs W.R., Gondoli D.M. 1989. Spousal violence among alcoholic women as compared to a random household sample of women. *J. Stud. Alcohol* 50:533–40.

National Institute on Drug Abuse (NIDA). 1992. *National Pregnancy and*

Health Survey: Drug Use among Women Delivering Livebirths: 1992. U.S. Department of Health and Human Services, Washington, DC.

Oleske J.M. 1977. Experiences with 118 infants born to narcotic-using mothers. *Clin. Pediatr.* 16:418.

Ostrea E.M., Chavez C.J. 1979. Perinatal problems (excluding neonatal withdrawal) in maternal drug addiction: a study of 830 cases. *J. Pediatr.* 94:292–95.

Ostrea E.M., Chavez C.J., Strauss M.E. 1976. A study of factors that influence the severity of neonatal narcotic withdrawal. *J. Pediatr.* 88:642–45.

Pasto M.E., Ehrlich S., Kaltenbach K., Graziani L., Kurtz, A., Goldberg B., Finnegan L.P. 1989. Cerebral sonographic characteristics and maternal and neonatal risk factors in infants of opiate-dependent mothers. *Ann. N.Y. Acad. Sci.* 562:355–57.

Pivnick A., Jacobson A., Eric K., Doll L., Drucker E. 1994. AIDS, HIV infection and illicit drug use within inner-city families and social networks. *Am. J. Public Health* 84:271–74.

Pond S.M., Kreek M.J., Tong T.G., Raghunath J., Benowitz N.L. 1985. Changes in methadone pharmacokinetics during pregnancy. *J. Pharmacol. Exp. Ther.* 233:1–6.

Regan D.O., Leifer B., Finnegan L.P. 1988. Generations at risk: violence in the lives of pregnant drug abusing women. *Pediatr. Res.* 16:77.

Robins L.N., Mills J.L. 1993. Effects of in utero exposure to street drugs. *Am. J. Public Health* 83(Suppl.):9–32.

Rosen T.S., Johnson H.L. 1982. Children of methadone-maintained mothers: follow-up to 18 months of age. *J. Pediatr.* 101:192–96.

———. 1985. Long-term effects of prenatal methadone maintenance. In: Pinkert T.M., ed. *Current Research on the Consequences of Maternal Drug Abuse.* National Institute on Drug Abuse Research Monograph, vol. 59, Department of Health and Human Services, National Institute on Drug Abuse, Rockville, MD, pp. 73–83.

Rosen T.S., Pippenger C.E. 1975. Disposition of methadone and its relationship to severity of withdrawal in the newborn. *Addict. Dis.* 2:169–78.

———. 1976. Pharmacologic observations on the neonatal withdrawal syndrome. *J. Pediatr.* 88:1044–48.

Schnoll, S.H. 1986. Pharmacologic basis of perinatal addiction. In: Chasnoff I.J., ed. *Drug Use in Pregnancy, Mother and Child.* MTP Press, Boston, pp. 7–16.

Schoenbaum E.E., Hartel D., Selwyn P.A., Klein R.S., Davenny K., Rogers M., Feiner C., Friedland G. 1989. Risk factors for human immunodeficiency virus infection in intravenous drug users. *N. Engl. J. Med.* 321:874–79.

Selwyn P.A., Hartel D., Wasserman W., Drucker E. 1989. Impact of the AIDS epidemic on morbidity and mortality among intravenous drug users in a New York City methadone maintenance program. *Am. J. Public Health* 79:1358–62.

Silverman K., Chutuape M.A., Bigelow G.E., Stitzer M.L. 1996. Voucher-based reinforcement of attendance by unemployed methadone patients in a job skills training program. *Drug Alcohol Depend.* 41: 197–207.

Silverman K., Chutuape M.A., Svikis D.S., Bigelow G.E., Stitzer M.L. 1995. Incongruity between occupational interests and academic skills in drug abusing women. *Drug Alcohol Depend.* 40:115–23.

Smith D.E., Wesson D.R., Tusel D.J. 1989. *Treating Opiate Dependency 1989.* Hazelden Foundation, Center City, MN.

Solomon L., Astemborski J., Warren D., Munoz A., Cohn S., Vlahov D., Nelson K.E. 1993. Differences in risk factors for human immunodeficiency virus type I seroconversion among male and female intravenous drug users. *Am. J. Epidemiol.* 137:892–98.

Stein M.D. 1990. Medical complications of intravenous drug use. *J. Gen. Intern. Med.* 5:249–57.

Stein M.D., Cyr M.G. 1997. Women and substance abuse. *Med. Clin. North Am.: Alcohol Other Subst. Abuse* 81:979–98.

Stevens S.J., Arbiter N. 1995. A therapeutic community for substance-abusing pregnant women and women with children: process and outcome. *J. Psychoactive Drugs* 27:49–56.

Stimmel B., Goldberg J., Reisman A., Murphy R.J., Teets K. 1982–83. Fetal outcome in narcotic dependent women: the importance of the type of maternal narcotic used. *Am. J. Drug Alcohol Abuse* 9:383–95.

Strauss M.E., Andresko M., Stryker J.C., Wardell J.N. 1976a. Relationship of neonatal withdrawal to maternal methadone dose. *Am. J. Drug Alcohol Abuse* 3:339–45.

Strauss M.E., Lessen-Firestone J.K., Chavez C.J., Stryker J.C. 1979. Children of methadone treated women at five years of age. *Pharmacol. Biochem. Behav.* 11(Suppl.):3–6.

Strauss M.E., Starr R.H., Ostrea E.M., Chavez C.J., Stryker J.C. 1976b. Behavioral concomitants of prenatal addiction to narcotics. *J. Pediatr.* 89:842–46.

Substance Abuse and Mental Health Services Administration (SAMHSA). 1997a. *National Household Survey on Drug Abuse: Population Estimates 1996.* U.S. Department of Health and Human Services. DHHS Pub. No. (SMA) 97–3137, Rockville, MD.

———. 1997b. *Preliminary Results from the 1996 National Household Sur-*

vey on Drug Abuse. U.S. Department of Health and Human Services. DHHS Pub. No. (SMA) 97–3149, Rockville, MD.

Svikis D., Golden A., Huggins G.R., Pickens R.W., McCaul M.E., Velez M.L., Rosendale C.T., Brooner R.K., Gazaway P.M., Stitzer M.L., Ball C.E. 1997a. Cost-effectiveness of comprehensive care for drug abusing pregnant women. *Drug Alcohol Depend.* 45:105–13.

Svikis D.S., Lee J.H., Haug N.A., Stitzer M.L. 1997b. Attendance incentives for outpatient treatment: effects in methadone and nonmethadone-maintained pregnant drug dependent women. *Drug Alcohol Depend.* 48:33–41.

Theis J.G., Selby P., Ikizler Y., Koren G. 1997. Current management of the neonatal abstinence syndrome: a critical analysis of the evidence. *Biol. Neonate* 71:345–56.

Tucker M.B. 1979. A descriptive and comparative analysis of the social support structure of heroin addicted women. In: *Addicted Women: Family Dynamics, Self-Perceptions and Support Systems.* DHHS, U.S. Government Printing Office, Washington, DC.

Wallen J.A. 1992. Comparison of male and female clients in substance abuse treatment. *J. Subst. Abuse Treat.* 9:243–48.

Wilson G.S., Desmond M.M., Wait R.B. 1981. Follow-up of methadone treated women and their infants: health, developmental and social implications. *J. Pediatr.* 98:716–22.

Wilson G.S., McCreary R., Kean J., Baxter J.C. 1979. The development of preschool children of heroin-addicted mothers: a controlled study. *Pediatrics* 63:135–41.

Wittmann B.K., Segal S.A. 1991. A comparison of the effects of single- and split-dose methadone administration on the fetus: ultrasound evaluation. *Int. J. Addictions* 26:213–18.

Zelson C. 1973. Infant of the addicted mother. *N. Eng. J. Med.* 288:1391–95.

Zuspan F.P., Gumpel J.A., Mejia-Zelaya A. 1975. Fetal stress from methadone withdrawal. *Am. J. Obstet. Gynecol.* 122:43–46.

13

OTHER MEDICATIONS FOR OPIOID DEPENDENCE

Rolley E. Johnson, Pharm.D., and Eric C. Strain, M.D.

Although methadone is the most extensively used pharmacotherapy for the treatment of opioid dependence, several other medications are available for both maintenance and detoxification treatment. Two medications, levomethadyl acetate (also called L-alpha-acetylmethadol, or LAAM, and marketed in the United States as Orlaam®) and naltrexone (originally marketed as Trexan®, and reissued as ReVia®) are approved for the maintenance treatment of opioid dependence. A third medication, buprenorphine, is currently marketed as an analgesic under the names Buprenex® and Temgesic®, and is available in some parts of the world for the treatment of opioid dependence as Subutex®. This medication is under active development for use in drug abuse treatment, and approval in the United States for this indication is expected in 1999. Last, alpha$_2$-adrenergic agonist agents (i.e., clonidine and lofexidine) have been used for the acute treatment of opioid withdrawal. Clonidine, a medication currently approved for use as an antihypertensive, has been extensively studied for symptomatic treatment during opioid detoxification, and lofexidine, a related compound, is approved for the use of opioid withdrawal in some European countries. This chapter reviews each of these medications, providing an overview to their pharmacologic characteristics, as well as summaries of their safety, efficacy, and optimal use.

L-ALPHA-ACETYLMETHADOL (LAAM)

Initial interest in the development of LAAM for the treatment of opioid dependence occurred during the 1970s—a time when methadone treatment was rapidly expanding in the United States. As methadone treatment became widely used, concerns arose that diversion of prescription methadone was leading to street trade of take-home doses of methadone within the drug-abusing community. In addition, daily clinic attendance for methadone treatment was inconvenient for many patients, and it was hoped that a medication administered on a less-than-daily basis, such as LAAM, would help decrease the need for frequent clinic visits without increasing the risk of diversion of take-home doses. Even though considerable research on the safety and efficacy of LAAM was conducted in the 1970s, approval of LAAM languished during the 1980s. However, in the late 1980s, there was renewed interest in gaining approval for the use of LAAM, and in 1993, approval of LAAM for the treatment of opioid dependence was granted by the FDA.

Pharmacology of LAAM

LAAM is a mu agonist opioid like methadone, and like other opioids, acute doses produce sedation and analgesia. However, the effects of LAAM are longer than those of methadone. This longer duration has generally been attributed to the active metabolites nor-LAAM and dinor-LAAM (McMahon, Culp, and Marshall 1965; Finkle et al. 1982). It was originally reported that the onset of effects for intravenous LAAM is slower than for oral LAAM. This was believed to be due to the time required for the active metabolites to be formed because LAAM must be metabolized by the liver to the nor- and dinor-metabolites. However, recent evidence suggests that intravenous LAAM exerts direct bioactive effects with a much quicker onset than the effects attributable solely to active metabolites (Walsh et al. 1996a).

Absorption, Distribution, and Excretion of LAAM

LAAM has good oral bioavailability and is rapidly absorbed from the gastrointestinal tract. There is considerable variability among individuals in the subsequent pharmacokinetics of LAAM, so generalizations regarding some effects may not reflect the profile of effects produced in a particular individual patient. Following acute oral dosing, peak plasma concentrations of LAAM typically occur within 3 hours, and conversion of LAAM to nor-LAAM and dinor-LAAM begins rapidly after absorption of LAAM (with peak concentrations of nor- and dinor-LAAM metabolites within 1 to 2 hours and 20–30 hours, respectively, after the parent compound's peak). LAAM is not converted directly to dinor-LAAM; rather, dinor-

LAAM is converted from nor-LAAM (i.e., there is a sequential series of demethylations of the parent compound). The $t_{1/2}$ for oral LAAM after an acute dose is about 0.5–1 day; for nor-LAAM, about 1 to 2 days; and for dinor-LAAM, about 3 to 4 days (although there can be considerable individual difference in these half-lives). The $t_{1/2}$ for oral LAAM after chronic dosing is about 2.6 days; for nor-LAAM, about 2 days; and for dinor-LAAM, about 4 days (although there can be considerable individual difference in these $t_{1/2}$s). Thus, the drug and its active metabolites remain in the body for prolonged periods of time. LAAM is excreted in both urine and feces, with a greater proportion via the latter route.

Efficacy

The effects of LAAM were studied in both humans and animals during the 1950s and 1960s (e.g., Fraser and Isbell 1952; Keats and Beecher 1952; McMahon, Culp, and Marshall 1965), but studies of LAAM for the treatment of opioid dependence were not begun until the early 1970s. Some of these studies were nonblind clinical trials (e.g., Zaks, Fink, and Freedman 1972; Taintor et al. 1975; Resnick et al. 1976; Wilson, Spannagel, and Thomson 1976; Senay, Dorus, and Renault 1977; Trueblood, Judson, and Goldstein 1978; Freedman and Czertko 1981; Marcovici et al. 1981) whereas others were double-blind trials with small samples (e.g., Jaffe et al. 1970; Jaffe and Senay 1971; Jaffe et al. 1972; Savage et al. 1976; Karp-Gelernter, Savage, and McCabe 1982). These studies demonstrated that LAAM was generally tolerated and similar to methadone in treatment efficacy. In the mid-1970s, two large sample studies of the efficacy of LAAM were conducted (Ling et al. 1976; Ling, Klett, and Gillis 1978). The first of these was a double-blind, multisite veterans' cooperative study with 430 male subjects. In this study, the outcomes of patients maintained on LAAM (80 mg three times per week) were compared with those of patients maintained on either 50 or 100 mg per day of methadone. Results from this study showed that the high-dose methadone group (100 mg per day) had better retention than the LAAM group. However, this could have been due to a dose difference rather than medication difference, because 80 mg of LAAM is currently thought to be equivalent to only 60–65 mg of daily methadone. Thus, similar rates of retention for LAAM might have been achieved if a higher dose of LAAM had been used. By contrast, LAAM and high-dose methadone produced similar rates of opioid-positive urines, and both of these groups had less illicit opioid use than the group that received 50 mg of daily methadone.

The second major study conducted in the 1970s was an open (nonblind), multisite cooperative study sponsored by the SAODAP (Ling, Klett, and Gillis 1978). This study enrolled 636 methadone maintenance patients who were randomly assigned to either continue on their methadone or switch to LAAM; a flexible dosing procedure was utilized. In this study, there was also better retention for methadone than for LAAM patients. However, because patients and staff knew medication assignments, this difference could reflect patient and staff biases toward a new medication. Overall, this study also demonstrated that LAAM and methadone were similar in terms of efficacy. Thus, results from these two large, multisite studies suggest that there could be some differences in treatment retention for the two medications but that overall, the treatment efficacy and safety of LAAM in the treatment of opioid dependence is similar to that of methadone.

More recently, another large outpatient clinical trial examined the relative efficacy of different LAAM doses in the treatment of opioid dependence (Eissenberg et al. 1997). In this double-blind study, patients ($N =$ 180) were randomly assigned to one of three (Monday/Wednesday/Friday) LAAM dosing schedules (25/25/35, 50/50/70, or 100/100/140 mg). Results showed no significant difference in treatment retention for the three dose conditions; 60 percent of subjects remained for the 17 weeks of the study. However, there were dose-related differences in the percentage of opioid-positive urines. For example, 34 percent of patients in the high-dose condition achieved 4 consecutive weeks of opioid abstinence (as determined by urine results), compared with 14 and 11 percent for the medium- and low-dose conditions, respectively. Self-report data regarding illicit opioid use also showed significant dose-related differences, with better outcomes (greater than 90% reduction) for the high-dose condition. Thus, like methadone, higher doses of LAAM are more effective than lower doses for suppressing opioid use during treatment.

Safety and Side Effects

LAAM is a safe medication when used properly. In a person who is not dependent on opioids, an acute dose of LAAM can produce the characteristic features of an opioid overdose, including respiratory depression and death. Because LAAM's active metabolites remain in the body a long time, ingestion of LAAM by a person who is not tolerant to the effects of opioids should be considered a medical emergency, and monitoring should be continued for at least one to two days. If the administration of an opioid antagonist (such as naloxone) is required, repeat dosing may be necessary, given the long duration of effect (i.e., respiratory depression) produced by

LAAM's metabolites. However, in opioid-dependent patients, LAAM is safe and produces few clinically significant side effects. Like other opioids, reports of excessive sweating, constipation, and decreased sex drive have been associated with the use of LAAM.

The multisite veterans cooperative study described previously included an extensive evaluation of LAAM's safety (Ling et al. 1976). Participants were monitored with self-reports of side effects, and biologic specimens (i.e., blood and urine samples) were obtained for testing as well. Overall, LAAM was shown to be safe: no significant adverse events (e.g., deaths) occurred, and side effects were infrequent and mild. In a more recent study of 623 patients who received LAAM, the most commonly reported side effects were difficulty sleeping, constipation, sweating, and nervousness (Fudala et al. 1998). Among the 41 serious adverse events reported in that study, only 1 was definitely related to LAAM (and was the result of a staff dosing error), whereas 20 were probably or possibly due to LAAM. Interestingly, of these 20, 12 involved signs or symptoms suggestive of a histamine response or an allergic type of reaction.

Clinical Use

Induction

There have been few studies directly examining the optimal schedule for starting a patient on LAAM. In the previously described veterans cooperative study, patients assigned to the LAAM condition received an initial dose of 30 mg, with subsequent dose increases of 10 mg each week until a weekly dose of 80 mg was reached (Ling et al. 1976). This dose induction schedule appears to have been well tolerated, and there was no trend for patients in the LAAM condition to drop out early compared with patients in the methadone conditions (i.e., there was no evidence to suggest that this rate of dose induction was too rapid).

A report directly addressing LAAM dose induction compared a slow versus rapid schedule (Judson and Goldstein 1979). The slow schedule consisted of doses of 20, 20, 30, 30, 40, 40, 50, 50, 60, 60, 70, 70, and 75 mg on each successive day of treatment (with clinic visits on Mondays, Wednesdays, and Fridays), whereas the rapid schedule consisted of doses of 20, 30, 40, 40, and 50 mg on successive days (again, using a Monday, Wednesday, Friday schedule). Patients in the slow-dose induction group were allowed to stop or speed up their dose increases according to their need, with a maximum dose allowed of 75 mg. Patients in the rapid-dose induction group could request dose increases above the 50 mg dose, as needed. This was not a double-blind study but, rather, was a report on clinical experience using the two different schedules, and the investigators concluded that the rapid schedule was safe, well tolerated, and preferred by patients.

Another report assessed the effectiveness and safety of LAAM during the first 28 days of induction after patients were assigned to one of three different fixed doses (Figure 13.1; Jones et al. 1998). Dose assignments were 25 (low), 50 (medium), and 100 mg (high) of LAAM. All patients were "street"-opiate dependent and received an initial 25-mg dose of LAAM. The patients assigned to the 50- and 100-mg LAAM groups received 30 mg of LAAM as their second dose, and then their dose was increased by 10 mg every other day until a dose of 50 or 100 mg was reached. All doses of LAAM were well tolerated by most patients. However, the greatest number of dropouts were in the high-dose group, and half of these patients dropped out because of side effects that suggested overmedication. Illicit drug use decreased in all groups; however, patients in the high-dose induction group used illicit opiates less than patients in the low- and medium-dose groups. Patients in the high-dose group also reported less craving for heroin.

From these studies and clinical experience, it is generally recommended that patients entering LAAM treatment directly from the use of illicit opioids (street addicts) start at a dose of 30–40 mg. Based on clinical re-

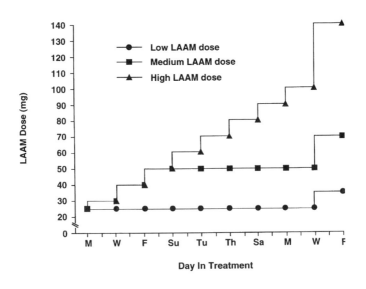

Figure 13.1. Examples of induction schedules for low-, medium-, and high-dose LAAM.

sponse, the dose can be increased 10 mg every other day during the induction period with little difficulty. However, it appears prudent to increase the dose more slowly after a dose of 65–75 mg is reached.

Induction onto LAAM for Patients Being Treated with Methadone

LAAM dosing may be particularly useful for patients currently in methadone treatment who are stable and doing well. For such patients, LAAM can decrease the frequency of clinic visits without the risk of diversion of methadone take-home doses. When converting a patient from methadone to LAAM, it is currently recommended that the methadone dose be multiplied by a factor of 1.2–1.3 to determine the LAAM dose. Thus, a patient maintained on 50 mg of daily methadone would be given 60–65 mg of LAAM, with a compensatory increase on Fridays to allow for the longer interval between Friday and Monday doses (as described subsequently). The transition from methadone to LAAM can be done on consecutive days—there is no need to taper the dose of methadone and gradually increase the dose of LAAM.

Maintenance on LAAM

Most research studies on maintenance dosing with LAAM have been conducted using a thrice weekly schedule—Monday/Wednesday/Friday—with a higher dose administered on Fridays to allow for the longer interdose interval between Friday and Monday. Typically, the Friday dose is 20–40 percent greater than the Monday/Wednesday doses. Because the Friday dose is being adjusted for adequate coverage over a 72-hour period, it may be useful to use a small supplementary dose of methadone on Sunday to avoid opioid withdrawal symptoms. However, some patients may continue to complain of withdrawal symptoms during the 72-hour dose omission period. For these patients, the LAAM dose may need to be administered on an every-other-day schedule, if possible. If this scheduling is impossible (i.e., the clinic is closed on weekends), the maximally recommended 40 percent increase in the Friday dose should be used. Chronic use of supplemental methadone is not recommended.

Patients maintained on LAAM should not receive a dose of LAAM every day; it is important to stress that LAAM is a medication that should be taken only every 48–72 hours. Dosing daily will result in a buildup of active metabolites of LAAM, and a person who consumes LAAM daily will experience a LAAM overdose. In the United States, take-home doses of LAAM are not currently permitted, even for patients who are receiving

LAAM maintenance therapy and who are clinically stable.

The majority of patients can be maintained on doses of 75 and 115 mg for the 48-hour and 72-hour dosing periods, respectively. Dosing of LAAM is complicated by patients failing to take the medication as scheduled, because of the long-acting metabolites. If only one dose is missed, patients can receive their regularly scheduled dose. If only two doses are missed, patients may receive 50 percent of their maintenance dose upon returning to the clinic, and then resume taking their regular dose at the next scheduled visit. However, if more than two doses are missed, patients can be reinducted onto their maintenance dose by receiving a dose that is approximately 50 percent of their scheduled dose, and then increasing the dose by 10 mg at each subsequent clinic visit. If patients miss a dose, return to the clinic on a nonscheduled dosing day, and the clinician wishes to return them to their regular clinic attendance schedule, the clinician may give them a dose of methadone and resume their LAAM dosing the following day. If the clinician is uncertain as to the correct dosing decision, the LAAM package insert should be consulted for guidance.

Discontinuation of LAAM

There have been few reports on the optimal mechanism for withdrawing a patient from LAAM, and it should be noted that in the United States, LAAM is not explicitly approved for use as a withdrawal agent. One double-blind study examined gradual versus abrupt LAAM detoxification (Judson, Goldstein, and Inturrisi 1983). Patients in the study were randomly assigned either to an abrupt detoxification group that had their LAAM dose (50/50/65 mg on a Monday/Wednesday/Friday schedule) abruptly switched to placebo or to a gradual detoxification group that had their LAAM dose (also 50/50/65 mg on a Monday/Wednesday/Friday schedule) decreased over a 15-week period. Interestingly, the study results suggest that the abrupt discontinuation was no worse than the gradual detoxification and, depending on the approach used in the data summarization and analysis, could even be better. Thus, for example, total scores for self-reported opioid withdrawal and total opioid use based on urine tests both were greater for patients in the gradual detoxification group. These results suggest that it may be safe and effective to withdraw LAAM rapidly.

In 1993 LAAM was approved by the FDA for use in the treatment of opioid dependence. Although LAAM is an extremely effective medication, as previously cited, LAAM has initially been underutilized for the treatment of opiate dependence in the United States. Several reasons can be identified for the limited use of LAAM. These include regulatory barriers found in many states, the slow process of bringing LAAM from the investigational stage to approval (25 years), unfounded safety concerns (e.g., hepatotoxicity, slow onset of active metabolites with associated problems during induction onto LAAM), inadequate dissemination of information to clinicians relative to the effectiveness of LAAM, and finally, the milligram-to-milligram cost of LAAM compared to methadone. As these problems associated with the use and acceptance of LAAM are addressed, it is expected that increased numbers of patients will be treated with this medication.

Naltrexone

The opioid antagonist naltrexone is theoretically an ideal medication for the treatment of opioid dependence: naltrexone effectively blocks the effects of opioid drugs such as heroin that may be used during maintenance treatment, but produces no opioid-like or other direct effects of its own. In the early 1970s, clinical development and testing of an antagonist treatment for opioid dependence was prompted by the SAODAP. Naltrexone was selected for development because of its good oral bioavailability, long duration of action, and lack of agonist-like effects (as reviewed in the next section). In November 1984, naltrexone was approved for use in the treatment of opioid dependence by the FDA.

Pharmacology of Naltrexone

Naltrexone is a pure opioid antagonist; that is, naltrexone occupies opioid receptors and prevents receptor activation by other opioid compounds. However, naltrexone does not exert discernible pharmacologic effects of its own—it simply prevents the receptor from being activated by another opioid. Although naltrexone binds to both mu and kappa opioid receptors, it has a higher affinity for mu than for kappa receptors.

In a person who is not dependent on opioids, a clinical dose of naltrexone produces no distinguishing effects. However, in a person who is physically dependent on opioids, the acute administration of a dose of naltrexone (or any of the other opioid antagonists, such as nalmefene or naloxone) will cause (precipitate) an opioid withdrawal syndrome. *Precipitated opioid withdrawal* is characterized by a set of signs and symptoms that is extremely similar to spontaneous opioid withdrawal. *Spontaneous opioid withdrawal* is the syndrome opioid-dependent patients experience when they suddenly discontinue their use of opioids. Characteristic signs of opioid withdrawal include gooseflesh (piloerection), runny nose (rhinnorhea), yawning, tearing (lacrimation), perspiration, dilation of the pupil (mydriasis), vomiting, diarrhea, and restlessness. Symptoms of opioid withdrawal include muscle aches, nausea, irritability, fatigue, anorexia, poor sleep, and dysphoria. Although precipitated and spontaneous opioid withdrawal syndromes are similar, they differ in their time course. Precipitated withdrawal is typically rapid in onset, and its duration is related to the length of time the antagonist is in a person. Spontaneous opioid withdrawal can have a more gradual onset and can last several days.

Naltrexone's Absorption, Distribution and Excretion

Naltrexone has excellent oral bioavailability. It is rapidly and almost completely absorbed from the gastrointestinal tract and undergoes rapid biotransformation to several metabolites, including 6-β-naltrexol (its major metabolite). Naltrexone, the parent compound, appears to be a more potent antagonist than 6-β-naltrexol, although there are higher levels of the latter when naltrexone is ingested orally. Naltrexone and its metabolites are primarily excreted in the urine.

Efficacy

In studies of the use of naltrexone in residential laboratories, where drug availability is controlled and life circumstances are eliminated, naltrexone has proved to be a remarkably effective medication for opioid abusers. In a study conducted by Mello et al. (1981), for example, heroin-dependent patients who lived on an inpatient research ward were maintained on either naltrexone (50 mg/day) or placebo, and given the choice of working to earn either money or intravenous injections of heroin. Patients maintained on naltrexone chose to administer heroin on less than 10 percent of the occasions when they could have received it, whereas patients maintained on placebo took virtually all of the heroin available. Similarly, another human laboratory study found that maintenance doses as low as 3.125 mg per day of oral naltrexone (the therapeutic dose is 50 mg/day) significantly reduced both the subjective and physiologic effects of intravenous hydromorphone, a pain medication much like morphine; when these same volunteers were maintained on 50 mg per day of naltrexone, essentially all hydromorphone effects were blocked (Walsh et al. 1996b). Human laboratory studies have shown that tolerance does not develop over time to the opioid blockade produced by naltrexone. Thus, naltrexone is, in theory, a highly effective medication for preventing heroin use.

Numerous outpatient clinical studies have reported on the efficacy of naltrexone for opioid-dependence treatment. In general, these studies demonstrate that naltrexone can be useful in some special populations (as discussed subsequently), but the most striking feature of these studies overall was the high dropout rate from naltrexone treatment. For example, one study reported on 386 patients who expressed an interest in naltrexone treatment, 242 of whom detoxified from opiates, remained drug-free for at least two days, and received at least one dose of naltrexone (Greenstein et al. 1981). Of these patients, 153 completed at least six days of a naltrexone induction period, 60 of the 153 completed at least two months of naltrexone treatment, and 3 took naltrexone for more than one year. Similarly, in a large, multisite, placebo-controlled study of naltrexone, conducted at several veterans affairs centers, 753 patients were screened, but only 192 started on medication (naltrexone or placebo), and of these patients, only 13 completed even eight months of treatment (National Research Council Committee on Clinical Evaluation of Narcotic Antagonists 1978). One interesting observation from this study comes from patients who had an opioid-positive urine sample and then provided at least one other urine sample. Those patients who were on naltrexone had significantly lower rates of opioid-positive urines for the follow-up sample compared with patients on placebo medication (10% vs. 33%). This observation suggests that subjects who tested the efficacy of their medication by using illicit opioids were less motivated to continue illicit opioid use if they were on naltrexone.

Although naltrexone's efficacy in the placebo-controlled study was poor, naltrexone has, nevertheless, been reported to be useful in special populations. For example, it has been reported to be highly useful in professionals such as business executives and physicians (Washton, Gold, and Pottash 1984), and also in federal probationers (Tilly et al. 1992). Finally, it may be possible to improve compliance rates if naltrexone ingestion is linked to a reinforcement schedule, such as a voucher-based program (as described in Chapter 10), or even to monetary payments (Grabowski et al. 1979).

Safety and Side Effects

Naltrexone is a very safe medication with few side effects in the typical therapeutic dose range. Some evidence suggests that higher-than-usual doses (e.g., 300 mg per day) can result in elevations in liver function tests (e.g., ALT, AST). The studies in which these elevations were observed were clinical trials examining the potential efficacy of naltrexone in the treatment of obesity, and in the treatment of dementia. Interestingly, a review of these results suggests that age is a risk factor for the development of elevations in liver function tests—no patient under 40 years of age who was treated with up to 200 mg per day of naltrexone developed elevations in his or her transaminases in these studies (Pfohl et al. 1986). In patients who do develop such abnormalities, liver function test values return to normal when naltrexone treatment is discontinued.

These studies of naltrexone and liver function tests have led to the recommendation that screening liver function tests (e.g., transaminase levels) be obtained prior to the initiation of naltrexone treatment, and caution should be exerted in patients with evidence of liver disease at baseline. Naltrexone treatment *can* be initiated in patients with mild elevations in liver function tests (e.g., up to threefold increases in transaminase levels). It is probably prudent to obtain monthly liver function tests for the first two to three months of treatment for all patients started on naltrexone, and patients whose test results suggest the onset of hepatic dysfunction following the initiation of treatment should be carefully evaluated and the discontinuation of naltrexone should be considered. However, it should be stressed again that the evidence for hepatotoxicity from naltrexone is limited and is associated with high doses in older age groups.

Two other side effects of naltrexone that have been reported are gastrointestinal complaints and dysphoria. Reports of abdominal pain or discomfort have been consistently noted in larger series of patients treated with naltrexone, although the percentage of patients with such problems is low (generally less than 5%), and such discomfort does not include vomiting. Dysphoria has been noted less consistently, although this effect has led to speculation that naltrexone-induced dysphoria could contribute to poor compliance in taking the medication.

Clinical Use

Induction

It is extremely important that a patient starting naltrexone treatment have a sustained period of opioid abstinence prior to the first dose of naltrexone. In general, a minimum of seven days without opioids (licit or illicit) is necessary. If the patient starting on naltrexone is still physically dependent on opioids, the administration of a single dose of naltrexone will produce a sustained precipitated withdrawal syndrome (and decrease the likelihood of compliance in continuing treatment). A common and useful mechanism for ensuring that the patient is not dependent is to administer a *naloxone challenge* before the first dose of naltrexone. Naloxone is also an opioid antagonist, but it differs from naltrexone in that it has poor oral bioavailability and a short half-life. A typical naloxone challenge involves the intramuscular, subcutaneous, or intravenous administration of 0.8 mg of naloxone, followed by close monitoring of the patient for evidence of a precipitated opioid withdrawal syndrome. Several different assessment instruments can be used to quantify opioid withdrawal, such as the Wang scale (Wang et al. 1974), the Clinical Institute Narcotic Assessment (CINA; Peachey and Lei 1988; Table 13.1), and the Weak Opioid Withdrawal scale (WOW; Haertzen 1974; Table 13.2). Signs and symptoms of withdrawal should begin within 5–15 minutes after the administration of naloxone and typically resolve within 1–1.5 hours. Some clinicians administer a lower dose of naloxone initially (e.g., 0.4 mg), and then give a second dose of naloxone (again, 0.4 mg) after 30–60 minutes if there is no evidence of withdrawal associated with the first dose. If the naloxone challenge test does not result in a precipitated withdrawal syndrome, it should be safe to administer the first dose of naltrexone. The recommended first-day oral

Table 13.1   **Clinical Institute Narcotic Assessment (CINA)**

NAUSEA AND VOMITING: Ask, "Do you feel sick to your stomach? Have you vomited?"—Observation
  0 = No nausea, no vomiting
  2 = Mild nausea with no retching or vomiting
  4 = Intermittent nausea with dry heaves
  6 = Constant nausea, frequent heaves and/or vomiting

GOOSEFLESH: Observation
  0 = No gooseflesh visible
  1 = Occasional gooseflesh but not elicited by touch, not prominent
  2 = Prominent gooseflesh, in waves and elicited by touch
  3 = Constant gooseflesh over chest and arms

SWEATING: Observation
  0 = No sweat visible
  1 = Barely perceptible sweating, palms moist
  2 = Beads of sweat obvious on forehead
  3 = Drenching sweat over face and chest

RESTLESSNESS: Observation
  0 = Normal activity
  1 = Somewhat more than normal activity (may move legs up and down, shift position occasionally)
  2 = Moderately fidgety and restless, shifting position frequently
  3 = Gross movements most of the time or constantly thrashes about

(continued)

Table 13.1 *(continued)*

TREMOR: Arms extended and fingers spread apart—Observation
  0 = No tremor
  1 = Not visible but can be felt fingertip to fingertip
  2 = Moderate, with patient's arm extended
  3 = Severe even if arms not extended

LACRIMATION: Observation
  0 = No lacrimation
  1 = Eyes watering, tears at corners of eyes
  2 = Profuse tearing from eyes over face

NASAL CONGESTION: Observation
  0 = No nasal congestion, sniffling
  1 = Frequent sniffling
  2 = Constant sniffling with watery discharge

YAWNING: Observation
  0 = No yawning
  1 = Frequent yawning
  2 = Constant, uncontrolled yawning

ABDOMINAL CHANGES: Ask, "Do you have any pains in your lower abdomen?"
  0 = No abdominal complaints, normal bowel sounds
  1 = Reports waves of abdominal crampy pain, active bowel sounds
  2 = Reports crampy abdominal pain, diarrheal movements, active bowel sounds

CHANGES IN TEMPERATURE: Ask, "Do you feel hot or cold?"
  0 = No report of temperature change
  1 = Reports feeling hot or cold, hands cold and clammy
  2 = Uncontrollable shivering

MUSCLE ACHES: Ask, "Do you have any muscle cramps?"
  0 = No muscle aching reported, e.g. arm and neck muscles soft at rest
  1 = Mild muscle pains
  2 = Reports severe muscle pains, muscles of legs, arms, and neck in constant state of contraction

HEART RATE: _____

SYSTOLIC BLOOD PRESSURE (Supine): _____

Scores are derived by summing items. For the items heart rate and systolic blood pressure, values are first divided by 10 and then added to the remaining eleven items.

Source: Peachey J.E., Lei H., "Assessment of Opioid Dependence With Naloxone," *Br. J. Addict.* 1988; 83(2):196–97. (Reproduced with permission from Carfax Publishing Limited, P.O. Box 25, Abingdon, Oxfordshire OX14 3UE, United Kingdom.)

Table 13.2   Weak Opioid Withdrawal Scale (WOW)

1. I am not as active as usual. (T)
2. I have had very peculiar and strange experiences. (T)
3. My sex drive is decreased. (T)
4. I have a pleasant feeling in my stomach. (F)
5. My face feels hot. (T)
6. I have felt my body drift away from me. (T)
7. The way I feel right now, I would rather be guided by someone I trust than to follow my own judgement. (T)
8. I feel as if I would be more popular with people today. (F)
9. I feel sluggish. (T)
10. I have often been frightened in the middle of the night. (T)
11. Something is making me break out in goosebumps. (T)
12. I seem to be able to see the comical side of things more than usual. (F)
13. I often feel that I must get up and walk around. (T)
14. I have spells of feeling hot and cold. (T)
15. I am often troubled by constipation. (T)
16. I would like to listen to music all day. (F)
17. People might say that I am a little dull today. (T)
18. My eyes are watering more than usual. (T)
19. I am afraid of losing my mind. (T)
20. My memory seems sharper to me than usual. (F)
21. Once in a while I notice my muscles jerking. (T)

Source: Modified from Haertzen (1974).
Note: Also known as ARCI scale #194. The patient responds as either true or false for each item. Those items followed by a "T" are scored with 1 point if the patient responds true, and those items followed by an "F" are scored with 1 point if the patient responds false. A total score is then derived by summing the responses.

dose of naltrexone is 25 mg. If the patient tolerates this dose, it can then be increased to 50 mg per day.

If an opioid-dependent patient inadvertently receives a dose of naltrexone, they should be closely monitored for at least 48 hours. Interventions should be supportive, and attempts to "reverse" the naltrexone by administering opioid agonists should not be attempted (because this could result in an opioid overdose as the effects of the naltrexone dissipate).

Because of the difficulties opioid-dependent patients often have in achieving a sustained period of abstinence as an outpatient, inpatient detoxification has been advocated as a useful first step in the initiation of naltrexone treatment. Unfortunately, inpatient detoxification from opioids is rarely a therapeutic option for most patients because of cost constraints (but should be considered in a highly motivated patient who might benefit from naltrexone treatment).

Naltroxene Induction Using Clonidine

A novel approach to starting patients on naltrexone is to use clonidine as a "bridging" medication to decrease opioid withdrawal signs and symptoms otherwise elicited after an initial dose of naltrexone is administered to an opioid-dependent person. Clonidine has been shown to be useful in attenuating opioid withdrawal, so this procedure capitalizes on this effect to aid in a more rapid initiation of naltrexone treatment in opioid-dependent patients. However, because of the frequent dosing of clonidine and naltrexone, and the risk of hypotension from clonidine during such a procedure, close and sustained monitoring of patients is necessary when using this procedure. Beginning naltrexone treatment with an initial clonidine phase can be accomplished on an outpatient basis (e.g., in a day hospital setting where patients are under supervision for most of the day).

Vining, Kosten, and Kleber (1988) have described an effective four-day outpatient procedure using clonidine and naltrexone. On the first day of treatment, after establishing physical dependence on opioids using a naloxone challenge, patients receive their first dose of oral clonidine (0.1–0.3 mg) and undergo blood pressure monitoring for evidence of hypotension (Table 13.3). Two hours later patients receive their first dose of oral naltrexone (12.5 mg), and then receive two additional doses of oral clonidine (0.1–0.3 mg each) over the remainder of the day (i.e., clonidine dosing should occur every four to six hours while awake). Clonidine doses should be selected to provide relief from withdrawal, but not produce significant

Table 13.3 **Sample Clonidine/Naltrexone Dosing Schedule**

	Dosing Time			
	9:00 A.M.	11:00 A.M.	2:00 P.M.	8:00 P.M.
Day 1				
Clonidine (mg)	0.1–0.3		0.1–0.3	0.1–0.3
Naltrexone (mg)		12.5		
Day 2				
Clonidine (mg)	0.1–0.3		0.1–0.3	0.1–0.3
Naltrexone (mg)		25		
Day 3				
Clonidine (mg)	0.1–0.2		0.1–0.2	0.1–0.2
Naltrexone (mg)		50		
Day 4				
Clonidine (mg)	0.1		0.1	0.1
Naltrexone (mg)		100		

Source: Modified from Vining, Kosten, and Kleber (1988).

hypotension. Blood pressure should be monitored throughout the day, and symptomatic treatments for opioid withdrawal (e.g., cramping) can also be given.

On the second day, clonidine is again given three times (every four to six hours), using doses of 0.1–0.3 mg each time. The day-two dose of naltrexone is 25 mg, and again given two hours after the first dose of clonidine. As on day one, blood pressure should be monitored throughout the day.

The procedure for day three is similar to day two's, except the dose of naltrexone used is now 50 mg, and clonidine doses should be lowered to 0.1–0.2 mg per administration. Finally, on day four the naltrexone dose is 100 mg, and the three clonidine doses should be 0.1 mg each.

Naltrexone Induction Using General Anesthesia

Several short research and clinical reports have described the use of general anesthesia for starting an opioid-dependent patient on naltrexone. In general, this procedure consists of inducing precipitated withdrawal with an opioid antagonist such as naltrexone while an opioid-dependent patient is under general anesthesia (i.e., asleep), so that he or she does not consciously experience withdrawal. After several hours, when the withdrawal syndrome has resolved, the patient is awakened and discharged (often on naltrexone treatment). There have been no large, double-blind, controlled studies testing the efficacy and safety of this procedure, although there have been reports of clinical experience (e.g., Loimer et al. 1989, 1991; Rabinowitz et al. 1997; for a review, see O'Connor and Kosten 1998). Note, however, that up to seven different medications may be used in the procedure and that there are significant risks (estimated 1 in 15,000 serious adverse events including death) associated with general anesthesia. These risks may be further increased by the use of these other concurrent medications for control of symptoms such as nausea, vomiting, and diarrhea. Although fear of withdrawal symptoms can contribute to continued opioid use in some patients, it is doubtful that the use of anesthesia has any greater long-term benefit than the use of safer means for treating opioid withdrawal.

Maintenance on Naltrexone

One of two dosing schedules with naltrexone is typically used. The first is 50 mg per day, with dosing every day. Because of naltrexone's sustained effects, dosing also can be on a less-than-daily basis. Thus, the second schedule frequently used is 100 mg on Mondays and Wednesdays and 150 mg on Fridays. Because naltrexone is a pure opioid antagonist, it exerts no pharmacologic effects in nonopioid-dependent patients. Abrupt discontinuation does not result in a withdrawal syndrome, and there is no need to detoxify patients off naltrexone.

BUPRENORPHINE

Pharmacology of Buprenorphine

Buprenorphine's Receptor Effects

Buprenorphine is an opioid mixed agonist-antagonist; that is, it exerts effects at both the mu opioid receptor, where it acts as a partial agonist, and at the kappa opioid receptor, where it acts as an antagonist (and hence the characterization as an "agonist-antagonist"). A brief explanation about agonists, antagonists, and partial agonists in the simplest terms is given here to provide some background for understanding these pharmacologic effects of buprenorphine.

An *antagonist* is a compound that occupies a receptor but does not activate it (e.g., naltrexone, as previously discussed). A *partial agonist* is a compound that occupies a receptor and activates it, but cannot produce as great an effect as a *full agonist*. Thus, partial agonists at low doses can produce effects very similar or identical to full agonists, but at higher doses a partial agonist does not produce greater effects, whereas a full agonist does produce greater effects. Therefore, a partial agonist does not activate the receptor as much as a full agonist. These features of partial agonists result in a unique effect. When a partial agonist opioid is given to someone who is not physically dependent on opioids, it produces agonist effects (such as mild euphoria); however, when given to someone who is physically dependent on opioids and has a high level of tolerance to opioids, a partial agonist could act like an antagonist (because it does not activate the receptor as much as the full agonist does). Thus, under these circumstances a partial agonist could precipitate withdrawal. (Obviously, if withdrawal occurred with regularity, this would be a distinct disadvantage of treating opioid-dependent patients with medications that are partial agonists.)

Although in general buprenorphine does not precipitate withdrawal when given to opioid-dependent persons, there is evidence that it can produce antagonist-like effects when a high dose is given shortly after an agonist. A study of subjects maintained on 30 mg of daily methadone and given an injection of buprenorphine two hours after their methadone dose found evidence of mild withdrawal in response to buprenorphine (Strain et al. 1995). However, note that a study investigating the use of buprenorphine in street addicts found that it was well tolerated when using a rapid dose-induction procedure (as described in more detail in the "Clinical Use" section).

There also are advantages to buprenorphine's partial mu agonist effects. Most important, because its maximal agonist effect is less than that of a full agonist, an overdose with buprenorphine should not produce the same amount of respiratory depression (something seen with an overdose of a full-agonist opioid). Evidence from studies on animals supports this belief, as well as some human research and a clinical report that suggests an overdose with buprenorphine alone will not result in clinically significant respiratory depression. However, there have been reports of deaths associated with the simultaneous injection of buprenorphine and benzodiazepines (Reynaud et al. 1998). Therefore, patients should be warned of this potential danger.

Buprenorphine is also a kappa antagonist. However, its ability to bind to kappa receptors is relatively weak when compared to its ability to bind to mu receptors. At higher doses this difference in binding affinity is less significant because there are more molecules of buprenorphine to bind to the kappa receptors. It has been suggested that the kappa antagonist effects of buprenorphine at higher doses may offset the partial mu agonist effects (this has been called *noncompetitive autoinhibition*). Noncompetitive autoinhibition has been used to explain the observation that buprenorphine has a bell-shaped dose-response curve; that is, as the dose of buprenorphine increases, measured effects (such as decreased gastrointestinal motility) first increase, but then decrease as the dose is further increased.

Buprenorphine's Absorption, Metabolism, and Excretion

When used as an analgesic, buprenorphine is typically given by injection. Buprenorphine has poor oral bioavailability, so it is not effective if given as a medication to be swallowed. However, it does have good absorption through mouth membranes if given sublingually, and clinical trials examining the efficacy of buprenorphine in the treatment of opioid dependence have used either sublingual solution or sublingual tablets. When administered as a sublingual solution, buprenorphine must be held under the tongue for 3–5 minutes to ensure complete absorption (Weinberg et al. 1988; Mendelson et al. 1997). Buprenorphine sublingual tablets are held under the tongue until they dissolve (i.e., 3–10 minutes). Several other novel delivery systems have been considered for buprenorphine, including intranasal

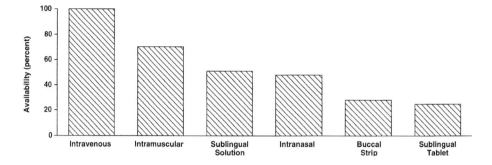

Figure 13.2. The relative bioavailability of buprenorphine when taken by different routes of administration.

spray and a transdermal patch. Figure 13.2 shows the relative bioavailability of buprenorphine given by different routes of administration.

Once buprenorphine is absorbed, a high percentage is bound to plasma protein and undergoes enterohepatic circulation. Sublingual buprenorphine is metabolized into norbuprenorphine and other products in the liver (and metabolized in the gastrointestinal tract wall when taken orally). In animals, norbuprenorphine is an active metabolite with analgesic activity one-fourth to one-fiftieth that of buprenorphine (Ohtani et al. 1995). With chronic dosing, norbuprenorphine may account in part for the long duration of effect noted with buprenorphine. Buprenorphine and its metabolites are excreted in both the urine and feces.

Buprenorphine Combined with Naloxone

Because buprenorphine has poor oral bioavailability, sublingual administration has been the primary route used in studies of clinical efficacy for treating opioid dependence. Initial clinical trials used a 1-ml alcohol-based solution (typically either 30% or 40% alcohol). More recent studies have focused on the use of a buprenorphine-containing tablet. There is an important difference in the bioequivalence of sublingual solution and sublingual tablets: it appears that tablets provide only about 50–60 percent of the corresponding sublingual solution dose. Depending on the formulation used (solution vs. tablet), a corresponding increase or decrease in the dose must be considered.

A water-soluble tablet containing buprenorphine could be abused. Buprenorphine abuse has been reported in many countries where it is available as an analgesic (Strang 1985; O'Connor et al. 1988; Gray, Ferry, and Jauhar 1989; Morrison 1989; Sakol, Stark, and Sykes 1989; Chowdhury and Chowdhury 1990; Singh et al. 1992; Robinson et al. 1993), and it is possible that a buprenorphine tablet could be dissolved and then injected. To decrease this abuse liability, a combination buprenorphine/naloxone tablet has been created.

The buprenorphine tablet capitalizes on the differential absorption of naloxone by the sublingual versus parenteral (i.e., injection) routes. Naloxone is a pure opioid antagonist that has poor sublingual absorption. Thus, a tablet taken by the therapeutic route (sublingual) will produce a predominant buprenorphine effect. However, a tablet dissolved and abused by injection will produce a predominant naloxone effect, because naloxone has good parenteral bioavailability. Thus, a person who is dependent on opioids other than buprenorphine would experience a precipitated withdrawal syndrome from injecting naloxone and, hence, would not abuse the medication by this route.

Buprenorphine/naloxone combination tablets are being developed for use in the treatment of opioid dependence. These tablets will contain buprenorphine plus naloxone in a dose ratio of 4:1 and will be available as combinations of 2/0.5 and 8/2 mg. By adding naloxone to buprenorphine in this way, it may be possible to give take-home doses of combination tablets and to decrease the risk of diversion and use by injection. Tablets containing buprenorphine alone (0.4, 2, and 8 mg) will be available, in the near future, to induct patients onto buprenorphine from methadone and other agonist opiates and for use during pregnancy.

Efficacy

Most studies of buprenorphine's efficacy have compared its use to methadone in the short-term (less than one year) outpatient treatment of opioid dependence. One study has compared buprenorphine to placebo, and several other studies have investigated the use of buprenorphine on a less-than-daily basis. Finally, although the focus of clinical trials has been on the use of sublingual buprenorphine for the outpatient treatment of opioid dependence, buprenorphine has also been used by both the sublingual and parenteral routes of administration for the short-term (e.g., three- to five-day) detoxification of opioid dependence. Each of these topics is addressed here.

Buprenorphine Compared to Methadone

Several clinical trials have compared sublingual buprenorphine solution to methadone in the outpatient treatment of opioid dependence. Generally, these studies have found the two medications to be equally effective for primary outcome measures such as treatment retention and rates of opioid-positive urine samples, as well as for secondary outcome measures such as amount of money spent on drugs and reports of dose adequacy.

In reviewing these clinical trials, it is important to recognize that the methodology of studies like these is significantly different from the clinical practice under which a medication would be used. For example, well-conducted studies use double-blind dosing: neither patients nor staff who come into contact with patients know what dose and which medication the patients are taking. Patient awareness of doses may enhance treatment compliance, so this double-blind dosing could contribute to poorer outcomes in a clinical trial compared to those achieved with routine practice. Similarly, most clinical trials have used an intensive urine testing schedule (e.g., collecting and testing urine samples three times per week). Such a schedule is dramatically different from most routine clinical practice and is designed to detect *any* drug use, but is poorer at detecting *changes* in drug use. Thus, rates of drug-positive urine samples can be quite high in these studies. Finally, the doses of buprenorphine and methadone selected should be roughly equivalent in efficacy. If they are not, a study difference may simply reflect a dose difference (e.g., comparing a high effective dose of methadone to a low ineffective dose of buprenorphine), rather than a true medication difference.

An early controlled clinical trial of buprenorphine versus methadone ($N = 45$) found that 2 mg of daily sublingual buprenorphine solution produced outcomes equivalent to 30 mg of oral methadone in a 90-day outpatient detoxification protocol (Bickel et al. 1988). A later study, which enrolled 162 opioid-dependent patients, found that 8 mg of daily sublingual buprenorphine solution was equivalent to 60 mg of daily methadone and that both of these conditions were superior to 20 mg of daily methadone, during a 17-week evaluation period (Johnson, Jaffe, and Fudala 1992). Whereas these two studies used fixed doses of buprenorphine and methadone, a third clinical trial compared the two medications in 164 opioid-dependent patients using flexible dosing (i.e., doses were adjusted during the study based on evidence of continued opioid use and patient requests). The results from this study showed that daily sublingual buprenorphine at an average dose of 8.9 mg produced outcomes equivalent to 55 mg of daily methadone (Strain et al. 1994).

Not all studies have found equivalent efficacy for buprenorphine and methadone. One large clinical trial, which enrolled 125 patients, compared four different groups (2 and 6 mg of daily sublingual buprenorphine solution vs. 35 and 65 mg of daily oral methadone) and found that all patients receiving methadone had better outcomes than those receiving buprenorphine (Kosten et al. 1993). Similarly, an outpatient clinical trial comparing 8 mg of daily sublingual buprenorphine solution to 30 and 80 mg of daily oral methadone, in 225 subjects, found that patients on the higher dose of methadone had better outcomes than patients on either of the other medications (Ling et al. 1996). Another clinical trial, with 116 patients, compared sublingual buprenorphine solution (4 and 12 mg daily) and oral methadone (20 and 65 mg daily) and found that 12 mg of buprenorphine and 65 mg of methadone were more effective than 4 mg of buprenorphine and 20 mg of methadone, but that 65 mg of methadone was superior to 12 mg of buprenorphine (Schottenfeld et al. 1997).

Overall, it appears that sublingual doses of buprenorphine in the range of 6–9 mg can produce treatment outcomes comparable to those seen with moderate (50–60 mg) doses of methadone. However, higher doses of methadone, such as 80 mg per day, may be more effective than doses of buprenorphine typically used in these clinical trials. Efficacy greater than that produced by 65 mg of methadone has not been demonstrated with buprenorphine doses up to 12 mg and may be difficult to achieve due to the partial agonist profile of buprenorphine. In general, results from these clinical trials demonstrate a maximal effect produced by buprenorphine, such that doses greater than 12–16 mg may not significantly increase the level of clinical efficacy but may increase the level of blockade and duration of action.

Buprenorphine Compared to Placebo

While studies comparing buprenorphine to methadone are useful, clinical trials comparing a medication to placebo are especially valuable in gaining approval by government regulatory bodies for clinical use. One study has compared buprenorphine (doses of 2 and 8 mg per day of sublingual solution) to placebo (0 mg per day of sublingual solution; Johnson et al. [1995a]). This study enrolled 150 opioid-dependent patients and used a novel design that lasted only two weeks. Results showed that active buprenorphine was preferred and had better efficacy than placebo.

Although not a placebo-controlled study, a large multicenter clinical trial ($N = 736$) compared different buprenorphine doses (1, 4, 8, and 16 mg). The 1-mg dose in this study can be conceptualized as an active placebo condition. The study found that 8 mg was superior to 1 mg on measures of treatment effectiveness but that there was no difference between the 8- and 16-mg doses (Ling et al. 1998).

Daily versus Alternate-Day Buprenorphine Dosing

Buprenorphine has been abused in several countries, and one means to decrease the risk of such abuse is to add naloxone to buprenorphine, as discussed previously. The addition of naloxone should decrease the potential of abuse by dissolving and injecting tablets, and could thus lead to the use of buprenorphine as a take-home medication.

Another means to decrease the diversion and abuse of buprenorphine is to administer buprenorphine on a less-than-daily basis. There has been considerable interest in using buprenorphine on an alternate-day basis, and several investigations have provided data supporting this use. This approach capitalizes on buprenorphine's long duration of action and allows patients to receive doses every other day or every third day. Some investigators have even administered buprenorphine every four days, but the efficacy for longer time intervals is less well established.

While some studies have simply given placebo on nonmedication days without a compensatory increase on active medication days (e.g., Fudala et al. 1990; Johnson et al. 1995b), it appears that corresponding increases in dose on active medication days result in improved outcomes (Amass et al. 1994). Thus, a patient maintained on 8 mg of daily sublingual buprenorphine would be switched to 16 mg of every-other-day sublingual buprenorphine, or 24 mg if the dosing interval was 72 hours (e.g., a Friday dose before a weekend with no medication).

Less-than-daily buprenorphine dosing has several advantages. As noted, it decreases the chance of diversion of a take-home dose. It also may improve patient cooperation, because it reduces the frequency of clinic visits. Finally, less-than-daily dosing provides a greater flexibility to clinicians. Although LAAM provides less-than-daily dosing, if a clinician wishes to switch an LAAM patient to daily dosing, he or she will need to switch both dosing frequency and medication. By using buprenorphine, the clinician can make changes in dosing schedule without the need to change the medication.

Buprenorphine for Brief Opioid Detoxification

Although considerable attention has focused on the development of a sublingual formulation of buprenorphine administered in a maintenance or short-term maintenance setting for the treatment of opioid dependence, buprenorphine has also been used for brief opioid detoxification. Such detoxifications generally last only a few days, appear to be primarily conducted in inpatient settings, and represent the use of a marketed analgesic

Title	Methadone Treatment for Opioid
Seller SKU	M 363508 38- 62
	Monday, October 04, 2004
ISBN #	0801861373
Sold Price	$7.60
order#	058-3145469-8629159
book condition	Used; Very Good
	Excellent Condition - no Markings! Ships out
	immediately!

Buyer Name	Brad Higginbottom
Ship Method	media mail
Return Address	Box 5, Inc.
	7026 Bellefontaine Ave.
	Kansas City, MO 64132

Dear Brad Higginbottom,

I sincerely appreciate your business and I want to do all I can to make this transaction a smooth and positive one. If in any way you are not satisfied with your order, please feel free to contact me personally. My e-mail address is brad@box5inc.com.

Please leave feedback which reflects the service I have given you. I will return the favor by leaving feedback for you. If you feel my service has been anything less than the best, please let me know so I can serve you better :)

Leave feedback by going to: www.amazon.com/feedback

-Brad

Table 13.4 **Buprenorphine for Brief Opioid Withdrawal**

Time of Administration	Buprenorphine Dose		
	High[a]	Low[a]	Injectable[b]
First dose	4 mg (2 × 2 mg tablets)	2.0 mg (1 × 2 mg tablets)	1.5 mg
24 hours	12 mg (6 × 2 mg tablets)	1.6 mg (4 × 0.4 mg tablets)	1.2 mg
48 hours	12 mg (6 × 2 mg tablets)	1.2 mg (3 × 0.4 mg tablets)	0.9 mg
72 hours	6 mg (3 × 2 mg tablets)	0.8 mg (2 × 0.4 mg tablets)	0.45 mg

[a]This schedule is based on the use of buprenorphine tablets.
[b]This schedule is based on the use of the injectable form of buprenorphine.

product for a nonapproved indication. When used in this manner, buprenorphine has been given intramuscularly one to three times per day, or sublingually one to four times per day. The doses used are generally lower than the dose used in the clinical trials comparing buprenorphine to methadone; for example, intramuscular dosing may be 0.3–0.6 mg three times the first day, 0.15–0.3 mg three times the second day, and then a single dose of 0.15–0.3 mg the third day.

When using buprenorphine for brief opioid detoxification, a high- or low-dose schedule may be used. The high-dose schedule takes advantage of the kinetics of buprenorphine and uses the tablet formulation, whereas the low-dose reduction schedule considers the off-label use of injectable buprenorphine, described previously (i.e., the analgesic formulation). Recommended dose reduction schedules utilizing these techniques are given in Table 13.4.

A limited number of studies have examined the use of buprenorphine for such brief detoxifications (e.g., Nigam, Ray, and Tripathi 1993; Cheskin, Fudala, and Johnson 1994). In general, these studies have found that buprenorphine is more effective than clonidine in relieving opioid withdrawal symptoms. In addition, some evidence suggests that a more gradual dose reduction is superior to a rapid detoxification.

Buprenorphine for Cocaine Use Disorders

Several preclinical studies found evidence that self-administration of cocaine decreased in animals maintained on buprenorphine . This intriguing finding suggests that buprenorphine might have efficacy for cocaine use disorders, in addition to its efficacy for opioid dependence. However, clinical studies have generally failed to find an anticocaine effect for buprenorphine.

Safety and Side Effects

The relative safety of buprenorphine was initially established when it was being reviewed and approved for use as an analgesic. The enhanced safety profile of buprenorphine is thought to be due to the fact that buprenorphine is a partial agonist opioid. Buprenorphine is a very safe medication, especially when administered alone. However, there have been a limited number of reports of clinically significant respiratory depression (McEvoy 1997). As with other opiates, buprenorphine should be administered with caution in patients with compromised respiratory function. In patients who have respiratory depression because of excessive buprenorphine dosing, naloxone (greater than 3 mg/70 kg) or doxapram (Dopram®) (a central respiratory stimulant) may be effective. Buprenorphine can cause sedation and hypotension. Increased CNS depression may occur in patients receiving buprenorphine along with other narcotic analgesics, general anesthetics, benzodiazepines, phenothiazines, other tranquilizers, sedative/hypnotics, or other CNS depressants (including alcohol). In addition, there have been reports of death in patients who inject buprenorphine and benzodiazepines simultaneously. Because buprenorphine is metabolized by the liver, the activity of buprenorphine may be increased or decreased in individuals with impaired hepatic function or in those receiving medications that induce or inhibit hepatic enzymes. In animal studies, buprenorphine has been shown to protect against the lethality of cocaine. Adverse effects observed with buprenorphine are similar to other opiates and, in general, include effects owing to under- or overmedication. The most common adverse-related events reported in a one-year clinical trial (ranked in order of frequency) were withdrawal, insomnia, sweating, asthenia (lack of strength or energy), rhinitis (inflammation of the nasal mucosa), headache, nausea, constipation, generalized pain, abdominal pain, anxiety, chills, somnolence, nervousness, diarrhea, watery eyes, back pain, vomiting, dizziness, depression, and flulike syndrome (Ling et al. 1998).

Clinical Use

Several issues are pertinent to the clinical use of buprenorphine for the treatment of opioid dependence and are discussed next.

Induction onto Buprenorphine

As a partial mu agonist, it is possible that starting a patient on buprenorphine could precipitate opioid withdrawal (as explained previously). In opiate-dependent individuals, under the appropriate conditions (i.e., buprenorphine dose, opiate maintenance dose, and duration since last opiate maintenance dose), buprenorphine at high doses can precipitate an opiate withdrawal syndrome. However, studies enrolling patients with illicit opioid dependence have generally used a dose-induction procedure of 2, 4, and then 8 mg of sublingual solution per day over the first three days of treatment, with good tolerability of these doses. It may be possible to precipitate withdrawal if the time interval since the last use of opioids is short (e.g., two hours), if the level of physical dependence is high (e.g., greater than 30 mg of methadone), and the dose of buprenorphine is high (e.g., greater than 4 mg). Precipitated withdrawal at the onset of treatment in individuals using short-acting opioids (i.e., heroin) is expected to be extremely rare.

Therefore, prior to administering the initial buprenorphine dose, consideration should be given to the (1) type of opiate dependence (i.e., long- or short-acting opiate), (2) time since last opiate use, and (3) degree or level of opiate dependence. After taking a clinical history the appropriate initial dose can be selected. The generally recommended induction dose of buprenorphine is 2–4 mg of sublingual solution (or 4–6 mg of sublingual tablet). The shorter acting the opiate of dependence (e.g., heroin), the longer the time elapsed since the last opiate use (e.g., 12–24 hours or longer), and the lower the level of physical dependence (e.g., using heroin one to two times per day), the higher the initial buprenorphine dose can be.

Maintenance on Buprenorphine

Studies of buprenorphine for the treatment of opioid dependence have used maintenance doses as low as 1 mg per day of solution, and as high as 16 mg per day of solution. Most of the clinical trials comparing buprenorphine to methadone used maintenance doses of about 8 mg of solution per day, and this dose appears to provide efficacy equivalent to about 40–60 mg per day of methadone.

As a partial agonist, higher doses may not produce corresponding increases in effects (such as a subjective sense of a high). However, higher doses may provide better cross-tolerance to other opioids over longer periods of time. Thus, it is possible that increasing the dose of buprenorphine at some point will produce no appreciable difference to the patient, but may provide further efficacy in reducing illicit opioid use. It may also be possible for the effects of buprenorphine, which are perceived as positive by the patient, to decrease as the dose of buprenorphine is increased. In one study, several patients who had been put on high-dose buprenorphine as part of a clinical trial asked for their dose to be decreased (Walter Ling, personal communication, 1998). Therefore, doses of buprenorphine greater than 16–32 mg per day may not demonstrate greater clinical efficacy but may increase the duration of the effects of buprenorphine.

An adequate maintenance dose, titrated to clinical effectiveness, should be achieved as rapidly as possible to prevent undue opiate withdrawal symptomatology, and the maintenance dose should provide the maximum benefit to the patient. There are three desirable clinical benefits during maintenance treatment: (1) suppression of withdrawal, (2) blockade of or cross-tolerance to other opiates, and (3) increased duration of effects for (1) and (2). Opiate withdrawal signs and symptoms can be attenuated in most patients for up to 24 hours with doses of buprenorphine solution as low as 2 mg. Therefore, a maintenance buprenorphine dose of 2–4 mg of solution is recommended to suppress the signs and symptoms of opioid withdrawal. Blockade and cross-tolerance to exogenously administered opiates by buprenorphine is dose related, and doses of 16 mg of solution administered daily significantly decrease both the subjective and physiologic effects of high-dose opiates. Hence, a dose of buprenorphine solution in the range of 4–16 mg is recommended for blocking the effects of other opiates. It has been shown that plasma levels of buprenorphine and its metabolites at 72 hours following a 32-mg dose of solution are higher than plasma levels observed at 24 hours following an 8-mg dose of buprenorphine solution. Thus, increasing the dose of buprenorphine increases the amount of buprenorphine in the body for longer periods of time. Therefore, doses greater than 8–16 mg of solution should increase the duration of effects and allow for a longer time period between doses (i.e., 24–72 hours).

Withdrawal from Buprenorphine

The use of buprenorphine in rapid withdrawal from opioids was discussed in a previous section. Although there have been some studies on the clinical use of buprenorphine for such rapid detoxifications (i.e., detoxifications generally lasting only a few days), studies examining the use of buprenorphine for longer detoxifications (e.g., three or six months) have not been reported.

Some reports have suggested that abrupt discontinuation of chronic buprenorphine dosing results in a very mild withdrawal syndrome (e.g., Jasinski, Pevnick, and Griffith 1978). However, evidence from the disengagement phase of some of the methadone/buprenorphine comparison clinical trials suggests that patients on buprenorphine relapse to opioid use and drop out of treatment at rates similar to those seen for patients receiving methadone.

Although studies of buprenorphine for opioid withdrawal are lacking, general recommendations that have been derived from methadone studies may also apply to the use of buprenorphine. Thus, detoxifications with gradual decreases in dose should be optimal. Dose changes should be made only after patients have achieved stabilization on their current dose, and patient awareness of the dose schedule and advance warning of dose changes may lead to better outcomes.

Conclusions Regarding Buprenorphine

In summary, buprenorphine is a safe and effective medication that can be useful for the treatment of opioid dependence. As clinical experience with buprenorphine's use in the treatment of opioid dependence increases, it may come to be considered a first-line treatment option for opiate dependence, given its safety profile, limited agonist activity, and reportedly minimal physical dependence–producing properties. If therapy is initiated with buprenorphine, successful treatment can result in a patient continuing on daily or less frequent buprenorphine maintenance therapy. Detoxification should be facilitated by the mild to moderate withdrawal problems generally associated with buprenorphine. However, in some highly dependent patients, the limited agonist effect of buprenorphine may result in unsuccessful treatment owing to such patients requiring a higher agonist effect. In such cases, the possibility of treatment initially with methadone or LAAM exists.

ALPHA$_2$-ADRENERGIC AGONISTS (CLONIDINE, LOFEXIDINE)

Two nonopioid medications that can be used for short-term opioid withdrawal are clonidine and lofexidine. Both are alpha$_2$-adrenergic agonist agents (see next section). Clonidine is available in several countries as an antihypertensive medication, and in the United States, its use in the treatment of opioid withdrawal is "off label" (i.e., it is not an FDA-approved indication). During the 1980s, the use of lofexidine as an antihypertensive was extensively studied but the development of lofexidine for hypertension was eventually abandoned because it was not as effective for this purpose as was clonidine. Lofexidine is available in the United Kingdom as Brit-Lofex®, where it is approved for the treatment of opioid withdrawal.

Pharmacology of Alpha$_2$-Adrenergic Agonist Agents

There is a significant adrenergic/noradrenergic component to opioid withdrawal symptoms, which include increased heart rate and blood pressure, heightened reactivity to environmental stimuli, restlessness, and agitation. Furthermore, opioid withdrawal is accompanied by hyperactivity in the locus coeruleus, a site in the CNS that controls noradrenergic function. Alpha$_2$-adrenergic agonist agents act on these CNS receptors to cause a decrease or dampening of noradrenergic hyperactivity, which, in turn, results in a decrease in certain opioid withdrawal signs and symptoms.

Absorption, Distribution, and Excretion

Clonidine has good oral bioavailability, with a peak effect occurring 3–5 hours after oral ingestion and a t$_{1/2}$ of 12–16 hours. It is primarily metabolized in the liver, although there is some renal clearance (and thus caution should be exercised when it is used in patients with impaired renal functioning). Clonidine is also available in transdermal patches, a highly convenient form of administration that greatly reduces the possibility of abuse.

Lofexidine also has good oral bioavailability, and peak plasma concentrations are reached two to five hours after an oral dose. Elimination is primarily mediated through the renal system, and the extent of biotransformation prior to excretion appears to vary considerably among individuals.

Efficacy

Clonidine

Several reports and studies have examined the use of clonidine in the treatment of opioid withdrawal, especially as a bridging medication that might allow an opioid-dependent patient to detoxify and remain drug free for a sufficient time to be started on naltrexone without precipitating a withdrawal syndrome. (See the section on naltrexone treatment in this chapter for a description of precipitated withdrawal, as well as a discussion of the use of clonidine in opioid-dependent patients being transferred to naltrexone treatment.) In general, these studies have demonstrated that clonidine can effectively diminish opioid withdrawal signs in a patient undergoing abrupt discontinuation of daily opioid use (e.g., Gold, Redmond, and Kleber 1978; Charney et al. 1981; Camí et al. 1985; Gossop 1988). For example, Jasinski, Johnson, and Kocher (1985) maintained opioid dependence in research volunteers living on a residential research unit by giving injections of morphine four times each day. When the injections were temporarily stopped, the volunteers experienced withdrawal symptoms. The study showed that clonidine was effective in decreasing the signs and symptoms of opioid withdrawal compared to placebo. Clonidine was more effective than morphine in suppressing the autonomic signs of withdrawal (such as rhinorrhea and lacrimation). However, morphine was more effective than clonidine in suppressing the subjective symptoms associated with withdrawal.

Another inpatient study compared buprenorphine to clonidine and showed that the two medications generally had similar efficacy but that buprenorphine relieved withdrawal symptoms better early in treatment (Cheskin, Fudala, and Johnson 1994). Other studies have reported on the outpatient use of clonidine for the treatment of opioid withdrawal, including in the form of patches, and have found that clonidine can be effective even though success rates appear to be lower than those achieved when it is used on an inpatient basis (e.g., Washton and Resnick 1980; Rounsaville, Kosten, and Kleber 1985; Spencer and Gregory 1989).

Lofexidine

Two double-blind studies comparing the efficacy of lofexidine versus clonidine in opiate withdrawal have been reported: an outpatient study with a small sample ($N = 28$) (Kahn et al. 1997) and an inpatient detoxification study with a larger sample ($N = 80$) (Lin et al. 1997). Both studies showed that lofexidine is generally equal in efficacy to clonidine for suppressing opioid withdrawal signs but that lofexidine is associated with lower rates of hypotension and other adverse effects, and thus may be a preferable medication from a safety viewpoint.

Conclusions Regarding the Efficacy of Clonidine and Lofexidine

Research has clearly shown that clonidine is more effective than placebo in the treatment of opioid withdrawal and that it is at least as useful as opioid agonists for some outcome measures. However, in general it seems that clonidine is better at suppressing the physiologic *signs* of opioid withdrawal than the subjective *symptoms* of withdrawal. At the clinical level, patients do not appear to be in withdrawal, but they may still complain that they feel like they are in withdrawal. Lofexidine appears to be as effective as clonidine for the treatment of opioid withdrawal. However, more research is needed on lofexidine, to better determine its efficacy and the optimal parameters for its use in the treatment of opioid withdrawal.

Safety and Side Effects

The primary concern associated with the use of clonidine in the treatment of opioid withdrawal is that patients may become hypotensive; patients treated with clonidine for opioid withdrawal frequently have significant decreases in both systolic and diastolic blood pressures (Gossop 1988; Cheskin, Fudala, and Johnson 1994). In addition, some clinical trials using clonidine in the treatment of opioid withdrawal have reported sedation (e.g., Charney et al. 1981), whereas others have noted that patients have problems falling and staying asleep when taking clonidine (e.g., Kleber, Gold, and Riordan 1980). Dry mouth and constipation are two other side effects reportedly associated with clonidine use. However, several of these effects may be related to opioid withdrawal rather than clonidine use, and the primary concern associated with clonidine use is the possibility of blood pressure changes. Two studies (Kahn et al. 1997; Lin et al. 1997) have noted greater decreases in blood pressure for patients on clonidine versus lofexidine, and the Kahn et al. study (1997) noted more adverse effects for clonidine, including more instances of serious decreases in blood pressure. Overall, it appears that lofexidine may be safer and better tolerated than clonidine.

Note, however, that some opioid-dependent patients appear to abuse clonidine. The extent of clonidine abuse is not well characterized, and it is not clear if this misuse is because of a psychoactive effect produced by clonidine, or if it is an effort to ameliorate withdrawal symptoms associated with opioid abuse. There is currently little information about the abuse liability of lofexidine.

Clinical Use

Clonidine

A description of the use of clonidine as a bridging agent from opioid dependence to treatment with naltrexone was provided in the section on naltrexone in this chapter (see Table 13.3). A similar procedure can be used if clonidine is being utilized simply to withdraw a patient from opioids (i.e., not transferring them to naltrexone treatment). Thus, for patients being treated on an outpatient basis, 0.1 mg of clonidine can be given orally as a first test dose on the first day, with close monitoring of blood pressure following this dose. If this dose is tolerated (i.e., no hypotension or other adverse effects, such as excessive sedation), then patients should receive a dose of clonidine (0.1 mg) every 4–6 hours while awake, with the frequency of dosing based on withdrawal suppression and toleration of the medication. Typical dosing of clonidine is three times per day (i.e., a total of 0.3 mg on the first day for outpatients).

During the second day of outpatient treatment, the dose of clonidine may be increased up to 0.2 mg, three times per day, depending on the balance between withdrawal suppression and hypotension. If necessary, doses can be raised further on the third and fourth days, up to 0.3–0.4 mg, three times per day. Thus, after three to four days of clonidine treatment on an outpatient basis, a stable total daily dose of 0.6–1.2 mg per day should be achieved. This dose can be maintained for several days, if needed, or a dose reduction procedure can then be instituted. Doses should be decreased 0.1–0.2 mg per day, as tolerated. If a patient is experiencing sedation associated with clonidine, dose reductions should initially be for the daytime doses, rather than the bedtime dose. Outpatients should be cautioned regarding the possibility of sedation associated with clonidine and should avoid activities such as driving if they experience such sedation.

If detoxification is being conducted on an outpatient basis, under optimal circumstances, supplies or prescriptions of clonidine should be given to a responsible, nondrug-abusing family member or friend of the patient (given the potential abuse of clonidine, and the potential for hypotension if a patient misappropriately ingests extra clonidine). If an outpatient is given a supply of clonidine to manage himself or herself, limited amounts (e.g., enough for one to two days) should be given.

If detoxification is being conducted on an inpatient unit, a more aggressive dosing schedule may be used, with doses increased over the first one to two days and withdrawal off clonidine accomplished within a week. Finally, if a patient is being concurrently treated for hypertension with antihypertensives, clonidine should be used with particular caution because there may be an increased likelihood of hypotension.

Lofexidine

Lofexidine treatment can be initiated with an oral dose of 0.2 mg (given either two or three times per day, for a total daily dose of 0.4–0.6 mg on the first day). Doses of lofexidine can be increased over subsequent days, with a maximum total daily dose generally in the range of 1.6 mg per day

Table 13.5 Summary of Medications for the Treatment of Opioid Dependence

Medication	Action	Use	Dosing Schedule	Opioid Blockade[b]	Abusable
Methadone	Opioid agonist	Maintenance, withdrawal	Daily	Yes	Yes
LAAM	Opioid agonist	Maintenance	Every other day[a]	Yes	Yes
Naltrexone	Opioid antagonist	Maintenance	Daily or every other day[a]	Yes	No
Buprenorphine	Opioid mixed agonist-antagonist	Maintenance, withdrawal	Daily or every other day[a]	Yes	Yes
Clonidine	Alpha$_2$-adrenergic agonist	Withdrawal	Multiple times each day	Unknown	Perhaps
Lofexidine	Alpha$_2$-adrenergic agonist	Withdrawal	Multiple times each day	Unknown	Unknown

[a]Also possible to dose every 72 hours.
[b]That is, will the medication block the effects of an opioid? With blockade, a patient will not experience the effect of illicit opioids while receiving an adequate dose of the medication.

(i.e., 0.4 mg, four times per day). In the United Kingdom, total daily doses as high as 2.4 mg per day may be given, and dose reductions of 0.2 mg per day can be made every day, as tolerated by the patient. Notably, evidence suggests that lofexidine causes fewer cases of hypotension and less sedation than clonidine, so it may be easier and safer to use lofexidine versus clonidine on an outpatient basis. However, lofexidine can decrease blood pressure, and, therefore, blood pressure should be monitored during treatment with this medication.

Summary

Although the mainstay of pharmacotherapies for opioid dependence has been methadone, several alternate medications are in various stages of development and regulatory approval (depending in part on the country). A summary of the different medications reviewed in this chapter can be found in Table 13.5. Currently, LAAM is a good alternative to methadone, particularly for stable maintenance patients who can benefit from the reduced dosing schedule (i.e., reduced clinic visits). Buprenorphine provides an additional alternative, with the potential for greater flexibility in dosing schedules (i.e., daily or intermittent dosing) and greater safety. Naltrexone is a potentially useful maintenance medication that may find application when combined with effective behavior therapy procedures that address poor compliance and retention, which have previously been seen with this medication. Finally, there are two nonopioid medications—clonidine and lofexidine—that have shown utility in detoxification treatment. Clinicians and patients will benefit from having a choice of medications, with medication selection being tailored to patient characteristics and needs.

References

Amass L., Bickel W.K., Higgins S.T., Badger G.J. 1994. Alternate-day dosing during buprenorphine treatment of opioid dependence. *Life Sci.* 54: 1215–28.

Bickel W.K., Stitzer M.L., Bigelow G.E., Liebson I.A., Jasinski D.R., Johnson R.E. 1988. A clinical trial of buprenorphine: comparison with methadone in the detoxification of heroin addicts. *Clin. Pharmacol. Ther.* 43:72–78.

Camí J., de Torres S., San L., Solé A., Guerra D., Ugena B. 1985. Efficacy of clonidine and of methadone in the rapid detoxification of patients dependent on heroin. *Clin. Pharmacol. Ther.* 38:336–41.

Charney D.S., Sternberg D.E., Kleber H.D., Heninger G.R., Redmond D.E. 1981. The clinical use of clonidine in abrupt withdrawal from methadone. *Arch. Gen. Psychiatry* 38:1273–77.

Cheskin L.J., Fudala P.J., Johnson R.E. 1994. A controlled comparison of buprenorphine and clonidine for acute detoxification from opioids. *Drug Alcohol Depend.* 36:115–21.

Chowdhury A.N., Chowdhury S. 1990. Buprenorphine abuse: report from India. *Br. J. Addict.* 85:1349–50.

Eissenberg T., Bigelow G.E., Strain E.C., Walsh S.L., Brooner R.K., Stitzer M.L., Johnson R.E. 1997. Dose-related efficacy of levo-alpha acetyl methadol for treatment of opioid dependence: a randomized clinical trial. *JAMA* 277:1945–51.

Finkle B.S., Jennison T.A., Chinn D.M., Ling W., Holmes E.D. 1982. Plasma and urine disposition of l-alpha-acetylmethadol and its principal metabolites in man. *J. Analytic Toxicol.* 6:100–105.

Fraser H.F., Isbell H. 1952. Actions and addiction liabilities of alpha-acetylmethadols in man. *J. Pharmacol. Exp. Ther.* 105:458–65.

Freedman R.R., Czertko G. 1981. A comparison of thrice weekly LAAM and daily methadone in employed heroin addicts. *Drug Alcohol Depend.* 8:215–22.

Fudala P.J., Jaffe J.H., Dax E.M., Johnson R.E. 1990. Use of buprenorphine in the treatment of opioid addiction. II. Physiologic and behavioral effects of daily and alternate-day administration and abrupt withdrawal. *Clin. Pharmacol. Ther.* 47:525–34.

Fudala P.J., Vocci F., Montgomery A., Trachtenberg A.I. 1998. Levomethadyl acetate (LAAM) for the treatment of opioid dependence: a multisite, open label study of LAAM safety and an evaluation of the product labeling and treatment regulations. *J. Maint. Addictions* 1:9–39.

Gold M.S., Redmond D.E. Jr, Kleber H.D. 1978. Clonidine blocks acute opiate-withdrawal symptoms. *Lancet* 2(8090):599–602.

Gossop M. 1988. Clonidine and the treatment of the opiate withdrawal syndrome. *Drug Alcohol Depend.* 21:253–59.

Grabowski J., O'Brien C.P., Greenstein R., Ternes J., Long M., Steinberg-Donato S. 1979. Effects of contingent payment on compliance with a naltrexone regimen. *Am. J. Drug Alcohol Abuse* 6:355–65.

Gray R.F., Ferry A., Jauhar P. 1989. Emergence of buprenorphine dependence. *Br. J. Addict.* 84:1373–74.

Greenstein R.A., O'Brien C.P., McLellan A.T., Woody G.E., Grabowski J., Long M., Coyle-Perkins G., Vittor A. 1981. Naltrexone: a short-term treatment for opiate dependence. *Am. J. Drug Alcohol Abuse* 8:291–300.

Haertzen C.A. 1974. *An Overview of Addiction Research Center Inventory Scales (ARCI): An Appendix and Manual of Scales.* DHEW Publication No. (ADM) 74–92, National Institute on Drug Abuse, Rockville, MD.

Jaffe J.H., Schuster C.R., Smith B.B., Blachley P.H. 1970. Comparison of acetylmethadol and methadone in the treatment of long-term heroin users: a pilot study. *JAMA* 211:1834–36.

Jaffe J.H., Senay E.C. 1971. Methadone and l-methadyl acetate: use in management of narcotic addicts. *JAMA* 216:1303–5.

Jaffe J.H., Senay E.C., Schuster C.R., Renault P.R., Smith B., DiMenza S. 1972. Methadyl acetate vs methadone: a double-blind study in heroin users. *JAMA* 222:437–42.

Jasinski D.R., Johnson R.E., Kocher T.R. 1985. Clonidine in morphine withdrawal: differential effects on signs and symptoms. *Arch. Gen. Psychiatry* 42:1063–66.

Jasinski D.R., Pevnick J.S., Griffith J.D. 1978. Human pharmacology and abuse potential of the analgesic buprenorphine. *Arch. Gen. Psychiatry* 35:501–16.

Johnson R.E., Eissenberg T., Stitzer M.L., Strain E.C., Liebson I.A., Bigelow G.E. 1995a. A placebo controlled clinical trial of buprenorphine as a treatment for opioid dependence. *Drug Alcohol Depend.* 40:17–25.

———. 1995b. Buprenorphine treatment of opioid dependence: clinical trial of daily versus alternate-day dosing. *Drug Alcohol Depend.* 40:27–35.

Johnson R.E., Jaffe J.H., Fudala P.J. 1992. A controlled trial of buprenorphine treatment for opioid dependence. *JAMA* 267:2750–55.

Jones H.E., Strain E.C., Bigelow G.E., Walsh S.L., Stitzer M.L., Eissenberg T., Johnson R.E. 1998. Induction onto LAAM: safety and efficacy. *Arch. Gen. Psychiatry* 55:729–36.

Judson B.A., Goldstein A. 1979. Levo-alpha-acetylmethadol (LAAM) in the treatment of heroin addicts: I. Dosage schedule for induction and stabilization. *Drug Alcohol Depend.* 4:461–66.

Judson B.A., Goldstein A., Inturrisi C.E. 1983. Methadyl acetate (LAAM) in the treatment of heroin addicts: II. Double-blind comparison of gradual and abrupt detoxification. *Arch. Gen. Psychiatry* 40:834–40.

Kahn A., Mumford J.P., Rogers G.A., Beckford H. 1997. Double-blind study of lofexidine and clonidine in the detoxification of opiate addicts in hospital. *Drug Alcohol Depend.* 44:57–61.

Karp-Gelernter E., Savage C., McCabe O.L. 1982. Evaluation of clinic attendance schedules for LAAM and methadone: a controlled study. *Int. J. Addictions* 17:805–13.

Keats A.S., Beecher H.K. 1952. Analgesic activity and toxic effects of acetylmethadol isomers in man. *J. Pharmacol. Exp. Ther.* 105:210–15.

Kleber H.D., Gold M.S., Riordan C.E. 1980. The use of clonidine in detoxification from opiates. *Bull. Narcotics* 32:1–10.

Kosten T.R., Schottenfeld R., Ziedonis D., Falcioni J. 1993. Buprenorphine versus methadone maintenance for opioid dependence. *J. Nerv. Ment. Dis.* 181:358–64.

Lin S., Strang J., Su L., Tsai C., Hu W. 1997. Double-blind randomised controlled trial of lofexidine versus clonidine in the treatment of heroin withdrawal. *Drug Alcohol Depend.* 48:127–33.

Ling W., Charuvastra C., Collins J.F., Batki S., Brown L.S., Kintaudi P., Wesson D.R., McNicholas L., Tusel D.J., Malkerneker U., Renner J.A., Santos E., Casadonte P., Fye C., Stine S., Wang R.I.H., Segal D. 1998. Buprenorphine maintenance treatment of opiate dependence: a multicenter, randomized clinical trial. *Addiction* 93:475–86.

Ling W., Charuvastra C., Kaim S.C., Klett J. 1976. Methadyl acetate and methadone as maintenance treatments for heroin addicts. *Arch. Gen. Psychiatry* 33:709–20.

Ling W., Klett J., Gillis R.D. 1978. A cooperative clinical study of methadyl acetate: I. Three-times-a-week regimen. *Arch. Gen. Psychiatry* 35:345–53.

Ling W., Wesson D.R., Charuvastra C., Klett J. 1996. A controlled trial comparing buprenorphine and methadone maintenance in opioid dependence. *Arch. Gen. Psychiatry* 53:401–7.

Loimer N., Lenz K., Schmid R., Presslich O. 1991. Technique for greatly shortening the transition from methadone to naltrexone maintenance of patients addicted to opiates. *Am. J. Psychiatry* 148:933–35.

Loimer N., Schmid R., Presslich O., Lenz K. 1989. Continuous naloxone administration suppresses opiate withdrawal symptoms in human opiate addicts during detoxification treatment. *J. Psychiat. Res.* 23:81–86.

Marcovici M., O'Brien C.P., McLellan A.T., Kacian J. 1981. A clinical, controlled study of l-alpha-acetylmethadol in the treatment of narcotic addiction. *Am. J. Psychiatry* 138:234–36.

McEvoy G.K., ed. 1997. *Opiate Partial Agonists 28:08.12, Buprenorphine Hydrochloride.* In: AHFS 97 Drug Information. American Hospital Formulary Service, published by authority of the Board of Directors of the American Society of Health-System Pharmacists, pp. 1593–98.

McMahon R.E., Culp H.W., Marshall F.J. 1965. The metabolism of alpha-dl-acetylmethadol in the rat: the identification of the probable active metabolite. *J. Pharmacol. Exp. Ther.* 149:436–45.

Mello N.K., Mendelson J.H., Kuehnle J.C., Sellers M.S. 1981. Operant analysis of human heroin self-administration and the effects of naltrexone. *J. Pharmacol. Exp. Ther.* 216: 45–54.

Mendelson J., Upton R.A., Everhart E.T., Jacob P., Jones R.T. 1997. Bioavailability of sublingual buprenorphine. *J. Clin. Pharmacol. Ther.* 37:31–37.

Morrison V. 1989. Psychoactive substance use and related behaviors of 135 regular illicit drug users in Scotland. *Drug Alcohol Depend.* 23:95–101.

National Research Council Committee on Clinical Evaluation of Narcotic Antagonists. 1978. Clinical evaluation of naltrexone treatment of opiate-dependent individuals. *Arch. Gen. Psychiatry* 35:335–40.

Nigam A.K., Ray R., Tripathi B.M. 1993. Buprenorphine in opiate withdrawal: a comparison with clonidine. *J. Subst. Abuse Treat.* 10:391–94.

O'Connor J.J., Moloney E., Travers R., Campbell A. 1988. Buprenorphine abuse among opiate addicts. *Br. J. Addict.* 83:1085–87.

O'Connor P.G., Kosten T.R. 1998. Rapid and ultrarapid opioid detoxification techniques. *JAMA* 279:229–34.

Ohtani M., Kotaki H., Sawada Y., Iga T. 1995. Comparative analysis of buprenorphine- and norbuprenorphine-induced analgesic effects based on pharmacokinetic-pharmacodynamic modeling. *J. Pharmacol. Exp. Ther.* 272:505–10.

Peachey J.E., Lei H. 1988. Assessment of opioid dependence with naloxone. *Br. J. Addict.* 83:193–201.

Pfohl D.N., Allen J.I., Atkinson R.L., Knopman D.S., Malcolm R.J., Mitchell J.E., Morley J.E. 1986. Naltrexone hydrochloride (Trexan): a review of serum transaminase elevations at high dosage. In: Harris L., ed. Problems of Drug Dependence 1985. Proceedings of the 47th Annual Scientific Meeting, Committee on Problems of Drug Dependence. National Institute on Drug Abuse Research Monograph 67, Rockville, MD, pp. 66–72.

Rabinowitz J., Cohen H., Tarrasch R., Kotler M. 1997. Compliance to naltrexone treatment after ultra-rapid opiate detoxification: an open label naturalistic study. *Drug Alcohol Depend.* 47:77–86.

Resnick R.B., Orlin L., Geyer G., Schuyten-Resnick E., Kestenbaum R.S., Freedman A.M. 1976. l-alpha-acetylmethadol (LAAM): prognostic considerations. *Am. J. Psychiatry* 133:814–19.

Reynaud M., Tracqui A., Petit G., Potard D., Courty P. 1998. Six deaths linked to misuse of buprenorphine-benzodiazepine combination. *Am. J. Psychiatry* 155:448–49.

Robinson G.M., Dukes P.D., Robinson B.J., Cooke R.R., Mahoney G.N. 1993. The misuse of buprenorphine and a buprenorphine-naloxone combination in Wellington, New Zealand. *Drug Alcohol Depend.* 33:81–86.

Rounsaville B.J., Kosten T., Kleber H. 1985. Success and failure at outpatient opioid detoxification: evaluating the process of clonidine- and methadone-assisted withdrawal. *J. Nerv. Ment. Dis.* 173:103–10.

Sakol M.S., Stark C., Sykes R. 1989. Buprenorphine and temazepam abuse by drug takers in Glasgow—an increase. *Br. J. Addict.* 84:439–41.

Savage C., Karp E.G., Curran S.F., Hanlon T.E., McCabe O.L. 1976. Methadone/LAAM maintenance: a comparison study. *Comprehen. Psychiatry* 17:415–24.

Schottenfeld R.S., Pakes J.R., Oliveto A., Ziedonis D., Kosten T.R. 1997. Buprenorphine versus methadone maintenance treatment for concurrent opioid dependence and cocaine abuse. *Arch. Gen. Psychiatry* 54: 713–20.

Senay E.C., Dorus W., Renault P.F. 1977. Methadyl acetate and methadone: an open comparison. *JAMA* 237:138–42.

Singh R.A., Mattoo S.K., Malhotra A., Varma V.K. 1992. Cases of buprenorphine abuse in India. *Acta Psychiatr. Scand.* 86:46–48.

Spencer L., Gregory M. 1989. Clonidine transdermal patches for use in outpatient opiate withdrawal. *J. Subst. Abuse Treat.* 6:113–17.

Strain E.C., Stitzer M.L., Liebson I.A., Bigelow G.E. 1994. Comparison of buprenorphine and methadone in the treatment of opioid dependence. *Am. J. Psychiatry* 151:1025–30.

Strain E.C., Preston K.L. Liebson I.A., Bigelow G.E. 1995. Buprenorphine effects in methadone-maintained volunteers: effects at two hours after methadone. *J. Pharmacol. Exp. Ther.* 272:628–38.

Strang J. 1985. Abuse of buprenorphine. *Lancet* ii:725.

Taintor Z., Hough G., Plumb M., Murphy B.F., D'Amanda C. 1975. l-alpha-acetylmethadol and methadone in Buffalo: safety and efficacy. *Am. J. Drug Alcohol Abuse* 2:317–30.

Tilly J., O'Brien C.P., McLellan A.T., Woody G.E., Metzger D.S., Cornish J. 1992. Naltrexone in the treatment of federal probationers. In: Harris L., ed. Problems of Drug Dependence 1991. Proceedings of the 53rd Annual Scientific Meeting, Committee on Problems of Drug Dependence. National Institute on Drug Abuse Research Monograph 119, Rockville, MD, p. 458.

Trueblood B., Judson B.A., Goldstein A. 1978. Acceptability of methadyl acetate (LAAM) as compared with methadone in a treatment program for heroin addicts. *Drug Alcohol Depend.* 3:125–32.

Vining E., Kosten T.R., Kleber H.D. 1988. Clinical utility of rapid clonidine-naltrexone detoxification for opioid abusers. *Br. J. Addict.* 83:567–75.

Walsh S.L., Johnson R.E., Stitzer M.L., Bigelow G.E. 1996a. Acute effects of intravenous and oral LAAM in human substance abusers. In: Harris L., ed. Problems of Drug Dependence 1995. Proceedings of the 57th Annual Scientific Meeting, College on Problems of Drug Dependence. National Institute on Drug Abuse Research Monograph 162, Rockville, MD, p. 199.

Walsh S.L., Sullivan J.T., Preston K.L., Garner J.E., Bigelow G.E. 1996b. Effects of naltrexone on response to intravenous cocaine, hydromorphone and their combination in humans. *J. Pharmacol. Exp. Ther.* 279:524–38.

Wang R.I.H., Wiesen R.L., Lamid S., Roh B.L. 1974. Rating the presence and severity of opiate dependence. *Clin. Pharmacol. Ther.* 16:653–58.

Washton A.M., Gold M.S., Pottash A.C. 1984. Successful use of naltrexone in addicted physicians and business executives. *Adv. Alcohol Subst. Abuse* 4:89–96.

Washton A.M., Resnick R.B. 1980. Clonidine for opiate detoxification: outpatient clinical trials. *Am. J. Psychiatry* 137:1121–22.

Weinberg D.S., Inturrisi C.E., Reidenberg B., Moulin D.E., Nips T.J., Wallenstein S., Houde R.W., Foley K.M. 1988. Sublingual absorption of selected opioid analgesics. *Clin. Pharmacol. Ther.* 44:335–42.

Wilson B.K., Spannagel V., Thomson C.P. 1976. The use of l-alpha-acetyl-methadol in treatment of heroin addiction: an open study. *Int. J. Addictions* 11:1091–1100.

Zaks A., Fink M., Freedman A.M. 1972. Levomethadyl in maintenance treatment of opiate dependence. *JAMA* 220:811–13.

INDEX

Buprenorphine: abuse liability, 32, 300–301, 304, 314; as analgesic, 199–300; antagonistic effects, 298–99, 307; as antidepressant, 158; as antipsychotic, 160; combined with benzodiazepines, adverse effects of, 299, 306; combined with naloxone, 32, 300–301; detoxification using, 302, 304–5, 308–9, 311; diversion, 304; dosing flexibility, 304; dosing forms, 299–301; dosing schedules, 32, 304, 314; efficacy, 301–5, 307–9; history of development, 12–13; induction, 307; interaction with cocaine, 305; maintenance dosing, 307–8; opioid blockade, 307–8, 314; partial agonist action, 39, 298–99, 307; pharmacology / pharmacokinetics, 32, 298–300; safety and side effects, 306

Caffeine use, related to psychiatric symptoms, 156
Cardiac complications of drug abuse / endocarditis: causes, diagnosis, treatment, 126, 253; and renal disease, 133; screening, 260
Child development, prenatal methadone effects on: brain growth, 270–71; cognitive and psychomotor function, 269–70; difficulties of assessing, 264–65
Clinic operation: automated dispensing, 29, 242; computerized tracking and documentation, 29; grievance procedures, 238; operating hours, 228–29; physical facility considerations, 225–28; professional conduct of staff, 239–40; rules and regulations, 237–38, 249; security / staff

safety, 225–29, 244–45, 247; staffing patterns, attitudes, supervision, and training, 229–32
Clinical trials, limitations of, 62–63, 302
Clonidine: abuse liability, 86, 121, 314; antihypertensive use, 309; clinical use in detoxification, 12–13, 281, 312–15; and depression, 155; dosing schedule, 313–14; history of development, 12–13; pharmacology, 310, 314; prescribing guidelines, 121; safety and side effects, 312–13; urine testing, 100, 121; use: —transition to naltrexone, 296–97; —treatment of withdrawal, 12–13, 296, 309–15
Cocaine: adverse effects, 89–90, 118, 125, 126, 132, 133, 245; behavioral strategies for controlling during-treatment use, 101–3, 170, 207–9, 211, 213, 234; decreases during psychotherapy, 177; and heroin use, 88; pharmacotherapy for, 101–2, 305–6; and psychiatric symptoms, 156, 158; urine testing, 96, 98; use: —during methadone treatment, 87, 101, 114; —as predictor of treatment response, 76
Community attitudes and concerns, 33, 224, 228–29, 247, 249
Confidentiality and duty to warn, 237–38, 240, 249
Contingency management: contracting methods and examples, 212–19; identifying and delivering reinforcers, 216–18; methadone dose alterations, 200–201, 205, 210, 212, 217–18; methadone dosing time, 229; methadone split dosing, 201–2, 210; methadone take-home, 202–6,

309–15; using lofexidine, 309–15. *See also* Withdrawal from methadone

Discharge from methadone: adverse effects / risks, 102, 190, 200, 202; as result of alcohol or illicit drug use, 91, 167; as behavior change incentive, 102, 185–86, 188–89, 199–200; costs of, vs continuing treatment, 23; as response to community concerns, 224; as response to problem behaviors, 244, 246, 263. *See also* Behaviorally contingent pharmacotherapy

Dispensing of methadone, 227–28, 241–42

Disulfiram: acetaldehyde reaction, 106, 110–11; contracting for in marital therapy, 180–81; delivery at the methadone clinic, 106–11, 154, 199; detoxification before starting, 109; dosing, 109–11; efficacy and role of compliance, 107–8, 111; safety, side effects, and contraindications, 110, 130; use in psychotic patients, 160

Diversion: of buprenorphine, 304; of methadone, 11, 15, 19, 227, 239, 246, 249, 282

Dole, Vincent, and Nyswander, Marie, 6–10, 20, 53, 64, 79

Domestic violence / sexual abuse, 135, 254, 256

Dosage forms: of buprenorphine, 299–301, 305; of methadone, 21, 43

Dose adequacy: and methadone blood levels, 78, 81; during methadone induction, 54; during methadone maintenance, 78; and psychiatric symptoms, 156; and urine pH, 44

Dose-related efficacy: of buprenorphine, 303, 307–8; of LAAM, 283–84

Dose-related efficacy of methadone: clinical trials of, 62–63, 68–76; double blind studies, 69, 72–76; higher vs lower doses, 70–76, 101, 303; history of, 64–65; interaction with nonpharmacological treatment, 75; vs placebo, 68–70; in pregnant women, 262; single blind studies, 70–72; survey research, 62, 65–68. *See also* Treatment evaluation / outcome

Dosing: with buprenorphine, 299–309; flexible / individualized, 62, 74–75, 81, 302; increases during treatment, 100–101; of intoxicated methadone patients, 247; with LAAM, 287–88; of methadone, during pregnancy, 261–62, 264; practices across programs, 66–67; schedules compared across treatment medications, 314; split dosing, 122, 201–2, 210, 262

Drug Abuse Reporting Program (DARP), 65

Drug Abuse Treatment Outcome Study (DATOS), 66

Drug combinations and interactions: with buprenorphine, 299, 306; with methadone, 122–23, 160–61

DSM-IV criteria for substance dependence, 233–34

Employment: counseling for, 170, 173–74, 256; as criteria for awarding methadone take-home doses, 170, 203; as function of time in substance abuse treatment, 24; gender differences in, 254; increase of, dur-

behaviorally contingent pharmacotherapy, 102–3, 189; detection in urine screening, 96–100, 155, 243; during LAAM treatment, 283–84, 286; effects of counseling intensity, 170; positive consequences for drug users, 167, 198–99; by pregnant women, 251–52, 256–57, 264. *See also* Benzodiazepines; Cocaine

Immunologic abnormalities, 134

Incentive therapies. *See* Behavioral contingencies; Contingency management

Induction: buprenorphine, 307; LAAM, 285–87, 289; methadone: —in pregnancy, 261; —schedule of increase, 54, 59, 64; —split vs once daily dosing, 53–54, 78; —starting dose, 53–54, 59, 64, 236; naltrexone, 292–97

Infections, 125, 253

Interim Methadone Maintenance, 30. *See also* Services delivery

LAAM: abuse liability, 314; cost of treatment, 25, 29, 34; counseling delivery in, 166, 168; discontinuation, 288; dose conversion from methadone, 287; dose induction, 285–87, 289; efficacy, 72, 283–84, 286, 289; history of development and approval, 12, 281–82, 288; maintenance dosing, 287–88, 314; opioid blockade, 314; pharmacology / pharmacokinetics, 282–83, 314; pregnancy testing, 29; regulation, 16–17, 19–20; safety and side-effects, 284–85, 289; take-home dosing, 282, 287; use in stable patients, 315; utilization barriers, 288–89

Lofexidine: clinical use in detoxification, 12–13, 281, 313–15; dosing schedule, 313–15; history of development, 12–13; pharmacology, 309–10, 314; safety and side-effects, 312, 315; treatment for withdrawal, efficacy of, 311–12

Managed care. *See* Financing of treatment

Marijuana: adverse effects, 91–92; detection in urine testing, 96, 100, 112, 243; and methadone treatment outcome, 92, 112; prevalence of abuse during methadone treatment, 87; and psychiatric symptoms, 156, 158

Medical care: delivery at the treatment site, 31, 70, 119, 135, 229–30; for patients with psychiatric disorders, 153; for pregnant women, 257–59. *See also specific medical disorders*

Medical methadone maintenance. *See* Services delivery

Medication development for treatment of opioid dependence, 11

Methadone: as analgesic, development of, 6; cost for methadone treatment, 25–26; countries with methadone treatment, 9; payment for methadone treatment, 27–28; pharmacology / pharmacokinetics: —accumulation, 44, 54; —bioavailability by oral route, 43, 50; —blood levels, 77–78, 81; —distribution / tissue and protein binding, 43; —excretion / elimination, 44; —half life and factors affecting, 43–44; —metabolism, 43–45, 123, 156, 262, 272; —receptor effects, 41–42; potency

Methadone *(continued)*
by route, 43; psychomotor / cognitive function effects, 50; structure and isomers, 42; tolerance to effects, 41, 45, 49–50, 64, 79–80, 121; treatment utilization: —acceptability of treatment, 69; —gender differences, 255; —internationally, 8, 13, 15; —number of patients, 8–9, 13, 15, 25; —over time, 8, 13; use for psychiatric disorders, 50. *See also specific topics*

Michigan Alcoholism Screening Test (MAST), 93–94

Mobile methadone treatment. *See* Services delivery

Mood disorders. *See* Bipolar disorder; Depression

Morphine: analgesic use in methadone patients, 122; blockade of effects by methadone, 47; detection in urine, 96, 98–100; maintenance on, 3, 8, 13; mu agonist activity, 41; similarities to methadone, 6, 38, 45, 49; withdrawal suppression by, 48, 311. *See also* Heroin.

Nalmefene, 40, 122, 289

Naloxone: challenge for determining opioid dependence, 292–93; combination with buprenorphine, 300–301; use in overdose reversal, 40, 306

Naltrexone: adverse effects in opioid dependence, 122; efficacy, 290–91; history of development, 11, 289; induction and withdrawal assessment, 292–97; induction with clonidine, 296–97; liver function testing, 292; maintenance dosing, 297–98; pharmacology, 289–90; safety and side-effects, 291–92; use in alcoholism treatment, 11, 106; use in treatment of opioid dependence, 40, 289–98

Needle exchange, 30, 119

Neonatal abstinence syndrome: assessment, 264, 266–67; and child cognitive and psychomotor function, 269–70; features and time course, 265–66; prevalence, 265; treatment of, 267–68. *See also* Withdrawal symptoms / syndrome

Neonatal status / outcomes: birth weight and head circumference, 268–69; difficulties of assessing, 264, 266–67; improved with methadone treatment, 258, 268; and methadone dose, 262, 266–69. *See also* Child development, prenatal methadone effects on

Neurological complications / seizures, 133–34

Nursing staff, role of, 230–31

Nyswander, Marie. *See* Dole, Vincent

Opioid use: cross tolerance blockade as mechanism of reduction, 48, 51, 87–88, 101, 167; decrease: —during buprenorphine treatment, 302–3, 308; —during methadone treatment, 64, 67–68, 71, 73–75, 81, 87–88, 100–101, 170; —with abstinent-contingent incentives, 199–201, 208, 210–11; detection in urine, 96, 98–100; during LAAM maintenance / withdrawal, 284, 288; during methadone induction / withdrawal, 55, 59; during placebo methadone treatment, 69; as predictor of treatment response, 76. *See also* Heroin; Illicit drug use; Morphine; Relapse

Pain management, 121–22

Patent medicines, 2

Personality disorders: assessment, 148, 260; prevalence, 142–43, 145, 162; and suicidal thoughts, 248; and treatment outcome, 152. *See also* Antisocial personality disorder

Physical dependence: during methadone treatment, 6, 89; features and assessment for treatment entry, 233–35, 261, 292–96; level related to buprenorphine effects, 307. *See also* Neonatal abstinence syndrome; Withdrawal symptoms / syndrome

Post-traumatic stress disorder (PTSD), 145–46

Pregnancy: and cocaine, effects of, 89; comprehensive care model of treatment, 255–56, 258–61, 271; drug use during and complications, 251–52, 256–57, 260, 264; methadone eligibility during, 235; methadone metabolism changes during, 262, 272; methadone treatment during, 257–63, 266–69; prenatal and obstetric complications due to drug use, 256–57, 260, 264; prenatal care, 256–59, 264

Prescription medications, prescribing guidelines for, 120

Prevalence of opiate dependence, 2–3

Program director, role of, 230

Psychiatric disorders / status: assessment, 93, 105, 146–51, 249, 260; —during disulfiram therapy, 110; —during drug use vs abstinence, 148–50, 162; and drug use vs abstinence, 148–49, 151, 154, 162; and medical disorders, 151; prevalence, 87, 141–46, 253; services integration / coordination, 152–53, 162;

substance-induced vs independent, 150–51; treatment, 27, 31, 151–62, 166, 176–77, 183, 253. *See also specific disorders*

Psychotherapy: availability in methadone clinics, 153; cognitive-behavioral, 175–76; compliance with, 178, 180, 184; efficacy, 175–78; goals and techniques, 174–75; interpersonal therapy (IPT), 177; long-term benefits, 178, 180; supportive-expressive, 175–76. *See also* Counseling; Family-based therapies

Pulmonary diseases, 130–32. *See also* Tuberculosis

Pure Food and Drug Act, 2–3

Receptors: affinity and intrinsic activity at, 39, 289, 299; opioid: —delta, 41; —kappa, 40–41, 289, 298–99; —mu, 40, 282, 289, 298–99, 307; —sigma, 40

Regulations: analgesic use, 46; Center for Substance Abuse treatment (CSAT), role of, 34; confidentiality, 240; detoxification, 55, 233, 238; Department of Health and Human Services (DHHS), role of, 17; dosing practices, 54; Drug Enforcement Agency (DEA), 15, 19; eligibility for methadone treatment, 232–36; exposure to hazardous and infectious materials, 242–43; FDA, 15, 17–19, 34; history of, 2–7; investigational new drug (IND) exemption, 32; LAAM, 289; methadone storage and dispensing, 226–27, 241–42; in other countries, 20–21; recommendation for change, 34; state and local, 19–20, 33; Substance Abuse and

Voucher payments. *See* Contingency management

Withdrawal from methadone: definition of, 53; and depressive symptoms, 156; dose change step size, 56; duration, 56, 60; effect on drug use, 59; federal regulations for, 233, 238; history of, 64; informed vs blind, 57, 60; inpatient vs outpatient for methadone withdrawal, 59; in pregnant women, 257, 262–63; prior to program discharge, 23, 188; rate of reduction, 56–58; readmission to methadone maintenance following voluntary detoxification, 235–36; as strategy to control during-treatment drug use, 102, 205, 210, 212; withdrawal schedule examples, 58. *See also* Detoxification

Withdrawal suppression: by buprenorphine, 308; by clonidine and lofexidine, 296, 310–13; dose-related, 48, 70, 89; during methadone induction, 55; by methadone, 42, 50, 167

Withdrawal symptoms / syndrome: adrenergic component, 310; assessment methods, 293–95; during buprenorphine treatment, 306, 309; changes during pregnancy, 262; in dependence assessment, 234, 261; features, 289–90; during LAAM treatment, 287; during methadone discontinuation, 44, 57; during methadone maintenance, 78, 81; and methadone dose, 266–67; and methadone metabolism, 266; in neonate, 257, 264–68; precipitated by opioid mixed agonist-antagonists, 122, 299; precipitated by pure antagonists, 39, 122, 289, 301; during prescription of enzyme-inducing medications, 123; spontaneous vs precipitated, 289–90; treatment with clonidine and lofexidine, 281. *See also* Physical dependence

Library of Congress Cataloging-in-Publication Data

Methadone treatment for opioid dependence / edited by Eric C. Strain
and Maxine Stitzer.
    p. cm.
    Includes bibliographical references and index.
    ISBN 0-8018-6136-5 (hbk. : alk. paper). —ISBN 0-8018-6137-3
(pbk. : alk. paper)
    1. Methadone maintenance. 2. Drug abuse—Treatment. 3. Narcotic
habit—Treatment. I. Strain, Eric C. II. Stitzer, Maxine L.
RC568.M4M476 1999
616.86'32061—dc21   98-50962
                                       CIP